A Life in Ragtime

A Life in Ragtime

A Biography of James Reese Europe

REID BADGER

New York   Oxford
OXFORD UNIVERSITY PRESS
1995

Oxford University Press

Oxford   New York   Toronto
Delhi   Bombay   Calcutta   Madras   Karachi
Kuala Lumpur   Singapore   Hong Kong   Tokyo
Nairobi   Dar es Salaam   Cape Town
Melbourne   Auckland
and associated companies in
Berlin   Ibadan

Published by Oxford University Press, Inc.,
200 Madison Avenue, New York, New York 10016

Oxford is a registered trademark of Oxford University Press

Library of Congress Cataloging-in-Publication Data
Badger, Reid
A life in ragtime : a biography of James Reese Europe /
Reid Badger.
p.   cm.
List of Europe's works: p.   Discography: p.
Includes bibliographical references and index.
ISBN 0-19-506044-X
1. Europe, James Reese, 1880–1919.
2. Jazz musicians—United States—Biography.
3. Bandmasters—United States—Biography.
4. Ragtime music—History and criticism.
I. Title.   ML422.E87B2 • 1995
781.65'092—dc20   [B]   93-42407

frontispiece:
Lt. James Reese Europe, Bandleader/Machine Gun Company Officer, 369th Infantry
"Hellfighters" Regiment, U.S. Army. February 1919. *Courtesy of James Reese Europe, Jr.*

9 8 7 6 5 4 3 2 1
Printed in the United States of America
on acid-free paper

This book is for

Virginia Marie and James Reese Europe, Jr.
And for their children:

Patricia Ann, Lynne Teresa, James Reese, III,
Virginia Marie, and Teresa Ann

Acknowledgments

J ames Reese Europe left a considerable legacy, but few personal documents, papers, or correspondence from which his life in American music could be easily reconstructed. Without the historic black newspapers, especially the *New York Age* and the Indianapolis *Freeman*, which regularly followed his activities, and the discovery of an important memoir by Noble Sissle, this book could not have been written. In addition, the contribution of James Reese Europe, Jr., throughout the process of research and writing, was essential. He supported the project by sharing the material he had collected over many years, and by assisting in the work at every stage. It is my hope that the picture of his father's life and music that I have painted here will seem to him a fair one and I offer it as a token of my esteem and affection.

Over the past eight years, I have been fortunate to receive the support and assistance of many wise and knowledgeable people and dozens of generous institutions. Suzanne Wolfe, the extraordinary editor of *Alabama Heritage*, provided the initial opportunity for me to write about Europe in the first issue of the University of Alabama's award-winning quarterly. An invitation from the University of Minnesota to participate in a conference on jazz helped me to focus specifically on Europe's contribution to the emergence and diffusion of that new music, while participation in a National Endowment for the Humanities Summer Institute at Howard University, directed by Doris McGinty, provided a solid introduction to the wealth of historical information (and perspective) contained in the black press. I am also grateful to the Endowment for the travel support that permitted several weeks of research in the Billy Rose Theater Collection of the New York Public Library.

Wayne Shirley and Debora Newman of the Library of Congress, Jay Higginbothan of the Mobile Municipal Archives, Penny Catzen of the Maryland Historical Society, and G.R.F. Key of the Washingtoniana Division of the Martin Luther King Memorial Library in Washington, D.C., were especially helpful in providing assistance and guidance in the important collections they supervise. I am grateful, as well, to the staffs of the Schomburg Center for Research in Black Culture of the New York Public Library, the Museum of the City of New

York, the National Archives, the Hogan Jazz Archive of Tulane University, the Vivian Perlis Oral History Archive of Yale University, Special Collections at the University of Alabama and at Samford University, the Mobile and Birmingham Public Libraries, and, especially, the Moorland-Spingarn Research Center at Howard University.

Individuals whose cooperation, advice, or scholarship contributed in important ways to this study, include Mrs. Lorraine Johnson, Reverend Ben Lewis, Donald Ashwander, Marva G. Carter, Lawrence Gushee, Robert Kimball, James T. Mayer, John Graziano, Dominique-René de Lerma, Ruth Glasser, Donald Thompson, Susan Cook, Edward Berlin, the late Martin Williams, William T. Robinson, III, David Jasen, and Steve Weiland.

I owe a special thanks to Albert Murray for being the inspiration that he is and for first encouraging my interest in Europe, and to Maurice Peress for the rare breadth of his musical understanding and for offering me the opportunity to play a part in his memorable recreation of the James Reese Europe/Clef Club Concert of 1912 at Carnegie Hall in the summer of 1989.

I am indebted to The University of Alabama and my colleagues and students in more ways than I can adequately express. The Research Grants Committee provided support for two summers of research and writing, and my department head, James M. Salem, was a steadfast champion of the project. His willingness to be there when I needed someone to talk through a particular problem, to help clarify my ideas and expression, made the book much more coherent and certainly more literate than it would otherwise have been. My thanks also to Lynne Adrian, Rose Gladney, Ralph Bogardus, George Wolfe, and the irreplaceable Margaret Vines, who endured the endless discussions and generously contributed their suggestions, and especially to George for his critical playwright's reading of the first draft.

Parts of this book appeared previously in publications of Wayne State University Press, Cambridge University Press, and the Sonneck Society (University of Illinois Press); I am grateful to these institutions for permission to incorporate some of that material in this work. Oxford University Press has been both generous in its encouragement and unusually patient and the book has profited substantially from Sheldon Meyer's editorial comments and recommendations.

Finally, my wife Lee and my family—Molly and Jerry, and Amy—not only weathered my preoccupation over these past years, but cheered and sustained me, as they have in all things, every step of the way.

Contents

A Life in Ragtime

Prelude

"Can't remember no time when I danced in the street but that one time when everybody did. . . . [T]he War had come and gone and the colored troops of the three six nine that fought it made me so proud it split my heart in two."

Toni Morrison
Jazz (1992)

On an unusually bright, faintly springlike morning in mid-February 1919 in New York City, a huge crowd of perhaps 1 million people gathered along Fifth Avenue all the way from Madison Square Park to 110th Street, and from there along Lenox Avenue north to 145th Street.[1] Along with Governor Al Smith, ex-Governor Charles Whitman, Acting-Mayor Robert Moran, Special Assistant to the Secretary of War Emmett Scott, William Randolph Hearst, Rodman Wanamaker, and other notables, they had come to welcome home the men of the 15th Infantry Regiment of New York's National Guard, who had fought so well in France as the 369th Infantry Regiment of the American Expeditionary Force.[2]

Under the command of Colonel William Hayward, the 369th had survived 191 days under enemy fire, received the Croix de Guerre, and was chosen by the French high command to lead the victorious Allied march to the Rhine. The 369th never lost a prisoner or a foot of ground that it was expected to hold, and it achieved every offensive objective save one—and in that instance the fault lay with a failure of artillery support. One hundred seventy-one of the regiment's officers and men received individual citations for bravery, a record among the American forces. Casualties, however, were also heavy: 800 of the original 2,000 who had embarked from Hoboken, New Jersey, on December 12, 1917, did not return. Many of those who did suffered serious and permanent injuries.

Having arrived in Manhattan at about 10 A.M. after traveling by rail and ferry from Camp Upton, Long Island, the returning veterans—the first fighting unit of World War I to parade in New York—assembled in formation on 23rd Street. At half-past eleven, led by a 100-member mounted police escort, they marched through the newly erected Victory Arch at 25th Street and up Fifth Avenue to receive as joyous a reception from the residents of New York as anyone could remember. New York's "finest avenue was the scene of a triumph," reported the *New York Herald* the next day. "From the windows of the mansions along that famous thoroughfare the city's socially elect looked forth and mingled their acclaim with the cheers of the multitudes that swarmed on sidewalks, rooftops and reviewing stands."[3] "Never in the history of Father Knickerbocker," wrote Lester Walton in the *New York Age*, "has such a rousing royal welcome been given returning heroes from the field of battle, not for many a day is it likely that thousands of white and colored citizens will participate in such a tumultuous and enthusiastic demonstration."[4] The soldiers, both officers and men, were astonished at the hundreds of thousands who turned out to see and cheer them. "It's been far beyond my expectations," said the colonel at the end of the day. "It has been wonderful!"[5]

The remarkable reception by New Yorkers reflected their patriotic pride in the recent Allied victory as well as relief that the nightmare of world war was over. It was also, in more specific terms, an expression of New Yorkers' affection and pride in their own booming city. This regiment may always be known officially as the 369th, commented the reporter for the *World*, but it was no such thing to those who lined the streets to greet it. "It was the old 15th New York. And so it will be in this city's memory, archives and in the folk lore of the descendants of the men who made up its straight, smartly stepping ranks."[6] "New York saw in them, one and all, the boys of the old 15th, whose heroic deeds had shed lustre on the city's name, and New York took them to its heart," added the *Tribune*.[7]

There was something else, however, that was special about these soldiers and this particular parade that accounts for the sidewalks being jammed with flag-waving spectators long before the troops appeared. Bernard Katz, a schoolboy who had no idea what the parade was about but was drawn to Fifth Avenue by the sounds of a marching band, immediately noticed something unusual. "Most of the other parades," he recalled, "came down Fifth Avenue—this one was moving uptown!"[8] He soon understood why.

With the exception of its officers, the old 15th was composed entirely of black Americans recruited primarily from the Williamsburg section of Brooklyn, the San Juan Hill section of mid-Manhattan, and, especially, Harlem. The Germans had named them "Blutlustige Schwartzmanner" (bloodthirsty black men), but it was by their French nickname, the "Hellfighters," that most New Yorkers and Americans had come to know them. "Swinging up the avenue, keeping a step springy with the swagger of men proud of themselves and their organization, their rows of bayonets gleaming in the sun, dull-painted steel basins on their heads," wrote a reporter for the *New York Times*, the regiment seemed "made up of men of seven feet or more." It was a "spectacle that might justify pity for the Germans."[9]

Indeed, marching in the dramatically dense French Phalanx formation unfamiliar to most American troops, and certainly to the New York public, the row upon row of dark faces, chins strapped high, eyes straight ahead, gave an impression of confidence and power and pride in being Americans, of being New Yorkers, and of being black. "Looking at their faultless ranks stretching in perfect alignment from curb to curb, their dignified, soldierly bearing," said the *Herald*, "it was hard to believe that less than two years ago many of these bemedalled veterans were parlor car porters, apartment house helpers, restaurant waiters, shipping clerks, bell boys, truck drivers, and what not."[10] "I'm taking off without asking the boss, for I just had to see these boys," one middle-aged white spectator was heard to remark. "I never will get another opportunity to see such a sight, and I can get another job."[11] "The feeling was terrific. Everybody was happy. Everybody was wonderful," recalled Melville T. Miller, a nineteen-year-old private. It was the "most wonderful day of my life, the day we marched up Fifth Avenue. That's one day that there wasn't the slightest bit of prejudice in New York City—that day."[12]

On February 17, 1919, antagonisms and prejudices were set aside, subsumed within a more generous spirit that seemed to promise a new era for America. "These Negroes have helped to win the war. Let us hope that their unflinching courage in the face of death will be remembered," commented a remarkable editorial in the *Jewish Daily News*. "Color, after all, is of no consequence."[13] If the day was without racial prejudice, however, it was nonetheless marked by a new sense of racial pride and determination. The questions that had attended the initial recruitment of the "colored regiments" in 1916 (i.e., Did blacks have an obligation to fight for a country that denied them full citizenship? Would demonstrating their loyalty and patriotism help advance their cause?) seemed answered. "Much as the white population of the town demonstrated their welcome to the Regiment, it was, after all, those of their own color to whom the occasion belonged," said the *World*.[14] "We wonder how many people who are opposed to giving the Negro his full citizenship rights could watch the 15th on its march up the Avenue and not feel either shame or alarm?" asked James Weldon Johnson in the *Age*. "And we wonder how many who are not opposed to the Negro receiving his full rights could watch these men and not feel determined to aid them in their endeavor to obtain these rights?"[15]

Among other ways, New York's officials recognized the special importance to the city's black community of the 369th Regiment's homecoming parade by reversing the usual direction of the march. Two sets of reviewing stands had also been set up, one between 61st and 62nd Streets on Fifth Avenue for residents of the San Juan Hill area, and the other spanning both sides of Lenox Avenue at 134th Street in Harlem. Nine-tenths of the seats were reserved for friends and relatives of the soldiers. In addition, the City Board of Education had ordered that all black children were to be excused from school. All along the avenue, white New Yorkers gave the front ranks nearest the curb to their black fellow citizens and their children.[16] Beaming smiles were everywhere, save on the faces of those who wore the black band on their left sleeve, but even these "held themselves just as proudly as the rest." As the soldiers marched past the reviewing stand at 61st Street, past Mrs. Vincent Astor waving an American flag in the window of her home at 65th Street and industrialist Henry Clay Frick cheering at the top of his voice at his on 73rd, the intensity of the reception increased. At one point, so many wives, mothers, and sweethearts had dashed out into the street with flowers and kisses for the men that the regiment's commander was forced to halt the march and wait for the police to escort the civilians back to the curb so that the parade could continue.[17]

While the collective achievement of the men of the old 15th was the primary focus of the celebration, three individuals were recognized by the crowd for being particularly responsible for making the occasion one that the *Age* could describe as "one hundred percent American in every respect."[18] Colonel Hayward, the regiment's commanding officer, came immediately behind the mounted New York Police in the order of march. Hayward had been responsible for the recruitment and training of the unit and it was largely due to his persistence that the 15th was ever given its opportunity. There were many who believed that black soldiers were capable of support operations only; Hayward was not one of them. He had broken a leg during the war, and there were those who expected to see him limp as he stepped out in the front of his troops, but there was none. "Didn't your leg hurt you, Bill," a friend asked. "Sure it hurt me," he said, "but I wasn't going to peg along on the proudest day of my life."[19]

Another easily recognizable figure was that of Sergeant Henry Johnson, a former chauffeur from Albany, New York, whose exploits on May 13, 1918, earned him the Croix de Guerre with Golden Palm and made him one of the most famous American heroes of the war. That night, Johnson's watch post was attacked by two platoons of German soldiers. He defended his position so ferociously that the enemy was driven off, leaving four of their number dead and twenty wounded.[20] To accommodate the crowd, which became nearly ecstatic whenever he was identified, Sergeant Johnson stood upright in the second touring car of a fleet of ambulances that carried the injured. Holding in one hand a bouquet of fleur-de-lis, pressed on him early in the parade by an admirer, and his overseas cap in the other, he looked for all the world like "some conquering prince coming home to his proud retainers."[21] "The Battle of Henry Johnson," an incident of little military significance, was celebrated by Americans as proof of the permanence of individual, democratic values—of the efficacy of personal courage against overwheming odds—even in an age of mechanized, impersonal warfare.

There was a third legend of the Great War in the parade that day whom New Yorkers strained both to see and to hear: Lieutenant James Reese Europe and his world-famous 369th "Hellfighters" Band. There were many excellent military bands, black and white, in the American Expeditionary Force, but it may well have been true as Irvin S. Cobb declared in the *Saturday Evening Post* that this one was the best. The men of the 369th certainly believed it ("Our band easily won all the competitions," recalled Captain Hamilton Fish) and took great pride in it.[22] By the end of the summer of 1918, the reports of the "Hellfighters" musical achievements had become a source of national pride as well. They were already a good band before going abroad, said the *New York Times*, but once in France it had become an organization that "all Americans swore, and some Frenchmen admitted, was the best military band in the world."[23]

As important as it was for Americans to believe that their country could produce a concert band that was superior in musicianship to the great national military bands of Italy, France, and England, it was perhaps more flattering to the national ego to celebrate Jim Europe's band as the first internationally recognized exporter of a new American cultural art, a new musical idiom that was being labeled *jazz*. Phonograph recordings by The Original Dixieland Jazz Band did bring jazz to Great Britain in 1917, but it was Jim Europe's and his assistant's (Gene Mikell) arrangements of American popular songs, marches, ragtime, and blues that brought the sound of live jazz to Europe less than a year later.[24]

Despite this reputation, it is difficult to be sure how the band sounded that February day in 1919. Europe began the parade with the French "Marche du Regiment de Sambre et Meuse," and it is very likely that most of the music consisted of similar marches performed in a fairly strict military manner. The *Philadelphia Tribune*, while acknowledging that it was as a "jazz" band that they had become famous in France, assured its readers that Europe confined himself on this historic occasion "to dignified marching music all through the parade."[25] These were serious war heroes, after all, and not entertainers. Still, there are indications that the band's rhythms may have been looser and more swinging. The *World*, which tended to agree with the *Tribune*, was nonetheless impressed both by the unusually energetic drumming and by an "additional undercurrent of saxaphones [sic] and basses that put a new and more peppery tang" into the music.[26] Major Arthur Little claimed that the band played no jazz until it reached Harlem, "but if what we along the curbs heard was not jazz, it was the best substitute for it I've ever heard in my life," Bernard Katz later recalled. "All I know is that my school friends and I stepped out into the middle of the street with great hordes of other spectators, and swung up Fifth Avenue behind the 369th and the fantastic sixty-piece band that was beating out those rhythms that could be heard all the way down at our end of the parade."[27]

The conductor of the band, thirty-nine-year-old James Reese Europe, was not difficult to pick out from among the ranks of soldiers who marched up Fifth Avenue. He presented a commanding appearance at 6 feet tall and weighing over 200 pounds, as he marched in the front of his musicians wearing the uniform of a combat officer rather than a bandmaster. Due to an unusual set of circumstances, Europe had served in two different positions with the regiment: bandleader and officer of a machine gun company. He became the first African-American officer to lead men under fire in the great war while serving in the latter capacity, when the 369th went into action in March 1918.[28] In addition, of the regiment's five original black officers, he was the sole representative in the homecoming parade that day.[29]

The height of public enthusiasm, as might be expected, was reached when the "Hellfighters" crossed 110th Street and turned up Lenox Avenue into the heart of New York's Black Manhattan.[30] There, the sidewalks were so jammed with people that it was impossible for them not to spill into the street, as was every roof, window, and fire escape of every apartment along the avenue. Everyone seemed to be wearing a badge that read "Welcome, Fighting 15th" or a pennant bearing the coiled rattlesnake insignia of the regiment, and every hand seemed to be waving a French or American flag. The greeting, according to the *Age*, "bordered on a riot" as the band broke into a familiar popular tune, "Here Comes My Daddy Now."[31]

At 145th Street, a halt was officially called and Colonel Hayward was presented with a resolution on behalf of the citizens of Harlem praising the courage, bravery, and patriotism of the men who had been largely recruited from its streets. Immediately thereafter, the soldiers were taken by subway to the 71st Regiment Armory at 34th Street and Park Avenue, where they and several thousand friends and relatives were feted by Delmonico's, toasted in speeches that went mostly unheard, and entertained by boxing matches and vaudeville acts (including an appearance by the great Bert Williams). Later, the 2,000 exhausted, but exhilarated men of the 369th U. S. Infantry Regiment returned to Camp Upton to await their final mustering out of service the following day.

For James Reese Europe, then at the peak of his career, the future appeared exceedingly bright, and he was eager to grasp the opportunities before him. Prior to the war, Europe had been one of the most influential orchestra leaders and musicians in New York, and, indeed, in the entire country. During the first decade of the century, he had been a prominent contributor to black musical theater and had organized the first effective black musicians's professional organization in New York's history. A dedicated champion of African-American music, he brought the first orchestra of black musicians to the stage of Carnegie Hall for a "Symphony of Negro Music" in 1912, and received the first major recording contract for a black bandleader the next year. It was as a composer and conductor of syncopated dance music, marches, popular songs, and orchestral ragtime, however, that Europe was best known to the vast majority of white and black Americans. He had been instrumental, through his collaboration with dancers Vernon and Irene Castle, in gaining national acceptance for a new kind of social dancing and a new style of native American music that both stimulated and reflected a major transformation in American culture.

This period of cultural transition and contradiction, framed by the World's Columbian Exposition of 1893 (where the American public first discovered a music called ragtime) at one end and by the return of the troops from World War I in 1919 (when a new term—*jazz*—had replaced it) at the other, constitutes America's Ragtime Era. Though far from precise, *ragtime*, as a term, is nevertheless as appropriate to the period as it is to the music that sprang from it. James Reese Europe, a unique black American, lived his remarkable life literally in ragtime, chronologically and musically, and his career—in its achievements and frustrations, triumphs and tragedy—is a portrait of the era itself.

1

"Down Home Rag"

> Jim Europe grew up part way down in Mobile, associating mostly
> with common Alabama banjos and fiddles until he became ac-
> quainted with an upright piano. His father could play about
> everything that would emit a sound when properly coaxed. . . . If
> a man is going to become the general superintendent of a jazz
> band, it is always well to select that kind of a father.
>
> Charles Welton (1919)

James Reese Europe was born on February 22, 1880, in Mobile, Alabama,
fifteen years after the end of the Civil War, seven years after the birth of
W. C. Handy, and one year before Booker T. Washington began his work at
Tuskegee.[1] Europe's parents were native to the port city, and had come of age
during the era of sectional crisis and war. James' father, Henry, who began his
life as a slave, was a student of law at Howard University before his death; his
mother, Lorraine, was the freeborn daughter of one of the earliest and most
prominent African-American members of the Episcopal Church of Mobile. Both
parents, his mother perhaps more so than his father, were among a small
number of African-Americans living in antebellum Alabama, or elsewhere in
the United States for that matter, who were able to experience something of the
modern condition, which Lawrence Levine has aptly described as the "simultaneous participation in a variety of social worlds."[2] The reasons for this partly
have to due with their individual personalities and backgrounds. They also involve the unusual nature of Mobile itself, whose colonial history and resultant
character, like that of New Orleans, differed considerably from other Southern
cities like Richmond, Norfolk, or Charleston.

At the time of incorporation into the new State of Alabama in 1819,
Mobile could boast of a 100-year legacy of colonial occupation under France
(1702–1763), Great Britain (1763–1780), and Spain (1780–1813). One result
of this multinational history was that a number of Creole families had become
firmly established in the area prior to the American occupation.[3] Mobilians,
therefore, were never as comfortable with the simple racial dichotomy of
white/free versus black/slave that characterized much of the rest of the antebellum South. This is not to say that the city's free population was particularly
sympathetic to antislavery arguments. The city's rapid economic growth, especially in the 1820s and 1830s, depended almost exclusively upon the cotton
trade, and cotton, it was then believed, required slave labor.

While there was little cotton to speak of growing within the city limits, there was a considerable need for unskilled and semiskilled labor, and the ownership of slaves was recognized—as it was in the countryside—as a mark of family status. Although ownership was confined to a small proportion of the population, the number of slaves in Mobile relative to the rest of the population remained large, averaging roughly 30 percent throughout the antebellum period.[4]

In addition to slaves, Mobile was also accustomed to the presence of a substantial number of legally free persons of African or mixed racial background. Some of these freemen, who had been required by law to leave their home-states at the time of their emancipation, had migrated to Alabama from nearby eastern states like Georgia or South Carolina. Some were related to the older Creole families and had never been enslaved; others had been manumitted by their owners or by the legislature or the courts; and a few had purchased their own freedom.[5]

Of greater significance than the legally free blacks, however, at least in terms of their numbers, were those who remained slaves in the eyes of the law but for all practical purposes lived as free persons. The precise size of this group will never be known with certainty, but it was by no means an unusual practice for slave owners in antebellum Mobile to permit their slaves to hire out their own labor and even to rent their own places of residence. Some owners simply let their bondsmen go free without legally manumitting them. As sectional tensions increased in the 1850s, city officials became concerned about the extent of the practice and tried without much success to stop, or by issuing permits, to control it. A Mobile Joint Police Committee report of early 1856 stated that "it is the opinion of those best informed that there are now in this city as many as 1,000 Negroes who are living apart from their owners or agents."[6] This was at a time when the total number of slaves in the city was estimated at less than 7,000. One such slave, perhaps one of those who was living as free, was Henry J. Europe.

Few specifics are known about James Reese Europe's father or his paternal ancestors prior to the Civil War.[7] It is known, however, that Henry Europe was born into slavery in Mobile in 1847 and that he was active in the Baptist Church before the war.[8]

All of the major religious denominations of the city ministered to Mobile's black population, slave and free. As elsewhere in the South, however, blacks preferred the evangelical faiths and they "flocked to white Baptist and Methodist churches in such numbers that both denominations established separate African missions for them."[9] Despite white efforts to maintain the subordination of black religious activities, the African branches, especially of the Baptist church, routinely tested the limits of their independence. Indeed, there is evidence to suggest that an African Baptist Church, usually called the Stone Street Church, had been organized informally by free blacks in Mobile more than two decades prior to the establishment of the white First Baptist Church in 1835.[10] In any case, on December 20, 1846, Mobile's two white Baptist Churches formally constituted their black members into a "separate body called Stone Street Colored Church."[11]

Whether or not Stone Street was the "mother" Baptist church of the state, it assuredly was the "mother" church for African-Americans of the Baptist faith in Mobile. It was also the church in which Henry Europe grew up and to which he remained loyal throughout his life.[12] It was in this church that he received the early religious training, and probably much of the general education that prepared him to become a successful professional as well as a leader among Mobile's African-American Baptists following emancipation.[13]

Somewhat more is known of the maternal side of James Reese Europe's family history during the antebellum period. Lorraine Saxon Europe, his mother, was the third of four daughters born to Armistead and Mary Ann Saxon, who were themselves free. Armistead Saxon, who was described by the 1860 U.S. Census-taker as "black" and whose occupation was listed as cotton sampler, had come to Mobile from South Carolina, where he was born in 1822; Mary Ann, who was described as "mulatto" in the same census, was fourteen years younger and was a native of Georgia.[14] By the late 1840s they had married, begun a family, and become active in Trinity Episcopal Church. In the spring of 1854, when it was determined that a separate parish should be organized for the non-white congregation, Saxon was one of the seven individuals confirmed by the Right Reverend Nicholas Hamner Cobbs (Alabama's first Episcopal Bishop) as founding members of the Church of the Good Shepherd, the first African Episcopal congregation in the diocese of Alabama.[15] Saxon's position of leadership in the church over the next decade is apparent from the nearly two dozen baptisms of both slaves and free blacks for which he served as sponsor.[16]

On the eve of Civil War in the early summer of 1860, the Saxons, including their four daughters (Emily and Silvia, twelve; Lorraine, eleven; and Leanna, eight), were living two blocks from the Church of the Good Shepherd in Mobile's Seventh Ward.[17] Before 1840, free African-American families like the Saxons could be found scattered throughout the city in racially mixed neighborhoods, but in the later antebellum period residential patterns began to reflect racial and class segregation. By 1850, three quarters of the free blacks in Mobile lived in Wards 6 and 7, outside and to the west of the central core of the city. A major reason for this was due to economic competition between free African-Americans and the large numbers of poor and unskilled foreign workers, especially Irishmen and Germans, who flocked to the city looking for work. By 1860, with the foreign born accounting for half of the free male labor force, residential separation provided one way of reducing friction between nationalities and races, as well as between classes.[18]

The spring of 1865 brought the end of the Civil War, the four-year blockade of the port of Mobile, the emancipation of some 4 million African-Americans (over 8,000 in Mobile), and, in early December, the premature death of Armistead Saxon.[19] A year and a half later, on April 30, 1867, Lorraine, the third oldest Saxon daughter, who had been employed as a teacher, and Henry J. Europe were married in the home of Reverend J. A. Massey, Rector of Trinity Episcopal Church and minister to the Church of the Good Shepherd.[20]

The period of Reconstruction was not a happy or prosperous one for Mobile. The city endured the postwar political struggles and economic decline common to Alabama and much of the South. In addition, it also suffered from the worst municipal scandals in its history, leaving the city bankrupt by 1870. Two serious yellow fever epidemics, in addition to the Panic of 1873, perpetuated the city's miseries into the next decade. The period of federal occupation and Reconstruction, however, was a time of optimism and hope for Mobile's black population, just as it was for African-Americans throughout the South. If their expectations remained generally unrealized, there were occasionally real political and economic opportunities in individual cases. After working at a variety of temporary occupations including teaching, newspaper reporting, and barbering, Henry Europe was appointed to a clerkship in the Mobile Post Office in mid-1872.[21] He resigned two years later to accept a position with the Internal Revenue Service as a gauger for the Port of Mobile. The transfer from one desirable job to another, however, did not require a change in location since the Mobile Customs House, built in 1852 by the federal government, housed both the local Internal Revenue Service branch and the Post Office. It is also quite likely that Europe's appointments to these agencies were, at least in part, the result of his support of the Republican Party, which was then firmly in control in Washington. It was later said of him that Republicans held him "in high esteem," and that members of both races in the party regarded him "as an unassuming and reasonably safe citizen."[22]

If he was hardly a political radical, then Henry Europe was nonetheless a strong supporter of the Republican position on national reunification and the extension of citizen's rights to the new freedmen. His short career as a newspaper reporter with the weekly Mobile *Nationalist*, the first black owned and managed newspaper in Alabama, is evidence of both his acquisition of a basic literacy as well as of his solid Republican convictions. During its four years of existence (December 1865 to October 1869), the *Nationalist* was essentially a mouthpiece for the victorious party of Lincoln.[23]

Until 1874 the Europes, who now numbered four (Minnie and Ida, two daughters, were born in 1868 and 1870, respectively), lived in Mobile's old First Ward not far from Royal Street, where the slave market and holding barracks had stood before the war. By this date most of the city's African-American residents had begun concentrating in the shanties and tenements that had sprung up west of the center of the city in the Seventh Ward. In the fall of 1874, however, the Europes purchased two lots of land in the Bernoudy Tract, one of the original Spanish land grants that lay to the south and which had only recently begun to be developed as a residential area.[24] Henry Europe contracted with James McArthur for lumber and building materials, and a house was constructed on Wilkinson between Montgomery and Virginia Streets. The Europes moved into the Wilkinson Street house the following year in time for the birth of their first son, John; this would be their home for the next fourteen years.[25]

In addition to his employment with the Internal Revenue Service, Henry Europe continued his activities in the Baptist Church, where he rose quickly to a position of leadership. Despite a resolution adopted by the white Alabama Baptist Convention in 1865 encouraging their black members to remain within the white congregations, there was a natural desire among the new freedmen to form their own churches and select their own pastors.[26] In Mobile, where the trend toward racially independent Baptist congregations predated the war, the demand for new church organizations and new ministers was especially strong. In November 1873, at the Sixth Session of the Colored Baptist Convention of Alabama held in Tuscaloosa (the first meeting was held in Montgomery in 1868), Reverend Henry J. Europe was received as delegate from Mt. Zion Baptist Church, Dog River, Mobile County. The Dog River area lies several miles to the south of Mobile; therefore, it is likely that Europe was simply representing this new rural congregation to the state brotherhood as a missionary from Mobile, rather than as a member himself of Mt. Zion Church. In any case, Europe was a conspicuous member of the 1873 session, delivering several sermons and receiving an appointment as Corresponding Secretary of the Convention and a member of the Executive Board for the following year.[27]

At the Seventh Session of the Convention held November 11–17, 1874, in Mobile, Europe—now Pastor of the Virginia Street Church—was again a prominent delegate. He was reappointed to the executive board, continued as corresponding secretary, and elected as one of five managers of a proposed theological seminary to be established in Alabama for African-Americans. On November 12, he spoke to the Convention on the topic, "What persons should be teachers in the Sunday Schools?" On November 13 he addressed them on the topic, "How to bring about a more cultivated ministry among the churches of the denomination in the State."[28]

Europe's position within the statewide organization lasted only a short time. At the Eighth Annual Session, held in 1875, once again in Mobile, "some trouble arose over contentions among the churches" of Mobile. Although Europe was permitted to address the convention, his Virginia Street congregation was determined not to be in good standing and was "erased from the church roll."[29] Despite the lack of official recognition, Europe continued as pastor of the Virginia Street Church (later renamed the Warren Street Church) into the mid-1880s, when financial difficulties resulted in a default on the mortgage. The property was sold in 1886.[30]

Reverend Europe was in no position himself to make good on the church mortgage, as he had resigned, in April 1885, from the position he had held with the Internal Revenue Service since 1876. It is unclear why he left federal service, but the timing suggests that it may not have been completely voluntary. The election of Grover Cleveland, the first Democratic president since the Civil War, and the installation of his administration in Washington in early 1885, could not have been viewed with anything but concern by someone in Europe's situation. Whether or not pressure was brought to bear upon him to seek other employment, his replacement, John W. Butler, was described in a letter to Cleveland's secretary of the treasury as an individual "in full accord with the administration and the Democratic Party."[31]

It is also likely that national politics had an influence upon the Europes' eventual decision to leave Mobile. Although Henry Europe had continued to serve his church in several different capacities—including that of editor of a religious weekly—he was never able to secure another public service position in Mobile.[32] In 1888, however, when Benjamin Harrison's victory over Cleveland returned the Republicans to the White House, Henry Europe's past loyalty to the party and his thirteen years of prior federal service were positive advantages. He accepted an appointment with the National Postal Service at its home office in Washington, D.C., in 1889, and the Europes left Alabama and the South for the greater opportunities of the nation's capital.

While economic motives were paramount, concern for their children's future played a role in the Europes' decision. Increasingly repressive and segregationist conditions in Alabama and the South, coupled with reports of greater racial tolerance and wider educational opportunity for African-Americans in Northern cities, constituted a compelling argument for leaving. Their oldest daughter, Minnie, had married and no longer lived with the family; however, a second son, James Reese, had been born in 1880, and the last child, a daughter, Mary Lorraine, had come five years later. In 1889, then, the Europe family consisted of Henry, (42), Lorraine (40), Ida (19), John (14), James (9), and Mary (4).

Educational possibilities for the Europe children had been limited, as they were for other African-Americans in Mobile, but both parents from their own experience understood its importance and had done what they could to take advantage of what was available. Lorraine Europe instructed her children in the fundamentals of reading and writing as soon as they were able to learn. Later, they were sent to church-sponsored private schools, like the American Missionary Association's Emerson Institute, that were established by Northern philanthropy during Reconstruction.[33]

Both Lorraine and Henry Europe were fond of music, which maintained a central place in their religious life, and they also possessed some musical ability.

Lorraine Europe played the piano and had learned musical notation at least well enough to provide each of her children with their first music lessons.[34] Henry Europe, whose approach was more improvisational than was his wife's, was a self-taught performer on several instruments. Writer Charles Welton would describe him years later as the perfect father for a future leader of a jazz band because he "could play about everything that would emit a sound when properly coaxed, and he wasn't particular what."[35] Musical ability was especially important, perhaps even a prerequisite, for effective leadership within the black Baptist Church in those years, so it is not surprising that he occasionally composed his own hymns. One of those attributed to him, entitled "Peace—Be Still," has the lyrics:

> Since, then, the storms in life and death
> Do all obey thy will.
> Lord, may we hear at life's last breath
> Thy sweet words, "Peace—Be Still."[36]

All of the children seem to have responded positively to their early instruction, and the strong influence of their parents can be seen reflected in the future course of each of their lives. Minnie, Ida, John, and James became teachers themselves during at least part of their professional lives, although teaching was something of a last resort for the two brothers. For Mary, teaching became a lifetime career of over thirty years in the public schools. The role of music in the lives of the Europe children is even more striking because they all showed—especially the three youngest—both aptitude and continuing interest.

John, James, and Mary Europe all eventually made their living in music. John and Mary achieved notable reputations as pianists—John as a performer and occasional instructor of ragtime and popular music in New York; Mary as a teacher and accompanist of religious and concert music in Washington. James, whose contributions would be the most important, seems to have been the most broadly musical of the three. Although only nine years old when the Europes left Mobile, he had already begun to demonstrate his abilities, both on the piano (under his mother's instruction), as well as in improvising on the fiddles and banjos (encouraged by his father), which were more common to the musical life of Mobile's black community.[37] Mobile was also well-known, before and after the Civil War, for the popularity of cadet drill tournaments and for the excellence of its drill companies who "entered competitions all over the nation and often were judged the best-drilled in their divisions. Fancy night drills on the wharfs were popular and drew large crowds."[38] The stirring sounds of the ubiquitous brass bands that attended such activities could not have been lost on a youngster like Europe. Whether or not he was the "infant prodigy" the New York News later claimed him to be, it does appear that Jim Europe's interest in music had already been significantly developed and that his attitude toward it had been significantly shaped before his family left the South.[39]

2

"Washington Post March"

> I cannot remember him as ever anything else than a loving brother; from the earliest childhood up to the last sight of him he was always expressing his intention to take care of "Ma" and little "Sis."
>
> Mary Lorraine Europe

Upon arriving in the nation's capital after a northern journey of 1,200 miles, the Europe family found a bustling city that was both quite different from, and yet surprisingly similar to, the one they had left "down home." One of the immediately obvious differences was size. Washington, the Federal District of Columbia, had grown dramatically since the Civil War in its public as well as private aspects. The city's population increased from 75,000 citizens before the war to 132,000 by war's end. In the 1860s, the increase in federal jobs in the district doubled the city's share of the national total and gave an early indication of the emergence of a new kind of administrative state. Entrepreneurs from the North, many of them part of a "carpetbagger generation" in search of new business opportunities in a changing South, descended upon Washington in large numbers. They helped to forge connections between the city and a postbellum national economic core dominated by the North and Midwest.[1]

In social terms, by the early 1880s it could be claimed—with some reason—that the northeast's elite society considered Washington an appendage of New York City, its "winter end . . . as Newport is the summer extension of the metropolis."[2] At the same time, it was true nonetheless that, beginning perhaps as early as 1874 when an increasingly conservative Congress took over the administration of the city government, Washington's traditional Southern orientation began to reassert itself.

Washington's black population accounted for roughly one-third of the total of the city throughout the nineteenth century, but the number of those who were free surpassed those who were slaves as early as 1830.[3] During the 1860s and 1870s, black Americans poured into the city in large numbers, giving Washington the largest black citizenry of any city in the country by 1880. They had initially come from Tidewater Maryland and eastern Virginia. Black professionals from the north, however, also viewed Washington as offering opportunities for business as well as civil service careers, and a fairly substantial property-holding black middle class began to appear. The district's newest black residents, however, came increasingly from the deeper South and south Atlantic states, and many of them arrived with little more than their freedom.[4] The result was that a definite class structure, with essentially two divisions—a lower and a middle class—appeared in Washington's black community.

Until the late 1880s, race relations in Washington seemed to be the reflection of a relatively open, Northern community. The city's Board of Trade was integrated, as was the city government (until 1878, when the district was placed under three commissioners appointed by the president), and Republican presidents through Teddy Roosevelt regularly reserved federal appointments for blacks.[5] In 1867, with the opening of Howard University, an explicitly national institution, Washington announced its intentions of becoming a prominent cultural and intellectual center for African-Americans, and it did attract many of the country's most highly educated and creative black citizens. Three years later, in 1870, the Preparatory High School for Colored Youth, the first public high school for blacks in the United States, opened its doors in the basement of the Fifteenth Street Presbyterian Church.[6]

In 1891, the Preparatory School moved to its first permanent location, a brick building on M Street N.W., and it became known as the M Street High School (it was renamed in honor of Paul Laurence Dunbar twenty-five years later). From the 1890s until the 1940s, M Street/Dunbar High remained the best public high school for African-Americans in the United States, educating "more notable black professionals and public servants than any other high school in America." It also remained the best public high school in the district for either whites or blacks, sending "80 percent of the graduates" on to higher education.[7] Washington's black middle class saw education as an opportunity for achieving "what they called racial uplift, and the performance of their sons and daughters in these schools dispelled the idea, widely held at the time, that blacks were either ineducable or incapable of high academic achievement."[8]

By 1889, when the Europes arrived in the city, despite the emergence of a self-conscious black middle class, race relations in the district had begun to harden. The initially integrated Board of Trade became all white, de facto segregation began to appear in public facilities, and Southern congressmen began pressing for formal segregation.[9] In 1901, the last black congressman to serve in the U. S. House of Representatives until after World War I left office. An editorial the following year in the Washington, D.C., *Colored American* lamented that "Washington prejudice is more intense than is found in most of the cities of the South."[10]

The Europes' first residence in the district was at 308 B Street S. E., in the section of the city that traditionally had the greatest concentration of black property owners.[11] Their house was two blocks from East Capital Street and in reasonable proximity to the Post Office Department where Henry Europe was employed. His initial position was as a clerk, but within two years he became a supervisor in the Mail Equipment Division.[12] He also applied to Howard University and was admitted to the Law Department in which he reached junior standing but was never graduated.[13] Lorraine Europe continued in her role as wife, mother, and principal piano teacher to the two younger children, James and Mary, while John, (15) was enrolled at the Preparatory High School. James, who was then nine and called "Jim," attended the third grade at Lincoln Grammar School on Capital Hill. It was about this time that he first began to study the instrument that would be his first love—the violin—under Joseph Douglass, the youthful grandson of the abolitionist, Frederick Douglass.[14] Joseph Douglass, then at the beginning of his career, became an admired soloist and teacher by the turn of the century.[15]

In addition to his musical aptitude, Jim Europe demonstrated a strong personality and a natural organizational ability. His physical size—as noted earlier, he was tall and stocky—certainly helped. "He would be sent to the store," his sister recalled, "but he would return with a little group of playmates tagging after him. Wherever he went boys flocked around him. He swayed them willingly. He organized them into clubs with wonderful names and still more wonderful purposes."[16]

The Europes also quickly reestablished a church affiliation, and Jim regularly attended religious services at Lincoln Memorial Congregational Church with his mother and younger sister. His father often accompanied them, but Henry Europe never became a member of a Washington church, faithfully retaining his membership in the Baptist Church of Mobile throughout his life. Reverend A. B. Miller, pastor of Lincoln Church at the time, was well liked by the young people and known for his effectiveness in engaging them in church activities. Jim admired Reverend Miller, happily participated in Sunday School and Christian Endeavor, and was in time baptized and confirmed a member of the church. One evening when he was about twelve, he returned home from a revival meeting to announce in a straightforward manner that he had been converted and "that he had given his heart to God and meant thereafter to follow in the footsteps of Jesus the Christ."[17]

Jim enjoyed the opportunities Reverend Miller gave him to assist in planning and organizing concerts and dramatic performances by the younger church members. He was popular among the other children, despite the fact that he tended to be rather decided, as well as outspoken, in his opinions. There were, of course, many "lively disagreements," Mary Europe remembered, but Jim—even as an adolescent—was able to keep such disputes from deteriorating into personal attacks. No wonder, then, that he was usually able to get his way without creating enemies or losing friends.[18]

In 1891, the celebrated leader of the most famous musical organization in the city and probably the nation, John Philip Sousa, moved with his family into the house at 318 B Street S.E., a few doors away from the Europes. Such an event could hardly have escaped the notice of the musical Europe family, especially that of the two Europe boys. The brass band movement in America was then entering its period of greatest popularity with an estimated 10,000 bands and 150,000 bandsmen actively performing across the nation.[19] Virtually every town of any size supported some sort of civic band, and larger communities— like Mobile—could boast of several such groups who had been performing regularly since the Civil War. In addition, there were numerous professional concert bands like that of Patrick S. Gilmore that toured the country extensively. In the nation's capital, brass band music seemed especially appropriate, and bands—white and black—provided popular entertainment for picnics, banquets, riverboat excursions, celebrations (like the annual Emancipation Day Parade on April 16), dances, drill contests, and serenades.[20] Most important, Washington was the home of the U.S. Marine Corps Band.

Since taking charge of the U.S. Marine Corps Band in 1880, John Philip Sousa had molded it into such a high-caliber organization that it was often referred to as *the* National Band.[21] Both Sousa, who had been dubbed the "March King" for such compositions as "The *Washington Post* March" and "Semper Fidelis," and the Marine Band itself had a long-standing relationship with the African-American community in Washington. The Marine Band regularly took part in such important events in the black community as Howard University's commencement ceremonies, and band members often provided musical instruction to promising black children. One of those youngsters was Jim Europe, who, along with his sister Mary according to some accounts, received instruction on piano and violin from Enrico Hurlei, the assistant director of the band. It is entirely likely that this early training provided the foundation for Europe's later successes as a composer of marches and as a leader of a military band during World War I.[22]

In 1894, Henry Europe resigned his position with the Postal Service to enter the promising real estate business. Washington was then undergoing a rapid expansion and transformation in residential housing patterns, and there was a need for African-Americans in the field. Once relatively integrated, with residential segregation limited to a block or an alley or to one side of a street, Washington's whites and blacks began resettling themselves along racial lines within larger neighborhood or sectional concentrations by the mid-1880s.[23] Class and status differences also became more clearly apparent. It was to one of these areas, the northwest section of the district centered on 7th Street north of M Street, that Henry Europe moved his family to embark on his new profession.

Seventh Street N.W. was one of the most important transportation routes to and from the city for many years. It was largely rural in 1880, but the northern end of the thoroughfare grew rapidly after 1893 as a racially mixed neighborhood when farms were broken up and streets were laid out.[24] Closer to the center of the city lay a large commercial and residential area (known more recently as "Shaw"). As racial attitudes hardened and blacks began to be excluded from the major stores downtown, 7th Street N.W. between Massachusetts and Florida Avenues developed into a secondary shopping area with both white- and black-owned businesses serving a largely black clientele.[25] By the mid-1880s African-Americans in the area could boast of several building associations, newspapers, realty companies, and (in 1888) the first black-owned bank in the United States.[26] Although the area began to become predominantly black in the 1890s, as Marcia Greenlee has written, "until 1900 and as late as World War I in some sections, Shaw was a preferred neighborhood for middle-class white residents."[27]

The most desirable neighborhood in the area, at first for white government administrators and professionals and later for Washington's most prominent and successful African-Americans, was LeDroit Park. Originally designed to feel like a refined rural village; the developers set the streets at angles to the city grid, encircled it with a fence and gates, and screened all applicants for the handsome James H. McGill-designed houses.[28] From the mid-1870s until the mid-1880s, LeDroit Park existed as the exclusive settlement it had been intended to be—the "flower garden" of Washington, as one former resident described it.[29] As the city spread northward along 7th Street, however, LeDroit Park's pleasant isolation was inevitably undermined. The fences had come down by 1891. Two years later, at about the time that Henry Europe moved his family to nearby 8th Street, LeDroit Park had its first black homeowner, and the gradual turnover from white to black began. LeDroit Park remained one of the most socially desirable, black middle-class residential neighborhoods in Washington until the Great Depression.

In the early 1890s, northwest Washington was an ideal place for Henry Europe to begin to develop his real estate business. In addition, Lincoln Memorial Congregational Church, M Street High School, and Howard University, the institutions of greatest importance to the Europe family, were located there. In moving to northwest Washington, the Europes also joined the tide of newly arriving black professionals and older established government workers who sought to purchase homes there that would demonstrate their rising status.

Having completed their schooling, the two oldest Europe children (Ida, 24, and John, 19) continued to live at home while seeking to establish their own careers. Ida Europe eventually secured a secretarial position with the U. S. Government Printing Office; John struggled to establish himself as a professional musician and music instructor. James, who was now enrolled at the M Street High School, and Mary, who would follow him in 1896, continued to receive regular private musical instruction, including, by some accounts, instruction in theory and instrumentation under Hans Hanke, a former member of the Leipzig Conservatory. They also began to provide positive evidence of their developing talents. Among the featured performances at a public recital on July 9, 1894, at the Vermont Avenue Baptist Church was a violin duet by "Jas. R. Europe and Mary L. Europe." That same year, at the age of fourteen, Jim entered a citywide contest in composition and came in second; his younger sister took the top prize.[30]

The curriculum at M Street High was challenging, regardless of whether a student chose one of the traditional courses of study (the academic track stressed Latin, Greek, and mathematics; the scientific track emphasized German, French, and the sciences) or the newer business course that Principal Francis L. Cardosa had recently instituted. "At the M Street High School,"a former student of those years recalled, "a dedicated and stimulating faculty fostered students' intellectual ambitions. Twenty of the thirty regular teachers had degrees from top-flight Northern colleges and universities, and five others had graduated from Howard." M Street students were accustomed to "long hours of study."[31]

One of the most popular extracurricular activities for high school boys was military drill. Military science instruction, which consisted of a weekly manual of arms and parade drill at the O Street Armory, was begun in 1890 under the direction of Civil War Medal of Honor winner Major Christian A. Fleetwood. Fleetwood and his wife, who was superintendent of the Training School for Nurses at Freedmen's Hospital, were among the first black couples to move into LeDroit Park. In the fall of 1892, Congress authorized the organization of a colored high school cadet corps, and the following year the M Street High cadets were invited to march in President Grover Cleveland's second inaugural parade. In May 1893, the first public competitive drill drew a large audience to Metropolitan A. M. E. Church, and the popularity of the activity with both high school students and the public grew dramatically thereafter. In fact, by 1897 the annual cadet drill competition had become a major spring social event in Washington's African-American community, attracting such large crowds that it had to be held in the new National League baseball stadium.[32]

With his outgoing personality and his musical interests, Jim Europe was quickly recruited into the high school cadets. During his two years at M Street High, he was a popular and enthusiastic member of Captain Joseph Montgomery's prize drill company and served as Color Sergeant for the corps.[33] Like many an ex-high school football star, he was proud of his high school experience and never forgot it. "Let me know when the competitive drill will be," he wrote his sister from New York in May 1915 during a very busy period in his career, "and I will come down."[34] Europe's cadet training would later prove useful when he sought to organize the black musicians of New York; it was undoubtedly helpful to him as an officer in the 15th New York Infantry Regiment in World War I.

In the late nineteenth and early twentieth century, skin color (or shade, as it was called) was thought to be a reflection of socioeconomic status and was, therefore, a prominent feature of relationships among black Washingtonians. The black middle class of the postbellum period consisted of a relatively small number of lawyers, teachers, doctors, clergymen, businessmen, and government employees. Within this fortunate minority, a disproportionate number were descendents of light-skinned antebellum free Negroes ("free persons of color"), and they tended to make personal judgments based upon skin color.

Given this general situation, it would have been surprising if M Street High had managed to escape such color distinctions (that it did not, in fact, has been one of the strongest criticisms of the school).[35] There is no evidence, however, to suggest that during his high school years Jim Europe ever felt personally disadvantaged or belittled because of the fact that he was dark-skinned and strong-featured. Mary recalled that when she joined her older brother at M Street High, he would take her hand and they would often stroll down the hall together holding hands—not the behavior one might expect from an adolescent male lacking in self-confidence.[36] Still, if such prejudice did not touch him in a directly personal way, he could not help noticing that it was a factor, perhaps, in the way that some of his other classmates were treated.

Class and status concerns were extremely prevalent in America in the last quarter of the century, influencing attitudes toward individually inherited physical features like skin color as well as virtually any outward manifestation of achievement (or the lack of it) including musical taste, where the formal European concert tradition provided the standard of respectability. Perhaps the most fully developed and widely practiced concert music in Washington, D.C., and indeed across the entire United States in the latter half of the nineteenth century in both black and white communities, was choral music. African-American practice was grounded, of course, in the informal singing and more formal sacred concerts of the black church choirs supplemented by such early touring groups as the Fisk Jubilee Singers, who visited Washington several times in the 1870s and 1880s. Washington's churches were known for the quality of their choirs as well as for the size of their auditoria, especially after the new Metropolitan A.M.E. Church—with an auditorium that could seat 1,800 in the main hall—was dedicated in 1885.[37]

Members of church choirs participated in vocal ensembles like the Original Colored American Opera Troupe, the Amphion and Orpheus Glee Clubs, and (after 1901) the Samuel Coleridge-Taylor Choral Society. They also contributed to such large-scale productions as the Gilbert and Sullivan operetta *H.M.S. Pinafore*, performed before a mixed racial audience at National Theatre in 1879, and Von Flotow's opera *Martha*, presented at the Grand Armory Hall in 1890. In addition, singers with national reputations like Thomas Bethune ("Blind Tom"), Anita Patti Brown, Madame Marie Selika, Flora Batson Bergen, Agnes Smallwood, Harry T. Burleigh, and Sissieretta Jones ("Black Patti") performed before receptive audiences in Washington. Touring concert instrumentalists were less common, perhaps because there were fewer of them in the country at the time, as was true also with regard to orchestras. In 1889, however, with support from both Frederick Douglass and Major Christian Fleetwood, a twenty-year-old violinist named Will Marion Cook undertook to provide Washington and its black community with an orchestra. Although Cook was eleven years older than Europe, the lives of the two Washingtonians would intersect later in significant ways.

Will Marion Cook was the second of three sons born to John and Isabel Cook, both of whom were graduates of Oberlin. The Cooks came to the district (settling in the northwestern section of the city, at 16th and M Street) from Kentucky in 1867 when John accepted the position of chief clerk of the Freedman's Bureau. A member of the first graduating class from Howard University's Law Department, John Cook subsequently practiced law in Washington from 1871 until he unexpectedly died of tuberculosis in 1878 at the age of forty.[38]

Young Cook was raised partly by his mother, a school teacher, and partly by other relatives in various parts of the country, including Chattanooga, Tennessee, until he was finally sent to his paternal aunt in Oberlin, Ohio, where he enrolled in the public high school and began violin studies at the conservatory. In 1888, Cook was back in Washington with a letter from Professor Doolittle, his violin instructor, recommending that he be sent abroad for further training to Berlin. Thanks to Frederick Douglass, an old friend of the Cooks, and to other leading musical figures in Washington's black community (including Major Fleetwood, Henry Grant, John T. Layton, and Dick Thompkins), a benefit concert at the First Congregational Church was arranged. Young Cook so impressed the mixed racial audience with his performance that, when the concert concluded, he had the funds he needed and in the fall of 1888 sailed for Germany.

Following a year of study in Berlin at the Hochschule für Musik (including, perhaps, some work with master violinist Joseph Joachim), Will Marion Cook returned to Washington, D.C. In September, a new orchestra was launched, with Frederick Douglass as president, Major Fleetwood as vice president, and Cook himself as director/conductor. The instrumentation consisted of six violins (Cook, Joseph Douglass, and four others), one cello, three cornets, two French horns, two clarinets, one flute, a saxophone, a tambourine, and a bass violin. Elsie Hoffman, saxophonist and later an orchestra leader, gave what was probably the first solo by a black American on that instrument at a concert of the orchestra given at the Grand Army Hall on September 26, 1889.[39] After a couple of tours of the eastern seaboard, however, the orchestra disbanded and Cook headed to New York to continue his studies at the newly created National Conservatory of Music, then directed by the celebrated composer, Antonín Dvořák.

Equally as ambitious as Cook, Jim Europe would likely have remained in Washington (and in school) had it not been for the sudden death of his father, Henry Europe, on June 21, 1899.

3

"On the Gay Luneta"

> Strictly speaking, I had no musical education myself. . . . Music I
> picked up as I went along. I gained much valuable training
> during six years I spent on the road as orchestra leader with
> negro musical comedies, for I was careful to keep always before
> me the ambition for a higher kind of work, and I was careful not
> to permit my sense of musical proportion to leave me.
>
> James Reese Europe (1914)

Shortly before he died, Henry Europe moved his family to 310 Oak Street in the LeDroit Park neighborhood. The unexpected loss of her husband, however, left Lorraine Europe in a difficult situation. It had been more than thirty years since she had earned a wage, and her two oldest daughters were living in Mobile. Her youngest daughter, Mary, had intended to continue her education at Miner Normal School for teachers. Neither of her sons, John (now 24), nor James (19), however willing to accept responsibility for supporting their mother and younger sister, had been successful in finding satisfactory employment as professional musicians in Washington.[1]

The newspapers in the district, however, had been carrying reports of increasing opportunities for African-Americans in the musical activities in New York City, and especially the recent successes of black musical theater, for several years. "Next season's bookings show a general rise in salaries," reported a typical article in the *Colored American* in July 1898; "there will be sixteen straight Afro-American companies on the road."[2] As a popular entertainer, said the *American* the following year, the Negro "has always been a success. Nearly all the leading vaudeville, speciality, and variety shows have engaged first class colored talent for next season. Coon songs are popular. So is the prize cake walk, and as minstrels they cannot be truly imitated." In addition, and more reassuring to Lorraine Europe, "refined concert talent among the colored people" was being sought and "booked by high class companies."[3] By the fall of 1900, it had become commonplace among black Washingtonians to see New York as *the* center for African-American professional musicians and entertainers (despite the dangers of corruption), and many of the District's aspiring talents had already joined the pilgrimage to the "Mecca for colored performers."[4] Among them was John Europe.

James remained at home in Washington with his mother and sister, studying and practicing as much music as he was able while holding down a series

of low-paying, temporary jobs. Finally, in late 1902 or early 1903, the combi-
nation of the return of his older sister, Ida, from Mobile, and the graduation of
Mary from Miner Normal School (and her subsequent employment by the
Washington City Schools), made it possible for James to leave his mother in
Washington and join his brother in the great metropolis.[5]

However high his expectations, or confident in his own abilities, Europe
did not immediately encounter much success in the popular entertainment
capital of America. At the time of his arrival, there were no clubs or employment offices or unions that would admit blacks or where an aspiring black
musician, newly arrived in the city, might apply for work. There was, however,
a widely accepted if informal procedure centered upon the clubs, saloons,
brothels, restaurants, and other places of entertainment that abounded in the
geographic center of Manhattan's nightlife, the area known as the Tenderloin.[6]
Tin Pan Alley, the famous concentration of popular music publishing houses
between Broadway and Sixth on West 28th Street, was located in the Tenderloin, and so were such legendary establishments as John B. Nail's saloon, where
many of the more successful and polished black performers gathered, or Ike
Hine's Professional Club, where some of the best ragtime piano players in New
York performed. Another club, Barron Wilkins's Little Savoy on West 35th
Street, was known as "the most important spot where Negro musicians got acquainted with the wealthy New York clientele who became the first patrons of
their music."[7] One of the regular piano players at the Little Savoy during this
time was John Europe.[8]

Theatrical producers and managers, song publishers, established performers (white and black), club owners, and their scouts, ever on the lookout for
new talent, attended such places partly for the purpose of auditioning aspiring
entertainers. A number of these clubs maintained an "open floor" policy where
promising musicians, like Jim Europe, or aspiring singers or dancers, were invited to perform, alone or with the club orchestra. Many later Broadway stars
owed their success to being discovered through such a process.

Deciding to put his best—and also his favorite—musical foot forward, the
younger Europe spent several lean weeks auditioning as a violinist in various
cafes and saloons. Although he was often applauded by the patrons, and sometimes even by the club musicians, no solid employment offers were
forthcoming.[9] The reason, he finally realized, was primarily not his skill; rather,
it was his instrument. The violin, especially when played in concert style, was
simply not in the popular vogue. Faced with a choice of conforming to public
taste or starving, and with a broken heart—as he later told Noble Sissle—he
put away the violin and took up the mandolin. Between this new instrument
and the piano, which he played well, although not as well as the violin, Europe
began to find regular employment in the district and to make his start as a professional musician.

Vaudevillian Tom Fletcher remembered Europe at the beginning of his career as a good piano player, as well as an ambitious and dedicated student of music theory, instrumentation, and conducting. "He was so interested in his studies," Fletcher recalled, "that while playing an engagement at the Brevoort Hotel in New York one evening, he brought a book of his lessons on the job and placed it on the piano so he could study while he worked."[10] Among those with whom he continued his music studies in New York were Harry T. Burleigh, a student of Dvořák's at the American Conservatory, and Melville Charlton, composer and noted organist at St. Philips Episcopal Church and the Temple Emanu-El.[11]

In the first decade of the twentieth century, the most important gathering place for successful and talented African-Americans in the world of music and the stage was the Marshall Hotel on West 53rd Street, just north of the Tenderloin. There were actually two hotels: the Marshall and the Maceo; both were converted brownstones, and both were run by blacks. The Maceo, however, catered more to the clergy and businessmen, while the Marshall became the headquarters of the actors and the musicians. Indeed, between 1900 and 1910, the Marshall was one of the "sights of New York," according to James Weldon Johnson, "for it was gay, entertaining, and interesting," and one could get a close-up view of the most famous actors, musicians, composers, writers, and better paid vaudevillians in New York. "To be a visitor there, without at the same time being a rank outsider, was a distinction."[12] As an ambitious young musician, Europe was understandably drawn to the Marshall as soon as he could afford to eat in its dining room, and it was there in 1903 that he made the acquaintance of John W. Love.

Love was private secretary to Rodman Wanamaker, whose father, John, was the developer of the department store and patriarch of the wealthy and socially prominent Philadelphia family. The senior Wanamaker had served as postmaster general in the Harrison administration from 1889 to 1893, and it was he who provided Henry Europe with the clerkship in the Postal Department that brought the Europes from Mobile to Washington, D.C. Whether or not the relationship between Wanamaker and Europe had been a personal one, as Lorraine Europe maintained, it is likely that the ex-cabinet member was at least familiar with Europe's name.[13]

In any case, shortly after Love and Europe met at the Marshall Hotel Europe's first musical group, a string quartet, was engaged to supply the music for Rodman Wanamaker's birthday celebration—a modest affair at Atlantic City, New Jersey, lasting three days. Europe and his music apparently pleased the Wanamakers so much, in fact, that from that day until his death in 1919, Europe was a part of "every celebration of the Wanamaker family."[14] The Wanamakers were important to Europe and his musical future in two ways: first, as employers they paid him well for his services and treated him as a professional; second, and most critically, they provided a valuable introduction for Europe, and indeed, through him for black musicians in general, to the social and financial elite of Philadelphia and New York. The patronage of the members of Eastern high society became especially important when black musical theater went into decline after 1910 and the demand for black musicians on the stage fell.

In 1904, however, at the time that Europe was beginning to establish himself in New York, the most exciting area of the black music profession, both artistically and in terms of popular acceptance and acclaim, was the musical stage. In the fall of that year, Europe got his first theater opportunity when he was asked by the John Larkins Company, virtually at the last minute, to direct the orchestra and chorus for a musical farce called *A Trip to Africa*.

The comedy opened on October 17, 1904, to a large and generally appreciative mixed racial audience at the Third Avenue Theater. The critical reaction, however, even in the black press, was also mixed. One reviewer, Sylvester Russell, the Indianapolis *Freeman*'s pioneering music critic, found the plot of the play only "fair" and the inclusion of vaudeville acts in the production objectionable. "If a Negro comedy can't go on its merits without resorting to variety," he wrote, "the botchworkers may as well stop writing comedy and return to the variety stage." On the other hand, he praised the individual stars (Larkins, Dora Patterson, and Bert Grant) and found the songs entertaining and the incidental music "quite well rendered."[15] Frank Clermont, in a special to the *Freeman*, offered a second opinion. In his judgment, the orchestra was simply "vile, cues were not taken up fast enough by the director," despite the fact that Mr. Europe, in a later interview, "said that he could not have done any better as they had just engaged him a couple of hours before the show."[16]

Clermont, a songwriter and bandleader in his own right, and Russell both received the impression that Europe was responsible for writing much of the music as well as for directing the orchestra, but neither could verify the fact. It is true that Europe had begun to have some success in Tin Pan Alley by the fall of 1904; five of his popular compositions had been sold to the music publisher Sol Bloom, the most successful of which was a song entitled "Blue Eyed Sue." It is possible, therefore, that his growing reputation as a songwriter could have encouraged the impression that he had moved on into musical comedy. Europe did write one song with John Larkins, called "Zola: Jungle Song," published in November 1904, but it is not known if this was sung in *A Trip to Africa*.[17] No programs for *A Trip to Africa* have survived, and none of the songs mentioned in the *Freeman* reviews ("Without You," "Shame on You," "Make a Fuss Over Me," "The Blackville Volunteers," and "Listen to the Big Brass Band") were ever published, so the composer or composers may never be known.

Subsequent events suggest that Europe was probably not the principal composer for *A Trip to Africa*. When the company left New York for Albany on November 2, Europe was no longer a member, having been replaced by nineteen-year-old Will Vodery as musical director.[18] Had he been the production's major composer, one would expect a longer tenure. In any case, *A Trip to Africa* began Jim Europe's career in black musical theater, an involvement that was to occupy him almost exclusively for the next six years and to which he planned to return at the time of his death. In December, the production began a tour of Southern states, which carried it as far from New York as Little Rock, Arkansas, and which ended in early March.[19]

Europe's horizons began to expand dramatically toward the end of 1904 and the beginning of 1905 due, in large part, to the connections he was making at the Marshall Hotel. He was now becoming known by many of the biggest names in black musical theater, among them Ernest Hogan, a multitalented entertainer whose career was at the center of the transformation of black musical theater from nineteenth-century minstrelsy to vaudeville and twentieth-century musical comedy.

Hogan, who was born Reuben Crowdus in 1865 in Bowling Green, Kentucky, got his start touring across the country with various tent shows and minstrel companies. In 1895, he composed his most famous (or infamous) tune, "All Coons Look Alike to Me," which was instrumental in creating the national fad for similar "coon" songs that lasted until World War I. Following two years as the leading comic, dubbing himself the "unbleached American" of the Black Patti Troubadours, Hogan was offered the starring role in Will Marion Cook's path-breaking all-black musical comedy, *Clorindy, the Origin of the Cakewalk*, which opened on Broadway on July 5, 1898. Despite the positive reception of *Clorindy*, other efforts along the same line failed to materialize, and Hogan spent the next half-dozen years touring America and abroad with various minstrel shows and variety acts.[20]

In early 1905, utilizing the experience and talent at the Marshall Hotel, Hogan began assembling a new song and dance group that he called the "Memphis Students," although none of its members was a student and none hailed from Memphis. The "Memphis Students," a singing, dancing, twenty-member orchestra, was originally intended simply as one of the features of a three act "musical melange" called "The Birth of the Minstrel," in which Hogan was to star and Will Marion Cook was to compose the music.[21] In an attempt to capitalize on the international fame of the Fisk Jubilee Singers (who were actually students from Fisk University in Nashville), numerous minstrel troops in the late nineteenth century adopted such names as the "Nashville Students." By 1900, there were at least four touring troops with such titles, including "Rusco and Holland's Original Nashville Students," with whom Hogan had himself worked.[22]

For his "Memphis Students," Hogan recruited Abbie Mitchell, a noted soprano and wife of Will Marion Cook, Ida Forsyne and Will Dixon, dancers, and perhaps twenty of the best instrumentalists/singers in the city, among them

Jim Europe.[23] The group made its debut at Proctor's Twenty-third Street Theatre in the early spring, and from there they were booked for a two-week
engagement at Hammerstein's Victoria Theatre, beginning June 19. The reviewer for the New York *World* found the first night's performance more than
entertaining:

> Far down the programme at the Paradise Garden, on the Victoria Roof, Ernest
> Hogan, the Negro singing comedian, assisted by Abbie Mitchell, a comely mulatto
> with a sweet soprano voice, and twenty-five others who performed a combined
> function of chorus and orchestra, gave a half hour specialty called, "Songs of the
> Black Folk" that came closer than any of the tinsel and burnt [sic] cork produc-
> tions that have been seen on Broadway in the last ten years. The roof garden
> fairly reeked with melody. There was a fervor in the rendering of the songs and
> choruses that could never have been supplied by white singers.[24]

Oscar Hammerstein was also pleased, and he quickly extended Hogan's contract until September. The troop had passed its one-hundredth performance by
mid-August, and Hammerstein was now offering a full-summer engagement
for the following year. "Rarely in the history of show business," gushed the *New
York Age* of August 24, "has such a decided hit been made as by Mr. Hogan, assisted by Abbie Mitchell Cook, and his Memphis Students at Hammerstein's
Roof Garden."[25]

Part of the reason for the popular success of the Memphis Students was
the novelty of a performing orchestra, one that both accompanied the star
vocalists, and also sang and danced in its own right. Will Dixon, the original
dancing conductor, epitomized this as he sometimes gracefully, and sometimes
grotesquely, danced out the rhythms of each piece. "Often an easy shuffle
would take him across the whole front of the band," James Weldon Johnson
later recalled, which seemed to get "the fullest possible response from the men
but kept them in just the right humour for the sort of music they were playing."[26] It could have been this emphasis upon performance that led Johnson to
characterize the Memphis Students as "the first modern jazz band ever heard
on a New York stage, and probably on any other stage."[27] There was also something special, however, about the instrumentation of the ensemble.

Johnson remembered hearing a saxophone, drums, and "a couple of brass
instruments," instruments common to the true jazz bands of a later period,
which are not reported in the contemporary accounts. Rather, the Students
seem to have consisted of about twenty instrumentalists predominantly playing mandolins, harp guitars, and banjos (with perhaps three celli added for
good measure).[28] All of these, with the exception, possibly, of the celli, are
plucked or strummed and, when performed by a tightly coordinated aggregate,
would provide the strongly rhythmical effect that was often noted. Such an
instrumentation would be effective both in conveying the kind of syncopated
music that Will Marion Cook was then composing as well as sound authentic

to the Southern African-American musical tradition from folk music and spirituals through minstrelsy. The success of this unusual instrumentation, both popularly and musically, had a particularly strong influence on Jim Europe, who would attempt to build upon it when he organized his large 100-member Clef Club, Tempo Club, and National Negro Orchestras in the next decade.

It was Hogan's intention, following the conclusion of the Memphis Students' run at Hammerstein's in early September, to continue managing the act on the vaudeville circuit both at home and abroad in England and on the Continent. His own part in the act was to be taken by Bobby Kemp, while Hogan himself worked on his long-cherished dream to mount a full-scale musical comedy of his own.[29] Cook apparently decided that he should manage the Students, and he convinced his wife and several of the other original members to break their contracts with Hogan. In late October, despite court injunctions granted to Hogan, sixteen of the ex-Memphis Students, now known as the Tennessee Students, sailed with Cook for Europe where, in the course of the next six months, they appeared at the Palace Theatre in London, the Olympia in Paris, and the Schumann Circus in Berlin.[30]

Europe, who remained loyal to Hogan, continued his studies and writing in New York. By mid-December Carle Browne Cooke reported that he was organizing and rehearsing a new version of "Ernest Hogan's Memphis Students at the famous Hotel Marshall in West 53rd Street for another engagement in vaudeville." "Mr. Europe," commented Cooke, "is talented, studious, and able. We wish him continued success in this new organization."[31] Europe's group performed widely in and around New York over the next three years, but it was not until the summer of 1908 that a major new edition of the Memphis Students, this time organized by Joe Jordan and starring Tom Fletcher, once again became headliners at Hammerstein's Roof Garden at Broadway and 42nd Street.[32] By then Europe, like Hogan before him, had chosen to concentrate his energies in musical theater rather than vaudeville.

In the late winter of 1905, Bob Cole and the Johnson brothers (James Weldon and J. Rosamond), who comprised the hottest songwriting team on Broadway and who were then enjoying large royalties for such songs as "Under the Bamboo Tree," "My Castle on the Nile," and "Congo Love Song,"—songs written for white musical productions—decided to write a complete musical for a company of their own.[33] The trio, who worked out of offices in the Marshall Hotel, would be the principle writers of the lyrics and songs, and Cole and Rosamond Johnson, who had already established themselves as an internationally successful vaudeville act, were also to be the major stars. A strong supporting cast, including Tom Brown, Sam Lucas, Theodore Pankey, and Anna Cook, was assembled, and James Reese Europe was asked to direct the orchestra and the forty-member chorus.[34] With a plot conceived largely by Cole, the musical was called *The Shoo-Fly Regiment*.

The Shoo-fly Regiment is best characterized as a musical farce in three acts set during the time of the Spanish-American War. The first and third acts take place at an industrial school for Negroes in Alabama, an obvious reference to Booker T. Washington's Tuskegee Institute, while Manila, in the Philippines, provides the setting for the second. The rather conventional plot involves a young graduate of the Alabama school, Hunter Wilson, who puts aside a teaching career to come to the defense of his country in the war against Spain. Everyone approves of his bravery and patriotism except his fiancée, Rose Maxwell, who, at the end of the first act, returns his ring. Hunter is sent to the Philippines, leads a successful attack on the enemy, and returns home to Alabama (and to Rose, who agrees to marry him), a hero.

Following a month of rehearsals, *The Shoo-Fly Regiment* began a lengthy pre–New York tour with performances in Washington, D.C., at the Majestic Theatre, and in Cumberland, Maryland, in late August. From there the sixty-member troop headed west "with some fairly good bookings and promises of more" on an exhausting seven-month road trip that took them as far from the lights of Broadway as the Oklahoma Territory, Texas, and Colorado.[35] Popular critical reaction to the production was generally positive, although the music and songs were thought superior to the melodramatic and predictable storyline.

Among the songs singled out by critics at the time as potential hits were "There's Always Something Wrong" (Cole's salute to Bert Williams), "If Adam Hadn't Seen the Apple Tree," and "Won't You be My Little Brown Bear."[36] The masterpiece of *The Shoo-Fly Regiment*, "Lit'l Girl," was not actually composed for the musical; rather, it was written by Johnson, with lyrics by Paul Laurence Dunbar, some five years earlier. It is, as Thomas L. Riis has written, "a gem of delicate writing, a three-section lullaby characterized by languid minor thirds placed over a well-crafted harmony in which major and minor chords are mixed with originality and suavity," and which sounds like the "hybrid offspring of art song and spiritual."[37]

In addition to leading the orchestra and chorus, Jim Europe also contributed the music for one of the hit songs of *The Shoo-Fly Regiment*. "On the Gay Luneta," a standard verse/chorus (each sixteen measures in length) love lament for a fair "Manila Belle," with lyrics by Bob Cole, was sung during the second act by the tenor, Theodore Pankey, and chorus.[38] As Riis suggests, the habanera rhythm in the bass line of the verse was undoubtedly intended to give a Spanish feeling to the piece and it does contrast effectively with the "snapping syncopation of the chorus melody over an ostinato bass."[39]

Despite an overall favorable response to the musical by local critics, *The Shoo-Fly Regiment* experienced more than its share of difficulties during its long road tour of 1906–1907. One problem was that a large percentage of the bookings turned out to be one-nighters in small-town theaters that could not raise their admission prices high enough to pay for such a large and expensive company. Even when the show played larger cities, the better theaters—those that could command top admission prices—were often closed to them. As James Weldon Johnson wrote, "not yet had the fight for colored companies to play first-class houses been won."[40] The financial situation eventually became so bad that Cole and Johnson had to use their own money to keep the company together and bring it back to New York.

In choosing a military theme for their first musical, Cole and Johnson were following a pattern that had proven popular with American audiences since Harrigan and Hart used rival military groups in their comedies of the 1880s. The intense nationalism stirred up by the Spanish–American War only increased the popularity of the military theme. George M. Cohan, of course, personified "Yankee Doodle" patriotism in the finales of his *Little Johnny Jones* of 1904 and *George Washington, Jr.* of 1906.[41] Military plots encouraged plenty of crowd-pleasing action on stage and provided an opportunity to exploit a resurgent national pride through patriotic songs. *The Shoo-Fly Regiment*, with the one modification of presenting black soldiers, was modeled on this successful pattern.

Rising nationalism in the United States at the end of the century was also unfortunately attended by increased hostility toward racial and ethnic minorities. Racial violence directed at African-Americans, especially in the form of large-scale riots, reached nearly epidemic proportions in the first decade of the century. The Atlanta riot of 1906 may have been the worst, but others occurred in the Northeast and Midwest as well as the South. In late August 1906 three companies of black troops from the Twenty-fifth Regiment, stationed in Brownsville, Texas—many of whom were veterans of the Philippine Campaign—were involved in a riot in which whites claimed they "shot up the town" in retaliation for racist insults directed at them by some local townspeople.[42] Tensions ran extremely high in the region throughout the fall.

In what could hardly have been a worse coincidence, *The Shoo-Fly Regiment* was scheduled for performances in Galveston, Houston, and Dallas, Texas, as well as other cities in the Southwest during September and early October. It is not surprising that a number of theater managers, fearing more outbreaks of violence, summarily canceled their previous bookings.[43] Given both the financial and psychological consequences of the situation, it is remarkable that Cole and Johnson were able to keep the company together.

Aside from the immediate and particular situation in Texas in the fall of 1906, some of the negative criticism leveled at *The Shoo-Fly Regiment* throughout its two-year life was due, as Woll suggests, to the resistance of white critics, and presumably the white theater-going public, to accept blacks in anything other than stereotypical roles and exhibiting anything other than familiar stereotypical behavior. *The Shoo-Fly Regiment* challenged such expectations in two ways. First, "all the male leads were brave, educated, and patriotic, a far cry from the shuffling stereotypes of minstrel origin."[44] Second, *Shoo-Fly* broke the taboo against having serious love scenes in black shows. The romance between Hunter and Rose is treated with tenderness, rather than as an opportunity for burlesque. In a sense, then, the Cole–Johnson play was, as some reviewers charged, imitative of white productions. *Shoo-Fly Regiment* was not, however, devoid of all African-American cultural content. One of the most interesting aspects of attending a performance of the show, one reviewer wrote, was "to watch the audience, for the white people laughed moderately at incidents that made no impression on the Negroes, while the latter shouted glee at the jokes that did not interest the white spectators."[45]

Back in New York, James Weldon Johnson described the effect of *The Shoo-Fly Regiment's* first eight months on his brother. "The wear and tear of 'trouping' coupled with anxiety had worn on Rosamond physically and showed particularly in the almost complete loss of his singing voice."[46] Cole, however, remained as optimistic as ever and convinced his partner to stick with the show for another year. Things would be better once they found new managers. *The Shoo-Fly Regiment* finally did make it to Broadway, opening at Grand Opera House on June 3, 1907, and then reopening at the Bijou Theatre on August 6. Summer's end found them embarking on their second tour of the country, this time including Canada and with Joe Jordan as musical director. It was a tour that proved to be much more successful than the 1906 ordeal. Jim Europe had left *Shoo-Fly* as music director in March to join S. H. Dudley and the Smart Set Company in developing a new musical play in which he would have greater writing responsibilities.

Sherman Houston Dudley was the same age as Jim Europe and, like Europe, considered himself a Washingtonian. Unlike Europe, however, Dudley had spent most of his life as a traveling showman, trouping around the South and West in various minstrel shows. He formed an act with Sam Corker (business manager of *Trip to Coontown* and *Shoo-Fly Regiment*), toured as a member of the cast of *Clorindy*, and in 1904 joined Gus Hill's Smart Set Company, a touring group that had previously featured Tom McIntosh and Ernest Hogan.[47]

The Smart Set's theatrical vehicle for the 1906 season was a three act musical comedy written by Dudley and Steve B. Cassin, called *The Black Politician*, that included such proven popular devices as a Southern setting and a horse race. As one veteran showman recalled, it was "one of those Simon Legree plots where all the colored people *suffered*. . . . The show opened with everybody singing, then one scene after another, according to the story not like vaudeville acts, with a chorus line of girls and lots of comedy and dancing."[48] James Tim Brymn, a conservatory-trained composer, conductor, and arranger from North Carolina, was responsible for the music.[49] For the new 1907 season, Dudley made a few changes in the script, added some new comedy lines and a female chorus, and asked Jim Europe and R. C. McPherson to write new music and lyrics. Europe was also hired to travel with the show as music director.

The Black Politician had its debut in Kingston, New York, on September 14, 1907, moved on to Montreal, Ottawa, and other Canadian cities, and then back across the border to Youngstown and Zanesville, Ohio, and Wheeling, West Virginia, in October. Playing mostly to white audiences, the troupe remained in the Midwest (visiting Indianapolis, Kansas City, Chicago, and Toledo, among other cities) until February 1908, when the company returned to the East.[50] Critics in both the white and black press found The Black Politician very entertaining despite the fact that it was hardly an original production. As one critic wrote, it was "put together in an original manner. Old tunes with new words (and some of them without this change)—old scenes with innovations and improvements, and one or two hybrid specialties, are brightened much with a thick sprinkling of really funny lines."[51]

Sylvester Russell of the Freeman was particularly complimentary of Europe's contribution both as composer and as the leader of the orchestra. "James Reese Europe," he wrote in his review of The Black Politician's opening performance, "whose reputation has not yet quite caught up with the length of his name, is accredited as composer of all the music. He is leader of the orchestra and a very good one. His music gives evidence that he possesses more ability as a composer than he has hitherto been given a chance to exhibit. . . . "[52] Only one of Europe's pieces from the show, a song entitled "Likin' Ain't Like Lovin'," was subsequently published, so it is not possible to corroborate Russell's judgment.[53]

The 1907–1908 season with The Smart Set was personally and professionally Jim Europe's most rewarding. After only four years in New York's expanding but extremely competitive popular music business, he had reached a level just shy, perhaps, of the most illustrious of black musical theater's composers and musical directors. There were few aspiring talents, even among those with greater formal training than he, who had risen so quickly. The Black Politician company of 1907–1908 seems to have been an unusually congenial group of performers, the credit for which belongs to Dudley's managerial ability and style. They performed mostly for white audiences in the Northern states and Canada, and they avoided most of the difficulties that Europe had encountered the previous year with The Shoo-fly Regiment.

Tom Logan's letters from the Smart Set Company, which were regularly printed in the Indianapolis Freeman's "Stage" column, convey a sense of the good-natured comradeship that existed in the company as well as an increasing appreciation for Jim Europe's contributions. In early November, for instance, Logan described Europe as "our genial musical director" who is "one of the most painstaking, conscientious men in the profession."[54] His letter in the November 30 issue reported that the principals and chorus were united in trying to see "who can best work and best agree," and that "Prof. James Reese Europe is greatly pleased with the development of his pet hobby (the choral department), and is happy, happy, happy."[55]

Logan's letters describe a relaxed and self-confident musical director as well as a playful Jim Europe, possessing a ready sense of humor that is only rarely revealed in his later photographs. One of Dudley's comic routines, for instance, in which Europe conspired, was a burlesque of the orchestra conductor himself in which Dudley replaced Europe and "mis-directed" the orchestra. "I have just been informed," Logan confided to his readers, "that the 'special selection' as directed(?) by Mr. Dudley was composed in an unguarded moment by J. Reese Europe and was written in D Moll—at least Dudley demolished every chair and music rack within his reach."[56] "Prof. James Reese Europe has been properly dubbed 'The Prince,'" Logan wrote in the March 28, 1908, *Freeman*, "and any time things get too warm for James, he says 'You got the Queen all jammed up; this is no place for the Prince; I'll exit.'"[57]

S. H. Dudley and the Smart Set Company continued to tour with various productions for several more seasons, most notably including *His Honor, the Barber*, which enjoyed a brief run on Broadway in 1911.[58] "The prince" of *The Black Politician*, however, exited the company after *Politician* closed in Boston at the end of April to rejoin Cole and Johnson in the preparation of an ambitious new production, called *The Red Moon*, for the 1908 fall season. Dudley, Europe, Cole, and Johnson did appear together, along with many of the luminaries of black musical theater, at the end of June in a benefit at the West End Theater on 125th Street for Ernest Hogan.

Hogan was attempting to recover from a general physical breakdown that he suffered in January while starring in *The Oyster Man*. Among theater people in New York, Hogan was liked as a person and widely admired both for his talent and for the key role he played in the emergence over the previous decade of a vital new era for black musical theater. This sense of personal obligation would have been reason enough to bring together what one participant described as "the greatest assembly of colored actors ever to appear in the same theater and on the same stage in one night."[59] A sense of the vulnerability each of them shared with Hogan in a profession without any organized health or social security protection coupled with a general uncertainty about the future without Hogan's energy and leadership may also have helped to draw the New York theater fraternity together. In any case, Hogan's death from tuberculosis the following year did seem to mark the beginning of the end of an era.

Hogan's unexpected illness did have the effect of convincing a number of the less-independently minded show business leaders of the need for a professional support organization. Several years earlier, Williams and Walker and a few others had planned to organize a Colored Actors Beneficial Association, but the idea never got very far.[60] In the month following the Hogan benefit, however, Bert Williams and George Walker and nine others (Bob Cole, Rosamond Johnson, Jesse Shipp, R. C. McPherson, Sam Corker, Alex Rogers, Tom Brown, Lester Walton, and James R. Europe), all of whom had been members of the planning committee of the Hogan benefit, formally organized themselves into a club dedicated to "promoting social intercourse between the representative members of the Negro theatrical profession and to those connected directly or indirectly with art, literature, music, scientific and liberal professions, and the patrons of arts." Secondary aims were to "aid in raising the standard of the theatrical profession" as well as "to elevate the race generally" by creating a permanent repository and library "relating especially to the history of the Negro, and the record of all worthy achievements" in the area of the arts, including folklore, "in which the Negro has participated."[61]

Despite its serious purposes, the good-humored social aspects of the association were apparent from the outset when it was agreed that the group would call themselves the "Frogs," after Aristophanes' comedy (and similar to the white "Rats"), and that their first sponsored activity would be a midsummer costume and novelty dance ("The Frolic of the Frogs") at the Manhattan Casino on 155th Street. "Get busy, make a noise like a Frog," advised the first announcement of the August affair in the *New York Age*.[62] All New York—white and black—got a chance to join in the fun when the *Tribune*, *World*, *Sun*, and several other papers commented (mostly tongue-in-cheek) on Judge John W. Goff's refusal to grant incorporation to the organization on the grounds that frogs and art did not go together. "The corporate name selected is so incongruous that I hesitate to cement the connection between the sublime and the grotesque," he said. Bert Williams, who represented the club in their petition, had clearly orchestrated the joke, and, of course, Goff's decision was hastily reversed by the New York Supreme Court.[63]

A splendid photograph exists of the original Frogs taken that summer of 1908. Ernest Hogan was still alive, though not present, and the eleven dapper representatives of black musical theater exude self-assurance, dignity, and optimism. It is a collective portrait of the Frogs, and also of the state of black musical theater achievement at that moment. There is no burnt-cork, no grotesque gesticulations, and no exaggerated characterizations. Minstrelsy seems a thing of the distant past. Twenty-eight-year-old James Reese Europe, bespectacled and smiling, stands just to the left of Bert Williams, the only Frog taller than he, and his expression seems to say, "Well, Ma and Little Sis, you can see I have done well."

George Walker was elected the first president of the club, Europe was appointed librarian, and a ten-room house was purchased on West 132nd Street that, when renovated, was expected to become "the finest clubhouse in America." Although the original members of the Frogs were all connected directly with the theater, it was not intended that future membership be restricted to such people.

Prominent black professionals and businessmen from New York and Philadelphia were also solicited to join, suggesting that the Frogs were interested both in developing support from outside the theater community as well as in revising the image of their profession (and raising their own status) among the prominent of the race.[64]

To be asked to be a charter member, and an officer, of the Frogs was clear evidence to Europe that he was now at the top level of his profession, and he was justifiably proud of it. He also believed in the value of organization itself, had demonstrated a talent for it early, and, it is clear, recognized this ability in himself. By the summer of 1908 he had determined that his future in music would be as a conductor, composer, arranger, organizer, and director of musical organizations rather than as a performer. The Frogs, which continued to exist up to World War I, never accomplished the lofty, progressive goals that they set for themselves, but they were effective as a sort of actor's and musician's benevolent society and as a focus (through their annual "Frog Frolics" and variety show tours) for generating social cohesion and fellowship within the black communities of New York, Philadelphia, and even Washington. It is not surprising that Europe remained a member throughout the life of the organization, serving as second vice president from 1911 to 1912. During August 1908, however, he had very little time to give to Frog activities because he was fully occupied—along with Bob Cole and J. Rosamond Johnson—in getting the orchestra and cast of *The Red Moon* ready for their debut performance scheduled for August 31 in Wilmington, Delaware.

The Red Moon, subtitled *An American Musical in Red and Black*, was the most ambitious, the most successful, and the last of Cole and Johnson's full-length musical comedy productions. The idea for the play, according to Cole, came from the team's experiences during an earlier trip through the Far West with their vaudeville act and from a desire to integrate traditional or folk elements from both African-American and Indian culture into a musical. A red moon, as Allen Woll points out, was long viewed as a bad omen by Southern blacks as well as by the Apaches, whose reservation Cole and Johnson visited, who interpreted it as a call to war.[65] *The Red Moon* storyline involves the adventures of Minnehaha, a young woman of mixed Indian and African-American parentage, who is kidnapped from her rural Virginia home by her father, Chief Lowdog (Arthur Talbut), and taken west, where she becomes the object of Red Feather's (an "educated Indian" played by Theodore Pankey) amorous attention. Minnehaha's boyfriend, Plunk Green, and his buddy, Slim Brown, set out after them and, following a number of misadventures (and several war dances), eventually succeed in rescuing the maiden, outwitting Red Feather, and even reconciling her parents. Cole and Johnson, who starred as Brown and Green, respectively, wrote the book, the lyrics, and most of the music. They also assembled a strong supporting cast, including Abbie Mitchell (recently divorced from Will Marion Cook) as Minnehaha, Theodore Pankey, Sam Lucas, and some forty additional actors, dancers, and singers.

As one might expect, predictable Indian elements (pentatonic melodies, repetitive eighth note "tom tom" rhythms, drones, etc.) appear in some of the music, including the songs "Big Red Shawl," "Land of the Setting Sun," and "I Want to Be an Indian." Such songs were generally well-received by the critics, but—perhaps surprisingly, given the plot—Indian musical cliché does not by any means dominate the score.[66] Many of the tunes, according to Riis, are both "charming and fresh" and "J. Rosamond Johnson's harmonic language is consistently richer than that of his contemporaries, Will Marion Cook excepted."[67] One of these, "I Ain't Had No Lovin' in a Long Time (an' Lovin' is a Thing I Need)," words by Cole and music by Europe, stands out from the others as an effective combination of "an especially catchy series of intervals that could be swung gently" and a cleverly humorous lyric that treats female sexuality with unusual frankness:

> Mister Romeo Bacon is a nice young man,
> But here's where I puts him on de frying pan,
> He's one o'dem gentlemen dat acts too nice,
> He sets up in de parlor, like a cake of ice;
> He never calls me "honey" an' he never says "dear"
> An' he never makes a noise like a cold glass of beer
> He don't give me nothing, but dat "weather" talk,
> And he never even asked me for to take a walk,
> Of course I'm "dickee doo,"
> But I Like a little lovin' too.
>   Chorus
> . . . You must call me by some sweet and tender name,
> It takes a lot of fire to start my flame,
> I ain't had no lovin' in a long time
> An' lovin' is a thing I need.[68]

Europe also contributed the music to "Sambo," words by Cole, which was sung with great spirit in the last act (back at the Virginia homestead) by Sambo Simmons (Edgar Connor), his sisters Sally and Susan Simmons (Leona Marshall and Daisy Brown), and the full chorus. The *Freeman*, in its review of *The Red Moon*, when the company played the Great Northern Theatre in Chicago in October, found Connor's individual performance so good as to start "the show all over again," the whole number being "beyond the limit."[69] Europe and Cole wrote the music for "Ada, My Sweet Potater," lyrics by Charles Hunter (stage manager for the show), which was sung by Slim Brown (Bob Cole) to the six Ada Girls. Chicago audiences gave the number numerous encores, and the *Freeman* called it "the hit of the show." Europe's efforts as musical director were also impressive. He "handled the orchestra and chorus in a masterly way. He worked every minute he was in the pit and between acts. The show has twenty-one big numbers and every one takes two or more encores. The musical director in the big league has to work these days."[70]

After opening its 1908 fall tour in Wilmington, *The Red Moon* company performed in several East Coast cities before moving into the Midwest. Late October found them in Chicago, and they spent a week in November at the Park Theater in Indianapolis, followed by runs in Louisville, and Dayton. The continuing enthusiastic reception by both white and black audiences, and the positive critical response by both the white and black press of Cole and Johnson's new production, suggests that American theater-goers were prepared to accept a new style of black musical that avoided much of the derogatory stereotyping of the past. It also showed that the black social and intellectual elite (who had been the group most sensitive to the demeaning images of African-Americans in popular music and the theater) were beginning to recognize that black musical theater and black artists themselves could contribute positively toward racial progress in America.[71]

A special to the Indianapolis *Freeman* by Gary B. Lewis in early December, "Many Social Functions in Honor of Cole and Johnson," reported that Dr. and Mrs. R. W. Oliver had hosted an "elaborate" dinner in Cole and Johnson's honor at their home in Louisville and that afterwards the "three 'Frogs' present, who were Messrs. Cole and Johnson and James Reese Europe," led an "intelligent conversation on the race." Cole discussed the Negro actor, Johnson talked about the Negro as musician and composer, and "Prof. James Reese Europe, who is regarded as one of the best musical directors of the race, talked optimistically of the Negro as a singer and recalled many of the nightingale singers who have challenged the admiration of the world."[72]

The less serious and more personable side of *The Red Moon*'s musical director is revealed in fellow Frog Lester Walton's columns in the *New York Age* written during the early months of 1909 as the company returned East. At the end of January, when the production was in Atlantic City, Walton published "Jim Europe's advice to chorus girls": "B sharp if you can; if you can't, B natural; but never, oh! never, B flat broke in Gotham in winter. Now we are wondering what prompted this bit of seemingly fatherly advice. Ask the man!"[73] In March, while the show was in Toronto, Walton humorously reported a "rumor" that "James Reese Europe is writing an article for one of our papers. We wonder will it be 'How to sing on the key?'" From Syracuse in April Walton printed a note from stage manager Charles A. Hunter describing Europe as a knowledgeable baseball fan. "The slogan in this company is: when in doubt about baseball, see Jim Europe."[74]

The highpoint of *The Red Moon* tour began on May 3, 1909, when the show began a week's run at the Majestic Theatre on Broadway at 59th Street in New York, only the second black company (following Williams and Walker's *Bandanna Land* of 1908) to play in that theater.[75] The reviewer for *Theatre*

Magazine did not think the dialog quite up to the standard of Johnson's score, which he found "tuneful and musicianly," but on the whole the production was "well mounted and there is a vigorous and comely chorus."[76] Most of the New York critics agreed with the *Mirror* that *The Red Moon* was "well worth seeing," and the Majestic extended the run for an additional two weeks.[77] When the curtain fell on the final performance, the

> white musicians [of the theater orchestra], numbering nearly twenty, marched on the stage and played several farewell selections, and gave three cheers for the musical director of the "Red Moon" Company, James Reese Europe. The members of the company returned the cheering and sang several selections while the orchestra played.[78]

In many respects, the 1908–1909 season had been a very good one for black musical theater. Despite suffering from some of the same problems that plagued *The Shoo-Fly Regiment* during its first year, including poor bookings at less than first-rate theaters, *The Red Moon* had enjoyed a successful year, and Cole, Johnson, and Europe planned to take the show on the road again in the fall. Williams and Walker, the other large African-American company, closed the second year of their highly praised production—*Bandanna Land* (book and lyrics by Frogs Jesse Shipp and Alex Rogers, music by Will Marion Cook) at the Yorkville Theatre in Brooklyn in April after playing Broadway as well as having been the first black show to play at the formerly white-only Belasco Theatre in Washington, D.C.[79] In February, however, George Walker became too ill to continue in the show and his wife, Aida Overton Walker, took over his part for the last two months. It was his last stage appearance. Coupled with the death of Ernest Hogan in May, the loss of Walker was a serious shock to black musical theater.[80] It was also a great personal tragedy for Europe and the other Frogs, and especially for Walker's partner of fifteen years, Bert Williams.

Despite the loss of Walker, Williams still had the core of the Williams and Walker Company and a reputation that had never been better. In September, therefore, he once again set out on the road with a new Jesse Shipp–Alex Rogers musical comedy, *Mr. Lode of Koal*. Williams (with significant assistance from J. Rosamond Johnson) was personally responsible for most of the musical score, but J. Leubrie Hill and Al Johns also made significant contributions. The simple storyline involved the antics of a servant on the island of Koal, one Chester Lode (Williams), who is installed as ruler when the former king is kidnapped. As Riis has written, the critics "unanimously agreed that *Mr. Lode of Koal* was a vehicle for Williams and not much more," although the music was occasionally praised.[81] *Mr. Lode of Koal* opened in Kansas City in mid-September and remained in the Midwest until November 15, when the show was booked for a week at New York's Majestic Theater.

Jim Europe remained the music director and orchestra conductor of Cole and Johnson's *The Red Moon* as it began its second season, like *Mr. Lode of Koal*, touring the midwest. He composed a couple of new tunes for the fall 1909 production—"Picanninny Days" and "Pliney, Come Out in the Moonlight"—to which Bob Cole contributed the lyrics. Following *The Red Moon's* run at the Globe Theatre in Chicago in mid-November, the *Freeman's* Sylvester Russell took note of Europe's increasing activity as a writer. "James Reese Europe, conductor of Cole and Johnson's 'Red Moon' Company," he wrote in early December, "is a composer of much merit. The music of 'Pliney,' 'Sambo,' and 'Picanninny Days' was all composed by Mr. Europe, as well as the 'Red Moon To-do-lo' two step chorus; it is expected that more will be heard from the professor later."[82]

Not everything, however, was going well with the company. Only one week later, Europe—along with star soprano Abbie Mitchell, stage manager Charles Hunter, and several others—abruptly left the show. Neither the *Age* nor the *Freeman*, who reported it, were willing or able to give any specific reasons, but it is known that the members of *The Red Moon* Company, despite the continuing favorable reviews of the show, were increasingly frustrated by the failure of the company's agents to secure adequate theater bookings.[83] One of the reasons for this was the growing commercial success of motion pictures. "The moving picture theatres," wrote Lester Walton the following July, "have, within the past year, played havoc with the more legitimate branches of the theatrical business, but in particular have the second-class playhouses suffered."[84] With only a few of the truly first-class houses open to even the best of the black productions, black shows always depended heavily upon revenues generated from the cheaper theaters. The effect of the expansion of the motion picture industry, however, was to depress the admission prices second-class houses could charge to the point that "even if a colored company played nightly to capacity in the second and third-class houses now available, the low prices of admission would not support a company of fifty or sixty people receiving only moderate salaries."[85]

Europe was immediately hired to replace James J. Vaughan as musical director with *Mr. Lode of Koal*, and he remained with the Bert Williams' show until it closed in early March 1910. Despite Williams' unfailing comic genius, audiences, critics, and Williams himself sorely missed the presence of George Walker, "whose flash and wit offered a sharp contrast to the slow and occasionally dour Williams persona." Williams left black musical theater the following season to accept Flo Ziegfeld's invitation to join the *Ziegfeld Follies of 1910*.[86] When J. Rosamond Johnson and Bob Cole announced that they, too, would not be taking out a large theatrical production in the fall—they would instead return to vaudeville with their two-man act—black musical theater was dealt a staggering blow. By the early fall of 1910, only the Smart Set Company was left in the field and hundreds of actors, singers, musicians, dancers, and stage production people felt a gloom settle over what had so recently seemed such a promising field for their talents. Although he was hardly pleased by the current situation in black musical theater, thirty-year-old Jim Europe was not discouraged about the future prospects for African-American musical development. His brother, John, had been doing well as a cabaret pianist in New York and his sister, Mary, was by now one of the most respected concert accompanists in Washington. From the standpoint of African-American music overall, therefore, there was some cause for optimism.

4

"Lorraine Waltzes"

In recent years we have been alarmed at the relatively great number of our talented young people who have sought fame and a livelihood before the footlights, to the neglect of more useful work of a higher order demanded by our race in this country.

The Washington *Bee* (1917)

The six years between 1904 and 1910, during which Jim Europe established himself as a leading figure in black musical comedy, were valuable ones for him—musically, professionally, and personally—and he profited from the experience. The years on the road widened his horizons while challenging him to develop his conducting and composing skills under pressure. Most importantly, he was introduced to a broad spectrum of black talent, and the experience forced him at first to question, and then to reject, the idea that popular entertainment and authentic African-American artistry were inherently antithetical.

The better part of each of these years was spent on the road, living out of suitcases in interchangeable hotel rooms in cities and towns where he rarely spent more than a few days at a time. While in New York, between tours and during the off-season, he continued to live at the Marshall Hotel, but he also made regular visits to Washington, D.C., and maintained sufficient residence there to be listed in the city directory as living with his mother and sisters from 1907 through 1909. His occupation during those years was given simply as "musician." Despite her son's successes and his growing reputation in the field of popular music and entertainment, it is quite likely that Lorraine Europe, like many others of her background and aspiration, hoped that her son would apply his talents toward what was then known as a "higher" class of music and musical activity, something more closely related to the kinds of respectable and respected musical endeavor his younger sister was pursuing.

Even before Europe left Washington to follow his brother to New York in 1903, Mary Europe had come to be recognized locally as a promising musical talent. After starting as an assistant pianist at the Park Temple Congregational Church (later Lincoln Temple), she became the principal piano and organ accompanist to the church's notable choir in 1901. She soon found herself in demand by soloists including Harry T. Burleigh, Joseph H. Douglass, and Clarence C. White when they performed in the city.[1] She was appointed to the staff of M Street High School as accompanist for the music classes in the fall of

1903. She was promoted ten years later to music instructor, a position she held for the next thirty years.[2] The personal highpoint of her career as a performer came in 1906 when she was asked by the celebrated Anglo-African composer, Samuel Coleridge-Taylor, during his second visit to the United States, to provide the accompaniment for his choral cantata *Hiawatha*.

Although the opportunities for black concert musicians and composers did not, in practical terms, rival those for popular artists, turn-of-the-century America was not without its encouraging signs for those African-Americans whose ambitions lay in the direction of "serious music." With the possible exception of Antonín Dvořák, Samuel Coleridge-Taylor had the greatest influence on aspiring African-American musicians of any European composer during these years.[3] Coleridge-Taylor was born in 1875 to Daniel Taylor, a native of Sierra Leone then studying medicine at University College in London, and Alice Hare (or Howe), an English woman. Named for the British poet, he was raised by his mother after Taylor returned to West Africa. Recognizing her son's musical gift, Coleridge-Taylor's mother enrolled him in the Royal Academy College of Music, where, according to his biographer, he "became possessed of a complete devotion to the works of Antonín Dvořák, a devotion which if anything increased with the years."[4] As a result of his admiration for Dvořák, then beginning his adventure in America, Coleridge-Taylor became personally interested in the United States, and specifically in the musical potential of its African-American people.

Among the many projects reflecting the rising tide of national consciousness in the United States in the last decade of the nineteenth century, and in accord with the most elaborate and conspicuous manifestation of that consciousness—the World's Columbian Exposition in Chicago in 1893—was the founding of the National Conservatory of Music of America in New York City. Chartered by Congress in the fall of 1892 in order to coincide with the four-hundredth anniversary of Columbus's landing, the goal of the National Conservatory as conceived by its founder, Jeannette Thurber, was to create a truly national music founded upon the native musics and languages of America. Mrs. Thurber found a musical figure of international stature in the distinguished Czech composer, Antonín Dvořák, who heartily supported her objectives, and she convinced him to leave Prague and to accept the directorship of the conservatory. Dvořák, it was hoped, would become the Columbus of American music (as Columbus was the first European to authenticate the existence of the New World, so Dvořák would authenticate the existence of music from the New World), and it is clear that he embraced the role. "I did not come to America to interpret Beethoven or Wagner for the public," he wrote in one of a series of letters to the *New York Herald* in May 1893. "That is not my work and I would not waste any time on it. I came to discover what young Americans had in them and to help them to express it."[5]

The influence of Dvořák's two-and-one-half year residence in the United States upon American musical culture was considerable. By virtue of his public statements, his direct influence on his composition students, and the example of his own arrangements and compositions, he helped to undermine the inferiority many Americans felt toward European musical culture. He also encouraged and helped to legitimize the development of a New World music. He indirectly pointed the way for a younger generation of Americanist composers, among them Duke Ellington, Aaron Copeland, and George Gershwin, each of whom studied formally or informally with one of Dvořák's students.[6]

The specific impact of Dvořák's tenure in America upon African-American music and musicians, and upon public attitudes toward them, has yet to be fully documented, but it appears to be even more significant. In his public statements, in compositions like his symphony *From the New World*, his encouragement of National Conservatory students like Harry Burleigh and Maurice Arnold (Strathotte), and his sponsorship of concert performances like the one at Madison Square Garden in January 1894 that featured Sissieretta Jones as principal soloist with the 130-member all-black choir from St. Philips Episcopal Church, he was an early and consistent advocate of African-American music and musicians.[7]

Dvořák left the United States in April 1895, and although negotiations concerning his possible return to America continued for some time, Mrs. Thurber's financial difficulties and his own concerns for his family led him to resign his directorship of the National Conservatory in August. The next seven years, until his death in 1902, were productive ones; however, with the exception of witnessing the worldwide acceptance and acclaim for his *From the New World*, his personal relationship with America had ended.

At the same time as Dvořák's American sojourn was coming to a close, Samuel Coleridge-Taylor's fame was beginning to spread to the United States. By 1895, although still a student in London, Coleridge-Taylor had won the prestigious Lesley Alexander prize in composition, and a number of his songs, anthems, and chamber orchestra pieces had been published and performed. When Paul Laurence Dunbar traveled to England in 1896 on a reading tour, he visited Coleridge-Taylor, and the two collaborated on several songs (Dunbar's words set to Coleridge-Taylor's music).[8]

During that same year, in Washington, D.C., a group of socially prominent African-American women organized the Treble Clef Club for the purpose of studying classical music. Several of the club's members, Mrs. Andrew Hilyer in particular, became enthusiastic about the compositions of Coleridge-Taylor and, following a visit to England in 1901, where she met the young composer, she and her friends began discussing the possibility of forming a choral group to perform the composer's works.[9] Two years later, the Samuel Coleridge-Taylor Society (eventually numbering 200 members) was incorporated with a slate of officers and directors that constituted "a virtual roster of the district's black aristocracy."[10] Mary Europe was selected as accompanist and joined the regular rehearsals of the group under the direction of John T. Layton. For a young musician, as Doris McGinty has pointed out, the prominence of this position can be appreciated only if one understands that the "Samuel Coleridge-Taylor Choral Society was at the heart of musical life in the black community of Washington, D.C., for many years."[11]

In the meantime, Coleridge-Taylor's interest in the musical potential of African and African-American themes was beginning to find expression in his compositions, including the operetta *The Dream Lovers* (another joint effort with Dunbar published in 1898), the *African Suite*, consisting of four sections (*Introduction, A Negro Love Song, Valse,* and *Danse Negre*—the latter inspired by a Dunbar poem), and the major choral work, *Song of Hiawatha*. The overture to the latter reflects the influence of the Fisk Jubilee Singers, who toured England in 1899, and in particular the spiritual "Nobody Knows the Trouble I See."[12]

As a result of a lengthy communication between Mr. and Mrs. Hilyer and Coleridge-Taylor, in which the composer was made aware of the musical sophistication of Washington's black community, the composer agreed to come to the United States to personally conduct his own works when a really "good coloured chorus" was available.[13] To provide this chorus, therefore, became the goal of the Coleridge-Taylor Choral Society. They were ready for their debut performance of *Hiawatha* by the spring of 1903.

On the evening of April 23, in the huge Metropolitan A.M.E. Church auditorium, an audience of several thousand of "Washington's best, both White and Colored [sic]" had the unique opportunity to hear 160 African-American voices directed by an African-American conductor perform a lengthy and difficult choral work by an Anglo-African composer. The soloists—Harry T. Burleigh of New York, Kathryne Skeene-Mitchell of Cleveland, and Sidney Woodward of Boston—were also black, as were the accompanists, Mrs. Robert Pelham, Jr., William Braxton, and Mary Europe. Such a concert was not without risk to the pride of black Americans, as the Boston *Guardian* noted, but if any "Negro choral society" anywhere in the country could do it, "Washington could." The performance was widely praised in both the black and white press.[14] It must have come as a revelation for many whites in the audience, as the *New York Times* concluded, to discover that blacks were capable of such "high class music."[15] Walter B. Hayson, writing in the Washington *Evening Star,* was particularly impressed by Mary Europe, whom he described as "a young musician, but of decided genius and played the score of *Hiawatha* so exacting in its readings, rhythm, time and tempo, with such precision, power and intelligence that she received the most cordial thanks of the soloists and almost extravagant commendation of the musical critics."[16]

Coleridge-Taylor, who had been following the events in Washington with close interest, indicated in June that he was prepared to come to America as long as a suitable orchestra could be obtained.[17] It took nearly another year and a half before the arrangements could be made, including securing the United States Marine Band for a three-day "Coleridge-Taylor Festival" to be held in Washington and Baltimore, during which time the choral society continued to rehearse and perform publicly.[18] Coleridge-Taylor finally arrived in Boston on November 2, 1904, and he remained in the United States until December 13.

The "Coleridge-Taylor Festival" took place on the evenings of November 16–18, with the first two concerts held before appreciative audiences estimated at over 3,000 (two-thirds black and one-third white) at Washington's Convention Hall.[19] The composer conducted the choral society and the Marine Band (with strings added) in his *Hiawatha Trilogy* the first evening, while the second evening consisted of a more miscellaneous program of his choral works. The third evening's concert, a repeat of *Hiawatha*, was held in Baltimore. Critical response was universally positive; Coleridge-Taylor was praised both as a great composer and also as a gifted conductor, and the chorus was described as the finest to ever appear in either Washington or Baltimore.[20] Following a reception by President Roosevelt at the White House, Coleridge-Taylor was quickly off to Chicago for a concert, and then back to England by way of New York, Philadelphia, and Boston.

The first visit to America by a black European composer was a great success, perhaps more so than Coleridge-Taylor's managers (and perhaps he himself) had expected. There had been some concern that he would not be treated well because of his race, but he was surprised to find that prejudice in America was curiously selective. "As soon . . . as people found out I was English they were quite different," he said in an interview shortly after returning home. "What is so deplorable to me is that there is as yet very little discrimination between the educated and decent-minded black and idle and semi-civilized man of colour." "The fact is, no Englishman can get quite inside the question, it is so subtle."[21] His discovery of "splendid orchestras, instrumentalists, and vocalists, and a public taste which enabled these to exist for their art," which he attributed largely to the German-American populations of Chicago and Philadelphia, was more pleasantly surprising. In addition to this, the high musical standards and enthusiasm he found in Washington led him to conclude that there was more widespread appreciation for musical art in America than in England, and "for some time, indeed, he contemplated the desirability of emigrating to this land of the future."[22]

The results of Coleridge-Taylor's first visit led to plans for a second tour to the United States in the fall of 1906. Although he was pleased with the performance of the chorus at the first festival, the composer had not been happy with the orchestral support provided by the Marine Corps Band. He suggested that in the future the string parts be supplied by a few "really fine string players" and the wind parts "be filled in on the pianoforte and organ by that extraordinarily clever Miss Europe and someone else."[23] Mary Europe had been introduced to Coleridge-Taylor during rehearsals for the *Hiawatha* concerts in 1904 and was immediately as impressed with him personally as she had been with his music. To be asked to provide the accompaniment for the second Samuel Coleridge-Taylor Society festival in Washington, conducted by the composer and held November 21–23, 1906, at the Metropolitan A.M.E. Church, was to her more than an honor—it was the high point of her career and, perhaps, of her life. According to the *Washington Post*, which noted that her "good tone and clear technique were observed all through the accompaniment," she rose to the occasion.[24]

An invitation from the Litchfield County Choral Union at Norfolk, Connecticut, led to Coleridge-Taylor's third visit to the United States in June 1910. Although he was unable to include Washington in his concert tour, he promised his Washington friends that he would surely do so the next time, and he asked to be remembered especially to "Miss Europe, Mr. White [Clarence Cameron White, the violinist], the Terrells, and the Grays and the Wormleys."[25] The 1910 tour, however, was his last as he died prematurely following a short illness in 1912.

The Coleridge-Taylor Choral Society continued to hold concerts featuring the Englishman's compositions in Washington and nearby cities for nearly a decade after his second visit, and Mary Europe's reputation continued to grow. Following a performance of *Hiawatha* at the Academy of Music in Philadelphia on April 19, 1906, for example, the *New York Age* described her piano accompaniment as "brilliant" and a "revelation."[26] The other accompanist on that occasion was organist Melville Charlton of New York, with whom her brother, James, was then occasionally studying.[27] By the spring of 1907, the Indianapolis *Freeman* was including Mary Europe in its list of African-American instrumentalists of the first rank.[28]

Washington's Coleridge-Taylor Choral Society was, throughout its life, self-consciously committed to cultivating an appreciation for "the best music" within the black community in order to contribute to the cultural uplift of the race and to the diminution of racial prejudice in America.[29] By virtue of his internationally recognized musical stature, Coleridge-Taylor was seen as a primary contributor to this goal. "In composing *Hiawatha* you have done the coloured people of the U.S. a service which, I am sure, you never dreamed of when composing it," Andrew Hilyer wrote to him in 1908. "It acts as a source of inspiration for us, not only musically but in other lines of endeavor as well."[30] A correlative of this attitude was that music conceived for other purposes than religious inspiration or "serious" concert performance (i.e., music designed for popular entertainment) was detrimental to cultural taste and therefore to racial progress. Coleridge-Taylor, himself, expressed such an opinion of current American popular music, decrying that broad spectrum of vocal and instrumental music then included under the term ragtime as "the worst sort of rot." "In the first place there is no melody and in the second place there is no real Negro character or sentiment," he said in a widely quoted interview.[31] "Will you accept thanks for your public condemnation published in this morning's paper of the abominable rubbish called 'coon songs' and 'rag-time,'" wrote a New Yorker to the composer in 1907. "There has been no greater detriment to the race in this country, nor can there be a greater impediment to its future progress."[32]

There can be little doubt that Mary Europe and her mother subscribed to this widely prevalent attitude and that James, brother and son, but also a noted "coon song" writer and conductor of "ragtime," was fully and painfully aware of it. His mother and sister had accepted the financial support that Europe's success in musical theater had allowed him to contribute, and, indeed, that had helped to make possible their purchase of a permanent residence at 1008 S Street (adjacent to fashionable LeDroit Park) in 1910. They would have been more pleased, however, to see him use his talents otherwise. His popular compositions, including even the charming "Lorraine Waltzes" that he wrote in their honor, could never quite be worthy. For his part, while accepting some of the criticism of ragtime, Jim Europe had already begun to formulate a defense of the music with which he—and, indeed, his older brother, John—had become identified.

In April 1909, Lester Walton, music critic of the *New York Age*, asked five of the "young and successful colored composers" for their response to John Philip Sousa's recent comment that the ragtime fad had run its course and was now essentially dead.[33] "Ragtime had the dyspepsia or gout long before it died," Sousa was reported as saying. "It was overfed by poor nurses. Good ragtime came, and half a million imitators sprang up. Then, as a result, the people were sickened with the stuff." Songwriters Chris Smith, Tom Lemonier, and Will Dixon, while admitting that there were many "worthless compositions thrown upon the market today," disagreed with Sousa. Good ragtime, their own songs and those of Will Marion Cook, J. Rosamond Johnson, and Harry Burleigh, they said, would continue to remain popular because "ragtime music is the only real melody that thrills the heart and moves the feet." Two current musical directors, Tim Brymn, then of the Smart Set Company, and James Reese Europe, of Cole and Johnson's *Red Moon*, were also asked by Walton for their comments. Brymn began by attempting to clarify the term *ragtime* by arguing that it was fundamentally a syncopated music that is produced by "effacing or shifting the accent of a tone or chord falling on a naturally strong beat by tying it over from the preceding weak beat." Syncopation can be found in the classics as well as in "coon songs," though the latter are "low-class" and are being replaced by "a higher or more artistic order" of song. "It has been said by an eminent composer [undoubtedly Dvořák] that true American music is ragtime," he concluded, and "I am proud to say that I think the Negro holds a stronger claim to the origin of ragtime than any other race."

Europe agreed with Brymn that a main characteristic of ragtime was its novel rhythms and that these were African-American in origin. In his view, however, what was passing was the use of the term, not the music, and he pointed to a recent Sousa concert as proof:

> In my opinion there never was any such music as "ragtime." "Ragtime" is merely a nick-name, or rather a fun name given to Negro rhythm by our Caucasian brother musicians many years ago. The phrase "ragtime" is dying. Why? Because in these days of theme famine, so many eminent Anglo-musicians have become inoculated with that serum—Negro rhythm ("ragtime"), and with their knowledge of musical theory embroider the plaintive ragtime theme with a wealth of contrapuntal ornamentation and a marvelous enrichment of tone coloring and complicated instrumentation, that the primal Negro rhythmical element—"ragtime"—is so disguised that a mere hint of a "motif" of the "ragtime" rhythm is lost to the popular ear. No! "Ragtime" is neither dead nor dying, but is undergoing a vast development, and is more popular now than ten years ago. Mr. Sousa always interpreted Negro music admirably, yet, as a composer, he remained immune from its contagion, although he closes a "suite" of his own composition with a reminiscent Negro theme.

If Europe were right, however, about the continuing popular appeal of African-American–inspired popular music, and even that its basic character was being buried through overelaboration, then could something more respectable than the comic and racially demeaning "coon song" ever be made of it while still preserving its essential character? The debate within the African-American community over this issue had emerged with the first appearance of ragtime in the early 1890s, and it continued to grow as the music achieved national and even—through the Cakewalk dance—international popularity. Despite the heroic efforts of Scott Joplin, who completed his first ragtime-based opera (*A Guest of Honor*) in 1903 and his second (*Treemonisha*) in 1911, to challenge the widely accepted distinction between high- and low-musical culture, throughout the first two decades of the new century most members of the black elite, and those who espoused the ideals of racial uplift, generally agreed with Coleridge-Taylor that ragtime was largely "rot," the "degenerate offspring" of the spirituals and jubilees.[34]

Europe and his associates in black musical theater and the black entertainment world in general, who regularly gathered at the Marshall Hotel in New York, had discussed the problem on numerous occasions. One of the reasons for organizing the Frogs in 1908 was to attempt to revise the low opinion of their profession and creative artistry. By the spring of 1910, black musical theater was beginning to enter a difficult period, and many professional entertainers found themselves without work. Jim Europe, among several others, however, recognized that an opportunity that black musicians could not afford to ignore lay in the continuing demand for musicians in New York's hotels and cafes.

5

"The Clef Club March"

Few white people had ever heard of the orchestra of the "Clef Club," a band of a hundred and twenty-five members organized a few years ago by the colored people themselves, at whose head now stands James Reese Europe, a man with a strong sense of organization and discipline, and with pronounced musical ability.

Natalie Curtis (1913)

Despite what James Weldon Johnson later called a "term of exile" for black performers from Broadway, black musical theater remained alive after 1910 in the growing Harlem district of New York as well as in other cities on the black theater circuit.[1] There were, however, far fewer of the large and expensive productions of the Cole and Johnson, Williams and Walker era, and fewer were seen by white audiences. At the same time, as a result of a general loosening in Victorian social patterns, individual black instrumentalists and singers found themselves in increasing demand by an ever-expanding number of fashionable hotels, clubs, restaurants, and cabarets that supported the lively nightlife of the city.

A few black orchestra leaders like Jim Europe, Ford Dabney, and Joe Jordan had been providing small ensembles for private social gatherings and entertainments of the eastern social elite for a number of years. As the country entered the second decade of the new century, however, increasing numbers of professional and business men and women, theatrical people and tourists, joined the fashionable and wealthy in seeking a "public social life outside the cloistered walls of home and business."[2] The desire of New Yorkers to participate in a more public style of nightlife resulted, naturally, in a corresponding need for musicians to accompany it; however, the dramatic change in public attitudes toward social dancing specifically encouraged hotel and cabaret owners to seek black entertainers and musicians.

In 1910 public dancing, with occasional exceptions, was still considered improper, if not scandalous, by most segments of American society; two years later, such attitudes had clearly begun to change.[3] So, too, were attitudes about the dances themselves, as "whites turned with ever-increasing frequency to the more primitive steps of black culture."[4] Ragtime dances, like the turkey trot and the Texas tommy, and the ragtime-influenced popular music that had already been given a certain sanction by the elite, fit this new informal social life perfectly. After 1910, according to Sigmund Spaeth, even "the publishers of popular music became more and more insistent that a song must be danceable in order to achieve real success."[5]

Prior to 1910, African-Americans, the universally acknowledged originators of both the music and the dance steps, found little success in gaining employment in the better and higher-paying public establishments in the city. Part of the problem was a lack of organization. Unlike their fellow white musicians, who had the benefit of Local 310 of the American Federation of Musicians, African-Americans were excluded from the local (and therefore excluded from performing with union musicians), and had no central place for potential employers to contact them or for them to gather while awaiting job opportunities. Neither, of course, were there any professional standards for performance, working conditions, or salaries. It is true that the New Amsterdam Musical Association had existed for almost ten years (although it was not officially incorporated until 1905), but it was not primarily interested in having popular musicians—especially those who did not read music well—as members.[6] There were also the two more recently organized theatrical support groups—the Frogs and the Colored Vaudeville Benevolent Association (C.V.B.A.)—but neither was designed to address the specific needs of singers, dancers, or instrumentalists who increasingly found employment opportunities outside the musical stage. In the absence of an alternative, and as demands for their services increased, many black musicians continued to use the traditional gathering place, the Marshall Hotel on 53rd Street, to meet, trade information, and wait for calls. It was there, according to Tom Fletcher, that one evening in early April 1910, in response to a not-very-disguised hint from owner Jimmy Marshall that "maybe the fellows ought to be getting a place of their own to hang out," a number of the Marshall regulars decided to form a new organization that they named the Clef Club of the City of New York.[7]

James Reese Europe—a charter member of the Frogs and a member of both the New Amsterdam Musical Association and Local 208 of Chicago, the first black unit of the American Federation of Musicians—was the leading figure in the formation of the Clef Club, and was elected its first president.[8] It is also likely that Europe was responsible for suggesting the name for the organization, patterning it after Washington's elite Treble Clef Club with which his sister had been associated, but avoiding that group's "high class" bias (neither "treble" nor "bass" clef was included in the title). The purposes of the new organization were nonetheless ambitious. The Preamble to the organization's charter states:

> We, the members of said organization, have established, organized, and incorporated the Clef Club of the City of New York, in order to inculcate the science of vocal and instrumental music, technique, and execution of vocal and instrumental music, and to promote good fellowship and social intercourse.[9]

Neither popular music, nor any of the current euphemisms for it, received mention. In fact, the stated social and educational objectives of the Clef Club were virtually the same as those of the New Amsterdam Musical Association, provided one overlooks the latter's restriction to instrumentalists who were "trained musicians."[10] The unstated objectives of both organizations were also similar in that the Clef Club was intended to function, like the New Amsterdam Musical Association, as a combined trade union and booking agency.

The idea for an organization devoted to furthering the professional interests of black popular musicians, singers, and dancers in New York City, given the rising demand for their services downtown, proved a timely and popular one. By April 28, when Lester Walton announced in his column in the *Age* that a new organization, composed of "well-known musicians and singers of Greater New York, the majority of whom play and sing in the leading hotels and cafes of New York City and provide entertainment for the smart set" had been formed, membership had already grown to more than 135.[11] Among the "well-known musicians and singers" were current or future band leaders Joe Jordan, Ford Dabney, Egbert Thompson, and Arthur "Happy" Rhone; singers Tom Bethel, Henry Creamer, and George Walker, Jr.; and pianists Clarence Williams, Irving "Kid Sneeze" Williams, and John Europe (Jim's older brother).[12] The majority of the original members of the Clef Club, however, played one or several of the stringed instruments then popular in the hotels and nightclubs. Among these were musicians trained in the standard instruments drawn from the European symphonic tradition (violins, celli, violas, and double basses), but the vast majority were players of instruments then associated with American minstrelsy and eastern European and Mediterranean folk music: banjos, mandolins, bandoris (a cross between the banjo and the mandolin), and harp guitars—an awkward double-necked hybrid of an instrument. The most significant technical aspect of the latter instruments is that they must be plucked or strummed, rather than bowed, in order to be played, and their sound, therefore, has a strong percussive, or rhythmic, quality. It is interesting that while there were a few true percussionists (timpani and trap drum players, the latter having recently emerged from the marching band, but considered at the time little more than a vaudeville novelty), there appears to have been no woodwind or brass players in the original Clef Club.

Attracting a large membership from among the more talented performers in the city was the easiest of several immediate problems that Europe and the other directors of the club faced. They needed to find a headquarters, to begin advertising, and to establish a reputation so that potential employers would know to call the Clef Club when black musicians and singers were wanted. It was also their intention to develop standards of professional performance and appearance for Clef Club musicians and, correspondingly, to command higher, more equitable salaries and better general treatment from white employers.

The first priority for the club's officers, following the positive reception of the idea for the club by a representative number of New York's black performers, was to raise the necessary funds to rent office space for their operations.

The C.V.B.A. had shown by the results of its first annual picnic and dance the previous summer that large-scale public entertainments, enlisting the talents of a group's membership, would be supported by New York's black community and could be financially successful. On August 12, the C.V.B.A. had combined an afternoon of games and outdoor sports with an evening of vaudeville and minstrel acts, including the requisite "Grand Prize Cake Walk," and an all-night dance.[13] Europe thought that a similar kind of social event, combining performances by individual Clef Club members and a dance, could work for the Clef Club as well, but he also wanted to try something novel— to introduce the New York public, black and white, to something they had not seen or heard before (and perhaps—at least among most whites—did not think possible): a symphony-sized concert orchestra composed entirely of black musicians.

There were considerable practical difficulties involved in attempting to organize a large orchestra from the Clef Club's membership. While many of the club's members were "legitimate" musicians—the term then used to indicate musical literacy—who had some familiarity with the standard orchestral repertoire, a greater number played only by ear and had experience only with popular forms of music. In addition, the instrumentation represented by the Clef Club's musicians was quite unusual, requiring substantial arranging of any piece of music to be performed. Organizing rehearsals presented yet another challenge, since most club members held regular (many nonmusical) jobs all across the city. It was therefore next to impossible to find a time during the day when they could be brought together.

There were risks as well as challenges in the project. If a concert orchestra composed of black musicians, directed by black musicians, was actually put together and then performed poorly in public, then the Clef Club itself would suffer, and great damage would also be done to the reputation of black musicians in general. An additional and even broader concern, always present when black Americans attempt something that the racially prejudiced society in which they live thinks is beyond their capabilities (black fighter pilots, black quarterbacks, etc.), is that a poor performance by a black orchestra would reinforce attitudes about black inferiority.

Europe was aware of both the problems and risks involved, but he had gained a great deal of confidence in his own musical and leadership abilities in the past six years in musical theater. He also had a number of equally talented and experienced musicians, like Joe Jordan, William Tyers, Tim Brymn, and Ford Dabney, upon whom he could count for assistance. More important, perhaps, was his recognition of the opportunity a Clef Club Orchestra could provide black musicians and composers, for the development of African-American musical culture, and his confidence in his own sense of how to make such an orchestra successful. Will Marion Cook had attempted to organize a concert orchestra of black musicians on a more modest scale in Washington, D.C., in 1890, but it had failed to last a year—despite the backing of Frederick Douglass and the leaders of Washington's black society—in part because it followed too closely the European "high culture" model. It may have been a competent (or even superb) black orchestra, but it was not—in instrumentation, performance, or material—an African-American one. Ernest Hogan had been more commercially successful with his Memphis Students orchestra of 1905 (whose material, instrumentation, and style of performance were clearly not imitations of European "high culture" standards), but the Students were a fairly limited musical organization. Europe saw an opportunity in the Clef Club for a large ensemble, capable of rendering a wide range of musical sound in an appropriately dignified manner, yet dedicated to expressing that which was unique to the African-American musical tradition. "Jim Europe was a man with a great personality," Tom Fletcher recalled, who was, moreover, "a shrewd fellow, [who] saw the great possibilities."[14]

On April 21, 1910, just ten days after the club was formed, the *New York Age* carried the first advertisement for the Clef Club's "Musical Melange and Dancefest" to be held the following May 27 at the Manhattan Casino on 155th Street and 8th Avenue in Harlem. The "big feature" of the evening was promised to be "the appearance of the Clef Club Orchestra of 100 musicians, singers, and dancers, under the direction of James Reese Europe, assisted by Joe Jordan and Daniel Kildare."[15] Europe had clearly decided very early on to include as many Clef Clubbers in the new orchestra as he could and also, as the Memphis Students had done so successfully, to integrate the elements of vocal and instrumental music and dance. Five weeks later, by the time the final ad appeared the day before the concert, Europe, Jordan, and Al Johns (who had replaced Kildare as an assistant director) had somehow organized and rehearsed the promised 100-member orchestra (now featuring ten pianos "on stage") sufficiently to offer a thirty-minute program as the "No. 1 Special Feature" of the evening.[16]

Lester Walton, in his review following the concert, was ebullient. "Never has such a large and efficient body of colored musicians appeared together in New York City in a concert," he wrote. The appearance of the orchestra was "striking," and the players "clearly demonstrated that they are capable of playing music as it is written," disproving what is "sometimes said of colored musicians that the only musical sign observed by them is forte." Walton applauded the program as well, noting that there were no "heavy operas," but that it was not all "ragtime" either. The music critic's choice for the best performance by the orchestra was Paul Lincke's "Beautiful Spring" ("Had the composer been on hand and heard his beautiful concert waltz so artistically rendered there is no doubt that he would have even a higher regard for his tuneful composition"), but he acknowledged that Joe Jordan's conducting of his own "That Teasing Rag" elicited the biggest response from the large audience. The variety acts that followed were also well received and made their contribution to the success of the evening, but it was the appearance of that orchestra that made the night special. "To see good colored singers and dancers is a familiar sight," Walton concluded, "but to have the pleasure of sitting and listening to nearly 100 trained colored musicians is an unusual treat." Furthermore, one may hope that "the time is not far distant when this organization will be afforded an opportunity to appear at Carnegie Hall or some large theatre and deliver the message to our Caucasian brothers that the race is making advanced strides in the musical world."[17] Walton would see his wish fulfilled in less than two years.

Europe had himself little time to celebrate the success of the Clef Club concert. The club's main object of systematizing black entertainment business was hardly begun, and profits realized from the dance were not adequate to permit the immediate leasing of permanent offices. He also had to attend to a previous ten-week personal engagement at Port-au-Peck, New Jersey, beginning at the end of June, and then there was the 3rd Annual "Frolic of the Frogs" scheduled for June 27, to which he was also committed. He was, however, pleased with the results of the first Clef Club entertainment and orchestra concert, and he and the other officers decided to hold a similar affair in the fall.

By early September, Europe was back in New York and concentrating his efforts on the new organization. The first general business meeting of the Clef Club was called for September 19, 1910, at the New Central Hall on West 53rd Street, and all members were requested to attend.[18] Aside from receiving various committee reports, the main business of the meeting was to agree upon October 20 as the date and the Manhattan Casino as the site for the "Second Grand Musical Melange and Dance Fest."[19] Although the basic format for the fall entertainment was similar to that presented the previous spring—a vaudeville program followed by the orchestra concert followed by a dance—several changes reflect Europe's increasing ambitions for the organization, and, indeed, for African-American music.[20] The most radical change was the addition of a third segment in the program, sixty minutes with the "Popular Colored Composers," designed to showcase the compositional talents of Clef Club members. According to the then-accepted hierarchy of musical arts, composition was accorded a higher status than performance. While the black musician as performer—especially of popular music—had achieved a certain respect and acceptance, the black composer, whatever his talents, found little of either. The struggles of non–Clef Club member Scott Joplin, then living in New York, are a poignant case in point. For the October 20 concert, William Tyers, Al Johns, Henry Creamer, Tom Lemonier, and Ford Dabney were each given an opportunity to present a selection of their recent compositions, most of which were songs written in the familiar ballad style of the day. Some, however, especially the instrumental pieces of Tyers, revealed greater than usual harmonic sophistication.

Europe wisely continued to keep the program fairly simple for the orchestral part of the concert (a few light classics, a schottische, a repeat, by request, of Lincke's "Beautiful Spring," his own "Clef Club March," a new composition,"Queen of the Nile," and Creamer's "Clef Club Chant" to close). The large aggregation was now called "The Clef Club Symphony Orchestra," and although no symphony-length work was performed, the program included a greater variety of music and was nearly twice as long as that offered in the spring. Europe also continued his practice of sharing the conducting duties with his assistant director, on this occasion William Tyers, and both were praised by Walton in his review of the concert for their ability and for emulating Toscanini, the celebrated conductor of the Metropolitan Opera, in knowing the music so well that they never appeared to look at the score.[21]

The second Clef Club entertainment was also well-attended, Walton reported, and, despite the length of the program, "no one left complaining that he did not receive for his price of admission 100 cents on the dollar." "In no other place except New York," he remarked, "could such a large and efficient body of colored musicians be brought together and furnish the form of amusement provided last Thursday evening." Even the scattering of whites in the audience, who appeared "very much surprised, with eyes, mouths, and ears wide open," had to acknowledge that The Clef Club Symphony Orchestra proved itself a credit to the city.[22]

Prior to playing the last piece, Europe was presented with a silver loving cup in recognition of his singular role in the development of the orchestra and in the progress of the association. Clef Club members are very enthusiastic, Walton reported, and "talk of doing great things," but they need to remember to "work shoulder to shoulder to make their organization one that will attract national attention. If they do a bright future is in store for the club."[23]

The members of the Clef Club had good reason to feel optimistic; under Jim Europe's leadership the organization had come a long way in its first eight months. The two popular Clef Club entertainments, coupled with the success of the novel concert orchestra, had begun to attract the attention of New York's black residents as well as of the city's wider musical and entertainment community. In addition, as signaled by the announcement toward the latter part of December of the opening of their official headquarters at 134 West 53rd Street, directly across the street from the Marshall Hotel, Europe had also been making progress in reorganizing the manner and conditions by which black musicians, singers, and dancers would participate in the entertainment business of the great city.[24]

With the opening of the Clef Club headquarters and the installation of a telephone line, Europe was able to begin the campaign to establish the club as the central clearing house, or booking agency, for black entertainment. Members who were not already on steady jobs now had a place to go to wait for the calls that began to come in—especially for dance orchestras of various sizes—with increasing frequency. He also began to effect major changes in the working conditions for black musicians. It was a common practice, heretofore, for the large hotels and restaurants in the city and by out-of-town resorts like the Poinciana Hotel in Palm Beach not to pay black musicians and singers for their services directly. As Tom Fletcher remembered it, they would be hired for some menial job, like dishwasher or floor sweeper, with the expectation that they also perform for the guests for tips. Europe began to require the employers of Clef Club musicians to pay them a fixed salary and to include nothing other than entertaining in their duties.[25] Moreover, if an engagement were out of the city, then the musicians were to receive their salaries plus transportation, room, and board. To increase name recognition, he also encouraged club members who had their own established combinations to bill themselves as "So-and-So and his Clef Club Orchestra and Entertainers." A standard dress code was instituted stipulating tuxedos for engagements booked in advance and dark suits, white shirts, and bow ties for pick-up dates. "No one was sent on a job if not dressed correctly," Fletcher recalled.[26] By the early spring of 1911, Europe was leading a Clef Club dance orchestra himself.[27]

For the Clef Club "Monster Melange and Dancefest" scheduled for May 11, 1911 (the popular entertainments at the Manhattan Casino now advertised as regular semi-annual affairs), Europe and the other directors planned a program integrating selections by the "Celebrated Clef Club Symphony Orchestra" with individual song, dance, and comedy routines drawn from "Ye Olde Fashion Minstrel" tradition. The minstrel acts could be expected to appeal to the widest popular taste while permitting Europe to continue to expand his musical ambitions for the orchestra by presenting a "Classy Concert" of new compositions entirely by "Eminent Colored Composers."[28] Europe was again billed as the principal conductor, with William Tyers as his primary assistant, but Will Marion Cook was listed as a second assistant conductor, the first time his name had appeared in any association with the Clef Club. The instrumentation of the orchestra had also undergone a slight modification from the previous fall concert with the addition of an organ, two flutes, and two clarinets—the latter constituting the first woodwinds to appear with the string- and percussion-dominated ensemble.

The May 11 Clef Club entertainment proved to be the most successful production, in both popular and artistic terms, yet presented by the organization. A capacity crowd, including a large number of visitors who came to New York specifically for the purpose of attending the event, found "about as much room for moving around as would a poor little sardine in a can."[29] Nevertheless, both parts of the lengthy program—the minstrel "melange" and the orchestral concert—were enthusiastically received. "From a spectacular standpoint," Walton wrote in his review of the evening, "the minstrels, stationed on the stage, carried off [the] honors"; however, the artistic hit "was registered by the Clef Club Symphony Orchestra, located on the floor of the Casino," which "demonstrated its versatility by playing sacred music, waltz, and rag-time compositions with equal skill and effectiveness."[30]

Europe's program included new compositions by Frederick Bryan, William Tyers, and Ford Dabney, with the only repeat performances from previous concerts being Tyers' "Smyrna" and his own "Clef Club March." Will Marion Cook's "Darktown is Out To-night," from the musical *Clorindy*, served as the rousing closing number for the entire company—although Cook apparently chose not to conduct it. Europe contributed the "Lorraine Waltzes" and "The Separate Battalion," the former dedicated to his mother (and sister) and the latter, a march, dedicated to the high school cadets of Washington, D.C., both clearly indicating his desire to meet the standards of respectability defined by his family and the Washington community. The greatest stylistic departure from prior concerts was the orchestra's rendering of Harry T. Burleigh's adaptations of the spirituals "A Jubilee" and "On Bended Knee." With the addition of these pieces based upon traditional African-American religious music, Europe also indicated his affirmation of a wider range of African-American musical expression.

The "Lorraine Waltzes" and "On Bended Knee" received special mention both as compositions and in the manner of their performance by the orchestra. All of the selections, however, each of which was written by a black composer, Walton was pleased to report, showed good "preparation and intelligent interpretation" by "New York's premier colored musical organization." The "man who is not moved by the music played by the Clef Club Symphony Orchestra," he concluded, "should at once have his mental and physical condition investigated." "Too much praise cannot be given James Reese Europe and the members of the Clef Club for furnishing New York with such a meritorious musical organization."[31]

During the spring and summer of 1911, Jim Europe was one of the busiest people in the city. When he was not rehearsing the Clef Club Symphony Orchestra in preparation for its next public concert, or composing new pieces for it to perform, he was overseeing the operations of the club, filling engagements with his own dance group, and responding to the increasing number of requests for contributions of his time and services to support various professional and community projects. In March, for instance, he conducted the 10th Cavalry Band, perhaps the most celebrated black unit of the U.S. Army (having served with Teddy Roosevelt in the Cuban campaign) at the 69th Regiment Armory in New York. In April, following the Clef Club concert, he was in Washington, D.C., preparing to conduct the "Lyric Orchestra" as part of a memorial for George Walker at the Howard Theater.[32] The Walker Memorial, a charity event to raise funds for a graveside monument in Walker's honor, which took place on two evenings at the end of May, must have been particularly pleasing for Europe, since he was joined by many of the leading figures in black music and entertainment (Aida Overton Walker, Harry T. Burleigh, S. H. Dudley, J. Rosamond Johnson, among them) as well as by a number of Washington's progressive social elite (Mary Church Terrell and Mrs. A. M. Curtis gave speeches).[33] Other evidence of Europe's increasingly prominent standing within the profession included his election as second vice-president of the Frogs; Bert Williams was reappointed president, while Lester Walton was named first vice-president.[34]

It was also during the early spring of 1911 that Europe began his association with David Mannes, son-in-law of Walter Damrosch and concertmaster of the New York Symphony Orchestra, in a project that became very close to his heart—the Music School Settlement for Colored People in Harlem. Mannes, who had received his early musical inspiration and instruction from the black violinist John Douglass and who wished to honor his former teacher, persuaded a number of philanthropists, including George F. Peabody and Dr. Felix Adler, individuals who were interested in helping the black people who had been moving to Harlem in large numbers over the past decade, that they could be of greatest assistance by helping to establish a music school there for black children.[35] Mannes, who had been successfully operating a similar school for poor whites on the lower East Side of the city for a number of years, argued convincingly that music was "the racial talent of the Negro, and through music, which is a universal language, the Negro and the white man can be brought to have a mutual understanding."[36]

A number of wealthy and influential white supporters of the idea (Natalie Curtis, Elbridge Adams, and Mrs. Percival Knauth joining Peabody and Adler) were initially organized into a board of directors or trustees for the new school, to which a number of prominent Negroes, including Harry T. Burleigh and W.E.B. Du Bois, were added.[37] Mannes, who was given the job of engaging a director and a faculty, contacted Europe, who, as president of the Clef Club, was in the best position to assist him in identifying those relatively few trained black musicians who were both capable of teaching violin, voice, or piano, and who possessed the time and means to be able to offer their services for little or nothing. John Douglass had been a master of the classics, and Mannes was therefore determined that the school should concentrate its instruction of black children in the tradition of Haydn, Schumann, and Brahms, a decision that made the recruitment of black instructors even more difficult. Europe, for his part, did not object to this, but he warned Mannes from the very first that to foster the pride of the black community it was "absolutely necessary that Negroes assume control of the school" as quickly as it became financially possible to do so.[38]

With Jim Europe's assistance, a staff of teachers—mostly volunteers, but a few on salary—was eventually assembled, and David I. Martin, a violinist in the Clef Club Symphony Orchestra, who had been operating his own studio since 1907, was appointed the Music School Settlement's first director.[39] The school had no permanent home at first, but various temporary locations were found and instruction began at a cost of twenty-five cents per lesson for children who could afford it, and free of charge (thanks to scholarships) for those who could not.[40] A permanent building was eventually acquired on 134th Street in Harlem. There, for a number of years, daily lessons were given in piano, violin, and wind instruments, as well as in theory, sight reading, and voice. Also, three orchestras of varying grades were organized there and they soon began holding weekly rehearsals.

At the first Clef Club smoker given at the club's headquarters on West 53rd Street in late September, Europe announced that the next Clef Club entertainment—the fourth semi-annual "melange and dancefest"—would be held on November 9 and that the program would include a "miniature cabaret show" in addition to the orchestra concert. By abandoning the traditional minstrel format for the non-orchestral part of the entertainment, the club's directors gave notice that the cabaret and dance-craze was in full sway by the fall of 1911, and that black musicians in New York intended to play an integral role in the phenomena.[41] Indeed, in his review of the concert, Lester Walton, for the first time in his column in the *Age*, noted that the orchestra itself was "one of the most unique musical organizations not only in the United States but in the world" in part because its members sang and danced as well as played their instruments.[42]

Walton was critical of the length of the overall program, which is easy enough to understand since it lasted four hours. While he appreciated the talents of many of the individual Clef Club acts (the best of which was dancer William Robinson—the future legendary "Bojangles"), he felt it was now time that the symphony and vaudeville elements be separated. "Each is strong enough to stand without the other," he wrote.[43]

Walton, as usual, was most interested in the evolution Clef Club Symphony Orchestra, which for the first time was augmented by a brass section under the direction of E. E. Thompson. A large photograph of the orchestra with Jim Europe reclining confidently in front accompanied Walton's review. William Tyers (who was recovering from an automobile accident) once again assisted Europe in conducting the orchestra in a program that the "large and elegantly attired audience" heartily applauded, requiring many encores. Everyone present seemed convinced that the orchestra was now "well qualified to give a symphony concert at Carnegie Hall or Mendelssohn Hall, and before a critical audience." Several of the selections were repeated from the spring concert and showed improvement from the additional rehearsals, but to Walton's ear the "most inspiring number of the evening" was a march, written and dedicated to the proposed black National Guard regiment of New York by Europe, entitled "The Strength of the Nation." "Each time I attend a performance of the Clef Club Symphony Orchestra," Walton summed up the evening, "I leave Manhattan Casino more deeply impressed with the idea that some day the organization is going to make the devotees of music in New York sit up and take notice, irrespective of whether they be colored or white; for there is really some class to the Clef Club."[44]

For the remainder of the year, Europe was engaged in planning the "most pretentious entertainment ever attempted in New York," as the consciously overblown advertisements for the Frogs' next "Frolic" scheduled for the end of January announced. He also appeared for at least one concert with Aida Overton Walker in Washington, D.C.[45] Despite their serious purposes, the Frogs (probably due to Bert Williams as much as anyone) continued to display a wonderful sense of humor and a true sense of fellowship in their activities that Europe fully enjoyed. In his December column in the *Age*, for instance, Lester Walton reported on a "Stormy Session of Frogs," where a "disagreement" among the members developed over who should play the female parts in a ballet planned for their upcoming entertainment. Some of the physically smaller Frogs refused to accept the assignment, so Europe, R. C. McPherson, and Captain W. H. Jackson volunteered. When they were not taken seriously because each "weighs nearly two hundred pounds and whose embonpoint is apparent without the use of glasses," the trio charged the group with unfair discrimination.[46]

On a more serious subject, Europe was very much interested in the progress of the Music Settlement School in Harlem, and he suggested to David Mannes that the Clef Club Symphony Orchestra give a benefit concert to help raise funds needed for the new building and its expanding programs.[47] At the Clef Club meeting on February 19, 1912, he announced that arrangements for such a concert, "on or about April 21, under the auspices of the Negro Settlement School," were underway. The club's treasury was reported at $5,000, monies accumulated mostly from the biannual concerts, and the membership agreed to contribute a minimum of $25 each toward the construction of a modern club house in Harlem where the "opportunity will be afforded the members to further their musical education, if desired."[48] The larger objectives of the Clef Club and the Music Settlement School were clearly seen to be interwoven. Mannes later recalled that the conductor of the Clef Club was among the most remarkable individuals that he worked with in the Harlem school project, and that he and "Big Jim" Europe also became friends.[49]

The idea that the Clef Club Orchestra should provide a benefit for the Music School appealed to Mannes, and it was probably he who took the next step by convincing the board of trustees that it should be held at Carnegie Hall. The board had initially been hopeful that one of the student orchestras would be able to offer a concert at the great hall "in which only Negro performers should render compositions of Negroes," but as of the early spring of 1912 none of them was thought ready.[50] Mannes and several of the others, who had heard the singing and playing of Clef Club Orchestra at the Manhattan Casino uptown, had no doubts that a largely white audience would find such a concert a pleasant surprise. The uninitiated members, however, were skeptical. It was one thing to expect a tolerant reception for a children's orchestra, but an orchestra comprised of popular entertainers from New York's theaters and cabarets was something else again. After all, a serious music concert was a sort of public ritual imposing certain formalities on both the audience and the performers; the concert hall was the temple of "high" musical culture in America at the time. Popular, or vernacular, music was accorded a lower status and its proper place was outside the concert hall.[51]

In response to such concerns, Mannes argued that if black musicians were to demonstrate their capacity to produce a suitably dignified concert for the first time in prestigious Carnegie Hall, the results could not fail to advance the aims of the Music School Settlement quite apart from any money that might be raised. Furthermore, the Clef Club Orchestra was "the outstanding Negro orchestra in the country," and its leader, "Big Jim Europe," was a man who could be trusted to do what he said he would.[52] Mannes and his associates were persuasive, and arrangements were subsequently made with Carnegie Hall for a historic first "Concert of Negro Music" by black American singers and instrumentalists for May 2, 1912.

The Carnegie Hall concert by the Clef Club was the greatest opportunity and the most difficult challenge that Europe had faced in his ten-year career. Unlike the earlier club concerts, there would be no lengthy vaudeville or minstrel program, nor any all-night dance to accompany the orchestral performance. The musical program also needed to be more broadly comprehensive than any Europe had previously attempted, to reflect the full range of African-American musical expression: secular and religious, traditional and modern, vocal and instrumental. The repertoire that he had developed for the orchestra over the past two years, in addition to popular songs and ragtime, fortunately included a number of suitably lyrical concert waltzes, stirring march pieces, and several works by Harry Burleigh and Will Marion Cook (representing the African-American sacred music tradition and the more recent music of black musical theater, respectively). In order to counter any suspicion that Carnegie Hall was being turned over to an evening exclusively of popular music, the St. Philips Church Choir was asked to offer a performance of Coleridge-Taylor's "By the Waters of Babylon," and the "Benediction" from an original mass composed by their principal organist, Paul C. Bohlen, and Burleigh, J. Rosamond Johnson, and contralto Elizabeth Payne were enlisted as vocal soloists (Johnson was also invited to perform a piano solo of one of his compositions).[53]

Current popular taste was eventually represented by two groups on the program: the Royal Poinciana Quartette, a vocal group that specialized in the

familiar Stephen Foster style "plantation songs" and which appeared courtesy
of Weisenwebers Restaurant, and the Versatile Entertainers Quintette, a virtu-
oso banjo and guitar ensemble drawn from the ranks of the Clef Club itself. All
of these additions were expected to contribute positively to the evening's concert, but there was hardly any question that the concert would succeed or fail
depending upon the performance of the Clef Club Orchestra.

Natalie Curtis has left a vivid description of the difficult conditions under
which Europe labored to prepare the orchestra for its most important concert.
Without a proper rehearsal hall, the men were "stuffed suffocatingly under the
low ceiling of a room that had seen better days," she later wrote. "No acoustics,
no elbow-room even, the bass tuba threatening with annihilation the poor
drummer next to him who could hardly lift his sticks without hitting the
cornet-player," and sheet music spread all over the chairs that served as music
stands.[54]

The musicians were arranged by the conductor in groups around the music,
and in each group was placed one or two of those who could read—the rest
"simply caught by ear what their neighbors played and then joined in." The Clef
Clubbers were all experienced musicians who, if they had not learned to read
music, had apparently learned to read each other, for "once they had caught the
main outline of the music, the whole band began to improvise." "I always put a
man that can read notes in the middle where the others can pick him up,"
Europe told Curtis. They "can catch anything if they hear it once or twice, and
if it's too hard for 'em the way it's written, why they just make up something else
that'll go with it."[55]

Despite Europe's confidence in his musicians and the orchestra, as the day
of the concert grew ever closer, fears began to be expressed that the Clef Club's
attempt to produce a serious and dignified program of African-American music
would prove to be an embarrassment. Even David Mannes, who was familiar
with the orchestra and who witnessed the final preparations during several all-
day rehearsals at Carnegie Hall, began to have doubts. His main concern was
that the orchestra was only able, because its members held other jobs, to be rehearsed in sections. "Even in the final rehearsal," he recalled, "the orchestra
was not complete," and despite Europe's assurances that he had dealt with this
problem in the past, Mannes "wondered if this scattered and disorderly rehearsal attendance could produce anything but chaos."[56]

The eccentric Will Marion Cook, who did not belong to the Clef Club but
whom Europe had earlier persuaded to appear as guest conductor of his own
works, now began to voice his opposition (as, indeed, did several other educated blacks) to the entire concert. According to Noble Sissle, Cook "raved all
over town about Jim not knowing anything about conducting and what right
did he have going to Carnegie Hall with his inexperience? Cook claimed that
Jim would set the Negro race back fifty years, and many of those remarks he
even made in Jim's hearing. . . ."[57] A potentially more serious situation arose

when the St. Philips Church Choir, out of fear of being "classed as sinners" for appearing "in the same hall and on the same platform" with theatrical performers, threatened to pull out.[58]

After failing to reassure St. Philips, the directors of the Music School Settlement called Europe in to see what he could do to persuade them. According to Tom Fletcher, Europe simply cabled the church officials and gave them twenty-four hours to make up their minds and, if they refused, threatening to have the Clef Club "take care of the full evening's entertainment." "Our club is full of good church members," Fletcher recalled Europe telling his sponsors, "and if the audience wanted church choir songs, 'just let me have a two or three hour rehearsal with the club members and we will sing some for them. I, myself, as well as the others, are members of some church and we know all the songs. But to make a living we have to sing and play what the public wants and will pay for.'"[59] The Settlement directors were satisfied and apparently so were the church officials.

Even if Europe and his supporters could finally convince their doubters that they would produce a dignified, serious program, there remained the question of whether the general public, which considered blacks second-class citizens and that had been reluctant to accord black artists—even "classical" performers— the respect that concert performance implied, would be receptive to a concert by black musicians of African-American music. By the day preceding the concert, May 1, 1912, all the box seats in the great hall had been sold, primarily through the personal efforts of the friends of the Settlement School. Fully two thousand (out of the total of three thousand) seats, however, remained untaken. At that point, something remarkable happened. An editorial appeared in the late edition of the New York *Evening Journal* that was so compelling that it seemed to convince New Yorkers that this concert was something special and not to be missed:

> The Negroes have given us the only music of our own that is American—national, original, and real. This concert, which is organized for tonight at Carnegie Hall, will be from beginning to end a concert by Negro musicians. The musicians volunteer their services. The proceeds of the concert will be devoted to the Music School Settlement for Colored People. This school is intended to encourage and develop musical talent in Negroes, and there is no doubt that those taught by it will contribute to the pleasure of the public and make valuable additions to the musical works of this country.[60]

Beginning in the late afternoon, the demand for tickets became so great that by the time of the concert the following evening all the remaining seats, and standing room, had been taken, and many persons had to be turned away.[61] When Europe stepped to the front of the 125-member Clef Club Orchestra and raised his baton for the opening number, "The Clef Club March," Carnegie Hall was "jammed to the very limit of the fire laws." When the chorus joined the orchestra to conclude the rousing piece, the audience—perhaps for the first time at any concert in the United States, composed equally of the two races—came to its feet and New York "woke up to the fact that it had something new in music."[62] "New York had not yet become accustomed to jazz; so when the Clef Club opened its concert with a syncopated march, playing it with a biting attack and an infectious rhythm, and on the finale bursting into singing, the effect can be imagined. The applause became a tumult."[63]

The entire program that evening was warmly, even enthusiastically, received, and numerous encores were required by the orchestra and soloists.[64] Lester Walton, in his review of the concert, attributed the palpable sense of the uniqueness of the evening to the absence of race prejudice. "Some of the leading white citizens sat in evening dress in seats next to some of our highly respectable colored citizens, who were also in evening clothes." No color line was drawn in any part of the house, as theater managers routinely did even where such Jim Crow practices were legally prohibited, said Walton, and yet "no calamity occurred because the colored citizens were not segregated." The reason for this was that "the whites present represented the best element of their race" as did the "colored people in attendance."[65] The common interests of class, as it was then still widely hoped, would triumph over racial prejudice.

The directors of the Music School Settlement were extremely pleased with the evening, both because it resulted in raising nearly $5,000 for the Harlem school, and because the orchestra performed so well. "Don't you worry," Europe had assured Ms. Curtis before the concert, "once those fellows hear that music and catch its swing they'll eat it right up." According to her, they did just that. "'Barbaric'!, one college-bred Negro called the Clef Club," she recalled. "'Barbaric,' we exclaimed in astonished admiration. That an orchestra of such power, freshness, vitality and originality could have remained so long undiscovered in novelty-hunting New York, was a silent and reproachful comment on the isolation of the 'Negro quarter.'" The large orchestra with its sections of banjos, mandolins, guitars, strings, and percussion, that entirely filled the stage, produced an "absolutely distinctive sound, a 'tang' like the flavor of pine-apple amid other fruits."[66] To David Mannes, the orchestra's sound was "very imposing and seductively rhythmic," and yet the great "surprise" was "the beautiful, soft sound of this strange conglomeration of unassorted instruments." "Its only prototype in tone," he thought, was "the Russian balalaika orchestra." As for the leader, Mannes described Europe as "an amazingly inspiring conductor. Of a statuesquely powerful build, he moved with simple and modest grace, always dominating this strange assemblage before him with quiet control."[67]

Mannes was impressed by the simultaneous singing as well as playing of orchestra members, who sometimes sang in a different clef or pitch than that of the instruments they played. There were also the fourteen upright pianos, placed back to back and played by fourteen of the best ragtime players in town, adding a "truly beautiful, rich and unusual" color to the overall sound.[68] Two aspects of the Clef Club Orchestra's use of the piano are worth noting. First, the instruments, which Elbridge Adams—an official of the American Piano Company—provided as Europe had requested, were not the concert grands that most Carnegie Hall patrons were used to hearing; rather, they were the smaller uprights of the type that so many of the Clef Club musicians played in their regular jobs as entertainers in the hotels and clubs. The choice was deliberate. Second, the pianos were treated as orchestral instruments, as contributors to the overall sound and not employed in their more familiar role as solo instruments or as single voices in a trio or quintet. As such, Natalie Curtis thought them particularly effective, "weaving a sonorous background of tremolos, deepening with tone-values the roll of the kettledrums, sharpening percussion effects with varieties of pitch, emphasizing rhythmic outline, coloring the accents, blending strings, brass, plectrum and drums into a vibrant unity of sound—a link between them all."[69]

The music critics in the audience were favorably impressed by the concert, although conservative papers like *Musical America*, while praising the performers, tended—patronizingly—to account for their accomplishment as a result of "that spirit of exuberance and freedom of fancy that mark the natures of these natural-born musicians."[70] Lester Walton's review in the *Age*, which did not devote as much attention to the music as usual because of his lengthy reflections on the social meaning of the evening, nevertheless indicated the positive response of the audience to J. Rosamond Johnson's singing of "Lit'l Girl," William Tyers' "Panama," the selection of songs by the Poinciana Quintet, and the St. Philips Church Choir. The undisputed hit of the program, though, requiring three encores, was the Clef Club Orchestra and Chorus's rendition of Will Marion Cook's "Swing Along."

According to Noble Sissle, Cook had only at the last moment decided to participate in the program, as a violinist, on the condition that Europe not call on him publicly to conduct his two works, "Rain Song" and "Swing Along."[71] Once they had been performed, however, and the audience began clamoring for the composer, Europe stepped down and, breaking his word, walked over to Cook's chair and introduced him. Tom Fletcher remembered that Cook was so overcome that he "began to weep tears of joy and when he tried to speak he couldn't say a word. All he could do was just bow."[72]

Although Europe and his orchestras were brought back to the stage of Carnegie Hall in 1913 and again in 1914, the Clef Club Concert of May 2, 1912, was the crowning achievement of Europe's Clef Club years. The success of that first concert, and the public attention it received, elevated Jim Europe's personal reputation as a composer, a conductor, and, especially, as an organizer to the top of his profession. Du Bois's *Crisis*, which named him one of its "Men of the Month" for June, stated that one of his most distinguishing characteristics was "his genius for organization" and quoted from a *New York Tribune* reviewer who said of his marches that "all in all, they are worthy of the pen of John Philip Sousa."[73]

The 1912 Concert also changed some long-standing opinions about black popular musicians and opened some new doors of employment opportunity for black musicians in New York, generally, and for Clef Club musicians in particular. Europe's effective use of violins, along with the banjos and guitars, was such that black violinists began to be more widely accepted, and Clef Club musicians found more calls for their use on jobs. Even some members of the black church, after seeing what the Club had done and the reception of the Carnegie Hall audience, "changed their feelings about these musicians and entertainers."[74] Prior to the concert, Clef Club musicians had been successful in furnishing entertainment for private parties given at such fashionable spots as the Waldorf-Astoria, Sherrys, Delmonicos, Martins, Rectors, the Hotel Astor, and the Ritz Carlton.[75] Afterward, members of the Clef Club were engaged to play for "nearly all of the best functions, not only in America, but in London and Paris. Combinations of from two to six pieces were hired to play at private parties in London and Paris and on private yachts cruising all over the world," and the public halls and theaters began to follow suit.[76] Indeed, the demand for Clef Club musicians as a result of the concert was so strong that, as James Weldon Johnson remembered, the Clef Club, for quite a while, held a "monopoly of the business of entertaining private parties and furnishing music for the dance craze which was then beginning to sweep the country."[77] "The colored musicians, all members of the Clef Club, had every amusement place outside of [the] legitimate theaters sewed up."[78]

6

"What It Takes to Make Me Love You—You've Got It"

> A society lady called up on the telephone a man who makes a business of supplying musicians, and asked the price for a band of ten men. The man she called up is a colored man and supplies colored musicians, but as his office is on Broadway, such a thought seems not to have been anywhere near the lady's mind. He told her what ten men would cost for an evening. She was amazed and said to him, "Why I can get colored musicians for that price."
>
> James Weldon Johnson (1915)

At the beginning of 1913, as James Reese Europe looked toward a new year of increasingly demanding professional responsibilities and challenges, it may have seemed to him an appropriate time to establish his personal life on a more stable, and perhaps more conventionally respectable, basis. He was now entering his thirty-third year, and circumstances external to his professional situation seemed to promise a greater measure of independence than he had previously enjoyed. In the nearly fourteen years since his father's unexpectedly sudden death, Europe had been a major source of support for his mother, Lorraine, and his younger sister, Mary. He had helped them through their most difficult period and seen them comfortably settled in the house they now jointly owned on S Street, near Howard University, in Washington, D.C.

For almost ten years, after graduating from Minor Normal School, Mary Europe had been employed part-time as an accompanist for various music classes which were then occasionally offered in the Washington public school system. By the end of 1912, however, her reputation as a soloist, accompanist, teacher, and choral director, was such that a regular position on the faculty of the prestigious M Street High School was offered her despite her lack of an advanced degree.[1] Since Mary was unmarried, and living with her mother, it was reasonable to expect that she would now be able to assume greater responsibility for their financial well-being.

Whether a growing sense of independence from his mother and sister played any part in Jim Europe's thinking cannot be known for certain, but less than a month before Mary Europe began her new position (and, coincidentally, five days after the fiftieth anniversary of the Emancipation Proclamation), on January 5, 1913, Jim Europe and Willie Angrom Starke were married in a quiet ceremony at Europe's residence at 67 West 131st Street in Harlem.[2] Willie Angrom, a widow almost exactly three years older than Europe, was recognized as a woman of some social standing within New York's black community at the time of her second marriage, and it is therefore somewhat curious that the New York City papers gave scant notice to the wedding.[3] How the couple became acquainted, or even when, is unknown, but it is certain that the new Mrs. Europe was not the first woman with whom James Europe had been seriously involved.

Among the members of the cast of Cole and Johnson's *Red Moon* in the fall of 1908 at the time Jim Europe became the company's musical director was a spirited, strikingly attractive young dancer named Bessie Simms. Born in 1889, Bessie was the youngest child of Joseph Simms, Jr., a bricklayer who had emigrated from North Carolina to Frederick County, Maryland, shortly after the Civil War, and Margaret Goins Simms, whose family resided in Buckeystown, a village near Frederick. After a brief teenage marriage from which a daughter was born in 1905, Bessie followed her desire to enter show business to New York, where she eventually landed a role as a chorus girl in Cole and Johnson's *The Shoo-Fly Regiment*. After touring with the *Shoo-Fly* Company in 1908—a period in which her on-stage and off-stage activities received occasional comment in the pages of the Indianapolis *Freeman*—she continued with Cole and Johnson's next effort, *The Red Moon*, where she was featured for two additional seasons as one of the six "Gibson Girls."[4]

From the fall of 1908 until December 1909, Bessie Simms, who was described by critic Sylvester Russell as "an artist's model," and Jim Europe were both working in *The Red Moon*, and it was during this period on the road that a close, perhaps intimate, friendship developed between them.[5] Casual relationships among theatrical people, especially those who spent months together traveling across the country, were hardly unusual, then or now, but the one that developed between Bessie Simms and Jim Europe seems to have been deeper than many. In later years, at least, it was the Simms' family's expressed assumption that the two had in fact been married at some point on tour with *The Red Moon*, and it is, of course, possible that they were.[6]

Given Europe's attachment to his mother and sister and his sense of responsibility toward them at the time, however, and given the social stigma then attached to entertainers and the theatrical profession (especially with regard to women on the stage), it would have been very difficult for Europe, regardless of the strength of his personal feelings, to have legalized their relationship. His mother would never have accepted her, and James knew it. At the same time, Bessie Simms, who had already weathered one marriage and whose stage career was beginning to look quite promising, may herself have felt some reluctance to marry again. In any case, Bessie Simms' and Jim Europe's relationship continued for a decade thereafter despite his legal ties to Willie Angrom; in fact, it ended only with his death in 1919.[7]

At the time of his marriage in January 1913, Europe had in truth very little time to attend to his personal life, since the second Clef Club concert at Carnegie Hall was scheduled to take place on the evening of February 12, barely five weeks away. The success of the ground-breaking first Carnegie Hall concert by the Clef Club Orchestra guaranteed that the 1913 concert would attract wider and, because the sheer novelty of such a concert would no longer be such a factor, greater critical attention. In addition, since it was advertised as one of the major commemorative events celebrating the Emancipation Proclamation, the concert would also be viewed, by whites and blacks alike, as a demonstration of the cultural progress of black Americans in general since the Civil War.[8]

The main feature of the second Carnegie Hall concert was, once again, the Clef Club Symphony Orchestra of 125 instrumentalists, performing for the benefit of the Music School Settlement in their now familiar combination of pianos, strings, and percussion. Another large chorus, drawn chiefly from St. Marks Methodist Episcopal Church Choir and consisting of almost 100 male and female voices (under the direction of Adalma E. Jackson) also contributed to the evening's program. In keeping with the spirit of the occasion (the anniversary of Lincoln's birthday), however, the combined chorus confined its performance to arrangements of such spirituals as "G'wine Up, Go Down, Moses," "Freedom," "Rise and Shine," "Run, Run, Mary, Run," and "Nobody Knows, the Trouble I See, Lord." No modern choral works were offered, as had been the case in 1912, and there were no examples of banjo virtuosity, or popular ragtime, and no black artists performed operatic arias or European-influenced piano solos.[9]

Five of the orchestra's numbers were repeated from the first concert ("The Clef Club March," Burleigh's "On Bended Knee," Tyers' "Tout a Vous," "Rain Song," and the now well-known "Swing Along," both by Will Marion Cook). Two pieces (Tyers' "Silhouettes: Dancing Shadows," and Vodery's "West Virginia Dance") had been performed previously at the Manhattan Casino by the orchestra, and to these were added four new (at least to the club's performances) compositions: "Deep River" by Coleridge-Taylor, "Maori—Samoan Dance" by Tyers, "Exhortation" by Cook, and Europe's own "Benefactors March," which he dedicated to the founders of the Settlement School. The orchestra's rendering of the Cook compositions, which are primarily choral works, was enhanced by the addition of a male chorus derived from the Clef Club membership. Europe and Tyers shared the conductor's podium, and, in between the first and second segments of the program, Major R. R. Moton of Hampton Institute spoke on the importance of musical expression to black Americans and encouraged the audience to support the work of the Music School Settlement. "I am glad that the people of New York are taking the Negro seriously in music," he said in closing.

> People are so apt not to take us seriously. It is so hard to disassociate him in the minds of many people from the Jim Crow buffoonery role in which he is so often placed in literature as well as in drama. The Negro is serious and often when he

joyously sings, his heart is burdened with sorrow and longings for the opportunities and privileges which he feels are his due, and I thank God for this
movement.[10]

The capacity audience, composed as before by the "prominent element of
both races," generously applauded the entire second Carnegie Hall "Concert of
Negro Music," but, as in 1912, reserved its strongest approval for Cook's "Swing
Along." The newspapers, especially the black press, also judged the concert a
major success. The *Freeman* reported flatly that the concert was perhaps the
"most notable event in commemoration of the 50th year of emancipation," a
strong endorsement, coming as it did from the Midwest.[11] All of the orchestral
numbers, according to Lucien White of the *Age*, were "rendered with precision and accuracy," though the performance of Europe's "Benefactor's March,"
written "in Europe's well-known style," could have benefited from the strength
of a brass section. He also liked the artful manner in which the "plantation
melodies" were sung by the chorus, though he did admit that the performance
lacked "the devotional fervor which made these songs expressive of the varying
moods of a downcast and oppressed people."[12]

The white press also reviewed the concert in a generally positive fashion,
though in some cases the reports were not quite as enthusiastic. *Musical
America*, for instance, carried only a brief, summary description of the evening's
program. It did, however, single out the performances of Cook's "Rain Song" and
"Exhortation," Coleridge-Taylor's "Deep River," and Will Vodery's "West Virginia
Dance" as particularly interesting.[13] The second successful concert of James
Reese Europe and the Clef Club Symphony Orchestra at Carnegie Hall did serve
to encourage a wider public awareness of, and debate about, the nature of
African-American music and its relation to American music in general.

The May issue of *Current Opinion* magazine carried a two-page article entitled "Legitimizing the Music of the Negro" that was clearly written in response
to the widespread interest aroused by the Carnegie Hall concerts. A photograph
of a bespectacled and seriously dignified Jim Europe, with the caption "Composer and Conductor," and a photo of the leader with the entire orchestra, "A
Multitude of Colored Music Makers," were prominently displayed on the first
page.[14] The actual article, however, pays little attention to the Clef Club Orchestra or its music; instead it is primarily devoted to summarizing the recently
published comments of two admirers of African-American folksong, H. E. Krehbiel and Natalie Curtis. Krehbiel, music editor of the *New York Tribune*, then
completing his *Afro-American Folksongs: A Study in Racial and National
Music*, was something of a purist and thus had been critical of the singing of the
large chorus (which he mistakenly thought was drawn from the Clef Club) at
Carnegie Hall on the grounds that the performance lacked authenticity. It was
"grievous to hear the Clef Club celebrate the emancipation of the slaves in a
song ('Freedom' is its name, and it is printed in the Hampton collection)," he

wrote, "which is compounded of phrases of 'Lily Dale' and 'Rally 'Round the Flag.'" Moreover, he continued, when the Clef Club did sing a song true to the tradition, like "Rise and Shine," "neither leader nor singers showed appreciation of its most striking melodic element—the use of the flat seventh." "Let not only the colored people but also the whites who love folk melody learn and perpetuate these songs as they were created and sung," he advised.[15]

Natalie Curtis, a friend and supporter of Hampton Institute and the Music School Settlement for Colored People in Harlem, was also, as has been indicated previously, a close observer and admirer of Jim Europe and the Clef Club Symphony Orchestra. *Current Opinion* referred to a recent article of hers that appeared in *The Craftsman* to the effect that of the modern composers who have remained true to the African-American tradition, Will Marion Cook stands out. Everything that he writes, she said, "is true in melody, rhythm, and form to the racial utterance, so that his music, even in its most external aspect, is distinctive and characteristic." "Tho [sic] his compositions so far are little more than an indication of the larger work that he might do, he is already seeking to interpret the character of his people in music, and to carry the untaught musical language of the Negro into the realm of art."[16]

The Clef Club's second successful Carnegie Hall appearance, and the critical notice it received, guaranteed that the popular reputation of the orchestra would continue to spread beyond New York City, and Europe began making definite plans to take the Clef Club on its first tour of several Eastern cities during the upcoming fall season. The kick-off concert was set for October 29, when "The Celebrated Clef Club" was scheduled to appear as part of an elaborate National Emancipation Exposition celebration in New York City.[17]

Organized by a nine-member commission appointed by Governor William Sulzer, the National Emancipation Exposition held at the Twelfth Regimental Armory at 62nd Street and Columbus Avenue from October 22 to 31 was one of the most ambitious of the Golden Jubilee celebrations. The headline event for the Exposition was a historical pageant, written by W.E.B. Du Bois, of the history of black people, featuring 350 actors and actresses in full costume. Special congresses of religious leaders, sociologists, lawyers, and women were scheduled, as well as an evening of athletic events, and special days were set aside to honor New York and other cities, organizations (like the Masons and Odd Fellows), individuals (Lincoln, Douglass), children, Southerners, businessmen, and even native New Yorkers. Three evenings were set aside for musical concerts by organizations chosen to reflect the achievement of black Americans in that field. In addition to the Clef Club, on October 24, David Mannes and David Martin led the Music School Settlement students in concert. On October 26 Will Marion Cook conducted the twenty-five-member Washington Conservatory of Music Folk Singers in a program of his recent compositions and his arrangements of traditional spirituals. All of the concerts were well received, and on the final night of the Exposition, both Cook and Europe (along with J. Rosamond Johnson, pianist Raymond A. Lawson, and Bert Williams in the field of musical arts) were named among the "100 distinguished freedmen" recognized for their achievements and each received a gold medal.[18]

Following the closing events of the National Emancipation Exposition, which included a costume ball and concert by the Exposition Band under the direction of E. E. Thompson (joined by Jim Europe) on the final evening, 125 members of the Clef Club Orchestra climbed aboard their special Pullman cars for the short ride to Philadelphia, the first stop on their ten-day tour. After performing in Philadelphia at the Academy of Music on November 4, Europe had scheduled successive concerts at Albaugh's Theater in Baltimore, City Auditorium in Richmond, the Howard Theatre in Washington, D.C., and Hampton Institute, in Hampton, Virginia. He was due back in New York by November 13 in order to appear with the organization for its regular fall concert and dance at the Manhattan Casino.

The 1913 Clef Club tour generated a fair amount of interest in the newspapers of the cities that were visited. "No more appropriate time could have been chosen for the tour of the now well-known Clef Club of New York than the present—the Fiftieth Anniversary of the Emancipation Proclamation," commented the *Afro-American Ledger*, for example, in anticipation of the concert in Baltimore on November 5.

> This organization of Negroes, whose aim is to preserve, encourage, and develop along natural lines, real racial expression of the Negro in music, and to dignify the place of the Colored Musician [sic], has, during the past four years, made a reputation in and around New York equal to that of any symphony orchestra in the country.

The concert promises to be a "revelation to many of those who are unaware of the musical proficiency of the African race."[19]

Europe appears to have made few changes in the composition of the orchestra for the fall tour. It was still dominated by mandolins, banjos and bandores, harp guitars, and pianos, but there was a single saxophone, played by John R. Burroughs, and a tuba.[20] The program, numbering twenty selections intending to demonstrate the musical progress of the race from the days of the "old camp meeting" and "days of long ago" to the present, included a number of the pieces that the orchestra had performed at Carnegie Hall in February.[21] No church choir was along on the trip, however, and therefore all of the vocal requirements, including soloists (tenor Louis Mitchell and baritones Harvey White and Emory R. Smith), were satisfied by the Clef Club members themselves.

As usual, the concerts began with Europe's "Clef Club March," followed by "On Bended Knee" and "A Jubilee," by Harry Burleigh, Cook's "Exhortation" (solo by White), "Maori" and "Tout a Vous" (conducted by the composer, William

Tyers), Vodery's "Virginia Dance," "I Hear You Calling Me" (sung by Mitchell), a banjo solo "Down South" by Vance Lowry (piano accompaniment by Hugh Woolford), and "Brazilian Dreams" (a tango written by Will Dixon). Will Marion Cook's "Rain Song," sung by the Clef Club Chorus, completed the first half of the program.

Europe's "Benefactors" march opened the second part of each evening's concert, followed by "Some Class" (an instrumental piece described as "A Down Home Tune"). Next came a sentimental song, "For the Last Time Call Me Sweetheart," and a piano solo "Araby," by the composer, Al Johns, followed by orchestral versions of two contrasting pieces: Coleridge-Taylor's "Deep River" and William Bryan's "Sugar Lump: A Syncopated Darky Expression." Emory Smith sang "For All Eternity" (by request) and the orchestra offered renditions of recent compositions by four of the Clef Club members: "A Negromance" by Woolford, "Trocha" (a tango) and "Contentment" (a waltz) by Tyers, "A Hot Step" by Europe, and Will Dixon's "Thoughts: A Darky Meditation." Cook's widely admired "Swing Along." Europe's "Strength of the Nation" march completed the lengthy program.[22]

Critical and popular reaction to the Clef Club's first series of concerts outside of New York City were, once again, generally very positive, even in Philadelphia where an unfortunate scheduling conflict resulted in a smaller audience than anticipated.[23] Douglas Gordon of the Richmond *Times-Dispatch*, for instance, called the Clef Club's appearance in his city "in many respects the most remarkable concert ever given in Richmond." The concerts in Baltimore and at Hampton Institute were equally well-received.[24] The crucial test for the orchestra, however—and for Europe, personally—was how well they would do performing before Washington's elite black and tan and white society, who, according to reports a week before the scheduled concert, were expected to be "out in force."[25]

The Indianapolis *Freeman*, which, like the *New York Age*, wished to claim the distinction of being the nation's national black newspaper, gave front page coverage to R. W. Thompson's glowing review of the Clef Club concert on November 7 at Howard Theatre. The theater, packed with 2,000 of Washington's best people, he wrote, were "delighted." "The music throughout was the work of noted Negro composers, the selections covering the folk song, the 'rag' and the modern tango, up to the purely classic," and each was played with "a precision, verity of expression, and technique that made the cultured audience gasp with surprise—an audience, too, that hears the Marine Band frequently, and has sat often with Sousa, Creatore, Gilmore, and the rest of the masters of the instrumental ensemble." "Prof. James Reese Europe," who Thompson identified as a "Washington product," wielded the baton and the "trained musicians responded to its every movement as if they were a part of it." The Clef Club, he concluded, "cannot be too lavishly praised" and it is "not too much to say that out of their visit the local musicians may get together and form an orchestra along similar lines in the near future."[26] The idea that New York had anything of value in music to teach Washington, D.C., would have pleased Europe enormously.

Back in New York, "fresh from their triumphant tour" and with talk of a second tour the next year, Jim Europe and the Clef Club held their eighth semiannual concert and dance at the Manhattan Casino on November 13.[27] It was, all in all, another "enjoyable program," said Lucien White, and James Reese Europe, who "swung the baton with authority," "is now so completely identified with the public appearance of the Clef Club that a concert without Europe would be similar to seeing Hamlet played with no Hamlet present."[28] Europe's name, however, could have become too closely associated with the successes of Clef Club over the previous year, at least in the minds of some of the club's members, because shortly after the concert the old jealousies resurfaced and Europe found himself accused of being more interested in furthering his own career than that of black musicians in general.[29] However widespread the sentiments, Europe was so stung by them that at the end of December he abruptly resigned from the organization he had led since its inception and announced the establishment of a new group, the Tempo Club, with himself as president.[30]

Despite the fact that Europe's reputation as principal conductor of the Clef Club Symphony Orchestra had risen along with that of the orchestra itself, the envy that developed within the club was not primarily do to his success as concert musician, nor to any general disagreement over his ambitions for the future of an African-American concert music.[31] Even those Clef Club members who were not included in the orchestra could appreciate that its success could help to raise the status, and increase the reputation, of all black professional musicians, especially those who belonged to the Clef Club. The dissatisfaction that emerged in the fall of 1913 was more likely the result of Europe's personal success in the dance orchestra field, both because New York's high society asked for him by name, and because, by the end of 1913, Europe had become the bandleader/music director for the extraordinary young dancing team of Vernon and Irene Castle.

7

"Castle House Rag"

> They were decisive characters, like Boileau in French poetry and
> Berlin in ragtime; for they understood, absorbed, and trans-
> formed everything known of dancing up to that time and out of
> it made something beautiful and new.
>
> Gilbert Seldes (1924)

Vernon Castle, whose future partnership with Jim Europe would help to revolutionize American attitudes toward social dancing, was born Vernon Blyth on May 2, 1887, at Norwich, England.[1] His mother died when he was ten, and his father, who owned a small pub, was left to raise Vernon and his four older sisters. A bright student, Blyth was admitted to Birmingham University and graduated with a degree in engineering in 1907. Prior to beginning his career, however, he decided to accompany his father on a holiday to New York. His sister, Coralie, and her husband, Laurence Grossmith, both of whom were actors, were also returning to New York to begin rehearsals for Lew Fields' fall production, *The Orchids*.[2] The elder Mr. Blyth found New York City not at all to his liking and returned to England after a week; however, Vernon, after attending several rehearsals and eventually accepting a small part (purely for the fun of it), became a victim of the stage virus himself.

Following his first role, where he adopted the name "Castle" (for Windsor Castle) in order to distinguish himself from his sister who used her maiden name on stage, Vernon Blyth—now Vernon Castle—continued to work with Lew Fields in a series of comic plays over the next four years, including *Old Dutch*, *The Girl Behind the Counter*, and *The Midnight Sons*. At a swimming party on Long Island Sound in the early summer of 1910, while he was appearing in the musical *The Summer Widowers*, Castle made the acquaintance of Irene Foote, the slightly rebellious daughter of a New Rochelle physician.[3]

Irene Foote, who was only seventeen at the time, was enamored with the theater (her idol was Bessie McCoy, who also lived in New Rochelle and who had made a big hit on Broadway singing "The Yama Yama Man"), and her attraction to Castle was at first as much a result of his stage connections as anything else. For his part, Vernon enjoyed escaping the city for Sunday dinners at the Foote's, and in return arranged an audition for Irene with Fields. Although no acceptable offer was immediately forthcoming, in January 1911, when a minor part in *The Summer Widowers* came open just two weeks before the production closed, Irene got the job. By that time, she and Vernon were formally engaged to be married, a circumstance that "all but broke the heart of a little girl in the show," a fourteen year-old named Helen Hayes, who "had fallen in love with Vernon, believing his blandishments, which were meant as a jest."[4]

Vernon Castle had his most successful comic role in the next of Fields' productions, this one called *The Henpecks*, which featured Blossom Seeley—one of the earliest of the female "coon shouters" who was also responsible for introducing New York to the "Texas tommy," one of the first of the ragtime dances that soon became so wildly popular.[5] Following their wedding in May 1911 and a two-month trip to England, the Castles returned for the fall tour of *Henpecks*. During the course of the tour, an agent for a French revue approached Vernon with an offer to put on a version of one of his comic skits at the Olympia Theatre in Paris in the spring. The glamour of Paris was an especially great lure at the time, and the young couple quickly agreed. Accompanied by Walter Ash, long-time black servant of the Foote family, they set sail for the continent in early 1912.

Predictably enough, once in France the couple found that things were not quite so wonderful as their romantic expectations had led them to anticipate. The revue was delayed in opening for several weeks, and what money they had brought with them soon ran out. Had it not been for Ash's skill at craps, a game then unfamiliar to the French, they would have been forced to give up and return home. Even so, when they finally appeared at the Olympia singing "Alexander's Ragtime Band" and dancing a version of Sheeley's Texas tommy that they devised from memory (since Vernon's comic sketch failed with the French audience), they found conditions in the theater so intolerable that they left the revue to audition at Louis Barraya's Café de Paris, a fashionable and very expensive supper club that had previously featured the noted demonstration dancers Maurice Mouvet and his wife, Florence Walton.

"We did some work rehearsing our grizzly-bear dance and wrote one other rough-and-tumble number to ragtime," Irene remembered, and then spent the last of their savings at the Café the evening before their audition to get a sense of the atmosphere.[6] It was very heady stuff for the relatively unsophisticated couple. Sitting at a back table, Irene felt more than a little intimidated as the room began to be filled by:

> [W]ealthy Argentinians with their dark and beautiful women; members of the French nobility; Russians from the court of the czar spending the spring in Paris. They did not come to be entertained, for it was not a restaurant where you sat down and waited for the entertainment to begin. They were the entertainment. They came to see their friends and to laugh, and later in the night they would go to l'Abbaye Thelèsme to dance and finally to Maxim's for breakfast.[7]

Shortly after midnight, the manager came over to the Castles and explained that one of his best customers, a Russian, had seen them at the Olympia and wondered if they would be willing to dance for him that evening. They re-

luctantly agreed and, to their great surprise, found themselves roundly applauded. "We were rotten, really," Vernon recalled, but "somehow our dance
pleased some Russian prince, an awfully rich fellow, and he sent 2,000 francs
over to us as a gift." Barraya also offered to reserve a table for them every night
and give them their meals if they would just come and dance.[8] From their first
impromptu cabaret performance at the Café de Paris until Vernon Castle left for
service in World War I, the Castles found themselves at the forefront of the
social dance craze that swept both Europe and America.

The Castles did not initiate the widespread popularity of social dancing, of
course, and they were not the first to successfully demonstrate the new dances
to the patrons of the cabarets of Europe or America. They were, however,
ideally suited—in appearance and manner, as well as talent—to give direction
to the phenomenon and symbolize the trend.[9] To those accustomed to Victorian standards of physical appearance, they seemed very young and exceedingly
slim, so slender that, as one reporter later wrote, "standing side by side [they]
are about as wide as one rather slim human being."[10] Vernon was tall and crisp,
without seeming brittle, while Irene was athletically boyish yet feminine, the
first embodiment of the American "girl next door," as opposed to the familiar
sex goddess–mother ideal. There was a careless, almost frivolous, informality
about them that was both fresh and engaging, and they were clever enough to
recognize the basis of their popular appeal and to capitalize on it.[11]

The sensational success of the Castle's nightly appearances at the Café de
Paris quickly led to invitations to dance at private gatherings of the fashionable
and well-to-do in Paris, in Germany, and even in England. In their eight weeks
or so at the Café they also made a favorable impression upon a number of
Americans, including Broadway producer and talent scout Charles Dillingham,
who proved important to the Castles when they returned to New York. Chief
among those who saw the Castles in Paris and who recognized their potential
were Elsie de Wolfe and her friend Elisabeth Marbury, two unusual women
whose progressive ideas and influential positions in American society were
critical to the rapid ascent of the Castles' star.

Elsie de Wolfe, a former actress and theater owner, has been described as
America's first professional interior decorator. Her decoration of the Colony, a
Stanford White–designed federal-revival home for the elite New York woman's
club in 1905, made her both highly sought after and highly paid. Her 1913
book, *The House in Good Taste*, which disdained Victorian overstuffed pretentiousness, became the first manual for decorators.[12] The second of these
remarkable women, Elisabeth Marbury, known to her friends as "Miss Bessie"
or "Pops," was a leading literary agent and dramatic producer who represented
(in America) Oscar Wilde and George Bernard Shaw, among others, and is
credited with encouraging a number of youthful playwrights, including
W. Somerset Maugham. Active in politics, she was the first woman from New

York to be named an official delegate to a national political convention and served in that capacity four times.[13]

Both de Wolfe and Marbury were charmed by the Castles' dancing, especially by their versions of ragtime turkey trots and grizzly bears. What pleased them most was that the Castle interpretations seemed to tone down, or refine, the most objectionable—that is, sensual—nature of these dances.[14] If properly handled and promoted, they concluded, the Castles could become an effective counter to the arguments of those reactionary elements in America who considered modern social dancing vulgar and morally corrupting, as well as symbolic of general social decay. Encouraged by predictions of success in the United States, when word came that her father had died following a long illness Irene and Vernon Castle returned to New York in May 1912.

Armed with an introduction from Louis Barraya to Louis Martin, the proprietor of the Café de l'Opéra (New York's equivalent to the Café de Paris), the Castle's were soon repeating their Paris dance routines for late-night Broadway crowds and with similar success. Invitations to do private "soirees" at the homes of America's high society were also forthcoming, but, at least at first, the Castles found themselves treated quite differently than they had been used to in Europe. At their first soiree, at the Long Island estate of the "colossally rich" Chatfield-Smiths, Irene recalled, she and Vernon were confined to a clothes closet where they were kept waiting until the guests had finished eating.[15] Perhaps having experienced such treatment themselves made it easier for the Castles to empathize with the lack of consideration often accorded musicians, and especially black musicians, who were similarly engaged, and to appreciate the efforts of someone like Jim Europe who was attempting to do something about it.

It is possible that Europe and the Castles actually crossed paths at one or another of the private parties at the Goulds, Garys, or Vanderbilts that summer; it is much more likely, however, that their first meeting occurred the following year, in the late summer of 1913. In September, the Castles were asked by Charles Dillingham to join him in Philadelphia where a new musical that he was producing, *The Lady of the Slipper* (music by Victor Herbert), was about to go into rehearsal. Neither of the two was offered important parts in the show, and when some objections were raised about Irene revealing too much of her bare legs during their only dance scene, the couple gave notice and left the show to return to their former schedule at the Café de l'Opéra.

By this time, the Castles had made two important professional acquisitions: a personal manager, Gladwyn Macdougal, and an agent, Elisabeth Marbury. Their popular following at Louis Martin's continued to grow, and Vernon, who had a natural talent for it, found himself in great demand as a dance instructor. While entertaining one evening at a private birthday party for Elsie Janis, one of the stars of *The Lady of the Slipper*, the Castles improvised a new step that they called the "Castle Walk" and which became an immediate sensation. "Instead of coming down on the beat as everybody else did," Irene remembered, "we went up. The result was a step almost like a skip, peculiar-looking I'm sure, but exhilarating and fun to do."[16] Thanks to Dillingham, who felt badly about the Castles' leaving *The Lady of the Slipper* before it even opened, Vernon and Irene Castle received another opportunity to appear on stage in the fall of 1912. This time they made the most of it. The show was called *The Sunshine Girl*, a musical production that had done well in London, and Vernon was given a major acting role by the producer, Charles Frohman, a friend of Dillingham's. Irene, who only appeared in a single dance (a modified turkey trot) sequence, nonetheless made sure that "nobody forgot I was in it," and the couple's American career was fully launched.[17]

The Castles stayed with *The Sunshine Girl* until it closed in the spring of 1913 and then were off again to France to repeat their first success—dancing for the wealthy and fashionable at the Café de Paris and at the Casino de Deauville in Normandy. Among those for whom they performed that summer were various members of Europe's aristocracy: Grand Duchess Anastasia of Russia, who demanded personal instruction in the one-step and the tango from Vernon; the Goulds, Vanderbilts, and Astors, all vacationing from New York; and Mrs. Potter Palmer, the wife of Marshall Field's former partner and a prominent figure in Chicago society.[18]

Upon their return to America in the early fall of 1913, the Castles found that the entire country had gone "absolutely dance-mad," and that the controversy over ragtime and ragtime dancing had now reached the level of a full-fledged national debate. Following the lead of the cabarets, the lower-class dance halls, and the amusement parks, New York's formerly sedate Fifth Avenue hotels had responded to the popular demand for dancing by installing dance floors and by scheduling tea dances, or thé dansants, that lasted from two or three in the afternoon until six in the evening. This extraordinary expansion of centrally located dance facilities and the hours of socially acceptable dancing had by 1913, as Erenberg concludes, established dancing as "a regular and public urban form of entertainment."[19] An article in the October 1913, issue of *Current Opinion*, entitled "New Reflections on the Dancing Mania," reported,

> [P]eople who have not danced before in twenty years have been dancing, during the past summer, afternoons as well as evenings. Up-to-date restaurants provide a dancing floor so that patrons may lose no time while the waiter is changing plates. Cabaret artists are disappearing except as interludes while people recover their breaths for the following number. One wishes either to dance or to watch and to criticize those who dance."[20]

"The winter of 1913–14," lamented humorist George Fitch, "will live in history because of the dances, which have spared neither young nor old."[21]

By the summer of 1913, however, social reformers, who had been concerned about the proliferation of unsupervised dance halls and the popularity of the more uninhibited ragtime dances like the grizzly bear and turkey trot among young people for several years, had joined forces with conservative music educators, critics, and church leaders in attacking the entire ragtime phenomenon (the syncopated rhythms and the often jeering lyrics of the popular songs, as well as the dances).[22] Anne Kaufman, a New York music teacher, for instance, after hearing a parody of the hymn "Nearer my God to Thee" ("Nero, my Dog, has Fleas"), pleaded for an end to this "system of ridicule" before it "shatters our every tradition and ideal."[23] In answer to the question, "Are we going to the dogs by the ragtime route?," posed by the New York *Sun* in early 1912, the *New York Tribune*'s music critic, H. E. Krehbiel, replied that "in this year of our Lord 1913, the [ragtime dances] are threatening to force grace, decorum, and decency out of the ballrooms of America."[24]

Vernon and Irene Castle returned to the United States in the midst of the controversy and found themselves taken up by proponents of both sides of the issue and, therefore, in great demand as demonstration dancers and as instructors.[25] "We were clean-cut; we were married and when we danced there was nothing suggestive about it," Irene explained. "We made dancing look like the fun it was and so gradually we became a middle ground both sides could accept."[26]

Prior to 1913, the Castles were restricted to dancing to the music of whatever orchestra was provided at the cabarets, tea dances, or private engagements. Most of these orchestras were capable of performing a tango, a waltz, or a two-step march, but few—other than the black orchestras—were adept at providing the syncopated rhythmic accompaniment that the Castles required for their adaptations of the ragtime steps. They were, therefore, forced to create their dances without musical accompaniment.[27] During a private party that fall, however, "society dancers" Irene and Vernon Castle found themselves dancing to the music of James Reese Europe's Society Orchestra. "Vernon was astonished," according to Douglas Gilbert, "first at Europe's rhythms, then at the instrumental color of his band." The Castles hired him on the spot "as their personal musician and thereafter demanded in all of their contracts that Europe's music be used solely."[28]

It was perhaps inevitable that the Castles and Jim Europe should eventually encounter each other. After all, Europe had been personally performing at New York's high society social engagements for several years before the dance craze swept the city, and musicians from his Clef Club had increasingly found themselves in demand as the number of cabarets and higher class dance halls grew. Apart from the formal Clef Club Symphony Orchestra concerts associated with Carnegie Hall and the Emancipation Celebrations, Europe's and the Clef Club's musical activities in 1913 clearly reflected the popular fascination with the new dances. The seventh semi-annual Clef Club concert at the Manhattan Casino on May 8, for example, featured a greater number of dance pieces than any previous entertainment. According to Lucien White's review of the evening, Europe's "Breezy Rag" and Luckey Roberts' "Junk Man Rag," were wildly applauded by the mixed black and white audience estimated at some 4,000 people. Most telling, however, was the addition to the program of Johnny (or Johnnie) Peters and Ethel Williams, whose demonstration of the Texas tommy was so exhausting that when they had finished it was "impossible for them to respond to calls for more."[29]

The Texas tommy, along with the turkey trot, the earliest of the new dances of African-American origin to gain wide acceptance, seems to have come to New York by way of Chicago from San Francisco's Barbary Coast in about 1910. By 1913, Johnny Peters and his partner, Ethel Williams, were dancing the Texas tommy with great success at Bustanoby's cabaret on 39th Street and in a featured number with J. Leubrie Hill's "Darktown Follies".[30] "It was like the Lindy," Ms. Williams recalled, "but there were two basic steps—a kick and hop three times on each foot, and then add whatever you want, turning, pulling, sliding." It also required the male to whirl or toss his partner and then catch her at the last moment. "Your partner had to keep you from falling—I've slid into the orchestra pit more than once," she said.[31] This particular acrobatic element in the Texas tommy, according to Marshall and Jean Stearns, constitutes the first example of a couple-dance incorporating "the breakaway, or the temporary and energetic separating of partners—a distinctly unwaltzlike and non-European maneuver."[32]

The Castles had seen Peters and Williams, probably when they were dancing at Bustanoby's. Irene Castle, who was much impressed, had asked Ethel Williams to teach her some of the steps. In the 1939 Hollywood musical, *The Story of Vernon and Irene Castle*, Fred Astaire and Ginger Rogers recreated the Castles' version of the Texas tommy, which Irlene Croce has described as a

> kind of breezy, rambunctious dance that the Castles shortly abandoned in favor of their own more sophisticated style. At one point the dancers whip around the floor with their hands clasped at the back of each other's neck, and at another there's a surefire vaudeville effect: she leans back with her heels together (like the Klopman, A Man You Can Lean On ad); he steps over her, turns her and steps over her again.[33]

During the late spring and early summer of 1913 as the popularity of social dancing continued to grow, the Clef Club found itself being called upon to furnish a large number of dance orchestras for society entertainments at the summer resorts of Saratoga, Newport, and the New Jersey eastern shore. Since Europe's reputation was already well-known among the 400, many of these requests stipulated Europe's own orchestra rather than any Clef Club ensemble. Given his other responsibilities, Europe could hardly fill all the jobs personally; neither did he wish to turn down opportunities for placing his musicians and their music before the elite of American society. His solution was to create a special aggregate called "Europe's Exclusive Society Orchestra" from among the members of the Clef Club that he would lead himself when he could, but that might also perform under such experienced veterans as Will Vodery or Ford Dabney when he could not. At the end of July, when the *New York Age* reported that the Frogs were organizing a tour by leading black vaudeville performers Bert Williams, Aida Overton Walker, and S. H. Dudley, "W. H. Vodery and the Exclusive Society Orchestra, under the direction of James Reese Europe" was announced as an equally prominent attraction.[34] Two weeks later, with a schedule for the tour having been arranged, the *Age* reported that "a special orchestra," known as the "Exclusive Society Orchestra, under the direction of James Reese Europe," had been secured for the entire tour. "This is the same orchestra which is playing for the Four Hundred at Newport, R. I.," the *Age* informed its readers, "and causing the society folk to dance the tango and turkey trot with unwonted enthusiasm."[35]

On Monday evening, August 11, the "Frolic of the Frogs" kicked off their week-long road trip (single performances in Philadelphia, Baltimore, Richmond, and Washington) in New York at the Manhattan Casino. Will Vodery and Jim Europe directed the music of "James Reese Europe's Exclusive Society Orchestra," and while the musical program was not reported, the composition of the twelve-member orchestra included:

> George Smith and Tracy Cooper—violins
> George Watters and Joe Grey—banjolines
> Chandler Ford—cello
> Walter Scott—bass violin
> Leonard Smith—piano
> Cricket Smith—cornet
> George Fairfax—trombone
> George DeLeon—baritone
> Edgar Campbell—clarinet
> Dennis Johnson—drums and traps[36]

As shown by the instrumentation, by the summer of 1913 Europe and his associates had begun to modify the predominantly string-based ensembles of the earlier Clef Club orchestras (at least in the groups dispatched to provide popular music) by making greater use of instruments traditionally associated with brass bands. In fact, by the end of August the *Age* had begun referring to Europe's dance orchestras as "bands."[37]

Following the August 11 performance in New York City, Europe's Exclusive Society Orchestra and the other members of the Frogs' variety show were transported by train to Philadelphia, where they appeared at the Academy of

Music, and then on to Baltimore and Richmond before finishing the week at the Howard Theatre in Washington, D.C. The audiences were reported to be large and enthusiastic, and, except for Richmond, the theater owners in the cities where they performed honored an agreement with the Frogs not to practice the usual segregated seating policy.[38] While Europe had been involved with the Frogs road tour from the initial planning stage, he may not have remained with the show for the full week because of a heavy schedule of society engagements. On August 22, Europe's orchestra was hired by Mrs. Stuyvesant Fish for the principal society dance of the summer Newport season. "Since the turkey trot craze, the colored musicians of New York have been kept busy dispensing syncopated melody for the Four Hundred," commented the *Age*, "but recently they appeared in a new role, thanks to the broadmindedness and appreciative qualities of Mrs. Stuyvesant Fish," who secured "James Reese Europe's Select Orchestra" to play for dancing, and "also for the reception and dinner."[39]

Since Mrs. Fish was both one of the society leaders who patronized Jim Europe and the Clef Club musicians for her dances as well as an acquaintance of Elizabeth Marbury, the Castles' manager and principal promoter, it is not unlikely that the August 22 party in Newport provided the occasion for the first meeting between Jim Europe and the Castles. In any case, by the late fall of 1913 when plans for the Castles' next professional ventures were being formed (Castle House and the Sans Souci), Jim Europe and his orchestra were understood to be a part of them both.

The inspiration and major force behind the organization of a school of dance, Castle House, was Elizabeth Marbury. A reformer, but a shrewd businesswoman, and master of public relations as well, Marbury decided that what the Castles needed to separate them from the other cabaret and ballroom dancers was their own dance hall. It should not be ordinary, however, and it should carry the endorsement (and financial backing) of New York's highest society. According to Irene Castle, Marbury convinced a number of society women that Castle House was needed because the dance craze then sweeping America lacked regulation and required "an uplifting influence to bring dignity to it. Castle House would be that uplift, a place where their children could go to learn the dance without being exposed to the discredited elements."[40] Aside from her friends Anne Morgan and Elsie de Wolfe, Marbury enlisted Mrs. Stuyvesant Fish, Mrs. Herman Oelrick, Mrs. William G. Rockefeller, Mrs. T. J. Oakley Rhinelander, Mrs. Anthony Drexel, Jr., Mrs. W. Burke Cochran, and Mrs. Amos Pinchot to the cause and convinced them to support the public-spirited enterprise with their names, their time, and especially their money.[41]

Bessie Marbury also found a suitably fashionable location for Castle House, a panelled and crystal-chandeliered house on East 46th Street across from the Ritz-Carlton Hotel that Elsie de Wolfe then undertook to decorate. The entrance was two steps down from the street, and it opened into a marble foyer with a fountain at the end surrounded by ferns and small palms, behind which was the balustrade of the stairway leading to a high-ceilinged ballroom above. A plush red tasseled rope served as the handrail of the stairs. There were actually two ballrooms, a main one and a smaller one that was used when the main room became overcrowded. "The smaller room had plain walls and cloth-covered lights, with mirrors going around the room. Both were furnished with benches and chairs covered by tie-on mats or cushions. The rooms were the height of the then customary New York private house."[42] James Reese Europe's Society Orchestra provided the music.[43]

"From the first day we opened our doors [December 15, 1913]," Irene recalled, "people poured in by the hundreds at two dollars a head on regular days and three dollars on Fridays. For this price they had their choice of two orchestras, a chance to be served tea [or lemonade] by a real society woman, an opportunity to see the Castles, and a slim chance of dancing with one of them, if their luck held."[44] Castle House gave the appearance of being open to the general public, but in fact its patrons came almost exclusively from the wealthy and upper middle classes. Lower class New Yorkers, even if they could afford the admission price found themselves unwelcomed. As Marbury later told the Worcester *Telegram*, "somehow or other those who do not naturally 'belong' find it a bit uncomfortable to be ignored, and they never come back."[45]

Also in late 1913, the Castles—and Europe's Society Orchestra—became involved in a second commercial venture. One of the headwaiters at the Café de l'Opéra, Jules Ensaldi, convinced Vernon that the couple could do much better as owners of their own supper club than as salaried employees of Louis Martin. Ensaldi proposed to manage all of the restaurant functions of the new cabaret for one-third of the total take; the Castles would handle the entertainment end of things and receive the rest. Irene was not too keen on the plan, especially when Ensaldi located a room under the sidewalk at 42nd Street and Broadway that had previously served as a "way station" for streetwalkers. The rent was cheap, however, and Elsie de Wolfe "painted it rose and gray" and "flooded it with lights until it almost glowed through the sidewalk."[46]

Beginning with opening night, the Castle's nightclub, christened Sans Souci—a name perfectly suited to the "carefree," yet glamorous, public image the Castles wished to convey—was a resounding success. "Tickets sold for a hundred dollars apiece," Irene remembered, discouraging "the wandering ladies of Times Square" but not Cornelius Vanderbilt, George J. Gould, Mrs. William Astor Chanler, Mrs. Herbert Harriman, William Rhinelander Steward, and even Diamond Jim Brady who came to eat, drink, and stumble through the Castle Walk, the tango, and the maxixe to the music of Jim Europe's Society Orchestra.[47] For the next six months, until the city's fire department closed it down due to a lack of emergency exits, the Sans Souci proved extremely popular; for the Castles, it was a "goldmine."

For James Reese Europe, associating himself with the rising star of the Castles presented a major opportunity, but it also inevitably led to problems for the Clef Club's president. The Castles' wanted Europe in part because Vernon, especially, was excited by the sound of the music he heard Europe's Society Orchestra play and by its infectiously danceable rhythms.[48] Europe was also a man of "considerable personality and wit," and he and Vernon seemed to understand each other immediately, and they became friends.[49]

Another part of it, of course, was that by the time they met, Jim Europe's name and his orchestra were already established among the leaders of New York and Philadelphia society. His was "the most famous of the colored bands," Irene later wrote, and Europe was a dignified and "skilled musician and one of the first to take jazz out of the saloons and make it respectable. All the men in his orchestra could read music, a rarity in those days."[50] Furthermore, both Europe and Ford Dabney, the Society Orchestra's coleader and principal pianist, were talented composers, fully capable of writing and arranging new music for the Castles' "refined" versions of popular dance steps. Although Europe used perhaps as many as 100 different Clef Club musicians in the various versions of "Europe's Society Orchestra" that played at the Castle House and at San Souci, many of the club members were not capable of performing instrumental dance music. Those left out were inevitably unhappy.[51]

On New Years Day, 1914, the New York Age reported that Daniel Kildare had been elected president of the Clef Club on December 30 at a meeting at the club house on 53rd Street and that Europe had tendered his resignation several days before "after successfully filling the position from the date of the organization's inception." Unwilling to take sides in the controversy, the Age's only comment was that "much of the Clef Club's success has been in a large measure due to the activities of Mr. Europe."[52] However hurt or discouraged Europe may have been personally, his split from the Clef Club seems to have had little effect on the direction or momentum of his professional career. That same day, the papers announced that the "Society Orchestra," under the direction of Europe and Tyers would be featured at the end of the month, along with soloists Harry Burleigh (baritone), Felix Weir (violin), Melville Charlton (piano), Mrs. H. G. Lucas (contralto), and Leonard Jeter (cello), in a charity ball at the Manhattan Casino. More significantly, four days later, on January 4, Europe formed a new organization, the Tempo Club (with offices on West 136th Street) and named himself president, Ford Dabney, vice-president, William H. Tyers, treasurer, and Warrick Cheesman, secretary.[53]

In establishing the Tempo Club, and modeling it after the Clef Club organization, Europe and his associates clearly indicated their intention to maintain control of the popular dance field and to continue to exploit the opportunities it offered black musicians. According to the "leaders of this new movement," the New York News also reported, "Europe aims to keep the colored musical world up to a certain standard morally, socially and artistically."[54]

By the time Europe resigned his position in the Clef Club, he and the Society Orchestra had already accomplished one breakthrough for black musicians as a result of his association with the Castles. On December 29, 1913, Europe and the orchestra had begun a historic series of recordings of dance music for Victor Records; it was one of the first contracts ever given by a major record company to a black musician and the first ever to a black orchestra.[55] Less than a month later, there was a second breakthrough. In mid-January, the Castle's accepted an offer of $2,000 a week to perform on the vaudeville stage at the Palace and at Hammerstein's Victoria Theaters, both of which were in Times Square. A problem developed when they insisted on using Europe's orchestra, Vernon claiming that "colored musicians are better qualified to play music for his style of dancing."[56] The segregated musicians union, fearing that black orchestras might come to dominate the theaters as they had done the cabarets, objected and threatened dire consequences for the theater owners if they permitted Europe's musicians in the pit of a Broadway vaudeville house where they had not been allowed before. The Castles refused to dance without their regular orchestra, and so on the afternoon of Monday, January 12, when they opened at Hammerstein's, Europe's Society Orchestra accompanied them from their seats on the stage. The union's demand had technically been honored, for black musicians did not play in the pit; in fact, as both the *New York Age* and the Indianapolis *Freeman* proudly reported, the barrier against black orchestras playing in first class theaters for white artists was broken.[57]

On February 10, Europe, Dabney, and the Society Orchestra were back in the Victor recording studio in New York for a second recording session of dance music. At the previous session in December, they had recorded Cecil Macklin's "Trés Moutarde" and Wilbur Sweatman's "Down Home Rag," both one-steps or turkey trots, a tango (Logatti's "El Irresistible"), and a maxixe (Storoni's "Amapa"), all of which reflected dances made popular by a number of recent teams, including, of course, the Castles. "El Irresistible" was in fact also known as "The Maurice Tango," named for Maurice Mouvet, the Castle's chief rival.[58] The first two pieces, written in 2/4 time but taken at a fast tempo, are particularly revealing of the rhythmic vitality and excitement that Europe's orchestra was capable of producing, and despite the repetitive melodies, one is forced to agree with Gunther Schuller that they "must have been electrifying to dance to."[59]

It is revealing to compare the Europe version of "Down Home Rag," his first recording, with that recorded eighteen months later by the Six Brown Brothers, a popular white saxophone sextet.[60] In both performances the four-strain form of the piece (AABBAACCDDCC) is faithfully followed, although Europe added a short introduction and a tag ending, and there is little textural variation among the strains. All the instruments play the melodies virtually all the time, either harmonized or in unison, in a clearly vertical fashion. Despite these similarities, the two interpretations of Sweatman's rag could hardly be more different. The Brown Brothers' performance, taken at an unbelievably slow tempo, is so stiff and mechanical as to be almost comical. There is a certain competence but no momentum, no rhythmic vitality, and no tonal variety. Except for the possibly novel sound of the saxophone family itself, it is difficult to understand the appeal of such a record. The Europe Orchestra's reading, on the other hand, is exuberant. Not only is the piece played very fast—twice the tempo of the Brown version—but the emotional intensity of the performance infects the performers themselves, who seem unable to resist joining the drum and cymbal punctuations with their ad-lib vocal shouts and laughter. Although things never get out of control and the orchestra follows the score, there is a clear sense in this first Europe recording that interpretation is at least equal in value to composition. How something is played is as important as what is played, especially if that something is intended for dancing. In addition, the performance parallels the Castle's approach, since it was the way they danced the new social dances, not their creation of new ones, that originally established their reputation.

The four tunes recorded by the Society Orchestra in February are even more closely associated with the Castles and their contemporary "refinements" of the ragtime steps. Three of the pieces, "Congratulations/Castles Lame Duck Waltz," "Castle House Rag," and "Castle Walk," were written specifically for the Castles (the first two by Europe and the last by Europe and Dabney), and the fourth, a one-step or turkey trot called "You're Here and I'm Here," was written by Jerome Kern for a current theater production. "You're Here" is of interest chiefly because it was one of two songs written by Kern in 1914 (the other being "They Didn't Believe Me") that mark a crucial turning point in his early career away from European operetta toward a more American style.[61] Europe's treatment of Kern's syncopated melody is straightforward and danceable, although the rhythm of the contrasting wood blocks and snare drums gives more than a suggestion of 4/4 time, rather than the 2/4 of the original sheet music. All of the recordings made at the February 1914 session are slower and less frenetic than "Trés Moutarde" or, especially, "Down Home Rag," recorded two months before, and it may therefore be true, as Lawrence Gushee has argued, that they "presage the turn from the one-step and turkey trot to the fox-trot."[62] This significant development would actually come about during the next few months, as a result of the impact of a new force in commercial music called the blues.

Of the other three instrumentals recorded in February, "Castle Walk" was intended to give the Castles a signature piece for their Castle Walk dance, a modified one-step and the earliest of their name dances to become widely popular. It is also, it seems, the only example during the Europe/Castles collaboration where the dance step was originated prior to and independently of the music. In the 1939 film, *The Story of Vernon and Irene Castle*, Fred Astaire and Ginger Rogers perform the Castle Walk to "Trés Moutarde," and it is easy to see its attraction.

The Europe Orchestra's recording of "Castle House Rag" is musically the most important, and it is something of a small revelation. The form of the piece follows that of Scott Joplin's classic (and commercially successful) "Maple Leaf Rag": it consists of four melodic strains played in an AABBACCDD pattern. The first strain, using fast sixteenth notes and shifting between minor and major keys, suggests several ragtime melodic and rhythmic ideas; the second section seems more related to march music, although it is quieter and dominated by the violins; and the third is a stop-time trio using contrasting instrumentation common to both orchestral ragtime and march music, and the drums lay out. The fourth strain, however, is quite different, exhibiting a less formal and more relaxed approach, as if the musicians unexpectedly abandoned the written score and, following Cricket Smith's cornet lead and the increasing domination of Buddy Gilmore's drum breaks, improvised a ferociously wild climax.[63] "With half a minute of recording time left," suggests Gushee, "Europe may have let his band loose for three choruses of ad-hoc basic rag, accidentally transmitting to us the only example from its time of orchestral ragtime extemporization."[64]

Although no additional dance records were made by Europe's Society Orchestra for the Victor Company (neither of the two pieces recorded at a third session in October were released), Europe and Dabney had secured contracts with Joseph Stern's publishing house for their dance music. Over the next two months a flood of Castle trots, waltzes, tangos, maxixes, hesitations, and one-steps appeared in print. So many pieces came from the two writers in March and April that, by May, they even tried combining and spelling their names backward ("Music by Eporue Yenbad") to give an impression of novelty. For their part, Vernon and Irene Castle had discovered that to stay on top of the dancing business the public required that they continually come up with new variations, some of which were hardly variations at all. One evening in January, Irene later remembered, they were engaged to dance at Mrs. Stuyvesant Fish's home and, as they were preparing to appear, Mrs. Fish informed them that she had already notified the newspapers that they would be introducing a new dance, especially for her party; Bessie Marbury had promised her. Ms. Marbury, however, had failed to inform the Castles, and they had nothing ready, so "we went out and did all of our old routines down to the last step. There wasn't the slightest variation." It did not matter as the next day the newspapers announced that a brand new dance had been created by the Castles for Mrs. Fish, and she was delighted.[65]

In fact, one of the Castle's dances that was a new creation was the Half and Half. Its genesis was simple enough: Europe and Dabney wrote a piece in alternating 3/4 and 2/4 meters (making a 5/4 overall time signature), and the Castles improvised the steps to go with it. The Half and Half received a great deal of attention at the time and, because it was relatively complicated, helped the Castles' reputation as clever artists. The dance itself, however, never became widely popular with the dancing public—and for the same reason. In an article written in 1930 for *Opportunity* magazine, Irene recalled how a number of the Castle dances, like the Half and Half, originated. In the early spring of 1914, the Castles purchased a sprawling country estate on Long Island to which they would escape on weekends, and Europe and Dabney "often came down to our Manhasset home on Sunday and played duets at the piano for hours at a time."

> We always had several weekend guests staying with us and no matter how full a program we had planned for Sunday—all bets were off when Europe and Dabney hove in sight and we would huddle around the piano, enchanted by some new dance number they were in the act of composing for us.[66]

8

"The National Negro March"

> Jim Europe would be talking about something, and you'd see him
> sit—he was a great big man, see . . . and all at once he'd say, let's
> buy tablecloths, or let's do so-and-so, let's do something. And
> everybody would look at him and say, "this guy's nuts," see. And
> he would be right. Every time. Never miss.
>
> Eubie Blake

In addition to the activities relating to his partnership with the Castles, in the spring of 1914 Jim Europe also faced a multitude of responsibilities attending his position as president of the Tempo Club. As leader of the Clef Club, he had helped to give that organization a national reputation among the members of New York's white society despite the preeminence of the Europe name. The Tempo Club, however, was a completely unknown entity. One of the immediate problems he had to address was what to do about the large concert orchestra, known as the Clef Club Symphony Orchestra, that he directed and that had appeared so dramatically before the public at Carnegie Hall and elsewhere over the previous several years. Europe was personally committed to the idea of developing a large orchestra of black musicians devoted to the performance of compositions by black composers, and he was supported in this by most of the musicians in the orchestra, even by those whose allegiances remained with the Clef Club. He also had an agreement with David Mannes for a third concert of the orchestra at Carnegie Hall for March 11, to be held again under the auspices of the Harlem Music School Settlement. For obvious reasons, the orchestra could no longer be called the Clef Club Symphony Orchestra, but Europe did not rename it the Tempo Club Symphony Orchestra, either. Instead, he chose to call it the "National Negro Symphony Orchestra" as a way of avoiding identification with either of the clubs while pointing in a positive way toward a future they might all agree upon.

For the 1914 concert at New York's most famous hall, Europe and the National Negro Symphony Orchestra, augmented by a larger number of strings, woodwinds, and brass than he had used in 1912 or 1913, was joined by a chorus from the Music School Settlement, by a new group called the Afro-American Folk Song Singers under the direction of Will Marion Cook, and by vocal soloists Abbie Mitchell, Harry T. Burleigh, and J. Rosamond Johnson.[1] During the course of the evening, David Mannes spoke for the Settlement and announced the results of a prize competition for the best work by a black com-

poser based upon African-American themes. Carl Diton was awarded first prize
for his "Four Mixed Choruses," which were arrangements of spirituals, and Nathaniel Dett received the second prize for his "Listen to the Lambs." William
Tyers, Will Dixon, E.E. Thompson, and Europe all conducted the orchestra in
works of their own composition, and Felix Weir (violin) and Leonard Jeter
(cello) performed a duet.

With the exception of the orchestral part of the program, the music performed by the choruses and soloists consisted primarily of arranged or harmonized versions of traditional spirituals and "plantation songs," or compositions
based upon African-American folk melodies or themes. The reviewer for the *New
York Times* found it to be an "interesting concert, and one calculated to stimu-
late the musical imagination," especially significant as "a demonstration of what
may be expected of negro [sic] composers trained in the modern techniques, as
they are affected by their racial traits in music," and showing "that these composers are beginning to form an art of their own on the basis of their folk material."[2] As the *Times* review indicates, by 1914 most white critics were willing to
grant the existence and musical importance of an authentic African-American
folk music tradition, to which Dvořák had called their attention some twenty
years before (and W.E.B. Du Bois ten years earlier), and to which H. E. Krehbiel
had recently added his voice.[3] Ironically, perhaps, the elevation of African-
American folk music led some critics to take a much harsher view of black efforts
in musical areas not clearly (to their ears, at least) rooted in that tradition. The
review in *Musical America* the following week was particularly pointed.

After praising much of the program as "more creditable than the two previous" concerts at Carnegie Hall and noting the positive audience response,
Musical America nevertheless thought the concert "fell short once more" of
what it called "the serious purpose to which these talents might be directed."
"Mr. Burleigh, for example, excellent musician that he is, after distinguishing
himself by singing his spirituals, spoiled his contribution to the musical excellence of the program by singing the popular 'Why Adam Sinned.'" Rosamond
Johnson's "Under the Bamboo Tree," Europe's "National Negro March," Tyer's
"Trocha: Characteristic Negro Dance," among others were also criticized for
being "popular" or "once popular," or "vulgar," or "common," or even "devoid of
even a single negro [sic] characteristic." "If the Negro Symphony Orchestra," the
article concluded,

> will give its attention during the coming year to a movement or two of a Haydn
> symphony and play it at its next concert and if the composers, who this year took
> obvious pleasure in conducting their marches, tangos, and waltzes, will write short
> movements for orchestra basing them on classic models, next year's concert will
> inaugurate a new era for the negro musician in New York and will aid him in being
> appraised at his full value and in being taken seriously. It is impossible to applaud
> in Carnegie Hall his imitations of the vulgar dance music of Broadway originated
> by the tone poets of Tin Pan Alley.[4]

One can only wonder what the *Musical American's* critic thought when he learned that three days after the Europe concert the "largest audience that Carnegie Hall has held in many a day" jammed the auditorium to its capacity to see Vernon and Irene Castle give an exhibition of the tango, maxixe, and the hesitation to the musical accompaniment of the revered New York Symphony Orchestra, conducted by Walter Damrosch himself.[5] He also might have understood better what he had heard on March 11 if he had read the comments of the director of the National Negro Symphony Orchestra that were published in the New York *Evening Post* on Friday, March 13.

It was rare for Jim Europe to consent to be interviewed by the press, either white or black. In fact, nothing of any length had appeared from him for nearly five years, since his opinion about "the death of ragtime" had been solicited by Lester Walton for the *New York Age*. When he was approached by a complimentary and genuinely curious *Evening Post* reporter following the concert, however, he took the opportunity to publicly explain his ideas about African-American music and its relationship to the kind of orchestra he was attempting to build. In addition, since Will Marion Cook had recently published some remarks about African-American music and its relationship to black choral societies like the one he was then organizing to appear with Europe at Carnegie Hall, the timing seemed appropriate.[6]

In introducing its readers to Europe and to his comments that would follow, the *Post* gave scant attention to the musical program recently offered at Carnegie Hall or even to the quality of the performance of the orchestra he directed. Rather, what seemed to the paper most interesting about the man they had sought out was that Europe was managing to combine success in both popular and symphonic music, fields then supposed to be inherently incompatible and separate. "In some ways," the article began,

> James Reese Europe is one of the most remarkable men, not only of his race, but in the music world of this country. A composer of some note—some of his serious efforts were played the other night, and his dance music is known wherever the Tango or Turkey Trot are danced—he is the head of an organization which practically controls the furnishing of music for the new dances, and at the same time, he is able to expend considerable energy upon the development of the Negro Symphony Orchestra. Unaided, he has been able to accomplish what white musicians said was impossible: the adaptation of negro [sic] music and musicians to symphonic purposes.[7]

Europe characteristically did not denigrate popular music nor apologize for his success or for that of other black musicians in that area. "The members of the orchestra are all members of my staff of dance musicians," he told the reporter, "who play at most of the principal hotels and at private dances in this city and out of town. I also furnish the dance music for the resorts at Aiken, Palm Beach, and other places, and frequently send men to play at weekend parties and special dances in country houses." In addition to which, "I furnish Vernon

Castle's music, and I have also composed most of the pieces for his dances." In
fact, Europe announced, "I have just concluded a contract with him to lead a
dance orchestra of forty negro [sic] musicians, all members of my staff, that will
accompany him to Europe next summer." The reason the African-American has
achieved a "monopoly of this kind of work," and is in such demand by the
wealthiest and most fashionable classes of white society, he explained, is simply
because he has an "inimitable ear for time in dancing," is "well trained," and is
an "instinctively good" musician. "The negro plays ragtime as if it was a second
nature to him—as it is." The same principal, he said, has directed and informed
his approach to the development of the Negro Symphony Orchestra.

"Our symphony orchestra never tries to play white folks' music. We should
be foolish to attempt such a thing. We are no more fitted for that than a white
orchestra is fitted to play our music." Neither should a black symphony orchestra be organized to sound like a white one. Some of the peculiarities of the
present orchestra, Europe admitted, were the result of practical necessity. Although he could call upon "between 150 and 187" musicians, he was forced, for
the moment, to make substitutions for the lack of good oboe or French horn
players. Other modifications, however, had a strictly musical and racial validity:

> For instance, although we have first violins, the place of the second violins with us
> is taken by mandolins and banjos. This gives that peculiar steady strumming ac-
> companiment to our music which all people comment on, and which is something
> like that of the Russian Balalaika Orchestra, I believe. Then, for background, we
> employ ten pianos. That, in itself, is sufficient to amuse the average white mu-
> sician who attends one of our concerts for the first time. The result, however, is a
> background of chords which are essentially typical of negro harmony.

The point is, noted Europe, that "we have developed a kind of symphony
music that, no matter what else you may think, is different and distinctive, and
that lends itself to the playing of the peculiar compositions of our race."

The *Evening Post* interview with Jim Europe is historically significant for a
number of reasons, as several contemporary writers have argued. Ron Welburn,
for example, writing in 1987, discovered in Europe's articulate statements about
African-American music (beginning with the *Post* article and including two later
interviews) the origins of a "genuine jazz criticism" that would in later decades
serve that new music well "by elevating it in the minds of his readers and by establishing a paradigm for later jazz criticism."[8] Olly Wilson, a contemporary
composer and educator, began an article, "The Black-American Composer and
the Orchestra in the Twentieth Century," by referring to the Europe interview.
"Although generally considered outrageous at that time," Wilson wrote in 1986,
"his basic idea of the orchestra as a viable vehicle for the expression of musical
ideas emanating from the black-American experience has not only continued to
flourish, but also has become a reality in the work of several generations of
black-American composers."[9]

It is interesting that Wilson found Europe's descriptions of his orchestra (his non-European primary emphasis on the way the music was performed and yet his use of the language associated with European orchestral practice) reflective of a "dichotomy in aesthetic approach" that is faced by any African-American artist "who works within the context of the broader American society," and which, in turn, stems from "the basic duality of the Black American experience."[10] At the time of the 1914 Europe interview, as Wilson points out, this sense of "two-ness—an American, a Negro; two souls, two thoughts, two unreconciled strivings; two warring ideals in one dark body" had been most vividly expressed by W.E.B. Du Bois in *The Souls of Black Folk*, so it is not surprising that Du Bois' influence is clearly present in Europe's thinking.[11]

Europe and the formidable editor of the *Crisis* had known each other personally for several years; Du Bois often attended Europe's concerts at Carnegie Hall and at the Manhattan Casino, and they had worked together in the National Emancipation Exposition in the fall of 1913. Du Bois was neither a musician nor a musicologist, but in the lyrical and plaintive final chapter of his classic work he wove together the themes of racial consciousness and national identity in a discussion of African-American folk songs, the "sorrow songs" of slavery, which he said constituted at once "the greatest gift of the Negro people," and "the singular spiritual heritage of the nation."[12]

Europe found reinforcement for his own racial consciousness and musical aspirations in Du Bois, as he did in Krehbiel's *Afro-American Folksongs: A Study in Racial and National Music* (1913), which described *The Souls of Black Folk* as "the most eloquent English book ever written by any one of African blood."[13] Europe, however, did not believe, as Krehbiel did, that the musical "soul of black folks" was frozen in the past. "You see," he told the *Post* reporter, "we colored people have our own music that is part of us." "It's us; it's the product of our souls; it's been created by the sufferings and miseries of our race." It is true that "some of the old melodies we played Wednesday night were made up by slaves of the old days, and others were handed down from the days before we left Africa." The orchestra also played the music of Will Marion Cook and Rosamond Johnson, Europe explained, adding that this is real African-American music as well because—unlike the music of Coleridge-Taylor—it comes from African-Americans who live as African-Americans, and that "to write real negro music, a negro must live with negroes. He must think and feel as they do." As long as the music "breathes the spirit of a race," Europe argued, it is authentic, and this matters far more than whether it is categorized as folk music or symphonic music, or even dance music. "Even the negro ragtime music of white composers falls far short of the genuine dance compositions of negro musicians," he said.

Black musicians have been hampered in the development of the symphonic dimension of the African-American musical continuum primarily because it "takes a lot of training to develop a sense of time and delicate harmony" and "up to now, we have not had the facilities in this country for developing negro symphonic players." Part of the problem, Europe claimed, echoing Du Bois' criticism of Booker T. Washington, is that the "schools and colleges for the negro are all of an industrial character. The artistic side has naturally been neglected as of less importance. That is our great difficulty." Nevertheless, we are gradually "finding the men and teaching them." "All of my men," he said, "are ambitious."

> They take to the symphonic work with enthusiasm. To give an idea of this, let me say that every member of the orchestra that played at Carnegie Hall the other night had been playing dance music during the afternoon at various places throughout the city, and after the concert was over every man was obliged to hurry back to take up the work of accompanying the tango dancers again. That's the way they make their living, of course; but every man is proud of his part in building up a representative school of real negro music that is worthwhile. I have at least two violinists and a cellist who, I venture to say, are equal to any in town.

The March 11, 1914, *Evening Post* interview with James Reese Europe provides a remarkably candid statement of his views about the relationship between his personal ambitions as a musician and his sense of race pride and commitment to racial progress. It is also notable, given the general state of race relations in the United States at the time, for the sense of confidence and optimism it conveys, suggesting that in music, at least in Europe's view, a door remained open for black Americans to create their own future within a largely hostile society.

As Olly Wilson has pointed out, when Europe used the term *orchestra* he was not using it the sense of the European symphony; rather, he used it in "its earliest and broadest sense: a group of mixed instruments playing together with more than one instrument on a single part."[14] Taken one step further, the expression *symphony orchestra* may be seen as a metaphor for the social group itself, and Europe's discussion of the "National Negro Symphony Orchestra" and his ideas for its future development, therefore, may also have broader social implications.

The first of these is that Europe appears to have intended that "national" be understood in racial and cultural, and not political, terms, and that while the orchestra was currently made up of African-Americans, he did not intend that it should necessarily remain so. In the *Post* article he said that he had already sent "to South Africa for two French horn players, and to the Sudan for an oboe-player." Two weeks later the New York *News* reported that

> several wealthy philanthropists, imbued with the belief that the colored race has constructed and furnishes the only genuine and native American music, are going to back James Reese Europe in assembling an orchestra of colored musicians from all parts of the world to complete in every detail his National Negro Orchestra.[15]

The second way in which Europe's comments may be taken in larger social or cultural terms is to see a reflection of his philosophy for how general progress could be achieved for black Americans as a whole in his prescriptions for development of the orchestra. In the concluding paragraph of the *Post* interview, he wrote that the "great task ahead of us, as I see it, is to teach the negro to be careful, to make him understand the importance of painstaking effort in playing and especially to develop his sense of orchestral unity."

The weeks following the Carnegie Hall concert were some of the most active, even hectic, of Europe's entire career. The New York *News*, which ran a brief sketch about him during this period, called him "the busiest man in New York," one who requires "three secretaries, all of them as busy as he."[16] In addition to his continuing engagements with New York's social elite and with the Castles, he found himself being called upon to furnish music for an expanding range of new patrons. During the last week of March, for example, Europe and his orchestra were in Richmond and Washington, D.C., playing for Virginia's Governor Stewart at the Jefferson Hotel and for President Wilson's daughter, Eleanor, at the new Willard Hotel in the nation's capital.[17] On April 1, "The New York Society Orchestra" with Europe and Abbie Mitchell made a hasty trip to Boston "to entertain the music lovers of that city" with a concert at Copley Hall and then rushed back to New York to prepare for the Tempo Club's first large concert and entertainment before its most crucial audience at the Manhattan Casino.[18]

Advertisements for the spring concert and dance had begun appearing on the front page of the *New York Age* as early as March 19, barely a week after the Carnegie Hall concert. Over the preceding four years, the Clef Club's biannual entertainments at the Manhattan Casino had proven extremely popular with the Harlem community and with the organization's members themselves, and had helped to establish the Clef Club's reputation as the leading organization of black musicians and entertainers in the city, perhaps in the country. Now there were two ostensibly competing organizations, and Europe, Tyers, and Dabney realized that they needed to act quickly and dramatically to give the public a sense of identification with their new enterprise.[19]

The front page of the March 19 *New York Age* carried the announcement that on April 8, 1914, the Tempo Club would present the National Negro Orchestra in "A Night in Tangoland," "A Joyous Festival of Music and Dance Revelry," during which Vernon and Irene Castle ("Creators of the Modern Dance") would positively appear. A brief accompanying article reported that the Castles, who "dance for high society and rarely appear in public," had accepted an invitation by James Reese Europe and Ford Dabney to appear in the benefit for the National Negro Orchestra.[20]

It is easy to understand why Europe and Dabney should wish to have the famous Castles appear with them at the first big Tempo Club entertainment in Harlem. It is also likely that the Castles accepted the invitation out of a sense of obligation to their musicians and, perhaps, because they sympathized with Europe's and Dabney's ambitions for the National Negro Orchestra. It is also true, however, that by the early spring of 1914, the Castles' professional career (still under the careful management of Elisabeth Marbury) had taken a different, and more broadly public, direction.

Prior to 1914 the Castles had established their reputation as "society dancers," performing at private parties for the wealthy and prominent and at Castle House and Sans Souci for the "select" classes who could afford the price of admission. They had become enormously successful financially, earning over $5,000 per week, but they had not won over the conservative critics of social dancing who continued to fear that the general public (and especially the young), having little opportunity to be exposed to the Castle's "refinements," were dancing their way into a state of moral depravity. That such concerns had even spread to the upstanding members of New York's black community is apparent from a 1914 New Year's Day sermon by Reverend Adam Clayton Powell, pastor of Abyssinia Baptist Church, entitled "The Negro Race is Dancing Itself to Death." "Our young people are too frivolous because they feed on too much trash," Reverend Powell said. "You can see the effects of the Tango, the Chicago, the turkey trot, the Texas tommy and ragtime music not only in their conversations but in the movement of their bodies about the home and on the street. Grace and modesty are becoming rare virtues."[21]

The problem, according to most of the critics, was not with the Castles themselves or with such places as the Castle House, where "the spirit of beauty and art" is allied "to the legitimate physical need of healthy exercise and of honest enjoyment," but rather with the public dance halls, where "girls 'pick up' escorts," dance in a manner that brings their "bodies into intimate contact," sit on men's laps, and go for "joy-rides."[22] The tango was the dance most often singled out for condemnation (it was banned from the Yale Junior Prom in 1914), but even the Castle's own steps, when danced by the untutored, could be dangerous. "The Castle Walk, one of the most popular dances of the day," said a report by New York's City Club Committee on Public Amusements and Morals, "requires the partners' feet to be placed in a position which, while it may be taken without bodily contact, usually results at the public dances of the city in an interlocking of the partners' lower limbs and a continual rubbing together of the bodies."[23]

Whether or not the Castles felt any burning personal responsibility toward the public controversy—to all appearances they seemed simply a charming young couple enjoying themselves—a progressive reformer like Elisabeth Marbury clearly did. It was she who convinced Vernon that they should embark upon a public crusade to raise the standards of social dancing among all segments of the society. "The modern dances," she told the Worcester *Telegram*, "cannot be banned. They have arrived, and they will remain." Furthermore, they are "not at all objectionable except when they are danced by people who do not know how to do them."[24]

Under Marbury's guidance, therefore, beginning in early 1914, the Castles became the "authors" or subjects of dozens of "how to" newspaper and magazine articles, a book (*Modern Dancing*, produced by Marbury), several short demonstration films, and even, by the end of the spring, a loosely biographic feature film called *The Whirl of Life*.[25] At the time, however, the most talked about of the methods of spreading the gospel of dance was the idea of a national "whirlwind" tour in which the Castles could demonstrate the correct way to dance in person before large audiences. "Our plans," Marbury told the Worcester *Telegram*,

> are to spread this proper instruction in dancing broadcast through every possible agency. That is one reason why the Castles are making this spring tour of twenty-one of the principal cities of the country. Not only will they dance the latest dances, but Mr. Castle will illustrate the mistakes usually made by the average dancers, and will address the audience, telling them how the dances should be danced. I do not believe that many people dance in a vulgar way except through ignorance of the proper methods, and I believe this tour of the Castles will be a wonderful dance crusade that will elevate the standards of dancing all over the country."[26]

Jim Europe had discussed the possibilities of touring with Vernon and Irene Castle in Europe, playing in Paris primarily, during the summer of 1914. In fact, he had mentioned it in his March 11 interview with the *Post*. The idea of a national tour with the dancers was apparently being conceived at about the same time, and this also appealed to him. As he began planning for the Tempo Club's first concert at the Manhattan Casino, the opportunity for featuring the Castles in their first really public exhibition—as a sort of preliminary to the projected national tour—presented itself. At first, the idea of having the Castles, a pair of white dancers who had learned or derived most of their dances from African-American sources, demonstrate the "right way" to dance the new steps to a black audience seems ironic to say the least. On the other hand, the Castles were known for not only using black musicians, but preferring them, and even for helping to break down the color line in Broadway vaudeville houses by insisting upon them. Also, the fact that these were white entertainers, darlings of the white upper crust who would be performing for the pleasure of a black audience (reversing the traditional pattern), could hardly be overlooked.

As a consequence, the *Age* gave expanded front page coverage to the upcoming Tempo Club entertainment, with discussions and photographs of the Castles, their music men Europe and Dabney, the National Negro Orchestra, and the impending historic national tour. By the April 2 issue, the one just preceding the concert, when the *Age* also listed the other black entertainers now scheduled on the program (J. Rosamond Johnson, Tom Brown, Jolly John Larkins, Abbie Mitchell, Criswell and Bailey, Smith and Burris, and Happy Rhone), nearly all the boxes and loges had been reserved, and the evening's success was assured.[27]

On Wednesday evening, April 8, the Manhattan Casino was jammed to overflowing by a large and enthusiastic crowd estimated at 2,500 that included many of the black community's prominent citizens and "more than 100 white people of fame and fashion."[28] Except for the Castles, who appeared in a separate section of the program, the Tempo Club concert followed the general pattern of the previous Clef Club entertainments.[29] It began with William Tyers conducting the large National Negro Orchestra in two of his recent compositions, "The Tempo Club March" and "La Mariposa—Tango." The orchestra then alternated selections with songs and humor provided by Happy Rhone, Jolly John Larkins, S. H. Dudley, Abbie Mitchell, and other well-known representatives of the black stage. As usual, nearly all of the orchestral pieces were written by black composers, and, in addition to Tyers and Europe, J. Rosamond Johnson, E.E. Thompson, Ford Dabney, and Joe Jordan conducted their own works. In keeping with the special nature of the evening, however, with few exceptions, the selections by the orchestra employed dance rhythms, and the finale to the first section of the program (prior to the Castles) was a rousing rendition of J. Leubrie Hill's "At the Ball, That's All," featuring the "Drummer Boys."

The addition of "At the Ball" to the program is significant in that it further underscores the Tempo Club's intention to focus on the dancing vogue and to make clear the connection between the modern dances, especially the Castle's refinements that were to follow, and their roots in traditional African-American custom. "At the Ball" was taken from the last act of Hill's musical comedy, *My Friend from Kentucky* (sometimes known as The Darktown Follies, the name of the company), which was then appearing at the Lafayette Theatre in Harlem and drawing favorable attention from both black and white audiences. Indeed, Florenz Ziegfeld had been so impressed with the production that he had purchased the rights to three of the numbers, including "At the Ball," which he called "one of the best ever staged in musical comedy," to use in his Follies. In addition, Oscar Hammerstein had booked the show for the roof of his Victoria Theatre on Broadway beginning June 1.[30]

In the musical production, Johnny Peters, Ethel Williams, and Eddie Rector performed a number of dances, including a "tango jiggle" and the turkey trot, and in the last number the entire cast shuffled across the stage in an improvised circle dance while singing "At the Ball." Leigh Whipper later told Marshall and Jean Stearns that the circle dance

> was a serpentine dance which goes back to the Ring Shout and Africa and its immediate inspiration was church "Watch Meetings," the custom with which colored people watch the old year out and the new year in. A little before midnight, someone starts shuffling and singing "Tearing Down the Walls of Zion, Goin' to See My Lord," and everybody puts his hands on the hips of the person in front of him and inches forward in a circle with a rocking motion."[31]

It is not reported whether the circle dance was performed as part of the "At the Ball" number by dancers from the Tempo Club or whether the orchestra simply played the music, and perhaps it does not greatly matter since many members of the audience were familiar with the piece and were aware of its association with older African-American dance practices. In any case, following a short intermission, the Castles took the stage, accompanied by Europe and the National Negro Orchestra (or a smaller contingent from within it), and demonstrated four of their most popular dances: the Half and Half, the Tango, the Castle Maxixe, and the Castle Walk. William Tyers then led the orchestra in a reprise of his "Tempo Club March," and the formal part of the evening was over.

It was a lengthy program, but well-paced and apparently well-executed. The *News* described it, overall, as "perhaps the finest musical and dance program ever given by and for colored people," one that commanded such "monstrous ovations" for nearly every number that it was difficult to say "whether or not the honors of the evening were bestowed upon James Reese Europe and his orchestra . . . or upon the greatest dance artists of the day, Mr. and Mrs. Vernon Castle."[32] Simply the fact that the Castles, "wizards of the dance, who are to terpsichore what Edison is to electricity," chose to appear "before the Tempo Club, one of the leading negro [sic] organizations of the city," was newsworthy to other white newspapers, like the New York *Sun*.[33] The *Musical Leader*, in its review the following week, explained that the "unique entertainment" at the Manhattan Casino was in part an experiment to try out the unusual combination of the Castles, "whose fame as dancers is widespread," and a very interesting orchestra, composed of "colored men," for a future tour of the country that may go "as far as the Pacific Coast." The director of the orchestra, James Reese Europe, the article continued, has written much of the Castle's music and is "a highly talented musician who has studied the folk music of his people and . . . has accomplished some remarkable things in composition as well as in the training of the orchestra."[34] Furthermore, the orchestra

> is not made up of mandolin, guitar, and banjo, but of regular orchestral instruments, and the quality of tone which these men produce is something indescribable. Just as the negro [sic] singer has a peculiarly individual tone which vibrates with emotion and which is unique in quality, so the tone of the orchestra has the same thrill, the same vibration, and in serious music this proves very moving.[35]

The success of the Castles' appearance with Jim Europe and his orchestra at the Tempo Club entertainment helped to spur arrangements for the much talked about national tour, and by the middle of the month a schedule had been set. As it finally evolved, and despite having to abandon the idea of including the Far West, the Castle tour was aptly christened a "whirlwind." Thirty large cities were booked—as far west as Omaha, as far south as Washington, D.C., and as far north as Toronto—all to be visited in the short space of twenty-eight days. To accomplish this the size of the traveling company was kept as small as possible: the Castles, Gladwyn Macdougal, Arthur Hopkins (the tour manager), three student couples from the Castle House, and Europe's eighteen-member orchestra. A special train consisting of three Pullman cars (one car for the Castle entourage, one for Europe and the orchestra, and one to serve as a combination baggage car and diner) was reserved to take them immediately from one city to the next.[37] At each of the stops, a single matinee or evening performance would take place at the largest theater or auditorium then available, after which the company would immediately pack up their costumes and equipment and scramble aboard the waiting Castle Special for the trip, usually overnight, to the next city on the itinerary.

Since there was little time available for creating or rehearsing new material, a standard two-part program was developed by the Castles and their music directors that was followed with only minor variations throughout the entire tour. Audiences in all thirty cities, therefore, saw and heard the same basic program. The first part consisted of the Castles' demonstration of several of the older style dances, like the polka, followed by an exhibition of their modern steps. Between dances, while Irene dashed out to change her costume—since many of the women in the audiences were at least as interested in how Irene dressed as in how the couple danced—Europe conducted the orchestra in its liveliest instrumental numbers, a quartet from the orchestra sang, Buddy Gilmore and Vernon Castle took turns giving acrobatic drum solos, and the Castle House dancers provided examples of the mistakes commonly made by novice dancers. In the second part of the program, the audience was invited to participate in a dance contest in which the Castles selected a winning couple and presented them with the Castle Cup. The winners were also awarded a trip to New York to compete for the "national championship" scheduled for May 23 at Madison Square Garden.

On Sunday afternoon, April 26, 1914, Europe conducted the National Negro Orchestra with soprano Abbie Mitchell in a benefit for the Howard Orphanage and Industrial School at the Majestic Theatre in Brooklyn. He joined the Castle company immediately thereafter for the trip to Boston, where the "Whirlwind Tour" opened at the Opera House the following evening.[38] As reported in the local papers, the predominantly white audience for the Castle company was large and enthusiastic, "establishing a new record for attendance" at the vast auditorium and reflecting the extensiveness of popular interest in social dancing and in the vogue of "Mr. and Mrs. Vernon Castle, dancers par excellence of the modern dances."[39] Since the fame of the Castles and the Castle House had spread to New England, a large turnout in Boston was perhaps to be expected, but the papers also reported that the audience was not disappointed in the "novel" and "delightful" entertainment they were given.

Primary attention in the published reviews of the evening, naturally, was given to the Castles' dancing exhibition, and Elisabeth Marbury, in particular, must have been pleased by what was said. "Mr. and Mrs. Castle," wrote Eugene Clark in one of the longer articles, "fully demonstrated that their new creations are, by far, superior to the old dances."[40] All of them "are very pretty and, when danced correctly, contain nothing that can possibly offend the most conservative." In addition to the instructive and entertaining dancing, the reporter found other features of the program—the music especially—equally enjoyable.

"There was music by Mr. Europe's orchestra, which alone would have been no bad form of entertainment," Clark wrote. "The orchestra not only played in a manner which made the whole audience eager to dance, but for the sake of variety it produced a quartet which sang surprisingly well." In addition, Buddy Gilmore—who, with his battery of traps and bells and cymbals, was the only orchestra member seated on stage—"demonstrated much cleverness and furnished a great deal of humor by the eccentric manner in which he manipulated the apparatus connected with his department."

The prominent role of the drummer in the program of the Castle Tour is significant for two reasons. First, the expansion of the drum set or traps to include a wide range of rhythmic tones (wood blocks, bells, cymbals, triangles, as well as the bass, snare, and other standard drums derived from the marching band) performed by a single drummer was familiar to the patrons of black vaudeville by 1914. Drummers like Buddy Gilmore had proven successful as "eccentric" novelty acts, although musical qualities were less important than was the acrobatic dexterity of the performer and the shear volume of noise created. The drum solos performed between dances in the Castle program by Gilmore and by Vernon Castle clearly fell in this vaudeville tradition. In Boston, they "produced such a hellish noise as no Tartar band ever could equal, drowning even the music of the orchestra, to the great delight of the audience."[41]

The second, and perhaps more important, way in which the roles of the drums and the drummer were significant was in the increased prominence Europe gave them within the orchestra to add rhythmic color and excitement to the dance music. Europe had been doing this for some time with the Society Orchestra at the Castle House, and the results of his expanding use of the instrument can be heard on the Victor records he cut in December and February, despite the primitive recording techniques then employed. One Boston reporter described the music he heard on April 27 as "Oriental." "One player on the end fairly worked with all fours to keep going the various cymbals and whistles and bell-like instruments which gave a wild, barbaric flavor to the dances," which "set the whole audience to swaying in rhythm."[42] One of their selections, something called "Queen of the Movies," "brought down the house."[43]

Following their appearance in Boston and a quick stop in Springfield, the company headed south to Washington, D.C. and Baltimore. They played the Academy of Music in Philadelphia on May 1, and then went west to Pittsburgh, north to Rochester, and on to Chicago and the great Midwest, where they spent over two weeks before turning back East to upstate New York and New England and, finally, home to Gotham. Virtually all along the way, the pattern was the same. Large crowds, dominated by young and middle-aged couples and by others curious to see what so excited Eastern society, filled the auditoriums and even, at some stops, met the train with banners shouting "The Castles Are Coming, Hooray, Hooray!"[44] The local press announced the visits, applauded the dances and the dancers, remarked appreciatively about the orchestra, and commented (usually favorably) about the noisy drumming exhibitions. As the Castle Tour moved farther west, however, the tone and emphasis of the newspaper coverage shifted noticeably, reflecting a greater sense of confusion about the larger social and cultural changes that the Castle phenomenon embodied. The Castles and their troupe were not simply entertainers; they were educating America, and their authority carried beyond the dances and dance lessons to a whole new code of acceptable personal and social attitudes and behavior. As Arlene Croce has said, they were "perhaps the first large expression of modern mass society and its cult of good taste, its How To Lessons, its obsession with The Correct Thing."[45]

Recent scholarship has called attention to Irene Castle herself as the first representative "New Woman" of the twentieth century, no longer frail and matronly, but active, free from unnatural physical and psychological restraints, and youthful. In sexual terms, says Erenberg, she "showed audiences how to alter traditional sex roles and create a life lived emotionally closer to men. She fought the sexual double standard and helped widen the conception of women's role," and she "did what seemed impossible in the old culture: She merged the virgin to the vamp and validated a wider range of behavior."[46] The fact that Mrs. Castle offered a new model for American women, and that this fact was widely understood in the spring of 1914, is apparent from the amount of coverage she personally received during the tour. Following the Castles' performance in Syracuse, for example, the *Post Standard* admitted that Irene is "probably the physical ideal of countless numbers of young women in this country," who must now "be as slender as one can be and still cast a shadow." Her costumes, the paper continued, might have been considered extremely daring "if Mrs. Castle's air of invincible virginity and fleshless statuesqueness could be daring. As it happens she resembles the sidewise shadow of a disembodied clothes pin so it makes little difference what lack of clothes she wears."[47]

Vernon Castle, Irene's male counterpart, also received attention, although considerably less than his wife, as a representative model for the new American male. Physically, Vernon was as slim, active, and as elegant in his movements as Irene. He wore his clothes "with a distinguished flair," Irene recalled, and had the ability "of being able to wear jewelry without being ostentatious or looking effeminate."[48] "Mr. Castle was in black—the narrowest dress-suit we ever saw," remarked a Toronto paper, "and Mrs. Castle wore white, so you could tell them apart when they danced."[49] Indeed, Vernon may have been the person most responsible for making the wristwatch acceptable to American men. Most important, perhaps, was the air of imperturbability he conveyed. "Nothing ever phased him," William Elkins, one of the orchestra members later remembered, "there was no situation that he was not master of, with his quiet dignified manner," including that of being the professional and romantic partner of the new woman without losing his masculinity.[50] Always careful to present themselves as the happily married couple, Vernon and Irene Castle epitomized the modern ideal of what Erenberg has termed the "fun couple," combining pleasure with business success, sensuality with grace, and increased individual freedom with social responsibility.

There was another message that the Castle Whirlwind Tour brought to the cities it visited during those four weeks in April and May, 1914, that, if the newspapers are an accurate reflection, seems to have been more difficult for many Americans, especially in the Midwest, to accept. This has to do with what the racial mixture of the company implied, especially what it seemed to say about the changing status of black entertainers (and, perhaps, of black Americans in general). The Castle company was not a truly integrated one—there were no black dancers and no white musicians—but there was a clear partnership between the dancers and the musicians in which the latter were presented as very nearly the professional, if not the social, equals of the former. The relationship was not unlike that of the two Castles themselves, where "despite her formidable business success and drive for self-achievement, Irene always depicted Vernon as the creator of their success and fame"; the "new woman" remained Mrs. Vernon Castle.[51]

The all-black Castle orchestra, led by Jim Europe was known, like the Castles, for carrying the endorsement of the Eastern elite, and Vernon Castle always reminded the audience when he invited them to the stage for the dancing competition that they were being given the opportunity to dance to the "best dancing music in the world by Mr. Europe's Orchestra."[52] As Irene Castle recalled, Europe was a "commanding figure," bespectacled, six feet in height and two hundred pounds, and "exceedingly intelligent," possessing a "profound knowledge of music," which was not the image of the black entertainer with which most Americans were comfortably familiar. All of the musicians wore formal black tuxedoes during their performances, and all of them both read the printed scores, and responded immediately to their conductor's instructions when he spontaneously shifted the time or the tempo of the piece being played, especially during the dance competition. "The best dancers were generally equally good enough to make the final decision a difficult one," Irene said, "so we had to depend on Jim Europe's ability to change the tempo of the piece he was playing without an apparent pause. Without changing the tune he would jump from one-step to waltz time and in this way we were able to weed out the couple or couples who did not at once perceive the change and swing easily into the new time."[53] In the first part of the program, the Castles demonstrated their considerable ability to integrate the movements of their bodies to the rhythms of Europe's orchestra so that music and dance—orchestra and dancers—were fused into a single performance. Lest there be any confusion about the status of the two components, the orchestra's drummer—the rhythmic heart of the dance orchestra—was seated prominently on the stage. In the second part of the program—the dance contest—the authorities of correctness, Vernon and Irene Castle, judged eager white couples on their ability to dance to the tune dictated by a black orchestra leader.

To publicly accord this level of dignity to blacks must have seemed a novel and, indeed, slightly disturbing experience, especially for many Midwesterners whose exposure to black entertainers had been limited to traveling minstrel shows. For such people, as well as for the newspapers who reflected the racial attitudes of their readership, the Castle Tour, deliberately or not, provided elements in the program that lent themselves to traditional interpretation. The vocal quartet that sang briefly during an interlude in the dancing was one, their music—as described by a Syracuse paper for example—being "that of the palmetto tree and the watermelon patch, with faint suggestions of the persimmons and the voodoo."[54] The second, and much more often noted element, was Buddy Gilmore's drum exhibition, which was done with such humor and athleticism that, while the audiences loved it, the papers could seize upon it as a way of dismissing or belittling the true substance and serious role of black participation in the overall program.

The *Minneapolis Journal*, for example, reviewed the Castles in a column by their "culture critic," an ex–prize fighter called Butch Johnson, a sort of Mr. Dooley persona whose perspective on high society and its activities was thought to be humorous. Naturally, Johnson could not see the appeal of the dancers (they were "too skinny—all legs"), and he could not understand Vernon's accent. This is innocent fun, reflecting as it does back on the obtuseness of the critic. When he spoke about the orchestra, however, the humor turned to ridicule:

> Chocolate Joe is on the stage playing a base [sic] drum, snare drum, cymbal, a whistle and one or two other instruments all at once, and no kid [sic], that's right. He plays with his feet, knees, and teeth. A lot of darky musicians sit in the regular music makers' places, and if it was a traveling medicine show I could sense it out, but what those society people are putting down good coin to see it for is what gets me.[55]

A comparison of the newspaper reviews of the Castle Tour for the purposes of understanding popular attitudes is useful only if it is kept in mind that the program that was put on in each of the cities remained constant. In some cities, by some reports at least, the Castle Tour seemed to raise no very serious questions, and the mixed racial performance could, therefore, be described straightforwardly without resorting to demeaning images and language. "A surprisingly good orchestra, one of large proportions and composed entirely of colored players, furnished the dancers music of the sort both to delight the ear and keep the feet a-tripping, their bodies swaying the meanwhile in rhythmic motion," said the Cincinnati *Tribune*, for example. "Europe, the leader of this special Castle congregation of players, has so thoroughly mastered the terpsichorean idea, and the Castle purpose in particular, that it seemed impossible not to dance while his baton was swinging."[56] The *Tribune* story also, like most of the others, remarks about Gilmore, but in doing so it says simply that he added a dash of humor to the program.

Most of the newspaper coverage of the tour appears to suggest a degree of confusion but not hostility toward the racial question. The St. Louis *Post*, in attempting to prepare its readers for the forthcoming Castle show at the Odeon, announced that the "Vernon Castles Dance to Music by [an] African Band." Moreover, this "special" orchestra is headed by the "Famous 'Europe.'"[57] One may wonder what the innocent reader made of this. More typically, following the May 6 performance in St. Joseph, Missouri, the local paper began its report with the comment that, when the Castles were thirty minutes late, the audience spent the time commenting "on the varying shades of the chocolate hue in Europe's eighteen piece orchestra and watched the maneuvers of the drummer." This familiar tack, however, was immediately dropped, and followed by the statement that the "music really was excellent and the drummer was even better, his versatility being unusual and his ability remarkable."[58]

Whatever difficulties the local press had in interpreting the challenges that the Castle Whirlwind Tour presented, the company itself seems to have experienced very few problems. Although they found little time to sleep, rushing from town to town, the enthusiasm of the crowds that greeted them and packed the theaters was infectious. "It was a happy, boisterous, crazy trip," Irene remembered, but one in which every member was expected to take his or her responsibilities seriously.[59] Orchestra member William Elkins remembered it the same way. The Castle company was "one of the most perfectly disciplined organizations and one in which everyone enjoyed themselves."[60]

One of the routine ways that the group combined both fun and discipline, and which also helped to pass the time they spent on the train between cities, was for the entire company to gather in the musicians' car for a mock trial of any member accused of misbehaving or being out of line in any way. This kangaroo court procedure was conducted with great seriousness, regardless of the nature or extent of the supposed offense. The usual charges amounted to such things as taking a drink before the show, chewing gum on stage, being late, missing steps in a dance, whistling in the dressing room, or wearing mismatched socks or shoes in the orchestra pit. The accused perpetrator of any of these heinous crimes was then summoned to appear before judge Elkins and a jury appointed by Vernon Castle to have his case tried. Jim Europe, the obvious choice for prosecuting attorney, would then deliver a ringing speech exaggerating the seriousness of the violation and the unshakeable nature of the "state's case." Gladwyn Macdougal, the defense attorney, would plead for "the poor wretch," imploring the jury to "consider the effects your condemnation will have on his young and innocent life, ruined forever by a chance of fate, by one innocent miscircumstance. . . ."[61] If, as was usual, the individual was found guilty, the punishment assigned was of the order of requiring him or her to supply the beer for the next evening or to submit to a noisy, but harmless, spanking. No member was above "the law," including the Castles themselves. On more than one occasion, when the headliners were charged with missing steps or being late for the train, they were required to pay their debt to society by providing champagne for the whole company.

Aside from the pure fun of the game, the mock trials helped to create a sense of comradeship and fairness among both white and black members of the troupe and to encourage responsible behavior by everyone. Thirty-four years later, William Elkins vividly recalled a particular incident, in some ways and in those times quite minor, that, to him, explained everything one needed to know about why the Castle company worked so well together and why the Whirlwind Tour of 1914 was so special. He told Noble Sissle:

> [O]ne of the white dancers, talking to a local stage hand, was overheard by one of the members of our troupe to use the word *Nigger*. The case was reported for trial. Well, that was the first of such an instance and I thought it best to speak with Mr. and Mrs. Castle before taking such a touchy subject up, for fear of how the offender might take it and knowing what could develop. But Mr. Castle spoke up, right away, and told me to bring him up in court and fine him fifty dollars. The case was called and the prisoner pleaded guilty. Instead of fining him fifty dollars cash, the fine was champagne, sandwiches, and refreshments for the whole troupe and that cost him at least fifty dollars. The victim objected, but Mr. Castle, who was standing in the door looking on, warned the offender that if he did not pay that the jury composed of the musicians might be a little rough. Needless to say, he bought the refreshments and on our special train that night, Mr. and Mrs. Castle, the offender, and the whole company had a wonderful party and after that there was never any other insulting remarks.

Bill Elkins, then seventy-six years old, remembered Mr. and Mrs. Castle as "really two great artists," but he also remembered them, more definitively, as the "the finest people I ever had the pleasure of working for in my whole career."[62]

On Saturday, May 23, the Castle Special brought the exhausted dancers and musicians of the Castle troupe home to New York City for the grand finale of the historic four-week national tour. Irene had been told that the "big and ugly" Madison Square Garden was a poor place for a dance contest, and when she saw it she agreed. The only thing in its favor was that its huge size gave the competitors plenty of room to dance in and the judges (Irene and Vernon) plenty of room to see them. They apparently needed the space because many of the couples, already winners of the competitions in their various cities, were quite accomplished, and despite Europe's efforts to trip them up by changing the tempos, it was late in the evening before a clear winner was chosen. By this time, the audience in the hall, which Irene recalled as "packed" when they started but which *Variety* reported as "disappointing," had thinned out considerably.[63] In the end, one of the two remaining couples—a brother and sister from Massachusetts— made a slip, and a rather dignified, middle-aged pair from New York, Mr. and Mrs. Sailing Baruch, were declared the national dancing champions.[64] The fact that Baruch was the brother of Bernard Baruch, a successful Wall Street financier soon to be appointed by President Wilson to the Council of National Defense, did not hurt the cause of the supporters of social dancing.

The monetary return from Castle Whirlwind Tour, reported to be $85,000, did not hurt the Castles' financial situation either, since they received about a third of the total.[65] Exactly how much Europe, the musicians, and the other members and promoters of the company received is unknown, but it is not reported that anyone was dissatisfied. Even the critics of the Castle dance campaign were given a temporary boost when Irene, after sleeping around the clock, checked into Woman's Hospital on Monday to have her appendix removed, and a few doctors were found to express the opinion that dancing had caused the attack.[66] Whatever comfort traditionalists received from this was quickly lost when Irene emerged from a week or so of recuperation with her hair cut in a short bob. Nothing she had done before seemed quite such a radical departure from past custom, and when it was immediately copied by thousands of women in New York and elsewhere, the battle was clearly over— the fatal blow having been struck by a pair of scissors.[67]

Europe's feeling about the Castle Tour, and about the Castles themselves, was conveyed in the caption of a photograph of the couple that was published while Mrs. Castle was recovering from her operation. They are "the best friends of the colored professional," it read, and while they are known for being

> artistic and exceptionally original in the terpsichorean art, they are also noted for their benevolence and congeniality. Race, color, creed nor religion mark their lives. Mrs. Castle, after a severe illness, is now convalescent and it is the hope of white and colored alike that she will be fully restored to good health.[68]

"They are outspoken for the Tempo Club at all times," concluded the caption, and "the Tempo Club wishes them success."

Watch Your Step

> I have had probably as good an opportunity to observe the various
> dances as anyone in the city, and I have found that dancing keeps
> husbands and wives together and eliminates much drinking, as no
> one can dance and drink to excess.
>
> James Reese Europe (1914)

By the early part of June 1914, Vernon and Irene Castle had decided against undertaking a full-fledged European dance tour in the summer; they did not need the money, Irene was still tired from the American Whirlwind Tour and still recovering from her recent surgery, and, since her father's death, Irene's mother had been living with them, and they wanted to do something for her as well. Their revised plans were simply to vacation in France, dance a little in Paris, and relax at the seashore at Deauville. Europe, in the meantime, had been approached by Mrs. R. W. Hawkesworth and her daughter, Margaret, with a proposition to provide his dance orchestra for a new restaurant, the American Supper Club, which they proposed to open on the Champs Elysées in Paris in July.[1] Like most Americans, neither the Castles nor Europe seemed aware of the ominous political events then taking place on the Continent, events that would both interfere with their summer plans and alter their lives, and the world, forever.

On June 4, the Clef Club, after six months without its former leader, held its first public concert and dance at the Manhattan Casino. Although the advertisements promised "everything new but the name," and in spite of the presence of the talented James Tim Brymn as conductor of the Clef Club Orchestra and Will Marion Cook as leader of the chorus, the evening's program and the composition of the orchestra appears to have been essentially the same as in prior years. Cook, Harry T. Burleigh, and J. Rosamond Johnson conducted works they had written, and the orchestra's composition reflected the familiar banjos, mandolins, bandoris, and pianos. The audience turnout was excellent, however, and Lucien White of the *New York Age* reviewed the evening very favorably. "Notwithstanding certain changes which have occurred during the past year, the most critical listener could find no fault with the musical achievement of the club," White wrote.[2] Despite the disagreements that had led to his resignation and to the formation of the Tempo Club, Europe and his associates were not antagonistic toward the Clef Club, and, indeed, several Tempo Club members, notably its treasurer and assistant conductor, William H. Tyers, performed with the Clef Club Orchestra on June 4.[3] The demand for black musicians and dance orchestras was so high during the late spring of 1914 that, economically at least, there appeared little reason for hostility between the two clubs; the public seemed willing to support them both.

On June 28, 1914, while the Castles were planning to sail to France and Jim Europe was putting together a suitable costume to lead the grand march in the annual "Frolic of the Frogs" scheduled the next day, Archduke Franz Ferdinand, the heir apparent to the Austrian throne, was assassinated in Sarajevo, and the war for which the Great Powers had been arming themselves for years was now virtually unavoidable. It would be another month before hostilities were actually declared, but as news of the assassination spread across Europe and the Atlantic, it became clear that this was no time to be traveling abroad, even if, as most people then expected, the war—when it came—would be short-lived. The Castles, who had left New York on July 18 anyway, continued on to Paris and actually danced a couple of weeks for "Papa" Louis, who had given them their first start, although, as Irene recalled, the "gaiety had drained out of the Café de Paris."[4] War was declared the day they left Paris for the coast, August 1.

Despite disappointment over the loss of the European engagement, James Reese Europe had an abundance of work with which to console himself during the summer. Eastern society, like most other segments of the American population, felt comfortably safe—and a little smug—from the madness enveloping the Continent, and continued to request his services. In mid-July, Florenz Ziegfeld contracted with Europe and his Society Orchestra to play for him at the New Amsterdam Theater roof, and Europe sent Ford Dabney to lead the contingent. Dabney was so successful that within a month the orchestra became almost an institution in its own right, no longer requiring the Europe name to bring in the customers.[5] Buddy Gilmore was dispatched with another Europe orchestra to Luna Park on Coney Island, where a large ballroom had been built to provide a summer version of the Castle House. The Brooklyn *Citizen*, which described the spot as a mecca for automobile parties, quoted Gilmore as saying that anyone "with dancing blood in his system has got to dance when he hears this music."[6]

With most of the Tempo Club musicians engaged in commercial or society jobs, many of them outside the city, there was little chance for Europe to continue the development of the Negro Symphony Orchestra during the summer. There was another area of his continuing interest, however, that he was able to give some renewed attention: black musical theater. In truth, Europe had never abandoned his hopes to see the return of black musical theater to the glory days of Williams and Walker and Cole and Johnson. He had, of course, spent six years with those celebrated companies, and he tended to view black musical theater as a coequal area of African-American artistic expression, along with popular song and dance, and symphonic composition and performance. Unlike most of his white, and many of his black, contemporaries (including his own mother and sister), Europe does not seem to have subscribed to the hierarchy of cultural or esthetic values that placed one area above another. A more important question for him than whether a musical activity was labeled folk, popular, or fine art was whether it was authentic and done well.

During the preceding four difficult years for black musical theater, Europe had remained an active member of the Frogs, and he had kept in touch with what was occurring on the black theater circuit (S. H. Dudley, who had moved to Washington, D.C., in 1912, had helped to put together a string of black-owned theaters called the Theater Owners' Booking Association, or T.O.B.A.). In the midst of all of his other activities in March 1914, for example, Europe accompanied Romeo Dougherty, dramatic editor of the *Amsterdam News*, to Washington to see a new production by the Smart Set Company at the Howard Theatre and to persuade its producers, Salem Tutt Whitney and J. Homer Tutt, to bring the show to New York.[7] The recent success of J. Leubrie Hill with *My Friend from Kentucky* provided further encouragement during the summer of 1914 for those, like Europe, who were interested in revitalizing black theater. On August 27, Lester Walton, dramatic editor of the *New York Age*, fellow Frog, and comanager of the Lafayette Theater, announced in his column that several "colored men prominently identified with the theatrical profession" were planning a new production "before many months" that would resemble those of "the days of Williams and Walker."[8] Cooperation was absolutely necessary, he said, "to bring colored musical comedy to the high position it once held," as well as a willingness to "take a long-shot chance as the promoters of 'A Trip to Coontown' and other colored organizations were forced to do some years ago." In addition to himself, Walton identified Jesse A. Shipp, Alex Rogers, R. C. McPherson, Henry Troy, and James Reese Europe as those principally interested. "The proposed production," Walton added, "will have its initial appearance at the Lafayette Theatre and if it bears the earmarks of a winner will be transplanted to Broadway." A month later, Walton and Europe were in Washington, D.C., talking with Dudley about the possibilities of a downtown theater site for their proposed (and as yet unwritten) new show. Walton expressed optimism about Dudley's New American Theater, an opinion that was "shared by Mr. Europe, whose home is here and who knows the Washington people like a book."[9]

Lester Walton and Jim Europe were not the only ones interested in revitalizing American musical comedy during the late summer of 1914. Producer Charles Dillingham had been working for several months on the idea of a new musical that would capitalize on the dance craze. Desiring also to exploit the popular "ragtime" song styles currently being cranked out by Tin Pan Alley, he approached Irving Berlin with an offer to write the entire score, something Berlin had not previously attempted. Up to that time, Berlin was known for writing single popular songs, like "Alexander's Ragtime Band" or "Everybody's

Doin' It," songs aimed at the sheet music and record market or intended to be interpreted individually into various musical comedies and revues. Berlin accepted the challenge to try something on a larger scale, and Dillingham hired Harry B. Smith (who has been called the "most prolific librettist and lyricist in the history of the American musical stage") to write the book.[10] In July, he cabled Vernon and Irene Castle with a contract to star in the new production, now titled *Watch Your Step*, as long as they could be back in the United States by the end of September when rehearsals were planned to begin.

As it happened, the outbreak of war in Europe forced the Castles to return earlier than they had expected, and so they spent a couple of weeks touring in vaudeville while waiting for *Watch Your Step* to start. Although neither Europe nor Dabney, nor their orchestra was with the Castles during their short period on the vaudeville circuit, the influence of their earlier collaboration was manifested in a new dance step, the fox-trot, which the Castles began performing publicly for the first time. The fox-trot, the most significant and endurably popular of the Castle dances, was born during the Whirlwind Tour of the spring of 1914 when Europe, who often experimented privately with new musical ideas at the piano, became fascinated by the slower rhythms of a tune called "Memphis Blues," written two years earlier by a young black composer from Memphis, Tennessee, named W. C. Handy. "Memphis Blues," was the first blues that Handy had published, and according to the composer, Jim Europe was the first bandleader to play it.[11] Europe, who thought of the piece as a dance rather than a song, asked Vernon, who had often heard Europe play it during the tour, if he thought it had possibilities as a contrast to their faster dance numbers, like the one-step (or Castle Walk). Castle was not at first enthusiastic. It was his feeling that the public would not take to the slow tempo, "the world of today demanding staccato music."[12] Nevertheless, the Castles compiled steps to the music and even tried it out at a few private parties while Irene was recuperating from her surgery. Much to their surprise, they found the dance an immediate success, so much so that when they were asked by Edward Bok to prepare an article on their dances for *The Ladies Home Journal*, they decided to include their latest sensation.[13]

As Thorton Hagert has written, while there was some confusion in the proper steps for the fox-trot, the earliest versions of the dance seem to draw upon a combination of steps that had been in general use for some years. The music "had an emphatic 4/4 rhythm at about forty bars a minute [a little less than half his estimate of the tempo of the one-step], peculiar structures of twelve or twenty bars in place of the customary sixteen, and some really crazy breaks in the rhythm—right in the middle of the tune."[14] Vernon Castle's description of the music for *The Ladies Home Journal* agrees with Hagert. "If you will play an ordinary 'rag' half as fast as you would play it for the one-step," he told the *Journal's* readers, "you will have a pretty good idea of the music and tempo."[15] Once you listen to the music, he continued, you will "find absolutely no difficulty in dancing to it, but the natural inclination is either to dance very fast steps double time to the music or very slow steps with it." Vernon's advice, however, was to combine the two, alternating between two and four steps to the bar. By doing so, he said, "you not only make the dance comfortable, but you also make it possible to do a great variety of easy and amusing steps." The article then gave several illustrated examples, each beginning with two slow steps (a glide, stride, or drag) followed by four quick ones (hop, kick, and stop). "This drag," Vernon explained, "is a very old negro [sic] step, often called 'Get over, Sal.'"

The historical importance of the fox-trot derives from two reasons. First, it provided the basis for many subsequent popular dances and the rhythm for many familiar American popular songs. Second is the fact that it constitutes the first manifestation of the diffusion of the blues into mainstream American culture. Without that diffusion, much of what developed as characteristic American popular song and dance, or jazz for that matter, would be inconceivable. It is also significant that the impact of the blues was first widely felt in dance (the first blues song would not be recorded for another six years), and that it was understood from the beginning as African-American in origin. As we have seen, the Castles credited Europe with the development of the modern fox-trot, but they also were quick to point out that the inspiration for the dance, its fundamental roots, lay in traditional African-American practice. When the *New York Herald* announced that the Castles, who had returned from Europe and were then appearing in vaudeville, were exhibiting a dance called the fox-trot, the article also reported that Mr. Castle explained that it was not really a new dance, "but had been danced by negroes, to his personal knowledge, for fifteen years."[16]

"There is much interest in the growth of the modern dances in the fact that they were all danced and played by us negroes [sic] long before the whites took them up," Europe told a *New York Tribune* reporter sent to interview him in late November.

> One of my own musicians, William Tyres, wrote the first tango in America as far back as the Spanish-American War. It was known as "The Trocha," and a few years afterward he wrote "The Maori." These two tangos are now most popular, yet who heard of them at the time they were written? They were the essentially negro dances, played and danced by negroes alone. The same may be said of the fox-trot, this season the most popular of all dances.

"Mr. Castle has generously given me credit for the fox-trot," he continued, "yet the credit, as I have said, really belongs to Mr. Handy. You see, then, that both the tango and the fox-trot are really negro dances, as is the one-step. The one-step is the national dance of the negro, the negro always walking in his dances."[17]

The extraordinary popularity of the fox-trot, which *Variety* said was being played so much in New York by the end of August that it was in real danger of being worn out, insured that the dance would have a featured place in *Watch Your Step* as the musical finally began rehearsals on October 3, 1914.[18] Most of the cast that Dillingham assembled were vaudevillians, including the Castles, rather than stage actors, but it did not make much difference since there was little in the way of a plot for anyone to follow. Vernon was given a major role that included one number, "the Dancing Instructor," in which he spoofed himself, and Irene simply played Irene, a temptress in a dance hall scene where she danced the fox-trot. The dance fad was expected to draw the crowds initially, but it was Berlin's music that was expected to sell the critics and keep the people coming. Berlin responded with some lively dance numbers, including "Show Us How to do the Fox Trot," "The Syncopated Walk," "The One-Step," and a waltz called "What is Love?" He also wrote several interesting songs, among them "Settle Down in a One-Horse Town" and "A Simple Melody," in which he used two melodies sung in counterpoint for the first time.[19] In view of the situation in Europe and the desire of entertainment-seeking American audiences not to be reminded of it, it may not be surprising that the hit of the show turned out to be an opera scene in which Berlin rewrote a number of familiar arias in ragtime (syncopated) style.

With its ill-fitting mishmash of vaudeville acts and musical drama, *Watch Your Step* took nearly two-and-a-half months of rehearsals and out-of-town trial runs getting in shape for its New York opening at the New Amsterdam Theatre on December 8. In the process, a number of acts and performers were cut from the production, including the comedian, W. C. Fields. James Reese Europe and his orchestra may have been another of the pre-Broadway casualties. According to Douglas Gilbert, when the Castles signed with Dillingham to do the musical they insisted that Europe and Dabney be hired to provide the orchestra for their dance numbers, and although it was "unusual and expensive" Dillingham agreed.[20] Europe does not seem to have ever been offered the position of arranger or musical director for the entire show (those jobs were given to Frank Sadler and DeWitt C. Coolman, respectively), but even had he and his orchestra of black musicians performed just for the dances, it would have constituted a major breakthrough for them and for American musical theater. As it turned out, however (again, according to Gilbert), "a few nights before opening" Europe resigned from the production and the opportunity, if indeed there had been one, was lost. Whatever the accuracy of the Gilbert account, *Watch Your Step* subsequently became the most successful show on Broadway that year, breaking all previous records for receipts at the New Amsterdam Theater and running for 171 performances, a remarkable record "when one considers that from an economic viewpoint the 1914–15 season was the worst the American theatre had known up to that time."[21]

Despite not working together in *Watch Your Step*, Europe and Castles continued to collaborate throughout the fall and winter of 1914. For the second

Tempo Club entertainment at the Manhattan Casino on October 13, the Castles were again a major attraction—as they had been in the spring—and the program (orchestra concert, dance demonstration by the Castles, and a dance competition) followed the previous pattern. Popular interest in the affair, however, was, if anything, greater than before, especially among white New Yorkers.[22] The white press gave the concert broader coverage, applications from whites for boxes exceeded the supply, and "more than 100 whites had to be refused."[23] There were also some modifications in the orchestra and in the concert program that preceded the dancers.

Six months earlier, the official program had referred to Europe's large concert orchestra as the National Negro Orchestra; now, the somewhat smaller (seventy-five member) aggregation was called, for the first time, the Tempo Club Orchestra. There appear to be two reasons for the change. First, Europe's former organization, the Clef Club, was still a large and viable enterprise, and its orchestra (and chorus) under the direction of Tim Brymn was still being called the Clef Club Symphony Orchestra. The instrumentation (dominated by banjos, mandolins, and harp guitars) of the orchestra and the music it performed also continued to reflect the original Europe formula. Moreover, in late September and early October the leaders of both the Clef Club and the Tempo Club had cooperated in a four-day musical benefit (at the Manhattan Casino and in Central Park) called the "Autumn Exposition and Amusement Festival," and the Clef Club Orchestra (which continued to open its concerts with Europe's "Clef Club March") was scheduled to repeat Europe's highly successful 1913 tour of five large Eastern cities in early November.[24] With all of this happening in the fall of 1914, Europe, perhaps, felt that it would be both ungenerous and an insult to the Clef Club to call the orchestra he was planning to use in the Tempo Club entertainment The National Negro Orchestra. His ambitions for a truly national Negro orchestra had not diminished, but they remained inclusive; if such an orchestra were ever to become a reality, he would need the contributions of the many talented musicians who remained loyal to the Clef Club.[25] Another and perhaps more compelling reason for the change of name to the Tempo Club Orchestra was that the program offered at the October 1914 entertainment was almost completely devoted to dance music. Had Europe advertised a concert by the National Negro Orchestra and then produced such a program, the ultimate goals that he entertained for that projected organization would have been undercut in the minds of the critics as well as his potential backers, both white and black. As it was, the only truly concert pieces performed that evening consisted of a violin/cello duet by Leonard Jeter and Felix Weir and a full orchestra rendition of William Tyers' "Admiration: A Negro Idyl." Lucien White, writing in the *New York Age*, was especially taken by the Tyers' piece. Tyers shows, he said, in nearly everything he produces that his ideals are not vitiated by the demand for ragtime and flimsy popular music. While catering to a popular demand he serves it musical food that tends to elevate the taste of the masses, and he is, in no small degree, educating the people to an appreciation of better than ordinary music.[26]

White's comments could easily be transposed to the classic performances of jazz artists of a later period like Louis Armstrong or Duke Ellington, or to the works of George Gershwin, and may offer a fair working definition of what a true "popular artist" really accomplishes.

The remaining selections in the rather abbreviated orchestra program included "Castle Walk," "Same Sort of Girl" by Jerome Kern, a new Europe waltz called "Fiora," "The Fox Trot" by Europe and Dabney and dedicated to the Castles, "Contentment d'Amour," another waltz—this one by Tyers, and "Reminiscent Tunes," apparently a medley of popular pieces from J. Leubrie Hill's Darktown Follies. Europe and Tyers alternated as conductors. White described Europe's waltz as one of his most charming ever, displaying a "wealth of harmony" and a "melody of sweetness and symmetry." White thought the first movement was "particularly beautiful," leaving a "haunting refrain running through one's head." White was also pleased by Europe and Dabney's latest dance creation. "The fox-trot number is a characteristic affair," he wrote, "with the rhythmic and tempting lilt Europe has developed lately, insidiously cajoling one into patting the foot and lifting the shoulder." Europe had recorded both numbers for Victor on October 1, and it is unfortunate that, for some reason, the record company never chose to release them. "Fiora," which Europe dedicated to Mrs. R. W. Hawksworth, was published later in the month by Ricordi, but the nature of Europe's intriguing "Fox Trot" remains a mystery.

Conspicuously absent from the program that evening were any of the usual vaudeville-style comedy or song and dance acts by other members of the club. The official program did list a ragtime quartet led by banjoist Tony Tuck and pianist Charles Mills, who had achieved notable success in England after performing as the Versatile Entertainers Quintet with Europe at the first Carnegie Hall Clef Club Concert in 1912. White, however, makes no mention of them in his lengthy review, and they may not, therefore, have actually appeared.[27] The program, however, did contain a dose of comic novelty employing moving pictures that was received by the audience with "uproarious applause." Following the performance of the Hill medley, the hall was darkened and a film of Europe, Tyers, and Dabney consulting upon "weighty Tempo Club affairs" was projected onto a large screen at the back of the stage. The orchestra, turning to face the screen, then began playing "Castle Walk" under the direction of the film image of Jim Europe. It was, White thought, "the most unique and surprising novelty which has been sprung on a New York audience."

While the audience was still buzzing over the film novelty the Castles emerged, and the orchestra accompanied them in their "most attractive and interesting dances," the fox-trot, the half and half, tango, polka, and one-step. At the conclusion of their exhibition, Mr. Castle, "with words appreciative of the services rendered by Mr. Europe and his orchestra," presented him with a bronze statue of themselves in a characteristic tango pose. Europe, apparently taken by surprise himself, was able to respond to the audience's demand for a speech only by calling "on the orchestra to help him out by playing the 'Castle Walk.'"[28] The amateur dancers then took the floor, the Castle Cups were awarded to the winners, and several hours of general dancing concluded an evening of "the best modern dance music this town has heard in many a moon," one that was "enjoyed to the utmost by the huge audience."[29]

Despite an evident "gay spirit which might be expected from the leaders of negro [sic] society of New York, Washington, and smaller places in between," there was nonetheless a general sense of sadness and loss at the Tempo Club entertainment.[30] Two days earlier, Aida Overton Walker, the leading female figure in black musical theater, had died of kidney failure. An accomplished dancer, actress, singer, and comedienne, Walker had been a major star since her first appearance with John Isham's Octoroons Company in 1895. She had performed since then in many of the major productions of the Black Patti Troubadours, Williams and Walker, Cole and Johnson, and the Smart Set companies, and had worked on numerous occasions with Jim Europe. Europe was a close friend and admirer of Aida Walker, as he had been of her husband, George, before his untimely death, and he felt the loss personally. The funeral, held at St. Phillips Protestant Episcopal Church on October 15, was described by Europe, who served as a pall bearer, as "a house of mourning."[31]

James Reese Europe's professional reputation had never been higher than in the late fall and winter of 1914. In its interview in late November, the *New York Tribune* introduced him to its readers as the Castles' composer and leader of an orchestra that "has all but secured complete control of the cabaret and dance field in the city."[32] Europe agreed. From among the 200 members of the Tempo Club, he said, I now supply "a majority of the orchestras which play in the various cafes of the city and also at the private dances," and the reason for this is that the Negro "is peculiarly fitted for the modern dances." "I don't think it too much to say," he continued, "that he plays this music better than the white man simply because all this music is indigenous with him. Rhythm is something that is born in the negro, and the modern dances require rhythm above all else."

Europe's Society Orchestra continued to supply the music for the dancing instruction at Castle House. In December, when the Castles took over the top floor of the Shuberts' 44th Street Theater for a new dancing cabaret venture (dubbed "Castles in the Air," or simply the "Castle Club"), Europe provided the twenty-piece orchestra they required.[33] He also continued his heavy schedule of society dates, including Marie Louise Wanamaker's debutante ball at the Ritz-Carleton Hotel in Philadelphia and a tea dance for Anne Morgan, Mrs. Vanderbilt, and Elisabeth Marbury at the Strand Theatre roof.[34] One of the most interesting of the Europe ensembles in the field at the end of 1914 was "Europe's Lady Orchestra," under the direction of Marie Lucas, which "headed the bill" at the Lafayette Theatre during December. Marie Lucas, a talented trombone player, was one of the earliest women dance band leaders, and she later headed the house band (under her own name) for some time at the Lafayette.[35]

Europe's popularity with New York society, and his effective organization of the Clef Club and Tempo Club as booking agencies for black musicians in the hotels and cabarets, had also created such serious competition for the formerly segregated Local 310 of the American Federation of Musicians in New York that the union was forced to change its policies. The union had voted earlier in the year to admit black musicians and to modify their standard examination and initiation fee to make it easier for them to join.[36] By the end of November, Europe joined and the Indianapolis *Freeman* reported that he and the union were now at peace, "so much at peace that he advises all musicians aspiring for a place to join the union with him." The newspaper, however, remained a bit skeptical, wanting reassurance that "under Europe, Kildare, Brymn, and Jordan, the colored musicians will retain their hold on Broadway."[37] Sixty years later, the president of the New Amsterdam Musical Association, the oldest black musical organization in the city, was clear about the importance of Jim Europe's role: "James Reese Europe," he stated simply, "was responsible for the sudden change of policy."[38]

These were assuredly positive developments for black performers, but as Europe was quick to point out in the *Tribune* interview, black composers, in particular, still faced substantial inequities in their treatment. "A white man would receive from six to twelve times the royalty" that he could get for his published and recorded compositions, Europe said, even when his music was more popular. "I have done my best to put a stop to this discrimination, but I have found that it was no use. The music world is controlled by a trust, and the negro must submit to its demands or fail to have his compositions produced." "I am not bitter about it," he told the paper philosophically, "it is, after all, but a slight portion of the price my race must pay in its at times almost hopeless fight for a place in the sun. Some day it will be different and justice will prevail."[39]

In the meantime, Europe and the other leaders of New York's black musicians intended to exploit fully the positive aspects of the situation as long as it existed. Over the next two years, until the United States entered the war in the spring of 1917, the demand for black musicians and orchestras to provide popular music for both public and private entertaining, if anything, increased. "This is the hey-day for colored musicians in New York City," reported Salem Tutt Whitney, then with the Smart Set Company, to the Indianapolis *Freeman* in late

May 1915. "Everywhere they are in demand. In fact, the demand is greater than the supply. James Reese Europe, J. Rosamond Johnson, Tim Brymn, and Ford Dabney have many musicians and they are diligently searching for others, real musicians, not fakers or bluffers."[40] The demand was not just at home. Two months earlier, Dan Kildare, president of the Clef Club, had left his position in New York to take an orchestra to Ciros, one of swankiest restaurants in London, where there was now an acute shortage of musicians. By the late spring of 1915, the Clef Club Orchestra was but one member of a contingent of African-American orchestras performing in the city.[41]

In September, a white musician, Eugene de Bueris, became so frustrated that he wrote to the Boston *Globe* complaining that the preference for black musicians (which he could not comprehend) had become so extensive that it "will not be long before the poor white musician will be obliged to blacken his face to make a livelihood or starve."[42] "Why should a famous dancing couple prefer a Negro orchestra for their dancing exhibitions?," he asked. The *New York Age* reprinted his letter with comments by its contributing editor, James Weldon Johnson. Johnson, who conceded that the situation for white musicians was as desperate as de Bueris described, endeavored to enlighten the "poor white musician" as to why it was so.

It might be thought, Johnson said, that black musicians are simply cheaper to hire, but the white musician does not make that claim because he knows it is not so. The fact is that black musicians charge more, and are still preferred, and the reason is that "not only is modern American music a Negro creation, but modern dances are also," so it is only natural "that when it comes to making music for modern dancing, the Negro musician should be the real thing." Indeed, the white musician can play ragtime as well as the Negro, Johnson concluded,

> that is, white musicians can play exactly what is put down on the paper. But Negro musicians are able to put into the music something that can't be put on the paper; a certain abandon which seems to enter in the blood of the dancers; and that is the answer to Mr. de Beuris's question, that is the secret, that is why Negro musicians are preferred.[43]

Jim Europe was, of course, one of those responsible for the "poor white musician's" misery, and he had, in fact, been singled out by de Beuris (though not by name) as a leading culprit. It was natural, then, following continued editorial comment on the matter in the Richmond *Times-Dispatch*, that the *Age* should ask for the devil's own response. "If the Negro musician enjoys any preference at all," Europe told the *Age* at the outset, "he does not enjoy it solely because of his color. In this occupation, as in all other desirable ones here in America, the Negro's color is a handicap; and wherever he achieves success, he does so in the face of doubly severe competition." The basic reason for the black musician's current popularity, Europe said, is due to the fact that he is especially adept at playing modern dance music. He then listed five reasons why he believed this to be so:

1. He [the Negro musician] is a natural musician, and throws himself into the spirit of his work with spontaneous enthusiasm; so that the music rendered by a Negro orchestra rarely has the mechanical quality which is fatal to dancing.
2. He has a superior sense of rhythm, peculiarly adapting him for dance music.
3. The art of playing the modern syncopated music is to him a natural gift.
4. He excels in the use of the guitar, banjo, and mandolin, instruments which are now being generally adopted by orchestras playing dance music to obtain the "thrum-thrum" effect, and the eccentric, accentuated beat, so desirable in dance music; and he was the first to discover the availability of these instruments for such purposes.
5. In addition to his natural talent . . . the modern Negro musician is well trained in his art. He reads readily, memorizes marvelously well, interprets naturally, and not only understands the principles of technique in the use of his instruments, but is remarkably skillful in execution—as is to be expected when one considers that the Negro possesses a rare facility for arts requiring physical skill.

In the past few years, Europe said in conclusion, "a new type of Negro musician has appeared," who combines a natural talent with "the serious study of his music," and in doing so has "contributed to American music whatever distinctive quality it possesses." It should not be surprising, therefore, that he should "interpret this music best."[44]

The president of New York's Tempo Club was in a fair position to know what he was talking about. In early 1915, Europe had complied with a request from William Morris of the New York Theatre Roof Garden for a dance orchestra that might rival Dabney's at the Amsterdam Theatre and the Castle's at the 44th Street Theatre Roof. On the evening of February 12, Europe himself directed three different orchestras at the New York Theatre (now called the "Jardin de Danse") in accompanying a twenty-five member dance chorus plus M. Albert and Mlle. Samya, Morris' featured dancers. Morris was so eager for a Europe orchestra that he permitted Europe to present a group called the "Emancipation Band," all of whose members, of course, were taken from the Tempo Club.[45] Whatever the competition between club owners or the dancing teams, Europe found himself in a no-lose situation; the Tempo Club was responsible for all of the orchestras. At the end of February, Morris challenged the Castles to a contest with his dancers for a $5,000 prize. The Castles were unwilling to risk their reputation on anything so silly, so they countered (perhaps after consulting Europe) with a proposal that the drummers of the two orchestras compete. *Variety*, in reporting the story, had a little difficulty figuring it out. William Morris's "colored drummer in the European orchestra at the New York Roof is called 'Battleaxe' [Carl Kenny]. Europe's Orchestra on the 44th Street Roof, where the Castles dance, has a drummer petitely known as 'Buddy' [Gilmore]." This was not the contest Morris wanted and refused to go along, so the Castles (and Jim Europe) got a substitute and held the contest anyway. To no one's surprise, the announced winner was Buddy Gilmore.[46]

Popular interest in the drums and in drummers had naturally increased with the popularity of social dancing and with the evolution of the role of the trap drummer in the dance orchestra. This interest was especially strong within the black community, and so Europe included a true drum contest, perhaps the first public event of its kind, in the spring Tempo Club entertainment at the Manhattan Casino. This time Gilmore and Kenny did perform against each other, but, according to the reports in the *New York Age*, the audience judged Si Moore, a third competitor, "the most fancy drummer."[47] A fourth percussionist (not competing), Vernon Castle, also favored the audience with a solo, but he was present primarily for other purposes—to give a dancing demonstration with his wife and to award the Castle Cups in the dance contest. The April 22 entertainment is notable for another reason; it was the first of such events with which Europe had been associated that did not include a formal, more or less serious, concert program. Perhaps the people who came that evening to enjoy "dancing from the time you arrive to the time you leave" and to hear the "great Tempo Club orchestra" furnish "one dance number after another," like those who flocked to see *Watch Your Step* that season, sought light-hearted distraction from the mounting uneasiness produced by the bleak reports from the Continent.

The war in Europe had not ended quickly, as most Americans expected; instead, it had settled into a bloody war of attrition with the two opposing armies dug in and facing each other in a nightmare called trench warfare. When Germany announced a submarine blockade of the British Isles in February, concerns about the ability of the American government to maintain its policy of neutrality grew dramatically, and when, on May 7, 1915, the British luxury liner *Lusitania* was sunk with a loss of 1,200 people, including 128 Americans, the country was shocked by the horror of a new kind of war in which civilians, including women and children, could be killed just as easily as combatants.

If one of the effects of the war prior to 1917 was to create a boon for black popular entertainers and dance musicians, the war years proved to be anything but beneficial for American symphonic and concert performers (both black and white). German music and musical practice, heretofore the acknowledged standard for concert artists, became increasingly unpopular, and the private funds upon which concert musicians and educators, white and black, depended, became increasingly difficult to acquire. One of the unfortunate casualties of this war-born situation was the Music School Settlement for Colored People in Harlem.

Just six months earlier, in the fall of 1914, prospects for the three-year-old music school had seemed bright. A new and larger building had been acquired at 4–6 West 131st Street, and the widely known and admired J. Rosamond Johnson had agreed to become the new resident supervisor of music. For the school's spring 1915 concert at Carnegie Hall, Johnson concentrated his efforts on developing a 160-member choral group (The Music School Choral Society) and a glee club to perform a program devoted primarily to vocal arrangements or adaptations of spirituals and to conclude with "Hiawatha's Wedding Feast" from Samuel Coleridge-Taylor's cantata *Hiawatha*. As in the past three Carnegie Hall concerts, James Reese Europe was expected to direct the orchestra, but barely two weeks before the performance, scheduled for April 12, Europe, his assistant conductor William Tyers, and the Tempo Club Orchestra withdrew, and Johnson had to replace them with the New Amsterdam Orchestra, a primarily dance-oriented ensemble.[48]

The incident is especially curious because on Sunday afternoon, March 28, Europe, Dabney, Tyers, and the seventy-member Tempo Club Orchestra had collaborated with Johnson and his pupils from the Music School in a successful benefit concert for the Howard Orphanage at the Lafayette Theatre.[49] It is possible that Europe, or Europe and his associates at the Tempo Club, were displeased with the subordinate role offered them on the Carnegie Hall program. It is also possible, though less likely, that Europe and Tyers found it impossible to convince their instrumentalists to take sufficient time from their lucrative dance jobs to properly rehearse for the concert. Europe, however, had faced the latter problem many times before. Given Europe's commitment to the objectives of the school, and his active participation since its founding, his actions suggest a deeper level of unhappiness with the general direction being taken by the school's administrators.

From the very first, apparently, Jim Europe, like many of the other black leaders who supported and contributed to the Music School Settlement, believed that "to foster the pride of the Negro people it was absolutely necessary that Negroes assume control of the school as quickly as possible."[50] Europe had warned his friend David Mannes that he and the other principal white backers (Natalie Curtis, George Peabody, Elbridge Adams, etc.) should understand this and be prepared to relinquish their control when the financial situation of the school permitted it. Johnson and the black members of the board of directors apparently decided that the time was right for them to take over both the school and the program for the April 1915 Carnegie Hall concert, and they acted quickly, perhaps even precipitously. Mannes's biographer suggests that the "ousting of the white philanthropists was done hastily and arrogantly," although Mannes himself never expressed such an opinion.[51]

Europe, who "had a business experience and skill very rare at the time among Negroes," and who "understood the problems of raising money to sustain a school" that "most other Negro musicians did not," was not consulted.[52] Europe also understood the public temper of the times, and had he been asked, he would not have recommended a program of African-American music for the 1915 Carnegie Hall concert, which was only classically oriented, especially one in which the major work selected for performance was by Coleridge-Taylor, a composer whose works Europe had on more than one occasion described as "not real Negro work."[53] Without white support, the school would be dependent upon the black community, most of whose members at that time, Europe knew from experience, were more enthusiastic about the current dance music (which he considered essentially African-American) than the spirituals or classics.

The April 12, 1915, Carnegie Hall concert was well-attended and received broad and sympathetic coverage by the New York press. Johnson was congratulated for his "earnest intent, hard work and real interest in music," and for presenting much "that was striking and suggestive of the significance and possibilities of the Colored Settlement's work."[54] Several individual soloists were also singled out for praise: pianist Ethel Richardson for her performance of Liszt's "Hungarian Rhapsody No. 3," and a young Boston tenor named Roland Hayes for his singing of works by Johnson, Coleridge-Taylor, and Harry T. Burleigh.[55] There were, however, some serious problems, especially with the orchestra, and Johnson felt compelled to explain to the audience that he had only been able to hold rehearsals for two weeks. Deficiencies in the concert aside, diminishing contributions due to concerns about the war, the lack of broad-based black support, and the consequences of decisions made that spring almost immediately led the school into financial difficulties, and barely six months later it closed. For David Mannes "undoubtedly, its failure was the greatest disappointment of his life," yet his only public response was that "our school came into life at least twenty years too soon."[56]

Another effective casualty of the continuing war in Europe during the early summer of 1915 was the partnership between Jim Europe and the Castles. As early as the previous fall, Vernon Castle had expressed to his wife his feeling of responsibility toward his homeland, and he often remained up late at night after their performances to read the latest news of the war. He had remained with *Watch Your Step* throughout its New York run until the late spring, but after the musical closed on Broadway and commenced its summer road tour, his sense of loyalty to England during the increasingly difficult crisis demanded that he volunteer for service. "Until the great war broke out," he later told a New York paper, "I almost imagined that I was an American. I had been here nearly ten years and all my friends, all my interests, were American," but "when the war came I could not forget that I was an Englishman."[57]

Given his celebrity stature, the British army would have been happy to use Castle as an entertainer, but, perhaps (as Irene believed) because he was a dancer, he felt his masculinity might be questioned if he accepted a noncombat role.[58] If he was to serve his native country he would to do so as a soldier at the front. Castle remained with *Watch Your Step* through its run in

Chicago and Boston, and then, having informed Dillingham of his decision, he left the production to obtain his pilot's license at Newport News, Virginia.

Like the submarine and the machine gun, the airplane was one of the new technologies that received its first widespread application to warfare during World War I. The planes themselves were flimsy and unreliable, and because they lacked even the most rudimentary navigational instruments, flying them took great personal courage and considerable athletic ability. It was also dangerous; aviators in the Great War had a life expectancy of less than a month. Although few military leaders then recognized the potential of the airplane as an offensive weapon, they were considered valuable for reconnaissance purposes, a role that placed both pilot and aircraft in extremely vulnerable circumstances. The result was that there was never a sufficient number of qualified pilots to meet the demand. Castle knew, therefore, that if he had his license when he enlisted he would immediately receive a commission in the Royal Air Force and be sent to the battlefront in France. He did not know when he and Irene danced at the Tempo Club entertainment in Harlem at the end of April, however, that it would be their last time to dance together to the music of Jim Europe's orchestra.

10

"The Rat-A-Tat Drummer Boy"

> What is the truth that rises stark naked from out [of] all the savagery and brutality of this war? It is the fact that twentieth century civilization, the so-called white man's civilization, is nothing more than a thin veneer, and underneath this thin veneer is the same cruel barbarism that Caesar found two thousand years ago.
>
> James Weldon Johnson (1916)

With Irene Castle on tour in *Watch Your Step* and Vernon Castle undergoing flight training in Virginia, the Tempo Club was forced to do without its headliners for the club's semi-annual entertainment in the fall of 1915. The war in Europe, now in its second year, no longer seemed so far removed, and Americans were beginning to feel nervous. Reverberations from the *Lusitania* tragedy coupled with a developing crisis in Latin America and Mexico had strengthened groups like the National Security League, which pressed for a shift in American policy from passive neutrality toward active preparation for war. While most Americans did not believe that "preparedness" ultimately meant involvement in the European conflict for their country, neither were they by the fall of 1915 feeling quite so comfortably secure in their isolation. In view of this general situation, and in the absence of their star attractions, Europe, Dabney, and Tyers decided simply to hold a dance at the Manhattan Casino on October 12, called "The Harvest Ball," at which the Tempo Club Orchestra provided music for general dancing and for a dance contest (the winners received a Castle Cup "Donated by Mr. and Mrs. Vernon Castle").[1] No formal orchestra concert, no vaudeville-style acts, no drum contests, nor any special "surprise" features seem to have been scheduled.

Despite the increasingly tense psychological climate, the fall of 1915 did witness the debut of one of the most highly anticipated and ambitious black musical comedies of the previous five-year period. Lester Walton, the show's organizer and producer, had been working feverishly for more than a year to put together a production that could launch "a new era for the colored musical show, which has not enjoyed the widespread popularity of former years since the passing away of the Williams and Walker, Cole and Johnson, and Ernest Hogan Companies."[2] He had most of the pieces in place by early September (with the exception of the show's title, the preliminary name of which was *Way Down South*). Both Will Marion Cook and James Reese Europe were reported to have contributed the music, Henry Creamer the lyrics, Jesse Shipp the staging, and Henry Troy the book. An impressive cast had also been assembled that included Flournoy Miller and Aubrey Lyles, Abbie Mitchell, Fannie Wise, Opal Cooper, Will Cooke, Ida Forsyne, DeKoven Thompson, and perhaps a dozen others whose names were familiar to followers of black musical theater and vaudeville—"truly the most representative group of theatrical geniuses of which the Negro race of the world can boast."[3]

Citing the Smart Set Company's *George Washington Bullion Abroad*, Will Vodery's recent contributions to Ziegfeld's "Follies," and the popularity of Alex Rogers' and Luckey Roberts' new song for Nora Bayes ("a headliner on the big time"), Walton believed that he sensed "a spirit of optimism" pervading "colored theatrical circles that has been missing since the days of Williams and Walker."[4] The chief evidence for this "Negro Renaissance," of course, was Walton's own production, now renamed *Darkydom*, which he was certain would be "a sensation on Broadway before many weeks have passed."[5]

The most impressive feature of *Darkydom*, perhaps, was the sheer size of the participating cast and the elaborate costumes and sets. The central scene of action for the two-act play, the picturesque black township of Mount Bayou, Mississippi, offered "untold opportunities to a playwright in depicting Negro life in both its gay and its somber aspects," and the time was set in the present.[6] The extensive musical score, largely composed by Cook, included three major choral productions ("All Kinds of People Make a Town," "Live and Die in Dixie Land," and "Bamboula") and more than seventeen song and dance numbers ranging in style and theme from the contemporary novelty ("Scaddle de Mooche"—a take-off on the tango fad—and "Rat a Tat"—featuring a female drummer and drill team) to the love song ("My Lady's Lips") to the sentimental "Southern" ballad ("Mammy," "Magnolia Time") to the burlesque ("Keep Off the Grass," "Chop Suey Sue").[7] The rather thin plot of the musical involves the antics of two tramps who inadvertently prevent a serious railroad collision. The president of the railroad, who was aboard one of the trains, sends his valet to find the pair to reward them. The tramps, however, believe they are being pursued in order to be arrested.

After an initial shakedown performance in New Jersey, *Darkydom* opened in Washington, D.C. at the Howard Theatre on Monday, October 18. R. W. Thompson, who reviewed the premier for the Indianapolis *Freeman*, described the evening as a distinct success. An expectant and "brilliant audience, embracing the wealth, culture and beauty of this cosmopolitan city," he wrote, heartily applauded an "aggregate of leaders in the firmament of Negro theatricals" such as has never "before been gathered together on a single stage."[8] However, despite good performances by the individual stars, "gorgeous" costumes, "fairyland" sets, and Will Marion Cook's energetic conducting ("Mr. James Reese Europe comes home today to lead the orchestra for the remainder of the local engagement," Thompson informed his readers), not all was right with the big production.

For one thing, there was an apparent problem of dramatic coherence. With so many major performers, each of whom required an opportunity on center stage, the show seemed like a string of climaxes, and the story, weak as it was anyway, was lost. In trying to bring together as many of the leading names in black stage as possible and giving them all a chance to perform, Walton had succeeded in creating essentially a very high-class and entertaining vaudeville production. This, however, was not what Thompson had anticipated seeing, for he had expected something new—something closer to a play about African-American life whose plot is carried forward through music and dance, and the disappointment in his review is apparent.

The producers of *Darkydom* who wanted to see black productions returned to the prestigious and high-paying Broadway theaters, devised the show too much, perhaps, with the singular object of giving white audiences what they had been used to—comic burlesque and vaudeville. "The show is said to be built largely to attract white patronage," reported the *Freeman*, "and its bookings, it is said, will be in white houses of the standard type."[9] Black audiences had been accustomed to such accommodations, of stooping in order to conquer, but times had changed, and what was more or less acceptable ten or even five years before now seemed unnecessary and even objectionable. Beginning with the first performance in Washington, the title of the show became the focus of such sentiments. "If the management consults the wishes of the masses of the colored patrons of the show they will select a title that will convey the idea that it is a genuine Negro entertainment without using a term that is banned by polite society," Thompson advised in his review of opening night.[10]

Darkydom, name unchanged, completed a well-attended week's engagement in Washington and moved on to the Lafayette Theatre in New York where personal invitations had been sent to Mrs. William K. Vanderbilt and other members of the 400 for opening night on October 25.[11] Despite considerable interest shown by white producers, writers, and a number of New York's high society, the production failed to attract the support it needed to survive, and the much hoped for "renaissance" of black musicals on Broadway never materialized.[12]

In retrospect, *Darkydom* may be seen as a "passing of the torch from the old generation to the new one" in that it was the last musical to which Will Marion Cook, among several others, would contribute. It was also the first musical comedy to feature Miller and Lyles, who later became major stars in the 1920s.[13] Aside from the personalities, however, as a musical production *Darkydom* was less a transition than an ending—the last installment of a chapter in black theater that began in 1898 with Bob Cole's *A Trip to Coontown*, the first musical to break clear from the minstrel tradition. The style and pattern of *Darkydom* (symbolized in the name itself) was, by 1915, simply passé; little if anything from it was passed forward. The show failed to live up to its expectations because, unlike *A Trip to Coontown*, *Darkydom* had nothing new to offer. In addition, the show's subtitle—"a medley of mirth, melody, and measured motions"—seems particularly frivolous and out of touch.

Jim Europe, given his commitment to dignifying and advancing African-American artistry, could not have been greatly surprised by *Darkydom*'s failure. This perhaps helps explain why his artistic contribution to the musical consisted of little more than alternating conducting duties with Cook. The week before *Darkydom* began its run in Washington, D.C., the featured performers at Howard Theatre's Sunday "supper show" were Noble Sissle and Eubie Blake, the two individuals who would become the closest of Europe's professional and personal associates during the last three years of his life.[14] Sissle and Blake would also, with Europe's inspiration, be the two most responsible for initiating, after his death, the next major chapter in the history of black musical theater in America.

Noble Lee Sissle was born on July 10, 1889, in Indianapolis, Indiana.[15] His father, the Reverend George A. Sissle, a Methodist minister, was born in Lexington, Kentucky, as was Sissle's mother, Martha Angeline Sissle, a school teacher and juvenile probation officer. Sissle was brought up in a fairly strict religious environment, absorbing the music from his father's church and learning the importance of precise diction from his mother. When the Sissles moved to Cleveland in 1906, Noble was enrolled in Central High School, where he encountered little racial prejudice, even though he was one of only six black students. He played baseball and football, and by his senior year became the leader of the glee club and elected class vocalist. There were hopes that he would enter the ministry, but by the time of his graduation Sissle had already begun to establish a local reputation as a singer and to appear professionally on the Chautauqua evangelical circuit.[16] Later, with Hann's Jubilee Singers, he traveled as far east as New York City and as far west as Denver.

In the spring of 1913, following the death of his father, Sissle returned to the family home in Indianapolis and entered De Pauw University in Greencastle, Indiana, on scholarship. He transferred to Butler University in Indianapolis in January 1914 "where he wrote parodies for the football games and sang, with a megaphone, in a local movie house frequented by Butler students."[17] By that time the dance craze spread by the Castles had created a demand for black entertainers "all over the state," and Sissle was hired as the vocalist for a local orchestra playing for students on the weekends. "The college kids were dancing till dawn, and I could dance around among them on the floor with my yell master's megaphone and whoop up the dancers," he remembered.[18] Early in 1915, he was asked by the manager of the Severin Hotel in Indianapolis, who had recently returned from New York where he had been impressed by the popularity of black entertainers in the hotels and cabarets, to organize an orchestra of black musicians on the New York model.[19] Setting aside his plans for the ministry, Sissle put together a twelve-piece string orchestra that performed successfully at the Severin until the late spring when he was offered a summer job with Joe Porter's Serenaders at River View Park in Baltimore.[20] Among the Serenaders' personnel was a talented pianist/composer, whose full name was James Hubert Blake, but who was called "Eubie" by everyone.

Nearly six-and-a-half years older than Sissle, Eubie Blake grew up in a vastly different world from that of his future partner. Both his father, John Sumner Blake, a stevedore and Civil War veteran, and his mother, Emily Johnston Blake, a laundress and devout Baptist, were former slaves.[21] Out of eleven children born to the couple, only Eubie lived past infancy. The Blake neighborhood in East Baltimore into which he was born was a rough one where a youngster had to learn to use his wits and his fists, often against whites, to survive. His interest in music surfaced early, and he was allowed to play "godly music" on the family organ and to take piano lessons from the organist at his mother's church. He also listened to the syncopated music of the period, the ragtime, coming from the bars and pool halls and bawdy houses (he thought the spelling was "body house" at the time), and he saw how much respect and admiration (especially from younger women) was accorded that first colorful generation of rag-pianists. By the time he was fifteen, he had heard Jesse Pickett play his "Dream Rag," with its sexy tango bass; he had been expelled from school for fighting over a girl; and his mother had resigned herself to her son's lost soul. He also found his first regular job as pianist at Agnes Sheldon's $5.00 sporting house.[22]

Blake remained at Sheldon's until 1901 when he went on the road with a minor touring group and later played various temporary jobs in New York and Baltimore. In 1907, he was hired by the Goldfield Hotel in Baltimore (a high-style establishment built by lightweight boxing champion, Joe Gans—whom Eubie had known in school). For the next eight years he alternated winter seasons at the Goldfield and summers in Atlantic City, playing such colorful resorts as the Boathouse and the Bucket of Blood. During these years, the dapper "Professor" Blake met and competed with some of the best-known pianists in the East, including One-Leg Willie Joseph, Luckey Roberts, Willie "The Lion" Smith, and a spindly youngster named James P. Johnson.

In addition to developing his technical abilities as a pianist and accompanist, Blake also continued to grow as a composer and writer. He later credited Franz Lehar and the English composer Leslie Stuart, whose light opera *Florodora* remained his favorite, for opening his ears to an expanded harmonic and melodic vocabulary. Another influence was Avis Lee, an accomplished classical pianist and "one of the ten most beautiful girls in Baltimore," whom Blake married in 1910.[23] Blake had written his first important piece, "Charleston Rag," in 1899, the same year as Scott Joplin's sensational "Maple Leaf Rag." By 1914, his first published rags—"Chevy Chase" and "Fizz Water"—had appeared thanks to an introduction provided by Luckey Roberts to publisher Joseph Stern. In the spring of 1915, when Sissle joined Joe Porter's Serenaders, Blake was looking for a lyricist to collaborate in writing popular songs. "Sissle," Blake recalled, "was a real square. A goody-goody. He never wanted to do nothin'," but he possessed a clear tenor voice, good diction, and a command of the language.[24] It was enough; the unlikely pair formed a musical partnership that lasted almost half a century.

As a songwriting team, Sissle and Blake started quickly. Their first effort, written only a few days after they met, was called "It's All Your Fault." The legendary Sophie Tucker was then appearing at the Maryland Theatre in Baltimore, where Sissle and Blake wrangled an audition and performed it for her. Tucker liked the song and incorporated into her act, and Sissle and Blake were on their way. After the Serenaders disbanded at the end of the summer, Sissle signed with Bob Young's sextet at the Hotel Kernan in Baltimore. In December he left with the group for Florida, where they were hired by the Royal Poinciana in Palm Beach.[25] Just prior to this, Blake and Sissle had a second song, "Have a Good Time, Everybody," picked up by Sophie Tucker, and their rising reputation led to the appearance at the Howard Theatre in Washington, D.C., in the first week of October.[26]

Playing with Young's group in Palm Beach during the winter of 1915–1916, Sissle got his first opportunity to perform before America's high society—the Astors, Warburtons, Harrimans, and Wanamakers—who regularly spent part of the winter season in the South. The Young orchestra was also featured with singer Nora Bayes in a benefit that the popular songstress had organized for the Red Cross. In early 1916, E. F. Albee, head of the Keith vaudeville circuit (who had seen the show), brought Bayes and the Young sextet, with vocalist Noble Sissle, to New York City to appear in a "Palm Beach Week" at his Palace Theatre.[27] At the end of the week's show at the Palace, Sissle brought a letter of introduction he had been given by socialite Mary Brown Warburton to James Reese Europe, and Europe, knowing that the Warburtons and his long-time patrons, the Wanamakers, were close friends, immediately offered Sissle a job with one of the society orchestras. Sissle also persuaded Europe to find a position for his partner, and Eubie Blake came north to join the Europe organization.

As performers, both Sissle and Blake fit the Europe model of the black professional entertainer perfectly. Sissle, as described by the *Freeman* in March 1916, always "appears in 'straight' dress—never resorts to slap-stick stuff," and his appeal "is to the higher senses" while adding "a bit of comedy relish to his numbers." Blake's ability as a pianist and composer, the paper added, has already "set a new pace in instrumental productions," and together the pair provides "an incentive to those in and out of the business to strive for nobler and higher ends in the art of 'holding the mirror up to nature' for the edification of mankind."[28] Furthermore, Sissle—perhaps to a greater degree than his partner—and Blake both had experience performing and writing for whites, and they both understood how to please them without demeaning their own personal or professional dignity.[29] Like Europe, they were capable of appealing to both black and white audiences because, as Blake said, "we were exposed to it all. It was all part of our heritage."[30]

Of course, James Reese Europe had been successfully cultivating Eastern high society for a number of years; therefore, it was not a difficult matter for Sissle and Blake to adjust to his system and to become two of his closest and most trusted associates. It also did not take long for them to appreciate the larger goals of the Europe strategy, such as his dream of establishing a permanent National Negro Orchestra, which he had been committed to since the early days of the Clef Club. Europe told Sissle in early 1916 that the reason why such an orchestra had not yet been created, despite his best efforts, was not that the country lacked the requisite number and quality of black musicians to fill such an orchestra, nor the composers capable of writing authentically African-American works for it. The basic problem was locating the financial backing required to support seventy-five musicians for an estimated three months of rehearsals and preparation. "I would never come before the public with a musical organization that I was not positive would be a revelation and a credit to the race," Sissle remembered Europe saying, "because it would hurt the race, and set it back in the minds of the world more than anything else inasmuch as any race's progress is rated by its artistic attainments."[31]

The prospects for finding an individual or a group of individuals able and willing to provide the needed backing for a National Negro Orchestra in the spring of 1916, however, did not appear bright. Nor was it likely, in light of the recent disappointment of *Darkydom* and the depressed state of the American musical stage generally, that adequate backing could be found to underwrite Europe's other long-term ambition of producing a true African-American Broadway musical.[32] Even if the war in Europe were to be settled somehow and opportunities improved, neither of these goals could possibly be realized in the foreseeable future, Europe told them, without the support of the wealthy. It was Europe's plan, therefore, to keep black musicians performing for the rich, in their homes and at their private parties and entertainments, so that when the time came, the people of means would know and trust him and he could expect a sympathetic hearing for his larger ambitions. "We were very lucky, Bill," Blake later told William Bolcom, "that we were with a master thinker, James Reese Europe."[33] "My God, he could see around corners. He could always figure out what was going to happen and be prepared for it. And he knew how to make a plan and stick to it."[34]

During the spring and into the summer of 1916, there were often as many as fifteen different Europe orchestras in the field at the same time. Europe, himself, seldom played piano or his violin any longer, but he did—because his patrons demanded it—always attempt to make a personal appearance. "He had so many orchestras," Sissle (who had during this time become Europe's assistant business manager) recalled, that

> every night I would accompany him around from one place to the other and by the time we visited every place, the night was gone. On several nights, he would have so many different places that I would have to visit some of the places, and try to make excuses for his non-appearance, a duty I dreaded because it was never satisfactory—everybody wanted "Jim."[35]

Blake, who had been promoted to an assistant orchestra leader from his first Europe job as a solo pianist, described the standard procedure. Europe would walk up to where the orchestra was, bow to the audience, and turn to the drummer. "All right, all right, Buddy—Buddy was the drummer—all right, let's go—all right. He'd take the stick—bing—downbeat—and hand the stick to me and he'd go out and sit with the millionaires' guests."[36]

Europe's musicians were well-treated and well-paid, Blake recalled, sometimes earning as much as $50 a date (the musicians' term *gig* for an engagement was invented by Europe, according to Blake), but they still found themselves having to make subtle compromises to their audience's preconceptions.[37] One of these, particularly galling to Blake, who with difficulty had taught himself, was pretending not to be able to read music. "Now the white bands all had their music stands, see," he told Rose, "but the people wanted to believe that Negroes couldn't learn to read music but had a natural talent for it. So we never played with no music." "I'd get all the latest Broadway music from the publisher, and we'd learn the tunes and rehearse 'em until we had 'em all down pat. Never made no mistakes." "All the high-tone, big-time folks would say, 'Isn't it wonderful how these untrained, primitive musicians can pick up all the latest songs instantly without being able to read music?'" Among those "primitive musicians" were Elliot Carpenter, William Grant Still, and Russell Smith.[38] The truth was that the "Europe gang were absolute reading sharks. They could read a moving snake and if a fly lit on that paper he got played," Eubie maintained.[39] The one possibly positive outcome of this, from the standpoint of the central importance of improvisation to jazz, is that by not having the music in front of them the musicians may have felt more freedom to interpret the actual score. "Of course," Blake admitted, "I'd always leave room for a little fakin,' and them guys that could fake, they did it."[40]

When they played private engagements for the Goulds, Vanderbilts, Schwabs, and Wanamakers, Europe's musicians also confronted other forms of the same sort of treatment. "We went into palaces," Blake remembered, "but never by the front door. We didn't use the regular Steinway, either. It was

locked up and covered with velvet and flowers that said 'Keep off the grass,'"
but we "gave them better music than any ofay ork could have played."[41]

In his instructions as well as by his own example, Europe tried to convince
his musicians not to react to the subtle insults they sometimes experienced.
One night, after they had been playing all evening for the Wanamakers, and all
the guests had finished eating, Europe asked the Wanamaker's butler, who happened to be black, to see about finding some food for the orchestra. "Now, the
butler," Blake recalled,

> he thinks he ain't like other Negroes. He don't like it when Jim complains. But
> anyway, in a little while they tell us to sit down at a table in this big room, and a
> waiter brings in this big china thing they use for soup, and he serves us all. I can't
> wait now, see—we're all dyin' from hunger. Now we grab our spoons and as soon
> as I tasted this stuff, I had to spit it out. And I see everybody else is doin' the same
> thing. This stuff, I'm still sure, is the water they washed the dishes in—soap, every-
> thing. And it's because the butler is mad, see. He don't like no colored people to
> complain. But Europe—I see Europe is eatin' the stuff just like it's soup, he don't
> pay it no mind, just keeps eatin'! My God, I thought, that Europe will eat anything.
> Now everybody else is watchin' him too, see. It ain't just me. I realize Jim Europe
> didn't get where he is with the white folks by complainin'. At home or in the White
> House, it was all the same to him. You couldn't make him mad.[42]

There was actually one thing that could get the Tempo Club's leader
extremely upset and that was when the behavior of one of the musicians threatened the reputation of the organization. Blake recalled such an incident when
he, Sissle, Europe, and a band of twenty musicians were hired to play for a yacht
trip from Atlantic City to Maine. Carl Cook, a performer not a part of the original group, stowed away, and when he was discovered Eubie convinced Europe to
let him stay and to do a number for the guests. Later, while Cook was doing his
imitation of Bert Williams, he suddenly "reached over, pulled an expensive
panama hat off one of the men's heads, and put it on his own head." "The crowd
was silent and the hat's owner," after Cook replaced it, "without a word, removed
his hat and threw it into the water. After an awkward moment everyone applauded, and the man . . . even gave Cook some money." When Europe, who had
been below decks at the time, heard about it, he was furious.[43]

There were other occasions when even his orchestra leaders caused him
problems. John Europe, James' brother, an excellent pianist and leader of the
popular Europe orchestra featured at the Copley Plaza Hotel in Boston, was
what would now be called a "binge drinker," someone whose abuse of alcohol
is irregular but (when it occurs) is so serious as to be debilitating. When John
went on one of his "drinking sprees," neither his brother nor anyone else could
control him, so Jim would call Eubie or one of the other pianists, pull him off
whatever job he was on, and send him immediately to Boston to cover for John
until he decided to sober up.[44] The procedure apparently worked well—well

enough, at least, that the managers of the Plaza in mid-November 1916 rehired the Europe orchestra for a second year.[45]

Although Europe's professional association with the Castles was, at least for the time being, put on hold, their personal relationship continued throughout 1916. In December 1915, when promoter Charles Dillingham brought the Castles to New York (Vernon from Virginia after completing his pilot's training and Irene from Pittsburgh where *Watch Your Step* was playing) to give a single "farewell dance" at the huge Hippodrome on 6th Avenue, the Castles joined Europe for an evening of vaudeville at the Lafayette Theatre in Harlem.[46] John Philip Sousa was the previously scheduled headliner at the Hippodrome for the following month when Dillingham arranged the Castle farewell appearance, and so probably for contractual reasons, the Sousa band rather than Europe's provided the Castles' accompaniment. Sousa was not their choice, and in spite of the popular success of the show (the crowd—estimated at 5,000 people—was so large at the first Sunday evening that a second "farewell" was held the following week), the Castle's were not pleased with the March King's mechanical accompaniment. "He ignored our frantic signals to pick up the tempo and his uniformed arms flailed away with the precise beat of a man conducting a military march, which was exactly what he was doing," Irene remembered. "I was boiling mad. I could have kicked him."[47]

Immediately following their appearance in New York, Vernon Castle left for England to join the R.A.F. for fighter training, and Irene returned to *Watch Your Step* until it closed in May. In February, Vernon wrote to his wife telling her of his discovery of some of the members of their old band in London, including Tuck and Johnson, and that they played "all our old favorites" bringing "tears to my eyes."[48] When she joined him in May and the Castles were persuaded to dance a benefit at the Drury Lane Theatre before the Queen, they chose their own accompanists. The result, because "we were so accustomed to the music of Negro musicians and they understood dance music thoroughly," was much better. "We never got a chance to rehearse on the stage," Irene recalled. "All we had time to do was to hum over a few tunes to our colored friends of the orchestra and to instruct them to watch and follow us closely. They were accustomed to doing this, and that part of our work was easy." "We forgot even the Queen Mother and danced as we had never danced before."[49]

After meeting and dancing in London in May, Vernon was awarded his commission and sent to the battlefront in France, and Irene accepted an offer from William Randolph Hearst to star in a pro-preparedness (and anti-German) motion picture serial for Pathé, called *Patria*. Even without the Castles themselves, the Castle name retained its popular appeal among New Yorkers, and the last of Europe's Castle orchestras—his "Castles in the Air Band"—continued to be much in demand.[50] In the fall of 1916, while Vernon was still serving in France, Irene Castle agreed to help Europe and the Tempo Club by appearing at the club's October entertainment at the Manhattan Casino. The Tempo Club had recently moved from its former location at 119 West 136th Street to the now empty Music School Settlement building at 4–6 West 131st Street and was sorely in need of funds to equip its new headquarters.[51] As with the several previous Tempo Club affairs, the last of which was held on May 2, the October 12 entertainment was devoted primarily to general dancing. Europe, Tyers, and Dabney (then completing his third year as leader of the orchestra for Ziegfeld's Midnight Frolics at the New Amsterdam Theatre) conducted the orchestra briefly. The Royal Hawaiians—an act from Ziegfeld's Follies of 1916—also performed, but the main attraction was Mrs. Vernon Castle's "first public appearance since Mr. Castle left for the European War." With her husband "now somewhere in France in the British Aviation Corps," Irene was not asked to dance, herself, but she did present the prize cup to the winning couples in the dance contest, and her presence did help to insure a large turn-out.[52] "All of colored New York met themselves at the great TEMPO CLUB entertainment last Thursday evening, at Manhattan Casino," reported the *Freeman*.[53] In a letter to his wife in November, Vernon indicated his support for her continuing loyalty to their former partner. "I'm pleased," he wrote, "to hear that Jim Europe's show was a success and that your decision [to appear] was a popular one."[54] It was also the last time that either Castle would appear with Jim Europe in public.

Although it was as active a year for Europe as an organizer and manager of musicians as any he had experienced, 1916 was not one of his most accomplished in strictly musical terms. There were no major concerts by the large symphony orchestras, and, in fact, his appearance as a conductor even of dance orchestras was rare. For the first time in over ten years, he seems not to have been involved in some capacity with the musical stage, and his published compositions consisted of a single piece, "Hilo: Hawaiian Waltz," compared with nearly twenty published the preceding year. There was the debut toward the end of October of the "Europe Double Quintet," featuring Noble Sissle and several other Tempo Club musicians, that was advertised as a novelty and did experience some success as a vaudeville act at the Lafayette Theatre and at Keith's Harlem Opera House.[55] The Double Quintet, whose inspiration was undoubtedly the singing/playing Memphis Students of 1905, however, did not introduce much that was new musically.

For Jim Europe as well as for most other professional musicians and entertainers, white as well as black (with the possible exception of those working in the film industry), 1916 was not a good year to invest in new projects or undertake new risks. Beginning in March when President Wilson sent American troops into Mexico after "Poncho" Villa's raiders—and despite the president's bid for reelection on the basis of having "kept us out of war"—the likelihood of the United States being drawn into international conflict either in Europe or North America continued to increase. By the fall, concerns about war and what it might mean for individual Americans and groups with old-world loyalties ("hyphenated Americans," Theodore Roosevelt contemptuously called them) as well as the nation as a whole overshadowed all other considerations. For black Americans, who until then had focused their attention on the deteriorating condition of race relations internally, the situation was especially problematic.[56]

Something of the confusion toward the prospects for war that was felt within the black community can be seen in the fall musical production of Salem Tutt Whitney and J. Homer Tutt's Smart Set Company—one of the very few black companies still active—which opened at the Lafayette Theatre in early October. The two-act musical comedy, entitled *How Newtown Prepared*, is set in the black township of Newtown, where the population is split between the old army veterans who favor a volunteer military or peace at any price and the young people who are for preparedness. When word comes of the gallant fight of the 10th (black) Cavalry against Poncho Villa's bandits in Mexico (the latest actual engagement of the most famous black outfit then in the U.S. Army), the town decides to organize its own regiment. Mexican spies, failing in their attempt to convince Newtown to join their side, trick the head of the regiment into boarding a ship that they control. After many vicissitudes, the Newtown regiment finds itself in Turkish territory and forced to fight against the Allies. They are eventually rescued by an American warship, and all ends happily.[57] The convolutions of the plot, however silly, nonetheless reflect the real sense of ambiguity in the black community, a feeling that must have been intensified in minds of those who sat in the audience by a knowledge that since the end of June, the theater in which they sat was also being used to drill the recruits of New York's first regiment of black National Guardsmen. Jim Europe, who was one of several celebrities reported in attendance at the Smart Set's opening night, was certainly aware of it; he had joined the regiment two weeks before.[58]

11

"The Separate Battalion"

A colored regiment has lately been organized in Harlem and the colored man is marching under the flag that often fails to protect him when alive but honors him when dead.

Reverend Charles Martin (1916)

In early 1916 as President Wilson embarked upon a speaking tour of the North and Midwest aimed at pressuring Congress to support his new policy of limited military preparedness, there were approximately 10,000 black soldiers on active duty in four segregated regular units of the U.S. Army. The most famous of these, the 9th and 10th Cavalries, had seen action with Theodore Roosevelt and the Rough Riders at the Battle of San Juan Hill, and the 10th would shortly be engaged in the dispute with Mexico. Although an additional several thousand black Americans were serving in various National Guard units, blacks had been systematically excluded from membership in the militias of the Southern states. In the North only Illinois had an established black unit of any substantial size, the 8th Illinois headquartered in Chicago. In New York, the state legislature had approved the formation of a black National Guard unit eight years earlier, but Charles Evans Hughes—the unsuccessful Republican nominee for president in 1916, but then governor of New York—had vetoed the bill on the grounds that additional reserves were not needed. Hughes successor, William Sulzer, subsequently signed a similar bill, but no action was taken until Charles S. Whitman entered his second term as governor in 1916.

Whitman was sympathetic to the petitions he had received from black New Yorkers—the most persistent of which was Charles W. Fillmore of New York City, a veteran of the Spanish-American War—that they should be given their own National Guard unit. When Whitman discovered that a law already existed that authorized an infantry regiment of black soldiers, he decided that "either that regiment ought to be built and given a fair chance of proving itself, or the law ought to be repealed."[1]

Modeled on the 8th Illinois, the original New York bill stipulated that black officers be used to staff the proposed unit. There were few experienced black officers available, however, and no provisions had yet been established for training them.[2] Whitman's former campaign director, William Hayward, however, had been a colonel in the Nebraska National Guard and, in addition, was currently serving as public service commissioner for New York City. Hayward was familiar with the black community of the city, especially the rapidly growing Harlem district, and was well known to New York's black leaders. He was also a supporter of a black National Guard unit, believing in the value of such institutions as a focus of community pride and as an instrument for encouraging civic mindedness. When Whitman asked him to undertake the organization of the black regiment in June 1916, Hayward accepted the responsibility "in all seriousness, and in full appreciation of the probable difficulties which lay before me," including the "necessary absurdity" of being colonel of a regiment of which the colonel was the only member.[3] In making the appointment, Whitman also promised that although white officers would be used at first, they would be replaced by black officers as soon as they were available.[4]

The 15th Infantry Regiment (Colored) of the New York National Guard thus began its existence with one white officer and little else: no rifles, ammunition, uniforms, armory to drill in, headquarters for recruitment, or troops. There was also little willingness in either the regular army or the National Guard Quartermaster Departments to assist Hayward in getting what he needed to get started. Had it not been for the public service commissioner's political connections in New York City and the personal support of the governor, to whom he was forced to appeal directly on a number of occasions, it is unlikely that the regiment would ever have been organized.[5] With the help of Mayor John P. Mitchell, however, Hayward was able to get the city to take a lease on the second floor of the Lafayette Theatre on 132nd Street to use as an armory (and a former cigar store at the corner of the same building to function as an office). Recruitment of the 15th New York Infantry began on June 29.

During the summer of 1916 while Hayward struggled to find uniforms, rifles, and other equipment, he also found that getting the number of volunteers needed to bring the regiment up to strength, both officers and rank and file, would not be easy. Whatever their attitude toward military service, a large number of the black citizens of New York were newly arrived in the city from the South and from the West Indies; most were poor, and few among them felt that they had time to spare for anything other than making a living. The appointment of the regiment's first black officers—Charles W. Fillmore, Harvard graduate Napoleon B. Marshall, and George C. Lacy, a veteran of the 8th Illinois—helped enlistment, as did the public endorsement of the *New York Age* and Ziegfeld Follies star Bert Williams (a former California National Guardsman), but as of the end of August less than a quarter of the men required to fill the ten companies of its four battalions had signed up.[6] On September 18, 1916, however, the 15th New York got one of its most important recruits. James Reese Europe, who had recently returned to the city from an orchestra engagement at the casino in Saratoga Springs, enlisted as a private and was assigned to a machine gun company.[7]

Europe's reasons for joining the regiment had little to do with general patriotism, national preparedness, or even with his fondness for march music and military drill. When he had first been approached about becoming a member, in the late spring, like many others he did not feel he could afford the time away from the heavy demands of the Tempo Club. Over the summer, however, he came to the conclusion that a national guard unit in Harlem could become an important organization of benefit to the entire community. "I have been in New York for sixteen years," he explained to Sissle, "and there has never been such an organization of Negro men that will bring together all classes of men for a common good. And our race will never amount to anything, politically or economically, in New York or anywhere else unless there are strong organizations of men who stand for something in the community."[8] Europe was encouraged in his decision by the support the regiment was beginning to receive from friends he respected, like Bert Williams and Lester Walton. He was also impressed by the interest being shown by substantial and well-meaning white New Yorkers, like Hamilton Fish, a former state assemblyman and nephew of Mrs. Stuyvesant Fish (Europe's and the Castles' influential society patron), who had become a captain in the 15th.[9] With the backing of the political and financial leaders of New York, there was a real opportunity that Harlem could get "a big Armory where the young men can have healthful exercise, swimming pools, and athletic training," and where the "moral and physical negro [sic] manhood of Harlem" could be developed.[10] It would not happen, however, Europe told his partner, if "the best and most sincere" members of the community, "men like you and I," simply "sit back and say we have not got time." A week later, on September 26, Noble Sissle was sworn in by the regiment's commanding officer as a private in Company K, the same day that Jim Europe was appointed first sergeant.[11]

Colonel Hayward understood from the first that successful recruiting depended in large part on showmanship, and that meant parades and uniforms, and the stirring music of a military brass band. Weekly drills by men in civilian clothes with broom sticks in the Lafayette Theatre or in Central Park in silence would not attract many recruits. On October 1, therefore, as soon as he thought it feasible, Hayward arranged for the 607 officers and men of the 15th New York Infantry (plus a few extras, notably Bert Williams) to parade down Fifth Avenue to the Union League Club where Governor Whitman officially presented the regiment with its colors. Music for the parade was supplied by Clef Club member E. E. Thompson and his band, which Hayward was forced to hire since few musicians had yet enlisted in the 15th. The band performed well enough, and Hayward convinced Thompson to try to organize and recruit a permanent regimental band.[12]

Two months later, despite his best efforts and several public concerts by the "15th Infantry Band," Thompson had been unable to make much progress.[13] The major problem was that few of the better musicians, the ones who could most easily make the transition from playing in dance orchestras to performing in a military concert and marching band, could afford to give up their evenings and the high salaries they earned for regular army pay. In addition, black brass and woodwind players were already at a premium for commercial jobs since there were far fewer of them than pianists and string players in New York at the time. Colonel Hayward was concerned both with Thompson's inability to recruit musicians as well as with the slow rate of enlistment in the regiment in general, and he believed the two were related. The only other black National Guard regiment, the 8th Illinois, had a concert band that had achieved an enviable reputation, and Hayward thought that it was one of the main reasons why the 8th Regiment had been given better equipment and a proper armory to drill in. In early December, therefore, Hayward called Jim Europe, whom he knew to be the most famous orchestra leader in the city, to his office to discuss the problem. Europe had by this time passed the officer's examination and was scheduled to be commissioned as a first lieutenant and given command of one of the regiment's machine gun companies. Since army bandleaders were noncommissioned officers, he had no reason to expect that Hayward wanted anything more from him than advice. The Colonel, however, wanted something more than that; he wanted Jim Europe to organize the best band in the U.S. Army.[14]

"I will never forget the worried expression on Jim's face that night as I met him coming out of the colonel's office," Sissle remembered. "'I don't see how I can do it!,'" Europe exclaimed, and then told his associate what Hayward had asked him to do and how he, Europe, had attempted to dissuade him.[15] In the first place, Europe was not particularly interested in military bands as musical organizations; he liked the sound of strings and thought them more appropriate vehicles for communicating the soul of African-American music. Military bands were generally too brassy and blasting. He was also proud of his new lieutenancy and was reluctant to be assigned to band duty; it was not what he had joined the regiment to do. Still, he was sympathetic to the colonel's argument that a really first-rate band could be helpful, perhaps essential, to the building up of the regiment, and he did not wish Hayward to think that personal reasons would keep him from doing what was best for the outfit.

After thinking through the matter for several days, Europe came to the decision that he would tell Hayward that he would agree to take on the organization of the band but only if several conditions were met. The colonel would have to provide him with the support he required to make the 15th Regimental Band the best of its kind in the country; he could not afford, professionally, to have his name associated with a second-rate musical organization. To do this, Colonel Hayward would have to be willing to bend army regulations and, in addition, make available a sizable special fund for the band.

Army tables of organization stipulated that a regimental band consisted of exactly twenty-eight pieces, and this was an "entirely impracticable combination of instruments to play well-balanced music," Europe explained to his commanding officer. "He had it all worked out and he figured that forty-four was the minimum number that a regimental band should have, and that sixty-odd would be better," Hayward recalled. He added:

> Well, of course, we couldn't get instruments for forty-four men when the tables
> of organization only allowed for twenty-eight men, and we couldn't get music
> scores, and we couldn't enlist bandsmen. We figured out that the latter difficulty
> could be met by having soldiers detailed for special duty with the band and ex-
> cused from the regular infantry company duties [including Europe, himself],
> while performing this special duty.[16]

Money was another issue. Europe told Hayward that he would need a few key men to lead each of the instrument sections, much like squad leaders and platoon leaders in line companies, and that he knew where he could find them. The problem was that such men could not afford to serve for the regular army pay unless it were supplemented. Adding this cost to the expense of extra instruments and music resulted in a budget, Europe estimated, of about $15,000 to put together the kind of band they both wanted. Hayward, to Europe's surprise, accepted his explanation of what was needed and agreed to try to find the money. His initial efforts, however, brought little success. Even after touching "the officers as far as it was safe to touch," the colonel recalled, "I was still short thousands of dollars on a reasonably set up budget."[17]

Europe later told Sissle that he had been sure that Hayward would not be able to find the funds and that this would "end them bothering him about taking the band." Much to his surprise, a few days after he gave Hayward his requirements, Europe was called by the regiment's commander and told that he had the money. Sissle, who was present in the Tempo Club office when the phone call came, remembered the comical expression on Europe's face when he received the news. "Well, they called your bluff," Sissle said laughing, and then ducked as a telephone directory came flying at him. "Colonel Hayward is sure a promoting old soul," Europe remarked. "[W]ho would have ever thought that anyone would put up that amount for a band?"[18]

The individual who provided the bulk of the funds was Daniel G. Reid, a director of U.S. Steel Corporation and American Can Company, to whom Hayward had appealed in a "spirit almost of despair." Hayward had called upon Reid to ask for letters of introduction to "thirty or forty of your rich friends," who the colonel planned to ask for a $500 donation each. "How many of the thirty or forty victims do you expect to land for $500 apiece," Reid asked. Hayward replied that he hoped to get at least twenty. "Mr. Reid reached into a drawer of his desk, took out his check book, and wrote me a check for $10,000 and said: 'That's a damn sight easier than writing you forty letters of introduction, and it will save you a lot of time too. Here are your twenty victims at $500 each.'"[19]

Having received the money to establish the special band fund, Europe and Hayward moved quickly to begin the process of organizing the new 15th Infantry Regiment Band. Europe and Sissle, whom Europe wanted as his assistant and eventually as drum major, were transferred from Company K to Headquarters Company and detailed to special duty with the band—which, of course, did not yet exist. Europe's enthusiasm for the project also increased as he began to think that if they were successful in putting together a truly great military band, it would help him obtain support for the National Negro Orchestra he wanted after the war period ended.[20] In order not to deplete the special fund while getting maximum recruiting value from the band, it was also agreed that the organization should be capable of giving public concerts (like Sousa's or Arthur Pryor's bands) in addition to providing music for parades and drills. Europe needed, therefore, to move quickly but also deliberately.

Prior to accepting his new assignment with the 15th Regiment, among other on-going professional commitments, Europe had been engaged by the Royal Poinciana Hotel to provide two dance orchestras to the Palm Beach resort during January and February 1917. This was an important, high-paying job for Tempo Club musicians requiring that Europe personally be away from New York for most of that period. Sissle, who had performed at the Royal Poinciana the previous season, had anticipated accompanying Europe to Florida, but Europe asked him to remain in New York to begin implementing his plans for organizing the band. Europe realized that there would be little time for training his musicians, and that he, therefore, needed to recruit already skilled instrumentalists. He was confident that if Sissle began a national advertising campaign while he was away, by the time he returned from Florida, Sissle could have a list of interested brass players and drummers from which he could select the most qualified. He was not so certain, however, that Sissle could find the number of skilled woodwind players he required. As Colonel Hayward recalled their conversation about the difficulty, Europe told him that

> reed instruments, that is, clarinets, flutes, saxophones, and one or two other instruments, served the same purpose in a military band that string instruments serve in a symphony orchestra, and he said there was a great scarcity of reed instrument players in the United States among the colored people.

Hayward asked what the answer was, and Europe, to his astonishment, replied that it was "Puerto Rico."[21]

It is not clear how Europe first came to know about the strong band tradition among Puerto Rican musicians, especially those of African descent. Prior to World War I, immigration from Puerto Rico had not been large, despite its becoming a possession of United States in 1898, and no sizable Puerto Rican community had yet developed in New York City. Judging from the lack of Spanish surnames among the members of the Clef Club and Tempo Club, the number of Afro-Puerto Ricans who had become part of the black entertainment profession in the city must also have been small. On the island, however, with the abolition of slavery in 1873 and the decline of the sugar industry, black and mulatto Puerto Ricans had begun migrating to the larger towns where popular musical performance became one means for many of them to attain "some measure of respectability."[22] Many of these musicians were reed players, and by the early spring of 1917 Europe had heard of them and was sufficiently sure of his information that he proposed to Colonel Hayward that he be sent to San Juan as soon as he returned from Florida to recruit woodwind players for the band. Hayward agreed.[23]

Following Europe's instructions, Sissle began advertising for musicians in the national black newspapers soon after Europe left New York for Palm Beach, and at first the Europe name seemed to have the desired effect. "There came a deluge of answers from everywhere," Sissle recalled.[24] However, as the sense of impending war spread across the country during the early months of 1917—first as a result of the German declaration of unrestricted submarine warfare and then, on March 1, when the Zimmerman telegram (revealing a German attempt to entice Mexico into a war against the United States) was made public—Sissle found that many of those who had previously applied for a position with the band now wished to have their names removed from the list.

During the early stages of their planning, Europe and Sissle had hoped to encourage recruits by promising them positions in one or another of his society orchestras, but as the clouds of war continued to gather, many of the society people who had previously wanted Europe's orchestras for their social affairs began turning their attention to Red Cross and other relief work, and the demand for Tempo Club musicians declined. As a result, Europe could no longer guarantee private employment to those who agreed to sign up with the regiment. By the time the actual declaration of war came on April 6, Sissle was completely discouraged. "Among the most desirable men who refused to join were those men right in New York, whom Jim so greatly relied upon," Sissle wrote. "I gave up and the only hope I could see now was when Jim returned he personally could get some of the men to join."[25]

Sissle's efforts had not been completely unsuccessful, however. Among the handful of recruits who honored their commitments were several veteran army musicians from the 9th and 10th Cavalries and the 24th and 25th Infantries, including Ila White, an experienced bugler. In addition to White, who was named head of the band's bugle corps, was Frank de Broit, one of the nation's premier cornet soloists, who joined the regiment from Chicago. Still, by the first week of April when Europe was finally back in the city, there were hardly enough musicians in the 15th Regiment to form a dance band, much less a marching band. General recruiting had also been slow, although by April 8, two days after the U.S. entered the war, the regiment managed to reach basic peace strength of 1,200 officers and men. One week later Hayward announced in the *New York Age* that his "street urchin of a regiment" had been officially recognized by the War Department and was now under government supervision.[26]

By the end of April, E. E. Thompson had resigned as bandmaster, and the 15th was without any effective musical organization at all. Europe, however, was prepared to devote his full energies to organizing the band; the previously scheduled spring Tempo Club entertainment at Manhattan Casino had been canceled, and the recruitment trip to Puerto Rico was now set for the first week of May.[27] Prior to his departure, Europe instructed Sissle to continue the domestic recruiting campaign as well as he could, and he asked Eubie Blake, his other partner, to take over administration of his professional music business, including supervision and booking of his and the Tempo Club's orchestras. Europe had never pressured Blake, as he had Sissle, to join the national guard—although both Europe and Sissle sometimes teased him about it. "They'd have some fun with me after they're in uniform," Blake recalled.

> Europe is a lieutenant now, see. And everybody knows they're goin' to war, but they're just gonna be musicians. Ain't none of us was a fighter, you know. But they'd introduce me to girls and they'd say, 'This is Eubie Blake, the slacker.' Now they don't tell the girls I'm thirty-five years old, see, way over the age for the army.[28]

It was not just his age, however, or the fact that, unlike Sissle, Blake was a married man. His prospects for becoming an officer, given the lack of a formal education or military experience, were slight (Sissle was promoted to lieutenant in 1918), and his musical talents were far less useful to Europe in the regimental band than as manager of his partner's business affairs.

Armed with new orders and a supply of cash for bonuses, Europe left New York by steamship and arrived in San Juan on May 2, 1917. Prior to landing, however, Europe received word that the 15th Regiment had been ordered to Camp Peekskill for two weeks of field exercises and rifle practice and he was directed to complete his recruiting mission as quickly as possible and return to New York. Europe spent only three days in San Juan, staying at the Hotel Inglaterra, but when he left, probably on May 5, he brought with him thirteen of "the most visible young players in San Juan," including former members of Manuel Tizol's municipal band, former performers with the Jolly Boys (a theater group who had recorded for Victor a few months earlier), and several "scions of illustrious musical families."[29]

Europe and his troupe of Spanish-speaking musicians debarked from their ship in New York harbor just a few short days before the 15th Regiment was scheduled to leave for camp. Colonel Hayward, the other officers, and most of the men were excited by the prospect of experiencing their first real opportunity to see what they could do as regular soldiers, but they were still poorly

equipped and woefully unorganized. Arthur Little, then a captain, has described
the general confusion and the innumerable problems that attended the regiment's preparations. "Getting ready for that tour of duty," he wrote, "was one
of the most exhausting bits of work that the officers of the regiment ever had
to perform."[30] The situation with the band was, if anything, even worse. There
were few instruments, no music scores, and precious little time to rehearse
even had the instruments and music been available. Added to this was the fact
that nearly half of the band members could not speak English and were experiencing varying degrees of culture shock. Europe did have one piece of good
luck, however. Just before he returned from Puerto Rico, a small, unassuming,
but widely experienced musician, named Francis Eugene Mikell, had signed up
for service with the 15th. Mikell, who was born in Charleston, South Carolina,
and was about the same age as Europe, had attended the New York Conservatory and taught music at Tuskegee Institute, the State College at Orangeburg,
South Carolina, Florida Baptist Academy, and the Bordentown (New Jersey) Industrial School. He had also been musical director of the Globe Theatre in
Jacksonville, Florida, and, for a time, head of the orchestra at the famous Pekin
Theatre in Chicago.[31] With Mikell, Europe now had a first class assistant conductor and bandmaster, and the newspaper ads that appeared following Mikell's
enlistment reflect Europe's renewed optimism:

ATTENTION!!!
Negro Musicians of America
Last Call   Golden Opportunity
If you want to do your *duty* in the present crisis.
IF you are not in a financial position to give your
services as a private volunteer.
IF you would serve should you be able to make a
living wage for your family.
IF you are a First Class Musician.
IF you have dreamed of belonging to a famous
Military Band.
IF you have longed for the time you could devote
All Your Time to your music.
IF you want to belong to a regiment whose officers
are sparing no means to make their regimental
band the Best In The World.
IF you want to be in a band that in the time of
Peace will devote its time to Concert Tours.
Then Wire Or Call
LT. James Reese Europe, care of 15th Regiment, N.Y.
Infantry, Harlem River Park Casino, 127th Street and
2nd Avenue, New York City.
P.S. There Are Only a Few More Vacancies Left, and
the Regiment Goes To Camp, Sunday, May 13th.
So Hurry! Hurry! Hurry![32]

At dawn on Sunday morning, May 13, 1917, the 15th Regiment of the New York National Guard assembled between 45th and 50th Streets and Fifth Avenue and prepared for the short march up to 56th Street and across to 60th Street and the Hudson River where special trains of the New York Central were waiting. After much delay and confusion, a marching line was established, and Colonel Hayward gave the order to march. Europe and the twenty-eight-member band had come down from the Lafayette Theatre on the elevated railway, and although they had virtually no rehearsal time, they responded by launching into "Onward Christian Soldiers." The crowd that had begun to gather started cheering, and as Captain Little has written, he

> forgot all about the mis-fit and incomplete uniforms hidden through the ranks of my company, I forgot all about the ignorance and other weaknesses of our command, I forgot that we were merely going to a state training camp for drill and for rifle practice, forgot that we were, as some newspaper cynic had said, merely a glorified organization of Mulligan Guards, and I felt, as I am sure 1,200 other men of that column felt that morning, that we were Christian and American soldiers marching on to war.[33]

Sissle, to whom Europe had assigned the responsibility of taking care of the new Puerto Rican recruits and of assembling the band, remembered quite a different scene. The drummers set three different marching tempos, the buglers did not play when they were supposed to (and when they did, could not be stopped), the Puerto Ricans seemed more interested in the crowds and the buildings than the music, and Europe was forced to run around among the ranks in a futile attempt to bring some order out of the chaos. If a movie had been made of all "the events that happened in those dozen or more blocks we paraded that morning," Sissle wrote, "it would have made many a comedy moving picture impresario blue with envy."[34]

The 15th Infantry Regiment reached the state camp near Peekskill, New York, on the evening of May 13, and for the next eighteen days underwent such rigorous field training that by the time they returned to the city the formerly ragged outfit was transformed nearly beyond recognition. All the officers and nearly half of the men had passed the qualifying tests as riflemen, and they could drill "as well as any regiment in the New York Guard." On May 30, when the 15th marched in New York City's Memorial Day Parade with the other state National Guard units, many of whose members were new and untrained recruits, there was a palpable sense that New York's Negro regiment was beginning to develop "the snap of experienced soldiers."[35]

Under the musical instruction of Bandmaster Mikell and his assistant, Sergeant de Broit, and the military tutoring of Sergeant White, the regimental band was also beginning to take shape. The Puerto Ricans, especially, demonstrated a remarkable ability to adjust to the situation, and their excellence as musicians began to become apparent. "The newly organized regimental band, under Lieut. Europe, now numbers nearly thirty musicians," reported the *New York Age* on May 24. "Half of them have been brought from Porto Rico [sic] and are adept on reed instruments. The band will soon be enlarged to sixty-five."[36] Europe did not personally spend much time at Peekskill; instead, he was dispatched to New York to assemble the band's music library and to work out the arrangements for their first public concert to be held as soon as it was feasible after the regiment returned from camp. There was a pressing need for a concert to aid enlistment as well as to replenish the special band fund. The 15th Regiment, while it had been accepted as a regular National Guard unit, had not as yet been mobilized as part of the regular army, and therefore salaries for the officers and men were paid only for the time they spent in weekly drills or while at training camp. Europe, however, had promised his musicians that they would receive full-time salaries for joining the band, and it was apparent that the original band fund would soon be exhausted. His plan was to hold a public concert and dance featuring the 15th Regimental Band at the Manhattan Casino as a replacement for the regular spring entertainment of the Tempo Club. Making the arrangements and preparing the band for their premier performance before the public, however, was not the only challenge Europe faced.

To Europe's closest associates, it had been clear for more than six months that he was suffering from some sort of progressive illness. Shortly after receiving his commission the previous December, he began appearing more nervous and easily fatigued than usual, and he began losing weight. Most disturbing to those who saw him without his glasses, his eyes seemed to be bulging from their sockets. His deteriorating health began to worry Europe as well. "Apparently," Blake recalled, "some people began to misread this. Finally Jim, one day, asked me to take a walk with him. Without even a One, Two, he hands me the stick: 'Eubie, do you think I'm crazy?' Jim was really worried. 'I might be, you know,' he said. 'When you are, everybody knows it but you.'"[37]

After returning to New York from Florida in April, Europe confided to Sissle that while he was working at the Poinciana Hotel, one of the guests, a specialist, had observed his symptoms and asked him to come to his suite. After a brief examination, the doctor told him that he had an Exopthalmic Goiter—what would be known today as Hyperthyroidism, an enlargement of the thyroid gland—which, if not operated on, could produce strangulation. Despite the doctor's warning that his condition was serious, because of his commitments to Hayward, the 15th Regiment, and the band, Europe continued to put off doing anything about it. He also made Sissle promise to tell no one, not even his wife.[38]

There was another personal matter, in addition to his physical condition, that weighed heavily upon Lieutenant Europe in the spring of 1917, something that he also wanted to keep private—especially from his wife, his mother, and

Mary Lorraine Europe in
Washington, D.C., circa 1930.
Author's collection.

Lt. James Reese Europe with Marion Gant Tyler and family in New Jersey, circa 1917.
Marion Tyler (the future Mrs. Eubie Blake) is standing behind Europe with her hand on
his shoulder. *Author's collection*.

James Reese Europe and Bessie
Simms in New York City, circa
1919. *Courtesy of James Reese
Europe, Jr.*

One of the numerous Europe Society Orchestras in the field during the spring and
summer of 1916 and 1917. In addition to Noble Sissle (second from the right), other
members include Leonard Jeter (cello) and Felix Weir (violin). *Courtesy of James Reese
Europe, Jr.*

Lt. James Reese Europe, at the front in France, 1918. *Author's collection.*

Lt. James Reese Europe, leader of the famous 369th Infantry "Hellfighters" Band. New York, 1919. *Author's collection.*

Mechanics Hall, Boston, Massachusetts, where James Reese Europe was fatally stabbed during a concert performance on May 9, 1919. *Courtesy of the Department of American Studies, University of Alabama.*

Members of the Hiram Masonic Lodge in Harlem pay their final respects as Europe's funeral procession passes on May 13, 1919. *Courtesy of James Reese Europe, Jr.*

Memorial card for James Reese Europe's public funeral in New York City, May 13, 1919. *Author's collection.*

The veterans of the 369th Infantry Regiment "Hellfighters" march up Fifth Avenue in New York City in their homecoming parade on February 17, 1919. *Courtesy of the Department of American Studies, University of Alabama.*

The Samuel Coleridge-Taylor Choral Society of Washington, D.C., photographed with the composer (arms folded) during his second American tour in the fall of 1906. *Courtesy of Associated Publishers, Inc.*

Entertainer Ernest Hogan (center) and his famous "Memphis Students" whose novel spirited performances were the hit of the summer season of 1905 at Hammerstein's Victoria Theatre in New York City. Twenty-five-year-old James Reese Europe stands to the left and just below Hogan.

The eleven original Frogs, a collective portrait of black musical theater achievement in 1908. *Courtesy of the Maryland Historical Society, Baltimore.*

Noble Sissle, photographed in New York during the summer following Europe's death. *Courtesy of the Maryland Historical Society, Baltimore.*

Europe's partner and friend, Eubie Blake. Photographed in New York, 1919. *Courtesy of the Maryland Historical Society, Baltimore.*

Composer-singer-teacher
Harry T. Burleigh. *Courtesy of
the Associated Publishers, Inc.*

Composer-conductor Will
Marion Cook. *Courtesy of the
Associated Publishers, Inc.*

Bob Cole (standing) and J. Rosamond Johnson, leaders in black musical comedy before World War I. *Courtesy of the Associated Publishers, Inc.*

James Reese Europe and the Clef Club Symphony Orchestra at the Manhattan Casino, New York City, circa 1911. The continuing popularity of the minstrel tradition is also apparent by the entertainers grouped on stage. *Courtesy of the Maryland Historical Society, Baltimore.*

James Reese Europe and his Society Orchestra, taken in New York City in the summer of 1916 or 1917. In this well-known (although mislabeled) photograph, Noble Sissle is immediately to Europe's left. *Courtesy of the Maryland Historical Society, Baltimore.*

A companion to the circular photograph of Europe's Society Orchestra, also taken in New York in 1916 or 1917. In addition to Sissle (center, rear) and Europe (seated at the piano), others present include Leonard Jeter (cello), Felix Weir (violin), and George Hicks (bass). *Courtesy of the Maryland Historical Society, Baltimore.*

Lt. Europe leads the 369th "Hellfighters" Band outside Hospital Number Nine in Paris, September 4, 1918. *Courtesy of the National Archives, Signal Corps 21789.*

Several members of the Hellfighters Band pose with the instrumental casualties of the war. Taken in New York in February, 1919. *Courtesy of the Maryland Historical Society, Baltimore.*

A flyer promoting the national concert tour of Lieut. "Jim" Europe and his 369th Infantry "Hellfighters" Band. Spring, 1919. *Courtesy of the Maryland Historical Society.*

James Reese Europe and his famous Infantry "Hellfighters" Band, their New York origins prominently displayed, sail home aboard the *S.S. Stockholm*, February, 1919. *Courtesy of the National Archives.*

Vernon and Irene Castle in characteristic dancing pose, circa 1914.

The sheet music cover for one of the many pieces that Europe and Ford Dabney wrote for the dancing Castles. Published by Joseph W. Stern in 1914. *Courtesy of the Moorland-Spingarn Research Center of Howard University, ABS 38.598.*

Vernon Castle as a drummer in
Irving Berlin's *Watch Your
Step* of 1914–15.

The sheet music cover for one
of Europe's earliest popular
songs. This one was written
with John Larkins in 1904.
*Courtesy of the Moorland-
Spingarn Research Center of
Howard University,
ABS 39.613.*

The sheet music cover for Europe's most popular composition of the war. Published by M. Witmark in New York in 1919. *Courtesy of the Moorland-Spingarn Research Center of Howard University, ABS 39.609.*

This sheet music cover of a typical "coon song". The piece, written by Europe early in his career, was published in New York City by Gotham Music in 1905. *Courtesy of the Moorland-Spingarn Research Center of Howard University, ABS 39.608.*

his sisters—until he could decide what he should do. On February 2, 1917, Bessie Simms gave birth to a son whom she named James Reese Europe, Jr. The birth certificate lists the father as musician James Europe, of 110 W. 137th Street, New York City, the same address as the mother, whose name was given as Bessie Simms Europe.[39]

Bessie Simms had been living and working in New York City since J. Leubrie Hill's Darktown Follies Company closed in the late spring of 1916.[40] The intimate relationship between Jim Europe and the attractive dancer had been a long-term, if intermittent, one, predating his marriage to Willie Angrom by some five years, and it was well-known to the black theatrical and musical community. There was, therefore, no question of Europe's responsibility, even had he wished to deny it—which he did not.[41] He was, however, married to another woman, who could hardly be expected, any more than his mother in Washington, to be pleased by the news. In addition, there was his public reputation, which he had so carefully cultivated and which he knew would have a direct bearing upon his future. For her part, Bessie Simms was, of course, fully aware of Europe's marital situation and, with the exception of financial support, she seems to have been unwilling—for the present at least—to make greater demands upon him.[42]

Despite the seriousness of his problems, Europe managed to complete the arrangements for the "Great Military Ball and Band Concert" and, with major assistance from Bandmaster Mikell, to ready the band sufficiently for the program he had selected.[43] On Friday evening, June 22, a large and enthusiastic crowd, perhaps "the biggest of the year" (including Mrs. Europe who occupied one of the boxes), gathered at the Manhattan Casino to see and hear the first public performance by the musical representatives of Harlem's own 15th Infantry Regiment.[44] The musical program was unfortunately not published, but the concert portion certainly included a number of stirring marches and patriotic pieces and even, perhaps, George M. Cohan's rousing "Over There," the song that, when Nora Bayes recorded it in July, replaced the hit of the previous year, "I Didn't Raise My Boy to be a Soldier." It may also have included W. C. Handy's "Memphis Blues," which Europe had been playing with his various ensembles for some time. Lester Walton was sufficiently impressed by the band's performance to predict that Colonel Hayward's desire "to see the regimental band gain distinction as being the greatest military musical organization in the United States, the Marine Band at Washington, D.C., not excepted," would likely be realized. Already, he said, "the dozen or more Porto Ricans [sic] who make up the reed section cannot be excelled, and the brass section is improving daily."[45]

Sissle also felt that the concert was well-played but that the audience and the musicians were especially anxious for the dance numbers to begin so they could really cut loose. "I will never forget the yell that went up after 'Jim' had conducted the first dance number," he later wrote. "What we thought was a wonderful demonstration of appreciation after each concert number, turned out to be but a ripple on the ocean compared with that mighty roar that followed the last strain of the first jazz tune."[46] Having accomplished his immediate goal, Europe turned the baton over to Sergeant de Broit and slipped out of the hall. A little while later, Sissle discovered him trembling and nearly collapsed in a doorway outside, and his wife was quickly summoned to take the bandleader home.

Europe was having such difficulty breathing by Monday morning that there was no longer any question about seeing a doctor. He was taken to a hospital on Second Avenue, where the first of two surgical operations was performed on Wednesday, June 27. Sissle, who, with Europe's wife and sister, Ida, visited him daily, wrote that in spite of his weakened physical condition—so weak that the doctors were afraid to use more than a local anesthetic—Europe remained in positive spirits and even joked with the nursing staff.[47] The preliminary operation, and the major one that followed ten days later, were both successful, but it would take nearly two months of recuperation before he was strong enough to rejoin his band and the regiment. In the meantime, events were moving swiftly.

Prior to June 1917, Colonel Hayward and the other leaders of New York's black regiment had been focusing their efforts toward the singular goal of organizing and training their men to take their place as a fully recognized unit of the National Guard. The further prospect that they might eventually be mustered into the regular army and prepared for combat duty overseas, especially in view of the army's hostility toward black soldiers, seemed more than remote. The Selective Service Act of May 18, it is true, made no distinctions regarding race—all able-bodied American males between the ages of twenty-one and thirty-one were required to register for the draft beginning on July 5—but whether or not blacks would actually be taken and, if so, how they would be trained, was not so clear. In the meantime, one black National Guard unit, the 1st Separate Battalion of the District of Columbia, had been called up for guard duty, and rumors began circulating that others would soon follow.[48] The effect of these developments upon the 15th, for a variety of complex reasons, was that recruitment increased dramatically. By the beginning of the second week of July the regiment had achieved war strength of 2,000 men and fifty-four officers, the first of New York's National Guard units to do so.[49]

With Europe convalescing in the hospital, the Regimental Band contributed positively to the success of Hayward's recruitment efforts by performing daily throughout the black districts of the city. Under the spell of the music, Sissle recalled, many a young man found himself a member of "Uncle Samuel's army" before he realized it. "Many a time in the rigorous camp life the regiment led during preparatory training here in the States," he wrote, "I would often hear a soldier say as the band would pass by on it's [sic] way to or from a formation, 'If it hadn't been for that d____n band I wouldn't be in the army.'"[50] By this time the band had also added a number of new members, the most valuable of which were six young musicians, students from Hampton Institute in Virginia, and a pair of clever drummers from the famous Jenkins Orphanage of Charleston, South Carolina.[51]

In July 1917, while Jim Europe was recovering, Eugene Mikell, who was born in Charleston and had taught at Jenkins Orphanage in the 1890s, drew upon his connections with the orphanage to recruit three of its band's leading performers—drummers Steven and Herbert Wright and trombonist Amos Gilliard.[52] Steven Wright, not related to Herbert, was the veteran of the group; at the age of twenty, he had played with the Orphanage Band in London and on Broadway when they appeared in the 1913 production of *Uncle Tom's Cabin*.[53] Gilliard and Herbert Wright were younger and somewhat less experienced, but all the Jenkins' musicians were used to playing a wide variety of music—including popular songs, dances, blues, and classical overtures—and they were adept at syncopated rhythms.[54] Noble Sissle remembered the two drummers as "below the standard educationally" of the rest of musicians in the 15th, but as being very similar in appearance and personality. "It was not very long," he wrote, "before the colonel and all of the regiment were wild over them. And when Jim finally rejoined the band, he, too, became equally wild about the boys and would always feature them on every program."[55]

On Sunday morning, July 15, 1917, with the anticipated call having been received by Colonel Hayward a few days before, the 15th Infantry Regiment of the New York National Guard was mustered into active service in the U.S. Army and ordered to Camp Whitman (near Poughkeepsie, New York) for field training.[56] Less than five weeks later, the 15th received orders to break camp, divide their forces, and take up guard duty at between forty and fifty separate posts in New York and New Jersey. Separate companies were dispatched to protect naval stores, railroad lines, and shoe factories, and to guard pro-German prisoners at Ellis Island, while Headquarters and Supply Companies were relocated in New York City. The two largest contingents of soldiers, the 2nd and 3rd Battalions were assigned to Yaphank, Long Island, and Wrightstown, New Jersey, respectively, where Camps Upton and Dix were being constructed. The Regimental Band accompanied the 3rd Battalion to Camp Dix, and it was here that Lieutenant Europe felt strong enough to rejoin the unit.

It is entirely probable that as a consequence of his recent illness Europe might have obtained a medical discharge, had he chosen to apply for one. From the positive reports he was receiving from Sissle and others concerning the progress of the band, as well as the personal commitments he had made, however, it seems never to have been a consideration. Indeed, a conversation earlier that spring with John Love (when they were traveling together to Newport for Captain John Wanamaker, Jr.'s, wedding) suggests that Europe had his mind made up regardless of the consequences. In response to Love's question of whether "there is no way you can get out of the army and stay in New York," he replied that "if I could, I would not. My country calls me and I must answer; and if I live to come back, I will startle the world with my music."[57]

Compared to the rigors of training camp, guard duty at Camp Dix was a relatively undemanding assignment, and the relaxed outdoor routine had an obvious beneficial effect upon Europe's health; his energy and enthusiasm returned and he began gaining weight. As at Camp Whitman, the band had the opportunity both to practice and to perform in concert almost daily. At Camp Dix, the commanding general ordered a special bandstand to be constructed so that thousands of new draftees could hear their evening performances. A vocal quartet from Captain Fish's company was added to the entertainments, and Europe and Sissle even began to offer duets (Europe at the piano, Sissle singing) of familiar popular songs and originals of their own composition.[58] As the reputation of the 15th Regiment's band began to spread, they began receiving invitations to perform outside the camp as well.[59]

New York's black soldiers carried out their responsibilities during their tour of guard duty more than adequately, but they also had the disappointing experience of watching while first the 27th Division (composed of the other regiments of the New York National Guard), and then the 69th Regiment, made their farewell parades down Fifth Avenue on their way to final preparation for war service in France. Colonel Hayward, in the meantime, appealed without success to the army to include his regiment among those assigned to combat training. His application for the 15th to be included in the farewell parade of the 27th Division was also denied, and when the 69th Regiment marched off to join the Rainbow Division in France, he was told that "black was not one of the colors of the rainbow."[60]

Despite the War Department's reluctance, however, Hayward's efforts were finally rewarded. A decision was made at the end of August to order the 15th New York Infantry to join the other regiments of the 27th Division of the New York National Guard then in training at Camp Wadsworth in Spartanburg, South Carolina.[61] Unfortunately, the timing could not have been worse. Incidents of friction between black and white troops and between black troops and white civilians had plagued the army from the outset of the war, but racial tensions exploded in the last week of August 1917 into full scale riot when soldiers from the 24th Infantry stationed in Houston, Texas, having taken all the goading and insults they could stand, engaged in a gun battle with local white citizens. When it was over seventeen whites were dead, and, although thirteen soldiers were summarily tried and hanged and forty-one others imprisoned for life, fears of further violence spread throughout the South.[62]

On August 31, 1917, the *New York Times* reported that the city officials of Spartanburg, fearful of a reoccurrence of the recent Houston riot, had vigorously protested the War Department's revised plan to include the 15th Infantry among the troops to be trained there. "I was sorry to learn that the 15th Regiment has been ordered here," Mayor J. F. Floyd was quoted as saying,

> for, with their northern [sic] ideas about race equality, they will probably expect to be treated like white men. I can say right here that they will not be treated as anything except negroes [sic]. We shall treat them exactly as we treat our resident negroes. This thing is like waving a red flag in the face of a bull, something that can't be done without trouble.[63]

"We asked for the camp for Spartanburg," a member of the Chamber of Commerce told the *Times'* reporter, "but at that time we understood that no colored troops were to be sent down." The mayor and the Chamber of Commerce feared that the black soldiers would not be satisfied with the town's "Jim Crow" shops and restaurants, which the *Times* confirmed to be "almost without exception dingy and poorly stocked," and would attempt to enter the "whites only" establishments, something a Southern black would know not to do. "I can tell you for certain that if any of those colored soldiers go in any of our soda stores and the like and ask to be served they'll be knocked down," the reporter was told.

The 2nd and 3rd Battalions of the 15th Regiment were not scheduled to be released from guard duty until October 8, so the officers and men had more than a month to discuss the *Times'* article and prepare themselves for the hostile reception they could expect in Spartanburg. They were encouraged by the War Department's refusal to be swayed by the mayor's dire predictions (or threats), and they were anxious to begin the combat training appropriate to an infantry unit, but the anticipation was also unsettling and tensions increased. Just a week before their departure, a confrontation between troops of the 3rd Battalion at Camp Dix and a group of Southerners from the 26th Engineers nearly erupted into violence. The Southerners had posted a sign reading "No Niggers Allowed" on one of the camp's buildings. When the sign, which had been torn down by one of the guards, was replaced by another that read "For White Soldiers Only," about 200 fully armed men of the 3rd Battalion marched on the building and destroyed that sign as well. Only a quick response from the battalion's officers kept the situation from escalating further.[64]

On October 10, 1917, troop trains carrying the enthusiastic, if somewhat apprehensive, New York 15th Infantry Regiment began arriving at Camp Wadsworth in Spartanburg. There was no question that they were not welcomed by the local population, but Colonel Hayward assured community officials that his men would not challenge local customs nor react violently to the predictable insults they would receive. Shortly after the troops were settled in camp, Hayward called them together in an open field and asked each of the men to pledge not to retaliate against any abuse, even physical abuse, that they might receive from the townspeople. The regiment faced a difficult situation born of igno-

rance and misunderstanding, he told them, but they also had a great opportunity "to win from the whole world respect for the colored race, with an
advance in the elimination of existing prejudices to follow" if they simply refused "to meet the white citizens of Spartanburg upon the undignified plane of
prejudice and brutality which had been so unfortunately advertised, by Mayor
Floyd, as the standard of the community."[65] When he finished, Hayward asked
them by a show of hands to promise to do as he asked.

The colonel next approached General Phillips, commanding officer of the
camp, with a proposal that the 15th Regimental Band be permitted to play at the
next scheduled public band concert. Open air concerts by various regimental
bands of the 27th Division were regularly given two evenings a week in Spartanburg's main public square where a bandstand had been erected for the purpose,
and Hayward thought that the band might be able to change some opinions in
"that community of unfriendliness."[66] On the first Saturday evening after their
arrival, soldiers from New York's black regiment gathered in the public square,
along with a crowd of local white citizens, to listen to a carefully prepared program by Lieutenant Europe and the 15th Regimental Band. Colonel Hayward,
Major Little, and a dozen other white officers from the regiment spread themselves throughout the crowd in order to intercede should any trouble develop.
"The talk which some of us overheard through that crowd, during the early
stages of the concert, was by no means reassuring," Little recalled:

> At first it seemed, almost, as if an error of judgment had been made in forcing
> the colored regiment into prominence at so early an hour after our arrival. But
> there must be something in the time-honored line about music and its charms;
> for, gradually, the crowd grew larger, but the noises of the crowd grew less and
> less, until finally, in that great public square of converging city streets, silence
> reigned. Lieutenant Europe conducted, as was his custom, with but a few seconds
> between numbers, and the program appeared to be short. When the final piece
> had been played and the forty or fifty bandsmen had filed out of the stand in per-
> fect order with the "Hep—Hep—Hep—" of the sergeants as the only sound from
> their ranks, the flower of Spartanburg's citizenry looked at each other foolishly,
> and one could be heard to say:—"Is that all?" while another would say:—"When
> do they play again?"[67]

Following the concert, Colonel Hayward was approached by a committee
of businessmen who, while being critical of the War Department's decision, assured him that the mayor's remarks did not represent the responsible
citizenship of Spartanburg and that they wanted to offer their full cooperation
to make the best of the situation. Colonel Hayward was invited to speak as
guest of honor at the next meeting of the Rotary Club, and the regiment's officers (the white officers) were to consider themselves honorary members of the
town's country club. Arrangements were also being planned with the leaders of
Spartanburg's black community to hold dances, church socials, and other ac-

tivities for the men. The colonel was finally asked if he would let the band, conceded the best in Spartanburg, play for a dance at the club the following week, if they paid for its services. Colonel Hayward's strategy, at that moment, appeared promising. Nevertheless, forces beyond the control of both Colonel Hayward and "the responsible citizens" of Spartanburg conspired against them.

During their first week of training, the soldiers from the 15th Regiment when on leave or on duty in the town submitted to the "Jim Crow" customs and reacted to the insults heaped upon them with admirable restraint. They did not try to enter or be served in places where they were not wanted, including the street cars, and they did not retaliate even when physically abused. "Our boys had some pretty bitter pills to swallow and all week we had been hearing stories of the ever increasing insults," Sissle remembered.[68] The white soldiers from the other regiments of the 27th Division, also—of course—New Yorkers, had made no promises to their commanding officers to avoid confrontations with the local civilian population; they sympathized with their fellow servicemen, and they increasingly resented the way they were being treated. When it was learned that black soldiers were being refused service by the small shopkeepers just outside the camp gates, a group of soldiers from the 71st and 12th Regiments visited them and told them that they better change their policy or close down because the "colored soldiers are all right. They're fighting with us for our country. They're our buddies. And we won't buy from the men who treat them unfairly."[69]

In another incident, several soldiers from the 7th Regiment witnessed a black soldier being attacked by two local men solely for the offense of walking on the sidewalk. When he did not fight back, muttering that he had promised not to, the white soldiers, saying they had not made any such promises, jumped on the civilians and knocked them into the gutter. The situation in Spartanburg was clearly becoming uncontrollable. "The white boys who were billeted next to our camp were from the 12th New York regiment [sic]," Sissle recalled, "They knew a lot of our boys from [the] 'San Juan Hill' section. Therefore they were always sympathizing with our boys and only awaited the opportunity to have an excuse to blow up the town."[70]

Early one morning at the beginning of the 15th Regiment's second week at Camp Wadsworth, the tragedy that was so widely feared was barely averted. Rumors had been circulating throughout the camp the previous evening that two of the regiment's men had been hanged at the Spartanburg police station for fighting with a local policeman. When the soldiers turned up absent at roll call, many of the men considered the rumors to be confirmed and declared their promise to Colonel Hayward was now off. At approximately 10:00 A.M. Colonel Hayward received word that half a company of men from the regiment had armed themselves and were on their way to Spartanburg. Fearing the worst, Hayward rushed into town and was surprised to find everything quiet; his men standing in perfect military order in the main street. Demanding an explanation, he was told that they were waiting to find out if their comrades had been lynched and if so, they intended to "shoot the police—all of them, if they could find them, and any other people of the town who might interfere or try to assist the police."[71] After taking charge of the soldiers, Hayward proceeded to the police station where, in response to his inquiries, he became satisfied that the story was groundless and he returned to the detachment, called them to attention, and marched back to camp. A crowd of civilians had in the meantime gathered nearby, and when the troops marched off rifles at right shoulder arms, they cheered. "Can you beat it," Hayward said to Major Little when it was over. "Just to think! That town was, for a half hour or more, just balancing between tragedy and normality, and they didn't know it."[72]

Hayward, naturally, wanted to keep the incident a secret from the towns-people, and he was successful in convincing the local newspapermen, who had gotten wind of it, not to report it in the papers. He could not, however, fail to inform General Phillips, and the general, despite his appreciation of the extraordinary efforts that Hayward and his officers promised to undertake to prevent a recurrence, concluded that the situation had become intolerable and that the army had to act. A few days later, General Phillips called on Colonel Hayward to tell him that he was recommending to the War Department that the 15th New York National Guard Infantry be sent immediately to France and that he had arranged for Colonel Hayward to meet with Secretary Baker in Washington, D.C., to present his report and recommendation.

Phillips had been deeply impressed with the way that the officers and men of the 15th had, for the most part, conducted themselves and avoided trouble, he told Hayward, but it would not be fair "to ask you and your regiment to continue working, indefinitely, under the strain which you have been compelled to accept since you came to Spartanburg." It would not be in the interest of the military service, either. Of course, the army could order the 15th Regiment to another camp in the United States to complete its training, but the general was opposed any course of action that might "admit of the violent element of this town claiming a moral victory," and this left only one option. Your "regiment should be rewarded," he told Hayward,

> To my mind, your regiment has established its right to be classed as "Disciplined." Having attained discipline, your regiment is fit to represent our country in foreign lands. In France, there is no color line. In France, your regiment can complete its training for modern warfare. To France, every fighting regiment of our army must go, sooner or later.[73]

On October 20, 1917, while Colonel Hayward was in Washington convincing the War Department to adopt General Phillips' recommendation for reassignment of the 15th to the war front, a confrontation between soldiers and townspeople in Spartanburg was narrowly averted that could easily have ended any chance that the regiment would be given the opportunity to prove itself in combat.

Lieutenant Europe, Drum-major Sissle, and several other soldiers were returning to camp after having attended evening services at a local church. Europe and Sissle had been invited by the minister to sing and play for his small congregation. While waiting with perhaps seventy-five other members of the regiment for their transportation to arrive, Europe asked one of the local townspeople where he might buy the New York papers and he was directed to a newsstand inside the lobby of a nearby "white" hotel. It was quite all right to go in there, the man assured them, "the colored people here in town go there for papers," and, in fact, "some of your boys were in there today to buy New York papers."[74] "Go on over 'Siss' and get every paper that has the word 'New York' on it. I never knew how sweet New York was until I landed here," Sissle remembered Europe saying, and, though he later confessed to some misgivings, Sissle did as he was asked:

> As I got there in front of the hotel I could see through the large window that there were quite a few white officers in the lobby and the newspaper stand was right near the door. I quietly opened the door and went directly to the newspaper stand. On the way from the door to the stand I passed a white soldier who was sitting reading. He looked up as I passed and smiled. As I got to the newsstand there was a white officer talking to the clerk behind the counter. At my approach the officer stepped back. I asked for the New York papers and was waited on with all the courtesy of a Boston clerk. Receiving my change I turned to leave all flushed with the idea of how ungrounded had been my fears.[75]

Before he could get to the door, however, Sissle was struck from behind, his hat knocked off his head, and a gruff voice roared, "Say, nigger, don't you know enough to take your hat off." Sissle, who was as slight and peaceable appearing a person as one might imagine (and who also wore glasses), could see that everyone else in the place—soldier and civilian—was wearing a hat. "Do you realize you are abusing a United States soldier and that is a government hat you knocked to the floor?," Sissle stammered as he grabbed his hat and scrambled towards the door, being cursed and kicked all the way by a man who turned out to be the hotel's proprietor.

None of the seventy-five black soldiers just down the street had seen what had happened, and Sissle pulled himself together and decided not to say anything until they were all back in camp. The situation, however, was beyond Sissle's control. The forty or fifty white soldiers, relaxing in the hotel, had witnessed what had happened, one of them yelled "Let's kill the so and so, and pull his dirty old hotel down about his ears," and the proprietor found himself in deep trouble. At the same time, the white soldier who Sissle had spoken to when he entered the hotel, "a Jewish boy from New York," had rushed outside and told the black soldiers and was leading them back to the hotel.[76]

Just as the black soldiers arrived and began to enter the hotel, "a voice of command was heard above all other voices," calling the soldiers to attention. In the midst of the confusion and strong emotions involved, the soldiers surprisingly obeyed. "Get your hats and coats and leave this place, quietly, and walk out, separately or in twos, to Main Street," the officer ordered. Again, they obeyed. When all the soldiers, white and black, were outside, the officer went up to the hotel owner, who seemed not to realize that his establishment and perhaps his life had just been spared, and asked him what had happened. Still raving, the proprietor said that nothing had happened except that "that nigger," pointing at Sissle, "did not take off his hat and no nigger can come into my place without taking off his hat and you take off your hat." Lieutenant Europe removed his hat very slowly, saying, "I'll take my hat off just to find out one thing; what did Sgt. Sissle do? Did he commit any offense?" "No," the man shouted, "I told you he did not take his hat off and I knocked it off, now you get out of here."[77] Europe made no response. "For a moment Jim Europe's eye held that of the man who was insulting him. There was no sign of fear in the glance of the negro [sic]. Then, with quiet dignity, he turned his back, and walked into the street."[78]

By this time the military police had arrived, and Europe was able to convince the men, despite their great reluctance, to let the authorities handle the matter and return to camp. Two days later orders came from the chief of staff of the 27th Division for the 15th Regiment to prepare immediately to move out, and on the morning of October 24, 1917, New York's black regiment marched out of Camp Wadsworth to the rail depot where the trains were waiting. The day was brilliantly sunny and warm, and "thousands of brave New York lads of the 27th Division lined the sides of the road-way, and sang us through, to the tune of 'Over There.'" Bidding farewell to Spartanburg, with mixed emotions, Major Little recalled, "we did not know exactly where we were going. We did know, however, and in the knowledge we felt thrilled with a number of emotions, of which by no means the least pronounced was—elation, we did know that—we were on the way."[79]

12

"Over There"

They were sent to hospitals and locations all over France. They were the best musicians on the Western Front, and that's no idle boast. Our band won all the competitions easily, under Jim Europe.

Hamilton Fish, Jr.

It is a sad fact that New York's black infantry could not be trained at home but had to be sent abroad to foreign soil to acquire the skills necessary to fight for their country, and the irony was not lost upon the officers and men of the 15th. Still, the anticipation of getting to France and into action helped to keep their spirits up, and as they traveled north to an as yet undisclosed port of embarkation, it was even possible to joke about the situation. "I'm sure sorry I sent you in after those papers in Spartanburg," Europe remarked to Sissle at one point. "[H]ere, the man has 'kicked' us right to France."[1]

As Colonel Hayward well knew, from the standpoint of the morale of his troops, the best thing that could have happened was for the 15th to be transferred from the trains directly to the ship assigned to them for the Atlantic crossing. Due to the threat of German submarines, however, transports sailed only in groups, or convoys, with warship escorts. By the time the 15th Regiment arrived in New York, the convoy to which they were assigned had unfortunately already sailed, and they were forced to wait at Camp Mills on Long Island and at various armories in the city for two weeks while new convoy arrangements were made.[2] On November 8, the regiment was reviewed in Central Park by General Hoyle, commander of the Eastern Department—Lieutenant Europe leading the band in "Auld Lang Syne," "Religioso March" (a "kind of half syncopated arrangement of 'Onward Christian Soldiers'"), "Come Ye Disconsolate," and "Over There,"—and three days later the men were transported to Hoboken, New Jersey, where the ocean transport *Pocahontas* waited to take the first black combat troops from America to France. That evening, Arthur Little recalled, "as we sailed for the battle fields of France, and realized that the 27th Division was in winter quarters at Spartanburg—we chuckled, and I must confess that, in a good-natured, friendly spirit, we even gloated a little."[3]

However widely such feelings may have been felt, they were shortlived; the *Pocahontas* was barely 150 miles out to sea when engine trouble forced the captain to return to port, and the 15th again found itself in camp for another delay of nearly three weeks. On December 2, with the repairs completed and a third convoy scheduled, they tried again. Unbelievably, before the unfortunate ship could get underway, a fire broke out in the coal bunkers, and the *Pocahontas* was stuck at the pier. Once more, the men of the 15th New York watched their convoy sail off without them.

Finally, on the evening of December 13, eleven days after the fire was discovered, the *Pocahontas* steamed carefully out of New York Harbor and dropped anchor at Sandy Hook. Two hours after midnight, while waiting for the other ships of her group to assemble, the *Pocahontas* was rocked by what felt like an exploding torpedo, and near panic ensued as the troops scrambled to get to their lifeboats. The true source of the disturbance was not an enemy submarine; rather, it was a British oil tanker that had dragged anchor and drifted down upon the *Pocahontas*, tearing a large hole in her starboard side. Thanks to the presence of a contingent of metal workers and their equipment on board—as well as Colonel Hayward's impassioned plea that they not return to port—repairs were made and ship was ready by evening. "I believe," Major Little wrote later, "that no less than ninety percent of the soldier men on that ship would have burst into tears, if we had failed for the fourth time to accompany the convoy to which we had been assigned."[4]

The Atlantic crossing of the *Pocahontas*, which took nearly two weeks, was accomplished without major incident, although the constant fear of submarine attack kept tensions high. Until the last three days of their voyage, when the *Pocahontas* entered the "danger zone" close to the continent, Jim Europe and the band were permitted to play on deck in the afternoons and accompany religious services on Sundays, and the music helped. The evenings were especially difficult, however; no light of any kind (not even a cigarette) was permitted on deck, the rest of the convoy vanished into the darkness, and feelings of loneliness and apprehension took over. The experience of these "blue haze" evenings, Sissle later wrote, "will linger long after all incidents of the war have grown old."[5]

On deck, the soldiers who leaned against the lifeboats or took a final stroll before going below spoke in whispers—though there was no prescription against talking in normal tones—and below deck the voices of men praying, or occasionally, singing could be heard. On such evenings, Lieutenant Europe would regularly extemporize at a piano placed on the upper deck while the other officers of the regiment and ship's company sat around. The melancholy atmosphere of these occasions brought out his sentimental side, and his playing, and the singing of the Company K quartet and Noble Sissle, who joined him, conspired to produce "very few dry eyes among those assembled."[6] "In all my experience of public and private entertaining," Sissle wrote, "never did I find such a submissive lot as those seventy-five or more lovesick, lonesome victims." Before things could degenerate into self-pity, however, Europe would launch into a syncopated up-tempo melody, and Sissle or the quartet would "immediately fall in and catch his spirit and start the feet to tapping out the time of whatever little ditty we would sing."[7]

On Sunday, December 24, the *Pocahontas* entered the "danger zone," and all hands were ordered to remain dressed with their life vests on at all times. No one was allowed to sleep below decks, and the life boats were kept manned and ready. Dawn on Christmas Day, however, brought a most welcomed present in the form of seven Allied destroyers, sent to escort the convoy to port and, with great relief and prayers of thanksgiving, the soldiers of New York's 15th Regiment enjoyed their holiday dinner of turkey and cranberries. Two days later the *Pocahontas* sailed into the picturesque harbor at Brest on the Brittany Coast, the easternmost part of France.

On New Years Day 1918, the first African-American combat unit to set foot on French soil marched ashore to receive the greeting of a large and curious crowd of French soldiers and sailors. Colonel Hayward had ordered Lieutenant Europe to have the band ready to play, and Europe immediately struck up the "Marseillaise." The response from the Frenchmen to the music of the American band is revealing, setting a pattern that would become almost commonplace wherever the band performed over the next eleven months. At first, to the great surprise of the Americans and, especially, the band members, the French soldiers seemed not to recognize the strains of their own national anthem. Suddenly, "as the band had played eight or ten bars there came over their faces an astonished look, quickly alert snap-into-it-attention and salute by every French soldier and sailor present." Only later, when the Americans heard a French band play the "Marseillaise" in their customary fashion, "like an organ playing a hymn," did they understand the reason. These Frenchmen had not been privileged to hear the sound of African-American music in the cafes and theaters of Paris before the war, and they were confused at first by the novelty of Europe's rhythmic arrangement and the band's spirited interpretation. Like those who had, however, they were also pleased and thrilled "to a far greater extent than their own band's playing."[8]

The 2,000 officers and men of the New York Regiment were allowed little time to adjust to their new surroundings as orders had been received from General Pershing, commander of the American Expeditionary Force, to proceed directly to St. Nazaire, a city farther down the French coast, where an American engineering detachment was constructing the facilities to support an American army of, eventually, several million men. Railroad track was in the process of being laid, storehouses built, docks renovated, and a large dam for a reservoir was under construction. This was important, perhaps vital, work, and many of the troops of the 15th recognized it as such. Even so, there was great disappointment when Colonel Hayward sadly announced that they had been temporarily assigned to labor duty and that they would have to exchange their rifles for picks and shovels.

It was clear that the American high command had no more idea about what to do with a black combat regiment in France, since the proposed black division was not yet formed, than the War Department did back home. American forces had been serving in the front lines since October, but, as Hamilton Fish later recalled, there "was an old law against black troops serving with white troops, and the War Department didn't want to mix them, but we had no other black units with which to form a division."[9]

The officers and men of the 15th reluctantly did as they were ordered, but as the days dragged on and no new orders were forthcoming morale began to drop. Even the regularly scheduled performances of the band (without its leader who accompanied his machine gun company each morning to "attack his assigned portion of the terrible dam") failed to raise the spirits of the men, who increasingly besieged Hayward with their question, "When are we going to fight?"[10] Neither the officers nor the men of the 15th, of course, had much understanding of the nature of trench warfare, but they had enlisted as fighting troops, and they "wanted to see good wartime service under fair conditions."[11] By the end of January, Colonel Hayward and the other senior officers also began to fear that although they had come to France as combat troops they were in danger of becoming permanent stevedores, and he wrote a lengthy letter to General Pershing pleading his case for front-line duty.

Aside from the inappropriate assignment of his regiment at St. Nazaire, Hayward hoped to impress the general by pointing out the progress, under the most trying of circumstances, that the 15th had made in its short lifetime. He was also able to demonstrate the regiment's remarkable record in avoiding or preventing infection from venereal disease, then viewed as a moral as well as physical evil and which had become the focus of a major campaign by the U.S. War Department. According to historian Allan M. Brandt, General Pershing was "virtually obsessed with the charge of making the AEF the first venereal-free army in military history," and Major Little recalled that "sixty percent of all orders and circulars from G.H.Q." that the regiment received at St. Nazaire were concerned with the subject.[12]

In drafting his request for a reassignment of the 15th, Colonel Hayward also benefited from the endorsement of General Walsh, commanding general of Base No. 1 at St. Nazaire. Walsh had commanded black troops himself in the regular army for more than twenty years and did not share the army's general prejudice against them. Most important, however, by the end of January, Hayward and the 15th Infantry Regiment possessed something that the AEF Headquarters decided it needed—Jim Europe's regimental band—and Hayward was convinced that if he complied willingly with the request for the band's services, his own petition would be given positive consideration. General Pershing's interest in the 15th Regimental Band was curiously not unrelated to the army's concerns about the morals and sexual hygiene of the American troops.

During the summer of 1917, the AEF decided that each soldier should receive a week's leave for every four months of duty. This would not permit them to return home, but it would be long enough for them to get into trouble, especially in France. The YMCA, which was given the responsibility for organizing the leave camps for American soldiers, therefore, chose areas away from the major cities, where the temptations of liquor and prostitution (legal in France) were not so prevalent, and they planned recreational activities and entertainment programs to keep the men occupied. Rates of venereal disease infection were inversely related to the quality of the amusements, the YMCA believed.[13] The first of these camps, at the resort town of Aix-les-Bains, some forty miles south of Geneva, was due to receive its initial group of American veterans in February, most of whom had their hearts set on spending their leave in Paris.

In mid-January, two members of the American theatrical profession, Winthrop Ames and Edward H. Sothern, who were then attempting to organize the entertainment for the troops at Aix-les-Bains, learned that one of the regiments at St. Nazaire had an unusually good military band, and they decided to investigate. "By this time we had heard a good many of the American military bands," Ames recalled. "They served as cheerful adjuncts of camp life; but from any musical standpoint, their performances were mediocre. In this case, I suppose, we expected the 'usual' thing."

> But we were immediately impressed by the number of players (there were forty of them) who gathered on the flat muddy parade-ground in front of the wooden barracks; and no sooner had they begun to play than it became obvious that we were not listening to the ordinary army band at all, but to an organization of the very highest quality, trained and led by a conductor of genius. We asked his name, and were told that he was no less a musician than James Reese Europe—already famous in America, but whom we little expected to find a soldier in France.[14]

Until then, Ames and Sothern had found little of the sort of entertainment they sought, the kind with a "flavor of America" and the "feel of home," but in the 15th Regimental Band they had discovered an organization that was "unequalled anywhere in the world in its own specialty," the performance of American syncopated music. "When they heard our band play, the quartette sing, and saw some of the boys dance during the hour-and-a-half program that we were able to give them," Sissle later wrote,

> [T]hey immediately said that we were the best entertainment unit that they had seen in France on their tour. It was so typically American that they were immediately going to get in touch with General Pershing, and have our band and entertainers sent to Aix-les-Bains for the opening of the rest center.[15]

A few days later, Colonel Hayward received word that the request had been made and that orders would soon be issued to have the band proceed to Aix-les-Bains to entertain the first soldiers on leave, due to arrive on Washington's Birthday.

Hayward and the officers and men of the 15th were not especially pleased to be losing their music men, but they appreciated the prospect that a good impression by the band on the Allied General Staff could help get the reassignment they wanted. There was concern, however, when rumors came from Chaumont (Pershing's Headquarters) that a white officer would be put in charge of the band and that Europe, who as a machine gun officer was not officially connected with the band, would not be permitted to go at all. Bandmaster Mikell was a fine musician, well-educated, and an excellent cornetist, but "as compared with Jim Europe as a leader of men, or as a band leader, he wasn't in the same class."[16] The consensus was that under Mikell's leadership, the band was much better than the average, but that when Europe led them there was a pronounced improvement in their performance; the 15th Regimental Band became something special.

Wanting Europe to go with the band, Colonel Hayward contrived to have General Walsh make a personal recommendation to General Pershing that he be assigned to do so. General Walsh had listened to the band play on several occasions, with Sergeant Mikell conducting as was the usual routine at St. Nazaire. Prior to a dinner party that he was hosting for the General and his staff in early February, however, Hayward told his adjutant to have Lieutenant Europe lead the band for the dinner concert. "General Walsh was up here a few nights ago and we gave him a good time," he said, "but if we can get Jim inspired tonight, we can stand that Headquarters crowd on their heads, and I think we'll have won our point about having Lieut. Europe tour France with the band, and in command of it."[17] Hayward's plan worked perfectly; General Walsh and his staff were visibly moved by the band's playing, and when Hayward explained to them the reason, Walsh promised to make a personal plea to Chaumont to have Europe included in the expedition.[18] On February 10, 1918, the special orders were received by Colonel Hayward detaching the 15th Infantry Regiment Band and support personnel, consisting of fifty-six men and *two* officers. Major Little, then a captain, was placed in overall command; the other officer, who was designated as director of the band, was Lieutenant Europe.

On the afternoon of February 12, 1918, Lincoln's Birthday, the musical contingent from the 15th New York Regiment began its three-day journey across the breadth of France, with a stopover in the city of Nantes, a short distance by rail from St. Nazaire. That evening, a public concert at the town's opera house had been scheduled in honor of the American holiday and for the benefit of a French charity, and Europe and the band got their first opportunity to perform before an audience of French civilians and to experience their reaction to American music. Prior to the 9:00 P.M. concert, the band played a few numbers for a large and appreciative audience that had gathered informally in the plaza outside the opera house. They then retired inside, where they found all the reserved seats and galleries filled, including standing room. "I doubt if any first night or special performance at the Metropolitan Opera House in New York ever had, relatively, a more brilliant audience," Little recalled.

> The French people knew no color line. All they seemed to want to know, that night, was that a great national holiday of their ally was being celebrated—and that made the celebration one of their own. The spirit of emotional enthusiasm had got into the blood of our men; and they played as I had never heard them play before.[19]

In a colorfully written article published four months later in the St. Louis *Post-Dispatch*, Noble Sissle described the concert that evening and the reaction of the crowd, especially when the band launched into its more uninhibited—and to the French, unfamiliar—ragtime numbers. The program began appropriately with a French march, followed by several overtures and vocal selections by the quartet, "all of which were heartily applauded." The second part of the program opened with Sousa's "Stars and Stripes Forever," and "before the last note of the martial ending had been finished the house was ringing with applause." Next followed an arrangement of Southern or "plantation" melodies, and then came "the fireworks, 'The Memphis Blues.'" Following Europe's example, the musicians relaxed their stiff military demeanor, half closed their eyes, and as the baton came down with a "soul-rousing crash" of cymbals, "both director and musicians seemed to forget their surroundings . . . . Cornet and clarinet players began to manipulate notes in that typical rhythm (that rhythm which no artist has ever been able to put down on paper)." The drummers hit their stride with shoulders shaking in syncopated time, and Europe turned to the trombones "who sat patiently waiting for their cue to have a 'jazz spasm.'. . . The audience could stand it no longer, the 'jazz germ' hit them and it seemed to find the vital spot loosening all muscles and causing what is known in America as an 'eagle rocking it.'" There now, Sissle said to himself,

> "Colonel Hayward has brought his band over here and started ragtimitis in France; ain't this an awful thing to visit upon a nation with so many burdens?" But when the band had finished and people were roaring with laughter, their faces wreathed in smiles, I was forced to say that this is just what France needs at this critical time.[20]

The first concert by the 15th Regimental Band at Nantes was perhaps the most memorable of the trip to Aix-les-Bains, and it was the only formally scheduled performance. It was, however, nonetheless representative of the reaction of the French people to the Americans whenever their train stopped and the band was permitted to perform. Leaving Nantes on the morning of February 13, they passed through a dozen towns and cities—including Angers, Tours, Moulins, Varennes, St. Germain des Fosses, Lyon, and Culoz—where time was found for at least a brief concert at the railway station or in a public square nearby. At Tours, where they spent the night of the 13th, no prior notification of their visit had been given to the local military authorities, but Captain Little (ever alert for opportunities to impress the Allied high command) suggested to the local provost marshal that the band be allowed to give a surprise serenade for Major General Kernan, the commanding officer of the region, who was quartered just outside the city. "Have you got a good band?," he was asked. "Pretty good," Little replied. "It's the only one I've heard over here; but I believe it's the best in the army." "Well, I dunno," said the provost,

> I dunno about that. Some of our young officers here came back from St. Nazaire a couple of weeks ago, and they've been talking ever since about some colored band they heard down there. They say that's the real thing in bands—about double the size of the regulation article, and wonderful to listen to. The leader, I believe, is a chap by name of Europe—Jim Europe, who used to play dance music in New York for Mr. and Mrs. Vernon Castle, when they were all the rage. Ever hear that band?

"That's the band I've got at your barracks, right now," Little answered. "Well, I'll be damned!," came the response.[21]

Transportation arrangements were quickly made, the concert given, and General Kernan was greatly pleased by the unexpected serenade. The general thanked the band afterward and predicted that their tour could not fail to be successful, but he also reminded the men of the 15th that they were going where no American soldiers had been before and that the reputation of the American soldier in general rested upon the impression they created with the French population. In addition, he said, they also carried the responsibility of representing their race and he admonished them not to be the cause of the establishment of a color line in the minds of the French people. "The eyes of France would be upon them," he said, "and through the eyes of France, the eyes of the world."[22] Returning to the city, the band gave a short concert before an appreciative audience at the Red Cross Club and then caught a few hours of well-deserved sleep before the train left early the next morning.

On the evening of February 15, 1918, much to the relief of Winthrop Ames, E. H. Sothern and the other members of the Entertainment Committee, the 15th Infantry Regimental Band arrived, as ordered, at the first American leave area at Aix-les-Bains. At noon the following day, a picturesque assemblage of American army officers, YMCA workers, French townspeople, and the mayor and his staff in high hats with red ribbons waited before the station for the train bringing the first contingent of "dough-boys" from their tour in the trenches. "It was a sight I'll never forget," Ames later wrote. A local band, consisting of schoolboys and old men, stood alongside, and as "the first American soldiers, unkempt from their forty-eight-hour train journey and still caked with the mud of the trenches, filed into sight, this little band set up a thin wail—a brave attempt at the "Star Spangled Banner."

> Our men did not laugh. They knew no able-bodied men could be spared for civilian bands in France in that year of grace 1918; but some of them could hardly repress a grin under their "tin hats" as they finally made out the air and came to a belated salute. But, as the wavering tune ceased it was followed by a thrilling burst of sound. Europe's band which had come the night before from the opposite side of France marched into the square playing "Marseillaise."[23]

The sight of such a large band composed entirely of dark-skinned musicians surprised the French almost as much as the sounds they heard. Among the French people at the time, there was a tradition that no foreign musicians could ever play the "Marseillaise" properly, and yet here "was a rendering of their national anthem that fairly swept them off their feet," Ames recalled. "Every head in the crowd was instantly uncovered; and I think not even a child stirred till the last notes had died away. Then there was a sudden and moving burst of cheers. An old man near me cried out: 'Mais, Mon Dieu, c'est magnifique!,' and there were tears on his cheeks."

The original orders for Lieutenant Europe and the band stipulated a two-week assignment at Aix-les-Bains where, although there were opportunities to play before French civilians, their primary assignment was to provide entertainment for the American troops. With its hot water baths, mountain setting, ancient Roman ruins, and wonderful mixture of French and Italian architecture, Aix-les-Bains had been one of the most famous health resorts in the world before the war, and many wealthy Americans, including J. P. Morgan, had frequented it regularly.

For the band, a routine was quickly established in which the mornings were set aside for rehearsals and the afternoons and evenings for concert performances for the men. Most of the concerts were held in the 1,000-seat theater, called the Casino, except for Tuesdays and Fridays when the band played in the park outside, and the evening performances were a main feature of the vaudeville show that Ames directed. The band also contributed several formal and informal concerts at Chambéry—an old cathedral city a short distance from Aix noted for its picturesque setting and for having been the home of philosopher Jean Jacques Rousseau—and provided the musical accompaniment for religious services on Sundays. From the first afternoon concert, when the band opened with "Over There" and the war-weary American soldiers responded by climbing on the tables, shouting, waving their caps, and demanding that it be played again and again, the band was a great hit. "No other form of entertainment appealed to them quite so much," Ames later wrote.[24] Indeed, the camp authorities found the band's contribution so important that they requested (and received) an extension of its services for an additional two weeks.

For the first time in his career, Europe experienced the luxury of being able to give his undivided attention to directing a musical organization whose membership was constant, who had no other responsibilities except their music, and for whom regular performances had been arranged before pre-dictably appreciative audiences. Given such favorable circumstances, the band's playing was bound to improve (Sissle believed it was 100 percent better by the end of the month), and Europe even began to think that there was a promising future for this kind of band once the war was over.[25] Aside from the rehearsals and concerts, most of Europe's time was spent finding new material and writing out new arrangements, since the band's program had to be changed daily. As a result, by the time they left Aix-les-Bains the band had expanded its repertoire of standard concert and popular pieces considerably.

Europe also took seriously the band's responsibility as an ambassador of good will to the French people. On a number of occasions during intermis-sions at the concerts in the park, civilians would hand him a sheet of music and request that the band play the piece at the next concert. It might be a song written by a daughter who had died or a favorite tune of a son now serving at the front, but these requests invariably had strong personal and emotional meaning, and they were never refused. "One morning," Captain Little remembered,

> I noticed that Mr. Europe's eyes had the appearance of great fatigue. I inquired if he was unwell. He said that he was quite well, but that he had been up most of the night, arranging the orchestration for one of those amateur musical compo-sitions. As Europe expressed it, he had written 3 million notes, representing over twenty different musical scores. Of course the 3 million estimate was an exagger-ation; but in Europe's Band [sic] no more than two men ever played the same score. His arrangements were always marvels of effective harmony.[26]

Another incident reflecting Europe's sensitivity and generosity that Little specifically recalled occurred when the band was giving a concert at an orphan-age in Chambéry. One of the children became fascinated by Europe's conducting and began to imitate his gestures. The conductor happened to turn, catching him in the act, and with

> a crash of brass wind and cymbals, Jim brought to a close the piece which he was playing. Then he walked over to the little fellow, placed the baton in his hand, led him out in front of the band, gave instructions to his men for the playing of a piece of simple time, walked over to the side lines to stand beside me—and the little French orphan led the band. That crowd just went crazy![27]

Winthrop Ames remembered Europe during the time they spent together at Aix as a "simple, quiet, and unaffected gentleman," "neither conceited nor self-satisfied," but a "sincere artist, full of respect for his work, and eager about his own future and that of his band." Above all else, however, he was a "passionate soldier. His great desire was to get into action,—to have his band play its regiment 'Over the Top.'"[28] The other band members, including even the Puerto Ricans, were similarly anxious "to get into the thick of the fray."[29] On March 14, 1918, when orders were received for the band to rejoin their regiment at Connantre in the Marne Division of the Western Front, not at St. Nazaire, it appeared that they would soon be given their chance.

While the 15th Regimental Band had been entertaining the American soldiers on leave at Aix-les-Bains, Colonel Hayward's persistent appeals for reassignment of his regiment—coupled with the splendid reputation the band was making—finally produced results. Still unwilling to break with army tradition and order the New York regiment to join an American combat division, the American high command gave Hayward a choice. He could return with his men to the United States and await the formation of one of the proposed black divisions, or be transferred immediately to the French Army. The French had already integrated African colonial troops into their forces and were desperate for combat reinforcements. Hayward did not hesitate. The option to join the French as a combat unit, the first American unit to do so, was received as a "fairy tale," a "beautiful dream come true," and at the end of the first week in March, the 15th Infantry Regiment—still officially carrying the colors of New York State—left St. Nazaire under sealed orders to join the 16th Division of the 4th French Army at the front.[30] "Our great American general simply put the black orphan in a basket, set it on the doorstep of the French, pulled the bell, and went away," Hayward wrote. When he told this to a French colonel "with an 'English spoken here' sign on him," the officer responded "'Weelcome leetle black babbie.'"[31]

The departure of the 15th Regimental Band from Aix-les-Bains was an emotional and memorable one. On the evening of March 16, at the conclusion of the vaudeville entertainment at the Casino, the YMCA official in charge attempted to give a speech biding goodbye to the band and thanking them for their services, but his words were drowned out by the cheers, whistles, and yells of the soldiers in the audience. The response of the civilian populace as the band attempted to depart the next day was equally heartfelt. The local chief of police was helpless to keep the mass of women, children, and old men (there were, of course, no young Frenchmen) from pressing bottles of champagne, handshakes, and babies to be kissed on Little, Europe, and the musicians. They were forced to stop and to listen to speeches from local authorities three times during their attempt to march to the railroad station. "When we arrived," Little recalled,

> a lane had to be forced, to admit of our getting through to where the trains were to be boarded. And when the train rolled (or rather crept) in, a guard of police and railroad attendants had to precede it, to clear the tracks to avoid wholesale carnage. During the delay attendant upon attaching our cars to the train, the band played its farewell; the crowd cheered without ceasing; women and children wept.[32]

The two-day journey to Connantre, which turned out to be a forwarding point, rather than their final destination, where new orders were issued to troops going into the front lines, took the 15th Regiment detachment east to Lyon and then north with stops at Dijon, Langres, Chaumont, and a number of smaller towns. As had been the procedure in the trip from St. Nazaire to Aix-les-Bains some six weeks earlier, the band piled out of its coaches at each opportunity, and Europe led them in an informal concert for local civilians or for the troops in the trains they passed.

On the morning of the second day, their train entered country that bore stark witness to the great battles of the first months of the war. Up until then, the Americans' understanding of the war had been based on the stories told them by soldiers who for the most part had escaped the worst of the slaughter and destruction. Now, for the first time, they began to see a country devastated by modern warfare—single buildings and entire villages reduced to rubble, miles and miles of meadowland horribly disfigured from cannon shells and tangles of barbed wire, and thousands of little wooden crosses marking the graves of the French and German patriots who had died. Hospital trains carrying the wounded away from the front began to pass with greater frequency, and the sight of their maimed bodies and the sound of their groaning shocked the musicians; until then, they could visualize only the enemy as the ones in the hospitals.[33]

Captain Little, Lieutenant Europe, and the rest of the band reached Connantre on the morning of March 20, 1918. There, they found a number of French officers, none of whom had ever heard of the 15th Infantry Regiment of New York. After almost two hours of struggling with the French language, Little and Europe finally found out who and where they were. It appeared that the 15th Regiment had "died a peaceful death in general orders" and was now known as the Trois Cent Soixante Neuvieme R. I. U. S., the 369th Infantry Regiment, U.S. Army, and as such had been temporarily assigned to the 16th Division of the French Army. The 369th was currently undergoing intensive indoctrination for front-line duty with the French in the advanced zone near Givry-en-Argonne, an overnight train ride away and near the city of Verdun, where 650,000 French and German soldiers had perished two years earlier. During the final leg of their journey, in the middle of the night, about half of the band members (including Sissle and most of the Puerto Rican musicians) were mistakenly placed on a troop car that was headed directly for the front. When they awoke and climbed off the train, Sissle recalled, they discovered that they had become separated from the rest of the band. They were unaware, however, of how close they were to the battle line "until all of a sudden, without any warning, there came a shriek through the air like the screaming of a pheasant, followed by a tremendous explosion of a large shell from the German line."[34] Two days later, by the time that Sissle and the Puerto Rican musicians finally found their way back to Givry-en-Argonne and the site of the 369th's encampment, they had recovered sufficiently from their frighting experience to take pride in the fact that they could claim the distinction of being the first members of their regiment, and the first African-American soldiers, to come under enemy fire in the Great War.

13

"On Patrol in No Man's Land"

> They wrote some music over there too. They wrote "On Patrol in
> No Man's Land" and "All of No Man's Land is Ours." Now I didn't
> have nothin' to do with those tunes. I did not write any part of
> them. But they put my name on 'em right alongside of theirs, be-
> cause that's the kind of partners they were.
>
> Eubie Blake

By the time that Europe, Little, Sissle, and the rest of band were reunited
with their comrades at Givry-en-Argonne, the newly designated 369th
Infantry Regiment was already intensely involved in the training required to integrate the American unit into the French Army. This was no
simple task. The French military organization was different from the American, and the French employed different methods of fighting and used different
ordnance and equipment. The soldiers of the 369th were permitted to retain
only their American uniforms; everything else, including their trusty Springfield rifles (which were useless without American ammunition), had to be
exchanged for French issue. Language differences and customs (the Americans
were not used to French rations, for example) also presented problems of ad-
justment, but the fact that the American troops had received such limited
combat training previously may have worked to their advantage. At the very
least, it meant that they had little to relearn when they began their indoctrination in the tactics of trench warfare.

To the surprise of their French instructors, who were assigned roughly one
to each platoon, the Americans seemed especially adept at two important aspects of close-in, hand-to-hand combat. "Our men who played baseball," Fish
recalled, "could throw grenades farther than the French, which amused the
French a lot."[1] Thanks to the popularity of boxing, the American soldiers also
showed talent in the use of bayonets; the techniques of the feint, thrust, and
parry are roughly the same.[2]

One problem they did not have to face, and it made all the difference in the
world, was bigotry. The French military—from the interpreters to the drill instructors to the staff officers to the commanding generals—showed none of the
prejudice toward the black American regiment that they had experienced in
the U.S. Army. From all accounts, a true comradeship developed between the
French officers and noncoms assigned to the 369th and their American
counterparts. "The French officers had taken our officers and made pals out of

them," Sissle wrote. "The noncommissioned officers in the French Army who held a little more elevated position than the noncommissioned officers in our army by virtue of their long military campaign, treated our boys with all the courtesy and comradeship that could be expected."[3] "We got along very well," Hamilton Fish remembered. General Gouraud, the near-legendary commander of the French 4th Army to which the 369th now belonged, had served in Africa and had "a high opinion of African troops." As for the Americans, "the French were glad to have them, and they were glad to serve."[4] The French, Hayward wrote to a fellow American colonel in late March, "are wonderful—wonderful—wonderful."[5] Two months latter, Europe wrote to Fred Moore, Editor of the *New York Age*, that the French were "models."

> Their broad minds are far and free from prejudice, and you, as a great champion of our people, I am sure will be glad to know that despite their contact, despite the desperate efforts of some people, the French simply cannot be taught to comprehend that despicable thing called prejudice . . . "Viva la France" should be the song of every black American over here and over there.[6]

With his special assignment to the band no longer a main priority, Lieutenant Europe turned over his musical responsibilities to Bandmaster Mikell and again took charge of his combat unit, Company I, of the 3rd Battalion. Less than a week later the entire regiment was ordered to move closer to the front where the sounds of exploding artillery and the sight, on clear nights, of rocket flares and flashes gave an increasing urgency and seriousness to their training. Like the other officers and men, Europe's energy and attention were focused upon learning everything possible from his instructors, from the proper use of the French Chauchat machine guns to the correct procedures for protecting himself and his men against the increasing use of gas warfare by the Germans. As the signs became clearer that the French intended to put the 369th into front-line duty at the first opportunity, Europe attempted to put aside his concerns about his personal and professional life back in New York.

On April 9, in reply to a letter from Eubie Blake in which Blake complained of the recent decline in jobs for musicians in New York, Europe wrote that he was aware that the music business was slow, but for Eubie to just "stay on the job and take your medicine." "If you think of the comforts you are having over there and think of the hardships we are having over here," he wrote, "you'd be happy I am sure to go on 'suffering.'"[7] "I have some wonderful opportunities for you to make all the money you need," Europe promised. "Eubie, the thing to do is to build for the future, and build securely and that is what I am doing. When I go up I will take you with me, you can be sure of that." The letter was signed "Your real pal, Jas. Reese, 369th Inf."

Other comments in the same letter make it clear that Europe had more worries than the current condition of his business affairs. He had learned from the

New York papers that his wife had been ill, but Willie Europe, who apparently knew about his relationship with Bessie Simms (and perhaps about their year-old son), was not writing to her husband. "I left N. Y. in Nov. and now this is april [sic]," he told Blake, "and not a post card (not to speak of a letter) have I received from Willie or Ida [Europe's older sister], nothing, nothing, nothing, nor I do not expect to hear anything." "Well at present, Eubie," he continued stoically,

> I am a soldier in every sense of the word and I must only take orders and be able to stand all sorts of hardships and make untold sacrifices. At the moment, I am unable to do anything. My hands are tied and tied fast but if the war does not end me first as sure as God made man, I will be on top and so far on top that it will be impossible to pull me down.[8]

As if these matters did not weigh heavily enough, just prior to receiving Blake's letter, Europe learned that Vernon Castle had been killed in an airplane accident on February 15 at Benbrook Field near Fort Worth, Texas. Castle had served the Royal Flying Corps with distinction, flying over 100 reconnaissance missions behind German lines and winning the Croix de Guerre for bravery. In 1917, after shooting down his first enemy aircraft and being shot down himself, he was relieved from combat duty and ordered to Camp Mohawk, Canada, as a flight instructor. Later that summer, he was nearly killed when the eighteen-year-old cadet he had been training froze at the controls, and their plane crashed. The cadet, who was in the forward cockpit, was not as lucky as his instructor, and Castle, who blamed himself, swore never to take the back seat in a training flight again. With the coming of winter, Castle's squadron was transferred south to Texas, and he was killed during a training flight when he attempted to avoid colliding with another plane. Riding in the rear cockpit, Castle's student escaped the crash without injury.[9]

Although Europe entertained few illusions about recreating the magic of the Castles/Europe partnership after the war (the days of the Castle House and the Whirlwind Tour must have seemed of a distant past), he felt grateful to Castle for his role in popularizing African-American music and broadening the reputation of black musicians (not the least of which was his own). Europe, however, also truly liked and trusted Vernon Castle, "one white absolutely with-out prejudice" who in private life was always "square."[10] Castle's death, therefore, was also a personal loss for Europe. "Can you imagine my grief," he wrote to Blake. "My one real and true friend gone."[11]

Vernon Castle's death, the military services in Texas, and the public funeral in New York were widely reported in the press accounts that made their way eventually to the soldiers at the front. When he read them, Europe must have felt somewhat better knowing that his old Society Orchestra was well-repre-sented at the funeral and that the Colored Musicians Union of New York had sent flowers.[12] Ford Dabney, cellist Charles Wilson, and violinist Allie Ross attended, but the most heartfelt tribute was given by drummer Buddy Gilmore, who insisted that Castle "had been his best friend" and who was so grief-stricken that Irene Castle granted him the honor of having the last look at her husband before his body was sealed. "For all the reverence displayed," a reporter for the *New York Tribune* wrote, "there had been something impersonal in the way in which most of the rest paid their respects to the dead. But 'Buddy's' mourning was for no dancer, nor soldier, nor hero, but for the champion trap drummer of the United States . . . and Buddy Gilmore had taught him how."[13]

Europe had precious little time to brood over the newspapers; on April 13, 1918, the entire 369th Regiment was ordered forward to the town of Maffrecourt, and there to establish a regimental base from which to direct the defense of its own sector of the line. The American soldiers had received barely half the training time that was originally planned, but the French command anticipated a major German offensive at any moment now that the Treaty of Brest-Litovsk had been signed and the Russians were no longer occupying the Germans' attention on the Eastern Front, and they felt that they could wait no longer. In fact, the 3rd Battalion had been sent forward almost a week in advance of the rest of the regiment, and among those first black soldiers from the United States to reach the trenches was Lieutenant Jim Europe, the 3rd Battalion's lone black officer. It was, almost to the day, the first anniversary of the American declaration of war against Germany.

"I will never forget the scene that cloudy morning in March [it was actually the first week in April] when we were called out with the band," Sissle later wrote, "to lead the first detachment of our soldiers to escort them to the outskirts of town on their pilgrimage down the roads of France into the trenches on the borders of no-man's-land."[14] The entire population of the town had come out to witness the Americans march off, and when, following the playing of the "Star Spangled Banner" and the "Marseillaise," the band struck up "Stars and Stripes Forever" and the command "forward march" was given, there was "hardly a dry eye amongst either the peasants or soldiers."

> As we got to the end of town and turned off for the troops to pass on by, at the colonel's command we swung into the favorite of both his and the regiment, the ragtime tune called "Army Blues," and the serious military attitude of the stirring march with which everyone had been overcome was immediately dispelled by the ragtime syncopated strains of the jazzed up "Army Blues."

The troops of 1st and 2nd Battalions who remained behind began to cheer, and the faces of those marching away broke into smiles as they waved their French helmets in return. "Much like the boys of the 9th and 10th Cavalry who went up San Juan Hill on that memorable charge singing, 'There'll be a Hot Time in the Old Town Tonight,' so was this farewell as the whole regiment, even the boys who marched away, began to sing the words of the 'Army Blues.'"[15] The band stopped playing once the battalion was beyond hearing range, but the musicians, "the entire regiment and quite a number of the people of the little village," remained watching until the column marched out of sight.

It was fortunate for both the French and the Americans that the anticipated German offensive did not take place, as feared, in mid-April. By the time it came, on July 14, the French had been able to bring up reinforcements, including the three additional black American regiments (the 370th, 371st, and 372nd) of the 93rd Division, who arrived from the United States by the end of April, and who, like the 369th before them, were then transferred to the French Army. For the officers and men of the 369th, the delay allowed them to become more fully acclimated to the French system and to experience their baptism in the trenches under conditions less harrowing than a full-scale attack.

For ten weeks, at first in close cooperation with French advisors and then on their own, the Americans learned the strangely routine, yet dangerous, business of trench warfare that had characterized most of the action on the Western Front since 1916. Dug in behind fortified lines that snaked 400 miles from the English Channel to Switzerland, the two armies faced each other across a no-man's-land of barbed wire, bomb craters, and crashed aircraft, in a virtual stalemate dictated by the adoption of the machine-gun by both sides. Major offensive action was suicidal without massive artillery support, and even then most commanders had learned (at great cost) that dislodging the enemy's machine-gun positions was extremely difficult. Warfare had thus, by the time soldiers of the 369th Regiment took their place in the line, become primarily defensive, neither side willing to risk a major frontal assault, and the fighting reduced to periodic slashing raids by small groups usually under the cover of darkness. There was, of course, the interminable, although sporadic, heavy artillery bombardment, but its major purpose (poison gas projectiles excepted) was intended to affect the minds rather than the bodies of the opposing soldiers.

Like most other troops who had expected something else, the black troops of the 369th found that front line duty did not, for the most part, mean fighting at all, but only a surreal "toying with death," as Sissle put it.[16] In a personal sense their introduction to the carnage of the war was gradual; although they had become almost accustomed to seeing the bodies of dead French and German soldiers, it was not until the regiment had been in the trenches for nearly three weeks that the first black soldier was killed in the line of duty. Most of the casualties and deaths the 369th suffered in the first weeks were the result of illness and accident, especially accidents involving grenades.

The nature of warfare the 369th first encountered was surprising. Instead of being organized in straight lines facing the enemy, the Americans found that the trenches, though continuous, consisted of very pronounced curves and irregularities. Rather than being placed side by side at intervals of two or three yards, soldiers were organized into small combat groups, ranging in size from half a squad to half a platoon, and placed at points separated by as much as one third of a mile, but which commanded a clear view of fire from one group to the next. "Without enemy artillery to assist in attack, a sector of defense properly organized and faithfully served would be impregnable against the attack of a body of twenty-five or thirty times the strength of its garrison," wrote the commander of the 369th's 1st Battalion. "Two groups and a machine gun section, with a total personnel of no more than twenty-five men, could hold a quarter of a mile of front against a battalion—if the ammunition held out, against a regiment."[17] The French operated on the principle of "increasing strength in depth" by which the first lines "were lightly held and were merely outposts for surveillance," while the heavy machine guns—and behind them, the artillery—were placed farther back in well-hidden and strongly protected positions.[18]

On April 20, 1918, the 369th Regiment assumed sole responsibility for a four-and-a-half-kilometer sector of the French line in the Bois d'Hauzy (Argonne Forest) bounded on the right by the Aisne River. Although this was not a great distance, it constituted 20 percent of all the territory held by American troops at the time, and it was the most, given the French principle of "increasing strength with depth" that could be expected of a three-battalion regiment. Employing the French system, one American battalion was assigned to front-line duty, a second was positioned in close reserve, while the third was at rest, or en repos, in the rear at the Regimental Headquarters at Maffrecourt. Conditions at the front were not as miserable as they were during the winter months, but there was plenty of standing water and mud in the dug-outs, and the men "slept with their clothes and did not take their shoes off during their tour in the trenches." The worst thing was the rats, "innumerable rats of all sizes which ate up everything within smelling distance. They ate through the men's pockets and musette bags, climbed over them at night, and were generally a pest."[19] The battalion assignments were rotated regularly every ten days.

Although Major Little, for one, confessed that the independent assignment frightened him, at the end of the first rotation Colonel Hayward felt confident enough by the way in which his troops had performed to write Special Assistant to the Secretary of War Emmett Scott and offer his evaluation of how the black soldiers in his charge were faring. "Of course," Hayward wrote, "it is still in the experimental stage, but two questions of the gravest importance to our country and to your race have, in my opinion, been answered."[20] The first question was how well would American Negro soldiers, including officers, get along with the French. This, Hayward said, had been answered "in a most gratifying way." The second was how they would stand up under "the terrible shell fire of this war," and to this Hayward admitted that although he might be premature "both my two battalions which have gone in have been under shell fire, serious and prolonged once, and the boys just laughed and cuddled into their shelter and read old newspapers."

They are positively the most stoical and mysterious men I've ever known. Nothing
surprises them. [M]y boys are public school boys, wise in their day and generation,
no caste prejudice, accustomed to the terrible noises of the subway, elevated and
street traffic of New York City (which would drive any desert man or Himalaya
mountaineer mad) and all are Christians. Also, that while the more ignorant ones
might not like to have a black cat hanging around for fear it would turn into a fish
or something, they have no delusions about the Boche shells coming from any
Heathen Gods. They know the d[amned] child-killing Germans are firing at them
with pyrocellulose and they know how the breech mechanism works.

The Germans do not know who we are yet, he said, but "I've been thinking if
they capture one of my Porto Ricans [sic] (of whom I have a few) in the uniform of a Normandy French regiment and this black man tells them in Spanish
that he is an American soldier in a New York National Guard regiment, it's
going to give the German intelligence department a headache trying to figure
it out." "We are proud to think our boys were the first Negro American soldiers
in the trenches," he concluded.

> Jim Europe was certainly the first Negro officer in. You can imagine how impor-
> tant he feels! In addition to the personal gratification at having done well as a
> regiment I feel it has been a tremendously important experiment, when one con-
> siders the hosts of colored men who must come after us. I wish I had brigade,
> yes, a division or a corps of them. We'd make history and plant the hob-nailed
> boots of the "Heavy Ethiopian Foot" in the Kaiser's face all right.[21]

Lieutenant Europe was the first African-American officer to lead troops
into combat in the Great War. He was also very likely the first to cross no-
man's land and participate in a raid on the German lines. When he told Sissle
about it back at Maffrecourt after his first tour at the front, Europe admitted
that it had probably been a foolish thing for him to do, but his explanation of
the incident, which Sissle recalled in detail, is revealing.[22] "You see," Europe explained, "it was like this:"

> Yesterday afternoon, I was visiting one of the French officers, next to our section,
> and while there in came two other officers and, as we were drinking wine, they
> commenced to tell of their experiences in the war.

Europe, like the other American soldiers, had seen little action thus far and so
he felt compelled to boast that they were anxious to experience some of the
"hair breath thrills of the modern warfare." "Bravo!," cried one of the Frenchmen patting him on the back, "We are going on a raid tonight, and you can go
with us. Get permission from your colonel." Europe made the request, hoping
to be turned down, but Colonel Hayward responded that he thought it would
be a good experience; he was stuck.

At 7:00 P.M., with his personal identification removed, Europe was dressed
in an old French uniform and given a cloth skull cap to wear instead of his
helmet:

We drank a bottle of wine and all the Frenchmen were as happy as larks, just as though they were going to a picnic. I was trying to laugh and smile, but the best I could do was give one of those "no good" grins. I was thinking of the band—how sweetly they could play—then I would hear the quartette singing "Sweet Emelina, My Gal";—then the scenes of dear old Broadway passed by. I could see myself standing before my old favorite orchestra in "Castles in the Air," and as I stood there, wielding my baton to those jazzing strains of "The Memphis Blues," I imagined I once again saw all those old familiar faces tripping by. When I came to myself, one of the officers touched me on the shoulder and said, "All right, lieutenant, the time has come to go."

Europe pulled himself together and was handed a small automatic pistol, about the size of a cap gun, which he looked at wondering "what good would it be shooting at one of those Boche Berthas, ten miles away—but the Frenchmen had them, and as I was with them, I thought I must just as well 'Rome' it."

Silently, we filed out in the darkness. Not knowing the ground over which I was trudging, I was constantly stumbling in the intense darkness. Every corner of the trenches I turned, leading down to the front line, I would pass the dark form of a member of the patrol, huddled up beside the trench, and not a word was spoken. It seemed to me that if someone would just clear their throat, I would have been relieved. First place, my throat was too dry to even make a sound; for a while I thought I was having a terrible nightmare and kept trying to wake up.

We finally reached the "jumping off" place, which the officer with me whispered was just opposite the place that led to where we were to cross No Man's Land. As we hesitated for a minute, I noticed how beautiful the night was. Every star seemed as bright as a shining silver light. It seemed they were mockingly winking their eyes at me, and how I wished I could change places with them, just at that time. At the same time, I wondered why such a bright night had been chosen to go on this detective job. One of the officers with me explained that as there was quite a bit of brush growing in front of our trenches, we were able to get through our wire without being detected, and the bright light would make our observing easier in the enemy's trenches . . .

"Let's go over, lieutenant," said my "ever-stick" friend, and blankly I struggled "Over the Top," and crawled on my stomach quietly till I reached the hole that had been left in the wire in front of our trenches, and before I was really conscious of the fact, I found myself in "No Man's Land" . . . I followed the lieutenant with me, still crawling, on past the soldiers, who were lying quietly in a straight line parallel to the wire, and finally we reached the enemy's wire, where I found [that] one of the French patrols the night before had cut an opening. Through this passage, a soldier crawled with a large ball of white tape in his hand, and my comrade whispered that he was going to lay that to the Boche trench, so as to mark the shortest route, and it would also serve as a guide back to the hole. That's the part that interested me, mostly—then getting back to the hole. He made the round trip, undetected, and he was no sooner back than I heard the boom of several of our light artillery guns, and like a thousand pheasants, several shells came whizzing over our heads, and burst about forty yards in front of me. Goodness gracious—I knew my time had come. Now they came thick and fast. All up and down the front they were pouring—all callibers—and were sweeping the enemy's trench. Talk about hugging the ground. Boy, no sod ever hung as close to Mother Earth as I was. You see, some of the shells would burst prematurely in the air and oh,—how they would scream—and shrapnel was hizzing hither and thither. Seemed mostly hither. After about two minutes of this—which seemed two hours—a pistol cracked right by my side and up whizzed a red flare from the Very pistol of the officer by me. Simultaneously, every man jumped to his feet—that is, in a crouching position, ready to run, and one by one, each slipped through the hole in the wire and formed a skirmish line a short distance from the wire. The shells had then begun to advance and at another crack of the Very pistol, every man leaped up and made a dash for the trenches.

"Come with me, lieutenant," whispered my companion, and I slipped through the hole in the wire, following the tape, and jumped over in the enemy's trenches, right where the white tape ended, and there I remained. By this time, all kinds of pretty lights were filling the air. It looked and sounded like the "Forty-Fourth" of July. All this time, our artillery was sweeping the back areas of the enemy's trenches, ahead of our men's' advance, and amid the din of the high explosives, could be heard the excited yelling of our men, as they darted first up one trench and down another, bombarding every nook and corner with hand grenades. For three minutes this continued, and then a green rocket was sent up by the lieutenant with me, at the place where the white tape marked the way back to the opening in the enemy wire. One by one the soldiers came scampering back, some carrying pieces of paper in their hands, some with a German coat, helmet, or anything that might convey information, but to my disappointment with no prisoners. The thing that caused me to hit the trail, right away, was when I saw the stretcher-bearers bringing back one of their men, wounded. Aw, Aw— right along that tape I tore out for the wire, and by that time most of the men were on the same route. Well, the whole time since the bombardment began hardly took over five minutes, but it seemed ages to me, and the worst scare I got was when I had just got back in the trench the German artillery opened up on our front lines. Don't tell me Frenchmen can't run. And that saying: "Don't know where I am going, but I'm on my way!" Listen, "Siss," I flew round those trenches, and the first dugout I spied, in it I hopped, and stayed till the Germans cooled off, which was fully fifteen minutes.

"Well, I finally found my way back to the abri [combat post] of my comrades," Europe concluded his story, "and only found two of the four there." Later he learned that the two missing officers as well as two other soldiers had been seriously wounded in the raid. "I found everything last night that I ever heard existed out there," he told his friend. "Next time I go, they will have to read orders to me with General Pershing's name signed and resigned to them."

In addition to regaling Sissle with stories of his adventures at the front, Europe used his ten-day rest period to work on new ideas drawn from his experience for songs that he hoped to publish once the war was over. He had taken a small folding organ with him when he was first sent forward to the support lines, and at odd times or in the evenings he would amuse himself and the soldiers in his dugout by extemporizing melodies or accompanying those who occasionally felt like singing. Back in Maffrecourt, he and Sissle borrowed a piano from a local family, moved it to Europe's barracks, and began trying to develop some of those trench-inspired songs. Most of their work was unfortunately subsequently lost, but of those songs whose titles and lyrics Sissle was later able to recall, a few seem to have had some promise. One of these was suggested to Europe by a fellow officer who asked him to write something that would reflect the feeling all the soldiers seemed to share of being far away from home and yet being constantly reminded by numerous small things of their loved ones. Europe composed "a beautiful melody" for the piece, which he called "Every-thing Reminds Me of You," and he and Sissle later wrote the lyrics:

> In the blue of the skies, I see the blue of your eyes
> In the thrilling song of a bird, your voice is heard,
> It thrills me, stills me, with love anguish fills me,
> I find the white fleur-de-lis an emblem of your purity,
> And as the bees kiss the vine, I feel your lips touching mine,
> The breath of the rose your perfumed tresses disclose,
> Everything reminds me of you,
> Everything reminds me of you.[23]

Another song that reflected a common concern, called "I've An Observation Tower of My Own," warns "Miss Butterfly" to remain faithful to her soldier while he's away because "I see every little thing you do." Other ideas that the pair worked on over the ten days in May, with titles like "Trench Trot" or "I've Got the Map of Your Heart," are perhaps just as well forgotten.[24]

Unlike Europe, who was assigned to combat duty, Sissle continued to carry out his musical responsibilities with the regimental band, which, although now led by Sergeant Mikell, was still universally referred to as "Europe's band." Aside from playing for various regimental formations, giving evening concerts for the French and American soldiers, and providing the music for the amateur vaudeville shows that Sissle organized, the band had the sobering duty of taking part in the funeral services for the soldiers killed at the front. During April and early May these involved mostly French and German casualties, brought back to Maffrecourt for burial, but by the end of the month the number of American graves with the small wooden crosses on them in the cemetery near the town was growing as well. The band also made periodic ap-pearances in various towns of the region, playing for the local French populace as well as for the mostly French troops quartered there, and whenever a gen-eral or high official passed through the area to call upon Colonel Hayward the band was invariably called out. During the second week of May, three civilian representatives of the American press, eager to report first hand about the un-usual service of black American troops with the French Army, had found their way to the 369th's headquarters in Maffrecourt, and as usual when military dignitaries were in camp, the band was called upon to play for them.

The writers included Martin Green of the *Evening World* and Lincoln Eyre of the New York *World*, but the visitor who attracted the most comment among the men of the 369th was Irvin S. Cobb. Cobb, a well-known writer at the time but now largely forgotten, was a humorist and a Southerner who had made his career in part by ridiculing black speech and black people. The soldiers were aware of Cobb's writing and "quite a few of them commented upon the nerve of Mr. Cobb's venture down into the front lines after having said and written so many damaging things about our people."[25] Some of the men thought that Cobb might learn something by his visit; however, others said that he would never change, and he received a very cold reception, especially from the non-commissioned officers who showed him nothing but their backs, "because everyone got busy finding something to do to keep from even having to look at him." "Well, if he gets back alive," one of the men commented, "it will be because he's standing beside the colonel."[26] Later, when the band was assembling to play for the regiment's guests after dinner, Mikell told Sissle that he felt like playing "Flee as a Bird," a traditional hymn the band often played as a funeral march during burial services.[27]

Europe was unavailable to offer his advice, having just returned to the front lines, but Sissle and Mikell decided finally that they would feature a selection of plantation melodies. "We were both of the same opinion," Sissle recalled,

> that if Irvin Cobb had any heart in him at all after going through the trenches and seeing our boys isolated from their own American army and cheerfully going about their allotted duties and then hear . . . some typical southern [sic] American melodies, his attitude would certainly be softened in some degree towards us as a race, and that "poisoned pen" . . . would be at least modified, if not stilled forever.[28]

The concert began with "Stars and Stripes Forever" and was followed immediately by the medley of "plantation melodies," featuring Sissle as vocal soloist on Stephen Foster's "Old Folks at Home." For his solo, Sissle was "accompanied by the trombone and a few other of the instruments that were to give an organlike effect."[29] As he sang, the night and the setting seemed to conspire with the sentiment of the song. A full moon shone across the shell-battered houses of the little town silhouetting the demolished steeples of a church nearby while in the background the muffled sounds of distant artillery and machine gun fire and the occasional drone of a French reconnaissance aircraft could be heard; all of this heightened the melancholy effect of Foster's "lament for lost home, friends, and youth."[30] For an encore, the band "stole into the strains of 'Dixie,'" at first very softly and then gradually building to a rousing crescendo of horns, cymbals, and drums. The effect of the band's performance on Mr. Cobb that night was described in his widely read article published in the *Saturday Evening Post* in August:

> If I live to be 101 I shall never forget the second night, which was a night of a splendid, flawless full moon. We stood with the regimental staff on the terraced lawn of the chief house in a half-deserted town five miles back from the trenches,

and down below us in the main street the band played plantation airs and hundreds of negro [sic] soldiers joined in and sang the words. Behind the masses of upturned dark faces was a ring of white ones where the remaining natives of the place clustered, with their heads wagging in time to the tunes.

And when the band got to "Way Down Upon the Suwannee River" I wanted to cry, and when the drum major, who likewise had a splendid barytone [sic] voice, sang, as an interpolated number, "Joan of Arc," first in English and then in excellent French, the villagers openly cried; and an elderly peasant, heavily whiskered, with the tears of a joyous and thankful enthusiasm running down his bearded cheeks, was with difficulty restrained from throwing his arms about the soloist and kissing him.[31]

Whenever he heard them during his stay, Cobb was impressed with the regiment's band. "On parade when it played the "Memphis Blues" the men did not march," he wrote at another point in the *Post* article,

the music poured in at their ears and ran down to their heels, and instead of marching they literally danced their way along.

"I think surely this must be the best regimental band in our army," he concluded. "Certainly it is the best one I have heard in Europe during this war."

Jim Europe's band had made an important convert, but it was not just the music that impressed Cobb and which made his account in the *Post* so remarkable. Unlike most other journalists who had seen the American black soldiers only as labor troops or stevedores and tended either to discount them or use them for comic relief in their reports, Cobb "saw the black soldiers under fire, was impressed with their bravery and discipline, and described their behavior with an eloquence fired by the perspective of a Southern background."[32] Up to the time of Cobb's and the other reporters' arrival, on May 14, 1918, the reputation of the American 369th rested almost exclusively upon reports of its exceptional band; Hayward's soldiers had not been tested by the enemy in any substantial battles. Early that morning, however, a German patrol of at least two-dozen men attacked Combat Group Number 29, a small and rather isolated post manned by four men and a corporal.

With the corporal and two of the men trapped inside the dugout and unable to lend assistance, the two privates who had been on guard duty—Needham Roberts from Trenton, New Jersey, and Henry Johnson, from Albany, New York—were outnumbered more than ten to one. Both Johnson and Roberts were immediately wounded by grenades, Roberts seriously, as the Germans rushed upon them; but they fought back ferociously. Even with his ammunition expended and his partner nearly unconscious, Johnson fought on, at first by using his rifle as a club and then with his eight-inch French bolo knife until the Germans retreated, dragging their dead and wounded with them. When the relief party reached them, Johnson and Roberts were both near death from their multiple injuries, but they had killed at least four members of the

German attacking party, wounded many others, and put the rest to rout. The enemy retreat was clearly marked by a large cache of abandoned equipment and "by pools of blood, blood-soaked handkerchiefs and first aid bandages, and blood-smeared logs, where the routed party had rested."[33]

The three journalists were given the official report of the battle and taken to the scene to appraise the evidence for themselves. Several days later, the correspondents for the daily papers, Green and Eyre, cabled their stories back to New York and shortly thereafter the details of "The Battle of Henry Johnson" were spread by the Associated Press to papers all across the country. Cobb's account appeared later in the lengthier piece he wrote for the *Saturday Evening Post*. As a result of this publicity, the "15th New York Infantry had passed out of the category of a merely unique organization of the American army, a regiment with its chief bid for fame based upon the music of Jim Europe's Band."[34] When Europe himself wrote to Fred Moore of the *New York Age* a couple of weeks later on June 13, his only reference to the band was to remark characteristically that he was no longer with it but now served in a machine gun company.[35] The main purpose of his letter was to make certain that the readers of the *Age* were aware of Johnson's and Robert's exploits so that they, the people of Harlem, could share in the pride of their black volunteers—that ragtag outfit who had now become one of the famous fighting regiments of the War. The Germans, too, had become respectfully aware of the American black soldiers, whom they now called "blood-thirsty black men," and the 369th Regiment had earned a new nickname—"Hellfighters."[36]

The German high command had by no means abandoned its plans for a spring offensive against the lines of the French 4th Army, which stood between them and French capital just fifty miles away. During the last week of May, German artillery bombardment increased significantly, but several probing assaults in early June resulted in no quick breakthroughs, and the Germans chose to delay their main offensive until early July, to coincide with the American (July 4) and French (July 14) independence day celebrations. The pressure, however, continued to increase. On June 6, Colonel Hayward directed his troops in support of a French force attempting to push the enemy back from a recent advance near Chateau-Thierry. "Previous to this," recalled Sergeant John Jamison, "we had fought through several small engagements, but this day we were fighting with the French, with whom we were brigaded. We came up to the German front lines and there we met the heaviest attack, which was a counterattack to our advance":

> Colonel Hayward tore off the "eagles" [from] his insignia, grasped a gun from a solder, and darted out ahead of the rest of Company K. We went through a barrage of German artillery that was poured down on us. A French general ordered us to retire. Colonel Hayward, who, of course was under direct command of this French general, said: "I do not understand you!" Then the French general raised

his arms above his head and cried: "Retire! Retire!" And then Colonel Hayward, with his hat knocked off, came running up and cried: "My men never retire. They go forward, or they die!"[37]

A few days later, another member of the 369th, Sergeant Bob Collins, was awarded the Croix de Guerre for bravery under fire. The 369th "Hellfighters" were making a name for themselves.

At the beginning of the third week of June, Jim Europe and his machine gun company found their position under intense German artillery bombardment, including a heavy barrage of poison gas bombs. Although no German troops followed up the shelling, Europe was overcome by the gas and had to be evacuated to the small field hospital at Geiscourt a few miles back of the lines. When Sissle learned that his friend had been injured, he and one of the Puerto Rican musicians immediately requested, and received, permission to see him.

To protect morale, the army tried to keep the soldiers from witnessing the often horrible injuries that their comrades suffered from the use of chemical warfare by the enemy, but word invariably got out. Sissle had heard some of the descriptions of how bad it could be and feared the worst. "I will never forget the terrible scene that greeted our eyes," Sissle remembered as they were directed into the gas ward. Pieces of sheet had been hung between the rows of cots, but it was still impossible to avoid witnessing the suffering.[38]

As they approached Europe's cot, the two soldiers could hear him "coughing one of those dry-hacking painful coughs," but when they came around the partition they found the lieutenant sitting upright and writing in a notebook propped against his knees.

> When he looked up through his big, shell-rimmed glasses and saw it was us, a big broad smile swept over his face, and instead of him telling us how seriously he was gassed, as we had expected, or how his physical condition was, the first thing that he spoke up and said was: "Gee, I am glad to see you boys! Sissle, here's a wonderful idea for a song that just came to me, in fact, it was [from the] experience that I had last night during the bombardment that nearly knocked me out."

The song, whose chorus he had just completed, was called "On Patrol in No Man's Land."[39]

Although his injuries did not appear to be serious, Europe was transferred a few days after Sissle's visit farther back from the front to a hospital outside of Paris for observation and treatment; the internal complications from a gas attack were not always immediately apparent. He returned to his unit sometime after the first week of July, perhaps, as Sissle says, with "the sad report that he was put in Physical Class 'B' [status], which meant he could not be active in the front line duty. . . ."[40] Whatever his official medical status when he reported back probably made little difference.[41] The Fourth of July had passed peacefully despite a growing anticipation among the Allies. On July 7, General Gouraud sent a general order to all of the French and American forces of the French 4th Army, advising them that "we may be attacked now at any moment."[42]

The Battle of Champagne-Marne began during the final minutes of July 14, Bastille Day, 1918, and was fought for two days along a fifty-mile stretch of the lines running from Verdun to Rheims. "All last night the cannonading was terrific and convulsing," Captain Napoleon Marshall wrote in a letter home, "the pen recoils from a description of the indescribable. . . . I do not know yet what toll it has taken of the lives of our brave men, for the action which lulled this morning is soon to resume. We are preparing for an infantry attack. May God be with us."[43]

Thanks to the brilliant planning of the French general, there was actually very little for the infantry soldiers to do in the early stages; it was primarily an artillery duel. Gouraud had ordered that the first line of allied trenches be almost entirely evacuated and that the allied artillery be zeroed in on them, while the infantry moved back to secondary entrenched positions. In effect, the Germans were simply invited in to the first lines and then blown apart. The strategy worked well; in the sector manned by the Americans less than one quarter of the enemy ground forces ever got past "the slaughter pits of our evacuated first line trenches."[44] "The first thing I knew," Colonel Hayward proudly recalled,

> all there was between the German Army and Paris on a stretch of front a little more than four miles long was my regiment of negroes [sic]. But it was fair enough at that; all there was between us and Berlin was the German Army. They tried pretty hard to get by, but they never did. No German ever got into a trench with my regiment who did not stay there or go back with the brand of my boys upon him.[45]

Along other sectors of the front the Germans were more successful, breaking through the first lines of defense before being stopped short at the second. By the afternoon of July 16, however, it was clear that the German thrust had failed, and General Gouraud again addressed his soldiers. "It is a hard blow to the enemy," he told them. "It is a beautiful day for France."[46]

The 369th Regiment had received several casualties as a result of the German artillery bombardment prior to the unsuccessful German advance, but they incurred many more when they were called upon to support the French 161st Division in a counterattack aimed at driving the Germans from their stronghold at Butte de Mesnil. It was the first major offensive in which the 369th had a part, and they both drove the Germans back and, for the next month, successfully defended the ground they had taken. In the course of this action, the regiment suffered its first serious officer casualty, Lieutenant Oscar Baker of the 1st Battalion, on the night of July 20, and eleven days later Lieutenant Arch Worsham became its first officer killed in action. Despite such losses, the 369th Infantry added two new heroes. Captain Charles Fillmore, one of the five black

officers who had been with the outfit from the beginning, was cited for conspicuous bravery and received the French Croix de Guerre, and the American
Distinguished Service Cross was awarded to Sergeant William Butler, whose exploits in mid-August against a German raiding party matched those of Henry
Johnson.[47] Shortly thereafter, having served 130 days in the trenches, the 369th
was relieved from the front lines and given a short week of much needed rest.

When the regiment returned to combat duty it was assigned, along with
the other black regiments of Gouraud's 4th Army (the 370th, 371st, and 372nd
Regiments of the 93rd Division), and augmented by the recently arrived 92nd
Division, important responsibilities in the great Allied offensive that began on
the night of September 25–26. Over 1 million American soldiers, black and
white, took part in the campaign to drive the German Army from the Meuse-
Argonne area north of Verdun, territory that the Germans had held for four
years and which, particularly in the Argonne Forest, was extremely well-
fortified. It was a lengthy, brutal, and costly battle (there were over 120,000
American casualties), and while the advance was slower than expected, the
German Army was eventually demoralized. Less than two months after the
battle began, hostilities ceased on the Western Front.

Fighting as part of the 161st Division of the French Army, the 369th Regiment gave a good account of itself. On the first day of the assault, the regiment
advanced four kilometers against fierce resistance. By nightfall, the 3rd Battalion, which had started the day with twenty officers and 700 men, ended it with
seven officers and 150 men; however, they had taken 125 prisoners, twenty-five
machine guns, and two 77-mm guns.[48] On September 30, the regiment drove
the enemy from the strategic town of Sechault, but it had cost a dozen officers
and several hundred men. First Sergeant Peterson reported to Captain Fish that
they had sustained 30 percent casualties. "We'd practically ceased to exist as an
organized combat unit," Fish recalled. "Yet, the 369th held onto the town,
through forty-eight hours of machine-gun and artillery fire, repulsing every
German counterattack, until we were relieved by a fresh battalion on October 2,
with my own unit placed in reserve. Sechault was declared secure on October
6."[49] For their actions, the entire regiment was awarded the Croix de Guerre, and
170 officers and men received individual citations. Over 150 men, however, were
killed in the battle (or later died of their injuries), and an additional 636 required
hospitalization. "Upon the evening of October 6th," Major Little wrote,

> the 161st Division of France was relieved from the offensive, and its American
> regiment the 369th infantry—what was left of it—marched through most of the
> night to the rear, and went into bivouac encampments, by battalion, near Minau-
> court—the place from which it had made its debut, some eleven or twelve days
> before, as an organization of shock troops, in the great victory drive of the Allies.[50]

14

Filling France Full of Jazz

Well old boy hang on then we will be able to knock them cold
after the war. It will be over soon. Jim and I have P[aris] by the
balls in a bigger way than anyone you know. . . . See that Nora
Bayes gets "To Hell With Germany." It's a big hit here.

Sissle to Blake (1918)

Jim Europe was not with his regiment when it fought with the French
161st Division in the bloody September Allied assault against the Germans.
Neither were any of the other five black officers who had come to France
with the old 15th New York Infantry. In late July, the A.E.F. adopted a policy of
having either all black or all white officers assigned to its black units. In its
wisdom, the U.S. Army had determined that since soldiers were to be segregated according to race, then so should their officers. Given the pervasive
prejudice against black combat soldiers and black officers in the service and the
army high command's unwillingness to tackle the issue directly, it is difficult
to conceive of a satisfactory general course of action that could have been pursued. It is nonetheless unfortunate that the fact that the 369th Regiment had
served in combat for five months with distinction and without significant racial
problems while having white lieutenants serve, in two instances, under black
captains, made little difference.[1] By August 1, Captains Fillmore and Marshall
and Lieutenants Lacy, Reid, and Europe had all been ordered to other regiments of the 93rd or 92nd Divisions, whether or not they had applied for the
transfer.[2] Colonel Hayward was forced to go along, although he was not pleased.
"Our colored officers were in the July fighting and did good work," he wrote to
Special Assistant Emmett Scott in Washington.[3]

Sergeant Sissle had also been transferred from the regiment, but for a
more positive reason. He was one of forty-two sergeants of the 369th who accepted Colonel Hayward's nomination for officer training in the knowledge that
if he were successful and awarded his commission, he would not be permitted
to return. Hayward wanted to send more. "There is splendid material there,"
he said, "but they declared they'd rather be sergeants in the 15th than lieutenants or captains in other regiments."[4]

Jim Europe was not keen about being ordered on a permanent basis from
the regiment either, nor did he want to leave his band. He was, however, happy
to be sent to Paris for several weeks of rest and recovery at the end of July. "My
Dear Little Mother and Sister," he wrote to his family in Washington,

After much work and worry in the dreadful trenches I am given a month's leave for nothing but pleasure and believe me I'm having it. This is dear old Paris from where I am writing this letter and believe me this [is] the fairyland of the world. No other place on earth like it. Even good old Washington is poor beside it. I have been here for fourteen days tomorrow. I am leaving for a tour of Southern France: Lyon, Nice, Marsailles, Bordeaux, & St. Nazaire. So you see now I am the lucky boy.[5]

The specific details of what transpired during Europe's leave in Paris at the end of July and beginning of August are unclear. It is certain, however, that he was not given a full month for recuperation; by the middle of August his transfer to the 92nd Division had been cancelled, and he was ordered to return to the 369th. The A.E.F. had apparently become convinced that the various bands of the black regiments (not just the famous 369th Infantry Band) were of such critical value to troop morale that the rule proscribing commissioned officers from being bandmasters should be changed.[6] "As you doubtless learned," Colonel Hayward later explained to Fred Moore of the *Age*, "all our colored offices were transferred to other units, two of them having made application. Lieut. Europe was transferred with the rest, but when the rule went through allowing bandmasters to be commissioned, he was sent back to us and to the band as bandmaster."[7]

It may have been that Colonel Hayward had something to do personally with the change in army policy, or even, as Douglas Gilbert later suggested, that Europe used his friendship with Major Barclay Warburton (who was married to Rodman Wanamaker's daughter and held a position with General Pershing's staff) to prevail upon the army high command to make the change.[8] One indication that Colonel Hayward may have done some bargaining, as he had done before, to secure Jim Europe as his band director is his remark made in a letter to Sissle after the war that when Europe was ordered to return to the 369th as bandmaster, "the authorities seemed to think the band belonged to the A.E.F. and not to the 369th Infantry."[9]

In the early spring of 1919 when Europe granted an interview with Grenville Vernon of the New York *Tribune*, he specifically recalled that when he rejoined the 369th Regiment in mid-August, it was Colonel Hayward who told him he was now reassigned to the band and that his first duty was to return to Paris.[10] "I can tell you that music was one of things furthest from my mind," Europe told Vernon, "when one day, just before the Allied Conference in Paris, on August 18, Colonel Hayward came to me and said: 'Lieutenant Europe, I want you to go back to your band and give a single concert in Paris.'"

I protested, telling him that I hadn't led the band since February, but he insisted. Well, I went back to my band, and with it I went to Paris. What was to be our only concert was in the Théâtre des Champs-Elysées. Before we had played two numbers the audience went wild. We had conquered Paris. General Bliss and French high officers who had heard us insisted that we should stay in Paris, and there we stayed for eight weeks.

Two African-American women, Addie W. Hunton and Kathryn M. Johnson, both YWCA delegates to the Conference of Allied Women War Workers, were in the audience that night and later testified to the accuracy of Europe's account.[11] "It was the last night of the conference," Hunton told the *New York Age*, "and a great gathering had assembled at the Théâtre Elysées for the final meeting."

> Just then someone remarked that a colored orchestra was in the pit, and instantly, I was on my feet. We could not see the men of the band, but just enough of Lieutenant Europe's head was visible for recognition. Scrawling my name on a card, I sent it by an usher and soon we were greeting each other.
>
> Then faded all the other events of the great conference; I was just concerned for the time being that OUR band should do itself honor on this important occasion—and it did. I can never forget how as President Poincaire and party entered it poured forth with splendid effect the "Marseillaise" and the audience came to its feet. Nor how with the roll call of the many organizations came forth National air after National air, always keeping the audience under its spell.
>
> Lord Derby, the British ambassador, presided. There were speakers, high in the affairs of the nation, and sweet singing, but it was the 369th Band, with Lieutenant Europe conducting, that maintained the enthusiasm of that final meeting. At its close women in many different uniforms, speaking different languages, pressed forward to shake the leader's hand. Mrs. Theodore Roosevelt, Jr., and others stood by and the band played on by request long after the lights had been lowered and most of the great throng had gone.[12]

With the Allies gearing up for the major offensive in September, it is hardly surprising that, following the inspired performance of the 369th Regimental Band on August 18, Europe and his musicians would be requisitioned from their parent regiment to remain in Paris and to provide their morale-boosting service for the men in the city and in the camps and hospitals in the immediate environs. Perhaps Sissle was right when he later wrote that it was at this time that Europe was able to "render his greatest service to his government and regiment."[13] There are several surviving photographs of Jim Europe leading the band in and around Paris at hospitals, rest areas, and gatherings of soldiers during this period, and he was, occasionally, even able to return to the 369th to perform for his own regiment before it entered the line, once again, in late September.[14] In the few letters of his that do exist during this period, however, there is an unmistakable note of apology—of a need to explain and to justify to himself why Lieutenant Europe, the line officer, would be directing a band in relative safety rather than a machine gun company when his comrades entered the battle. "I will not write much today for we are moving out," he wrote to his mother on September 10. "I am now back with my old regiment in charge of the band permanently. This will be good news to you. I did my bit in the line and I think I've earned the rest."[15] At the end of a somewhat longer letter the following week, he wrote:

> I am very contented now that I am with the band . . . I spent five months in the trenches and God was with me, for I had some miraculous escapes, for unless I walk into some lost stray shot I'll come back to you and ma.[16]

In mid-October, the 369th Infantry Regiment, having been given a week to recover from their role in the bloody Meuse-Argonne offensive, was ordered south to relieve forces of the French 84th Infantry, then guarding a relatively quiet sector of the lines in the Valley of the Thur (Alsace) in the Vosges Mountains. After nearly two months in Paris, Lieutenant Europe and the band were also permitted to leave and join them enroute. "The band is as fine as ever under his [Europe's] direction," Colonel Hayward wrote following their reunion, "and has been the source of great solace and comfort, not only to us, but elsewhere. It has played for hundreds of hospitals, rest camps and on the occasion of many functions, so that we have not been selfish in the enjoyment of its good music."[17]

As they had done the previous February at Aix-les-Bains, Europe's band had again made an important contribution to the Allied war effort. Thousands of wounded soldiers—American, British, French, Belgian, and Italian—would testify to the benefit of their music. The experience of playing in Paris, however, was of significance to Europe in a purely musical way because there he had the opportunity to compare his band with many others and to witness the reactions of both soldiers and civilians to the kind of music his band was playing. "Everywhere we gave a concert it was a riot," he later told Grenville Vernon,

> but the supreme moment came in the Tuileries Gardens when we gave a concert in conjunction with greatest bands in the world—the British Grenadiers' Band, the band of the Garde Republicain [sic], and the Royal Italian Band. My band, of course, could not compare with any of these, yet the crowd, and it was such a crowd as I never saw anywhere else in the world, deserted them for us. We played to 50,000 people, at least, and, had we wished it, we might be playing yet.[18]

Why was this? If it was not that the Americans were superior or even equal, technically, to the great military bands of Europe, was it because of the novelty of a black band? Or because the Europeans wanted to express their gratitude for the American intervention in the war? Or was it because Europe's band played better music? Europe did not think so. "After the concert was over," he said, "the leader of the band of the Garde Republicain came over and asked me for the score of one of the jazz compositions we had played."

> He said he wanted his band to play it. I gave it to him, and the next day he again came to see me. He explained that he couldn't seem to get the effects I got, and asked me to go to a rehearsal. I went with him. The great band played the com-

position superbly—but he was right; the jazz effects were missing. I took an instrument and showed him how it could be done, and he told me that his own musicians felt sure that my band had used special instruments. Indeed, some of them, afterward attending one of my rehearsals, did not believe what I had said until after they had examined the instruments used by my men.

The important thing, Europe concluded, was not so much what his band played but rather how his musicians played it; and his musicians did not play like the Europeans. By the fall of 1918 a peculiar word had begun to enter the general vocabulary as an appropriate descriptive term for that way of playing. The word was *jazz*—or *jass*, as it was first introduced through the popular 1917 recordings of the Original Dixieland Jazz Band—but its meaning was not immediately clear (other than simply being a replacement for *ragtime*, a term that seemed passé). With the highly publicized reaction of the Europeans to the music of the black military bands during the war, however, journalists needed a term to identify what was novel in the playing of these black organizations. The term they appropriated—still, without much precision—was "jazz." The *New York Age*, for example, in an article published in October 1918, entitled "Jazz Music Makes Hit With French Officials," reported that French army officials were "exceedingly fond of the 'jazz' music furnished by the colored bands," and that no less a person than General Petain, himself, "had 'the time of his life' listening to a colored band playing the popular 'jazz' music, with some Negro dance stunts in keeping with the spirit of the melodies."[19] By early 1919, Europe was comfortable enough with the term (or, perhaps just resigned to it) to attempt to give it some specific musical definition.

Charles Welton, who was assigned by the New York *World* to write "the jazz chapter for the history of the great conflict" in the early spring of 1919, focused his entire piece on Jim Europe and his band. His article, based primarily upon interviews with the bandleader, apparently done in early 1918, perhaps while Europe and the band were still at Aix-les-Bains, is interesting for its tone—which is personal and humorous—as well as for his description of what constitutes jazz.

> To understand jazz, it is well to know that it isn't merely a series of uncontrollable spasms or outbursts of enthusiasm scattered through a composition and discharged on the four winds, first by one wing and then by another of the band. Of course if a player feels an attack of something which he believes to be a jazz novelty rumbling in his system it is not the Europe rule to make him choke it back and thus run the risk of cheating the world out of a good thing. Any player can try anything once. If it doesn't come out a fliv on harmony it can remain as a toot to be used whenever there's a place where it won't crowd regular notes over the bars.
>
> The basic fundamental of jazz, however, is created by means of a variety of cones inserted point down in the bells of the horns. These cones are of two kinds. One is of metal and the other of leather. The leather cones are usually soaked in water before the band goes out for a blow. The metal cones muffle and modify the natural tones of the instruments and make them come across with new sound values.

When a leather cone is wrung out and fitted into the vestibule of a horn, and the man back of the works contributes the best that is in him, it is somewhat difficult to explain what happens in mere words. You get it with both ears, and almost see it. The cone being wet, the sound might be called liquefied harmony. It runs and ripples, then has a sort of choking sensation; next it takes on the musical color of Niagara Falls at a distance, and subsides to a trout brook nearby. The brassiness of the horn is changed, and there is sort of throbbing nasal effect, half moan, half hallelujah. Get me?[20]

Europe's own explanation is more measured, as he always was when he was talking to the white press, but he also endorsed the notion that jazz was something done to music in performance. "It is accomplished in several ways," he said:

With the brass instruments we put in mutes and make a whirling motion with the tongue, at the same time blowing full pressure. With wind instruments we pinch the mouthpiece and blow hard. This produces the peculiar sound which you all know. To us it is not discordant, as we play the music as it is written, only that we accent strongly in this manner the notes which originally would be without accent [i.e., syncopation]. It is natural for us to do this; it is, indeed, a racial musical characteristic. I have to call a daily rehearsal of my band to prevent the musicians from adding to their music more than I wish them to. Whenever possible they all embroider their parts in order to produce new, peculiar sounds. Some of these effects are excellent and some are not, and I have to be continually on the lookout to cut out the results of musicians' originality.[21]

Although Welton's and Europe's comments concerning the kind of music Europe's band played were published within a few months of his return to the United States, it is reasonable to assume that they constitute a relatively accurate description of the unusual aspects of the way the band sounded when it performed in Paris in the fall of 1918, if not earlier. Those unusual aspects—slight alterations (smears, slurs, unusual tonguing techniques, rhythmic or dynamic shifts), occasional "blue" notes, tonal coloration through the use of mutes, and improvised or paraphrased breaks—are understood today as important elements of jazz interpretation, and they contribute to the essential nature of jazz as a performers' art rather than a composers' art. As a performer's art, the emphasis is placed upon conveying a musical experience that is both personal and immediate, and it should not be surprising that, when it is done well, an audience might be compelled to respond in kind. "Everywhere we gave a concert," Europe had said of the reaction in Paris to his band (although not what most orchestra conductors of the time would take as a compliment), "it was a riot."

If it is true, as seems to be the case, that Jim Europe and his band introduced to Paris audiences a primitive sort of big band jazz, the question remains why their audiences—not just the black American troops for whom they played, but white Americans, Frenchmen, Englishmen, and Italians, soldiers and civilians alike—responded so positively to this music. A good part of the answer may

well be found in the nature of the music, its emphasis upon the personal, immediate, and kinetic (as opposed to the presumably authoritative and eternal
virtues of the European musical tradition), and in the experience of the war
itself. World War I was the first modern war, the first to be fought with de-
personalizing weapons of mass destruction—submarines, aircraft, long-range
artillery, tanks, gas, and machine guns—which blurred the line forever between
previously sacred categories like combatants and noncombatants. By the fall of
1918, few Europeans, and few Americans who had experienced it, needed to wait
for a "Lost Generation" of postwar writers to define for them their sense of dis-
illusionment. There is a certain irony, and yet a certain appropriateness, in the
fact that it was a black American lieutenant named Europe—a commander of
machine guns, that most perfect symbol of depersonalized mechanical warfare—and his band that brought the welcome compensation of jazz to wartorn
France. "Attached to the old 15th Colored Infantry, which later became the
369th under Col. William Hayward," Welton wrote, "this band operated with B-
flat trombones or machine guns, just as it happened, all the way from Brest to
Armistice. It cleaned up everywhere. It filled France full of Jazz."[22]

At 11:00 A.M. on November 11, 1918, the hostilities that began four years
and three months earlier and which were waged at a cost of 10 million lives
(20 million wounded) and hundreds of billions of dollars in material destruction
ceased on the Western Front. In New York and Paris, and dozens of other major
cities, the news was received with wild, almost orgiastic, celebrations. In the
streets and public squares of every small town and village across France, some
kind of public celebration was held; bands played, and people danced and
cheered and cried. Still holding their sector of the line in the Vosges Mountains,
the black soldiers of the 369th Infantry Regiment and their officers greeted the
Armistice with relief and thankfulness more than with wild revelry, but there
was no shortage of champagne or deeply felt emotions as they watched the fireworks "being set off from the trenches of the enemy and listening to their
cheers. Yes—the Germans in the front line trenches—they were happy too."[23]

Six days later, on November 17, the 369th Regiment was given the honor
by the commander of the French 4th Army to leave its trenches, cross no
man's land and the German lines, and enter Germany as the advance guard of
the victorious Allied Forces. At first, the Americans passed through silent and
evacuated villages near the front. By the second day of their march, however,
when they entered Ensisheim, they began to encounter large numbers of
German citizens who had clearly been preparing to receive them. "Every house
had its display of flags," Major Little wrote.

> Across the streets, great banners were hung. Pictures of President Wilson appeared
> in hundreds of windows. Girls and young women in the gay costumes of native Al-
> satian dress, threw flowers into the streets to make a carpet for soldiers to walk
> upon; and wherever the troops were at rest and the discipline of the moment per-
> mitted, these young women bestowed kisses upon the men in uniform.[24]

"As the advance guard of the 4th French Army, we were the first troops to go into the enemy territory, in Alsace-Lorraine—beautiful place," Meville Miller, a private in the outfit, recalled years later:

> As we marched in to this particular town—I don't quite remember the name, I think it was Bittsvilla—the colonel before we marched in gave us the command to get into formation and we straightened up and struck up the band, the flag of New York State was flying for the 15th New York Infantry—our colors flying—and as we approached the town, at the outskirts of the town . . . you could see the German troops leaving. They're marching out of the town and we come in with the band playing "The Army Blues." And Jim Europe and—Noble Sissle was not our bandmaster, drum major, at the time—it was a fellow named [Sergeant Gillard] Thompson, since passed. And we marched into that town and the people on both sides and were waving; they didn't know whether we were coming as conquerors or liberators, but they were playing safe and cheering—whether they were cheering and happy out of fear, to win us over, or because they were happy, I have no way of telling. But that day the sun was shining and we were marching and the band was playing and everybody's head high and we were all proud to be Americans, proud to be black, and proud to be the 15th New York Infantry . . . We had a ball.[25]

On November 18, the regiment reached Blodelsheim, on the left bank of the Rhine—it was the first unit of the Allied armies to do so—and four days later, Colonel Hayward received a letter from General Lebouc, commander of the division, congratulating him for having "collected the water of the Rhine in your hand and [having] placed the 'Black Watch' along the river." "I shall never forget that the opportunity has been given me in the course of this war," the general continued,

> to have under my command an American regiment which, with little previous training, has fought with extreme bravery, and which since the last combat has applied itself to such regular and steady work that as far as attitude and military discipline are concerned, this American Regiment can compare with any of my French Regiments. . . . When the citation is approved [the Croix de Guerre], I shall take great joy in decorating your flag and in kissing you in front of your Regiment. And that day we shall not only drink water from the Rhine, we shall drink Champagne, and it will be a beautiful day for your General Commanding the Division.[26]

Colonel Hayward's soldiers remained another three weeks guarding the west bank of the Rhine before orders were finally received for them to move back to the west to prepare to leave the French Army as the first step toward going home. By then, the thoughts of the men had turned with happy anticipation toward reunions with their loved ones and their futures after leaving the army. "I think I told you that we are now guarding the Rhine," Europe wrote to his sister, Mary, on Thanksgiving Day. "I have so much to give thanks for this time for I have been throu [sic] the valley and shadow of death so often and still I am unscathed."

> Now dear little loved one, have a merry cherry time but remain away from large gatherings until that terrible epidemic of influenza has passed over.

I am so tired of the army life now that I do not know what to do. I want to
get home and to get to work and make some money. It costs all we earn over here
to live and clothe ourselves. Now I must close. I've so many things to do.[27]

On the afternoon of December 13, 1918, on the Plains of Munchausen, a
"great parade ground made by nature," General Lebouc, faithful to his promise, pinned the Croix de Guerre to the top of the 369th Infantry's regimental
colors and kissed the regiment's commander and four other officers on both
cheeks. The next morning, the first black American combat regiment to arrive
on French soil began what would seem, in their eagerness to return, an almost
intolerably long journey from the Rhine and back home to Harlem. The first
week of the trip was accomplished on foot over often steep and snow-covered
mountain roads and where billeting in the small towns en route was unpredictable. On December 20, the first of the regiment's battalions reached Belfort,
the first town of substantial size, and there they rested while the other battalions and Headquarters Company caught up.

Christmas Day found the regiment quartered at various villages on the
outskirts of Belfort. The officers of the 1st Battalion, like those of the 2nd and
3rd, tried with limited success to make the day as "merry" for the men as possible. The weather was poor, an uncomfortable mixture of heavy rain and snow,
and most of the men had not been paid for several months. In addition, the
regiment had never been supplied with the special rations issued to all other
American troops on Christmas so that the officers were forced to use company
funds to purchase what they could from the local markets to construct their
holiday dinner.[28] Despite these problems, the regiment did have one unfailing
source of good cheer, their band. "At about three o'clock in the afternoon, just
after we had gone through that regular Christmas dinner function of letting
out the belt three holes," the 1st Battalion's Commanding Officer wrote,

> came the sounds of martial music. In an instant our banquet table was deserted.
> Down the rickety stairs we rushed, out through the shed into the open, and there
> in our barnyard, facing us, standing in the crescent of "concert formation," and
> playing my favorite march of Aix-les-Bains, "Our Director"—was "Europe and his
> band. . . . We had a happy hour—all the men of our town and the civilian popu-
> lation too, crowded into that barnyard, to listen to the best music of the
> American army, to dance and to sway to the rhythm of the jazz.[29]

Beginning on December 31, the three battalions of the 369th Infantry
Regiment entrained for Le Mans where the A.E.F. had established its main
center for the processing of American troops prior to their return to the United
States. When they arrived on January 4, 1919, they were both pleased and surprised to find the other regiments of the 93rd Division (the 370th, 371st, and
372nd Regiments) already in camp, and among them were nearly all the surviving members of the original 15th New York Infantry. It was a memorable

moment, according to Sissle, who was there with the 370th. "It was the same as a family reunion—smiles and tears."[30] At Le Mans, the quarters were crowded and uncomfortable, the activities (delousing, reequipping, preparing embarkation lists, etc.) were routine and boring, and there was a great deal of rain and mud, but the general atmosphere was positive. After all, Little wrote, "We were going home. We were happy."[31]

After about a week at Le Mans, the soldiers departed by train to proceed to Brest, the designated port of embarkation for their ships to take them home. All along the way, the men speculated and wagered about whether they would be on the first ship leaving for America the night of their arrival or on one departing a day or two later. "Those boys all hoped we might wait until morning," Little wrote. "Of course everybody would want to see us; and, of course, everybody would want to hear the band; and, of course, the commanding general of Brest would want us to pass in review before him."[32] What they found was nothing like that at all. The army command was apparently worried that the black American troops had been infected with an egalitarian virus ("foreign radicalism" was the standard euphemism) from their experience in France and that this would cause problems when the men returned home. The military police at Brest, therefore, were instructed to treat the black soldiers harshly, to help them remember their inferior status back in America. There were immediate problems: a black soldier from the 369th was assaulted by the MPs without provocation, and when Major Little asked for an explanation he was told that the MPs had been warned that "our 'Niggers' were feeling their oats a bit and that instructions had been given to 'take it out of them quickly, just as soon as they arrived, so as not have any trouble later on.'"[33] "We arrived at Brest January 11th," Little said. "We embarked from Brest for home, January 31. During that three weeks, no day passed (and but few hours) during which we failed to get some notice of petty fault-finding coupled with a threat of disciplinary action against the entire organization by placing its name at the bottom of the list for embarkation."[34] This was, of course, the ultimate threat—to hold up the regiment's departure for home until a satisfactorily obsequious attitude had been demonstrated. One of the soldiers wrote in his diary that at Brest "it seems as if we at last had struck something worse than the Germans. . . ."[35]

Finally, the embarkation orders for the 369th Infantry were issued to Colonel Hayward. Headquarters Company (with Jim Europe and the band) and Little's 1st Battalion were scheduled to leave Brest aboard the *S.S. Stockholm* on January 31. The 2nd Battalion, Supply Company, and 3rd Battalion would follow the next day. On the afternoon of the 31st, the first contingent marched from Camp Pontanezen through the streets of the city and down to the docks where tenders waited to take them to their transport anchored in the harbor. They marched in silence. "Every man had been warned and every man had taken his warning seriously."[36] As the last of troops filed aboard, the chief of staff of the base noticed the band. "Can they play?," he asked Major Little. "Yes, sir," Little replied. "Well, why don't you give us a tune as you leave?" "I'm sure it would be very welcome to us, sir," Little answered, "but I'm not taking any chances of losing our sailing place. If you so direct, sir, I will give the order." "Yes, yes, by all means, let us have some music!," replied the chief of staff, and Little turned to the bandmaster. "Mr. Europe," he said, "you may play!"[37] And so the officers and men of the 15th New York National Guard Infantry, the 369th "Hellfighters" of the First World War, said farewell to France with "the music that they loved so well stirring their hearts," just as it had when they first stepped ashore in anxious anticipation thirteen months before.

This time, the Atlantic crossing was uneventful—no fires, no collisions, no submarine threats, but the anxieties were just as great, and the miles passed just as slowly. During the daytime and evenings, there was little for the men to do except lounge about the decks and exchange war stories, reflect on their comrades who were not coming home, or talk about who would be waiting for them and what their plans were for the future. Those who were lucky enough to be on board the *Stockholm* could at least listen to the band play each afternoon.

The transport carrying the regiment's 3rd Battalion, the *S.S. Le France*, made the best time and arrived in New York on February 9, 1919; the other two ships with the rest of the regiment steamed past the Statue of Liberty and into the harbor on February 12, Lincoln's Birthday. New York was waiting, and the dramatic welcome was duplicated for each ship's arrival. Tugs and harbor craft came out to meet them with their horns blaring, and fire boats shot their streams of water high overhead. The piers were lined with thousands of family members and friends, all straining to catch a glimpse of their own soldier and cheering and waving handkerchiefs. When the *Stockholm* finally tied up and Europe's band played the men ashore, the "scenes of joy and excitement, of the bursting of pent up emotions, I cannot describe," Major Little wrote.[38]

General orders instructed the regiment to proceed directly to Camp Upton on Long Island and there begin the processing necessary for demobilization. It can be imagined how difficult it was to pull the men away from their families, get them in line, and march off to the ferries to take them to Long Island, much less to hold them there that night. The day of arrival was a day for families and friends of the men; there was little in the way of formal ceremony. Five days later, however, February 17, had been set aside for all of New York to welcome home its black soldier heroes with a parade up Fifth Avenue. Denied the opportunity of a going-away parade, Colonel Hayward had promised his men that when they returned he would insure that they had a homecoming parade that would erase the memory of those early disappointments. Ever since the Armistice was declared in November, the regiment's victory parade in New York had become a favorite topic of daily discussion among the men. The officers, therefore, had little trouble insuring that their troops were back in camp by the

16th "because no one was going to miss that opportunity of parading up Fifth Avenue."[39] On the morning of February 17, all of New York, it seemed, turned out to cheer the 15th Heavy Foot as it marched from the Victory Arch on 25th Street up Fifth Avenue and home to Harlem. "During the entire progress of that seven mile march," Little, who followed just behind Jim Europe's band, wrote, "I scarcely heard ten consecutive bars of music. So great were the roars of cheers, the applause, and the shouts of personal greetings!" "I doubt if any of us shall ever again be privileged to share in such thrills. . . ."[40]

Beginning the following morning at Camp Upton, the lengthy and tedious process of mustering the regiment out of service was initiated. It would take nearly ten days to complete all the paperwork, but most of the men had turned in their gear, verified their service records, received their last pay check, listened to their final farewell speech, and received their formal discharge by February 21. As an officer, Jim Europe had additional responsibilities, and despite his eagerness to begin picking up the pieces of his civilian career, his own discharge was not made official until February 25. By then, Europe had characteristically already begun to act upon his promise to reward those who had stuck with him at home and in the service. His immediate plan was to capitalize upon the fame the 369th Regimental Band had achieved by embarking upon a national tour by the band that, according to an announcement in the *Chicago Defender* on March 1, had left the service "in a body" to join him. Following this, he intended to take the band to England, where the Prince of Wales had requested a concert, and then, perhaps, for a tour of the continent.[41] If the tour was as successful as he had every reason to believe it would be in revitalizing interest in African-American music, it might also ultimately help spawn a return of black artistry to the theaters of Broadway and even lead to the establishment of permanent national organization dedicated to the performance of African-American music, his greatest ambition.

"All of No Man's Land Is Ours"

Since his return from the battlefields of France, Europe's jazz band has made a sensational tour in this country, playing to packed houses in every city. Everyone that has heard this remarkable music has gone wild about it.

The *Talking Machine World* (1919)

The demand for black musicians and entertainers had fallen off even before Jim Europe and Noble Sissle joined the National Guard, and it continued to decline throughout the last years of the war. From the correspondence with Eubie Blake and others back home, and from the New York papers, Europe was kept informed of the discouraging situation, and it concerned him. By the spring of 1918, the Tempo Club had virtually ceased to function as a booking agency, and Blake had himself been forced to go on the vaudeville circuit with singer Broadway Jones. America's entry into World War I, it seemed, had created a situation in which the gains that black professional musicians and entertainers had made were in danger of being lost. Thanks to the positive response of the French to the black American soldiers and to the music of their military bands, however, the war also provided a genuine opportunity—if only, as Europe had written to his partner in April 1918, they could hold on and "build for the future."[1]

The Clef Club, Europe's original musicians organization, managed to survive the war years under its third president, Fred "Deacon" Johnson, but it, too, had experienced declining revenues and membership. Compounding the problem was the fact that the office of club president was an honorary, unsalaried one, and as a consequence during difficult economic times the president found himself having "to hustle just like any other member to make a living."[2] This made it nearly impossible for him to give much attention to managing the club's affairs or even to organizing the big public concerts that had been so important in establishing and sustaining club's reputation in prior years. Nonetheless, there were a few notable Clef Club concerts. One of these, held at the Academy of Music in Philadelphia on April 22, 1918, is of historical significance because it introduced a local singer of considerable promise. Her name was Marian Anderson.[3]

Later in the same year, Will Marion Cook—who had been inactive for some time due to illness—returned to organize the Clef Club Orchestra and Chorus for a concert tour of major Eastern cities beginning in November. His aim, the papers announced, was to foster "the development and exploitation of the best Afro-American music," which meant that music ranging "from the old spirituals to the standard works of the modern Negro composers including Coleridge-Taylor, Burleigh, Rosamond Johnson, and Will Marion Cook." "We are endeavoring to strengthen and uplift the Clef Club so that all the Afro-American musicians of the United States will become actively associated with its growth, and through this association a national school of Afro-American music will be established," he said.[4] It is apparent from this that Cook, for personal or artistic reasons, did not wish to identify himself or the Clef Club with the "jazz" music that former Clef Club leaders like Europe and Tim Brymn were becoming celebrated for performing with their military bands.

As Gunther Schuller has written, "Cook regarded both Europe's brand of brassy jazz and the novelty bands on Broadway, which claimed to represent the Negro's music from New Orleans, as unworthy reflections upon the dignity of Negro music."[5] This may have produced some friction within the club itself, but in any case, before the tour could begin, the unpredictable Mr. Cook had divorced himself from the Clef Club and formed a partnership with lawyer and businessman, George Lattimore. Calling his new organization the New York Syncopated Orchestra, Cook was able to keep a number of former Clef Club musicians and singers, including Europe veterans Buddy Gilmore and William Tyers, and over the next seven months they toured, with varying success, much of the eastern and midwestern United States.[6] In February, London theater manager Andre Charlot met with Cook and booked the New York Syncopated Orchestra for a six-month engagement in London beginning in July 1919. Ironically, it was this orchestra (with the crucial addition of New Orleans clarinetist Sidney Bechet, and under yet another name—this time the Southern Syncopated Orchestra) that impressed the Swiss modernist conductor, Ernst-Alexandre Ansermet, and which has been credited by most historians with first bringing jazz to the attention of Europe's "serious" musical community.[7]

In the meantime, the Clef Club membership decided that, with the war over and business picking up, it needed someone who could devote full time to managing the business. Jim Europe had continued his membership in the club and had kept in touch with Deacon Johnson while he was in France, and his reputation, despite his defection to form the Tempo Club in 1914, remained strong. In early 1919, therefore, when a special meeting of the Clef Club was called, at which time it was decided that the next president should receive a salary, "it was also agreed from the outset that the most desirable man for the job was Jim Europe, the Club's first president, as soon as he was mustered out of the army."[8] However flattered, Europe could not respond immediately; his first responsibility was to bring some order to his personal affairs, and to do this he needed to reestablish himself professionally and financially. Until then, he could do little about the future of his marriage to Willie, his relationship with Bessie Simms and their son, or his mother and sister in Washington—all of whom depended upon him financially to one degree or another.

At least since the time of their well-publicized successes in Paris, Europe had been planning to take his military band on a tour of the United States as soon as the members were released from the army. He needed to move quickly, however, to exploit the recent publicity they had received both for their music and for their membership in the most celebrated black unit of the war. Black Americans would support them because they could share in the general pride of the race for their achievements during the war; white Americans would want to hear them to learn for themselves what it was about their music that had so excited the Europeans. The initial advantage the "Hellfighters" enjoyed in being the first to return home would also be short-lived; by the end of February Jack Thomas and his 368th Regimental Band, E. E. Thompson and the 367th "Buffaloes," and George Dulf and the 370th "Old Eighth Illinois" were all back and planning concert tours.[9] Europe's most serious rivals for the public's attention, because of their skill in playing blues and employing similar jazz effects, were Tim Brymn and his 350th Field Artillery Band (known as the "70 Black Devils") and Will Vodery's 807th "Pioneers," and both of them were scheduled to return in March.[10] Thanks to his friends in the Clef Club, however, even before the ships carrying the old 15th Infantry had docked in New York, the "Hellfighters" had an advantage over their rivals.

On February 15, 1919, two days before the 15th's great victory parade, the *New York Age* announced that a "big welcome concert" was being sponsored that evening at Carnegie Hall by the Clef Club to honor the 15th Regiment, its medal winners, and Lieutenant Europe and his band.[11] Radiograms informing Colonel Hayward of the event had been sent to the *S.S. Stockholm* at sea five days earlier, and special invitations had also been issued to Secretary of War Baker, Governor Smith, ex-President Taft, and even opera star Enrico Caruso. An advertisement for the concert on the same page of the paper promised that New Yorkers would be treated to James Reese Europe and his "Big Ragtime Soldier Band" for the "First Time in America."[12]

> Hear the songs that the Doughboys of the Fighting Old 15th sang as they went "over the top" and put the Huns to run! Hear the Jazz Tunes of Lieut. James Europe's Famous Ragtime Soldier Band which set all France whistling and dancing! Hear Sergt. Gene Mikell's great song hit "Camp Meetin' Day" which created such a furor at the big Armistice celebration in Paris, London, and Rome.

Aside from the exaggerations (the band, of course, had not performed in London or Rome and it is unlikely that Mikell's tune was played there by some other group), the advertisement, presumably written by Deacon Johnson and the Clef Club, is interesting because it suggests that New York's leading black musicians' organization had embraced the new "jazz" label, however unclear they were about the differences between it and ragtime.

As it happened, those who bought tickets to Carnegie Hall in the expectation of hearing Europe and his famous band would have been disappointed. Europe and Mikell were present and did take a turn conducting the Clef Club Orchestra, but the 15th Regimental Band did not perform.[13] With two exceptions, the music and entertainment for the evening was provided by the Clef Club. One of these was an organ solo by Meville Charlton, and the other was a guest appearance by W. C. Handy, who directed the orchestra in several of his "blues" compositions. For anyone truly interested in exploring the musical basis for the semantic shift from ragtime to jazz, Handy's blues would have been worth their attention. In his autobiography, *Father of the Blues*, Handy recalled that he first met Jim Europe in early 1918 at the Clef Club and that Europe received him warmly as the author of "Memphis Blues," which Europe had been performing for nearly five years.[14] The year is inaccurate, since Europe was then in France, so it was likely the following year, at the time of the Clef Club's welcome home concert at Carnegie Hall, that the two major figures in the development of African-American music actually became personally acquainted.

It is hardly surprising that Europe and Mikell did not bring the regimental band with them to Carnegie Hall that evening. The men had only just arrived home from the war, and if they had passes from their quarters at Camp Upton, those who had families and loved ones in the area would naturally want to be with them. Their big parade was only two days away, and there was much to do in preparation, including repairing and replacing a number of the band's instruments. In addition, Europe was then in the midst of negotiating arrangements with Pat Casey, a well-known New York booking agent, for the band's upcoming national tour, as well as making the necessary program and personnel decisions.[15] A number of the musicians in the original 15th Infantry Band, including Europe's assistant Gene Mikell and several of the Puerto Ricans, decided to return home after their discharge, and Europe also wanted to augment the band with additional singers and instrumentalists who had not been with him in the army.[16] From the standpoint of the "Hellfighters" tour, upon which Europe had pinned such high hopes, a public appearance by the 15th Infantry Band prior to marching with their regiment up Fifth Avenue would have been premature.

On March 16, 1919, "Lieut. James Reese Europe and His Famous 369th U.S. Infantry Band," featuring "Superstar Lieut. Noble Sissle" as tenor soloist, launched their ten-week tour of eighteen Eastern and Midwestern cities with an evening concert at Hammerstein's Manhattan Opera House in New York. To Sissle, who had not been with Europe when his orchestras performed at Carnegie Hall before the war, the fact that a group of black "jazzsters" appeared on the stage of this "musical sanctuary" of "immortal composers" was nearly overwhelming.[17] When, judging by the "spontaneous applause from the jewel-bedecked patrons in the stage boxes," it was clear that the "stirring marches, favorite overtures, and jazztime strains to the moaning blues" had actually won the audience over, he could hardly describe the experience. The New York papers the next day did somewhat better. "There was a flood of good music, a gorgeous racket of syncopation and jazzing, extraordinarily pleasing violin and cornet solos and many other features that bands seldom offer," reported the New York *Sun*.[18] There were "echoes of camp meetings and of the traditional darkey life that seems almost to have disappeared," and quartets and octets sang "tone pictures of the gayety with which the colored brother takes his religion." The centerpiece of the evening, however, was the "perfectly welded" band. At the outset, "under Europe's firm hand," the band played the French march, "Sambre et Meuse," followed it by a "tempestuously applauded 'Plantation Echoes,' passed to suites of the Western world and then launched into a medley of jazz tunes." "All the old favorites were played and played with unfamiliar charm," and Europe closed the program with "Echoes from Broadway" and an "ear splitting crash of jazz music that caused the audience to explode [with] cheering and laughter." "Seeing him in New York again, hearing him play the 'St. Louis Blues' in Hammerstein's Manhattan Opera House just as he had played it in France," Handy later wrote, "my gratitude and admiration reached new Heights. I felt then as I feel now, that the gifted president of New York's Clef Club was not only a loyal friend but a great musician and leader of men."[19] There was only one aspect of the evening that might have concerned the leader. During the snare drum duet by the "Percussion Twins," as Herbert and Steve Wright had been labeled, Herbert was unable to control a fit of giggling, and though the audience laughed along with him, he nevertheless made a fool of himself.

All told, however, it had been a positive beginning, and "when the final curtain finally descended after having been raised for so many encores, there was a public reception held on the stage which was participated in by all classes, from the various sections of the auditorium."[20] Following a second New York concert on March 22 at the Academy of Music in Brooklyn, the troupe left the big city for two days of concerts at Philadelphia's more famous Academy of Music and then headed north, where they enjoyed the distinction of being the first military band ever booked into the prestigious Boston Opera House. By this time, Tim Brymn's "70 Black Devils" Band was also playing to large audiences and receiving good reviews, and with the Clef Club Orchestra and Cook's New York Syncopated Orchestra also appearing at major theaters in New York, it was possible to believe that a resurgence of interest in black music and popular support for black musicians was truly underway.[21]

Following the concert at Boston, the "Hellfighters" contingent boarded their two private Pullman cars to begin the western part of their tour, which consisted mostly of one and two day stopovers at Wooster, Springfield, Albany, Syracuse, Buffalo, Cleveland, Dayton, Indianapolis, Terre Haute, Fort Wayne, Battle Creek, Toledo, and Pittsburgh, with longer visits to St. Louis and Chicago. All along the way, the local press praised the band and commented upon the poise and geniality of its leader. In Buffalo, for instance, the local paper described Europe as "one of the snappiest and peppiest [band leaders] in the country. He injects his own dash and spirit into the playing of the organization."[22] "That there has been no better musical entertainment in Buffalo in many seasons seemed to be the general opinion among the hearers last night, to judge from the applause and enthusiasm with which the program was received," said the paper. Most distinctive in the band's performance was its "jazz." "How those boys do play slouchy supersyncopations, strange tones from squealing saxophones, slide trombone 'blues,' the muted cornet, exotic rhythms and barbaric chords—these are the elements which the musicians have used in developing their musical novelty," and yet the band was "one of the best bands along conventional lines," not just a "novelty."

The program for the "Hellfighters" matinee and evening concerts followed a basic variety format that began and ended with an appropriately rousing march. In between, Europe led the band in straight (or "High Brow" as the program sometimes explained) renditions of classical or operatic selections, medleys of popular Broadway and Tin Pan Alley tunes, familiar "plantation" or Southern melodies, short recent compositions by black composers (like William Tyers' "Panama"), and their own jazz specialities. In addition, and one of the biggest crowd pleasers, was the band's syncopated arrangements (the papers called them "jazzations") of themes taken from Grieg's "Pyr Gynt Suite" and Rachmaninoff's "Prelude in C Sharp Minor," known as the "Russian Rag." Aside from the numbers played by the full band, there were cello and violin duets by Leonard Jeter and Felix Weir (with Europe at the piano), songs by Creighton Thompson, Al Johns, and a vocal sextet (called either the Singing Serenaders or the Southland Singers), a snare drum duet by Herbert and Steve Wright, and a selection alternately featuring either the saxophone or trombone sections from the band. Just prior to the finale, Europe accompanied Sissle at the piano for his singing of two of their wartime songs, "On Patrol in No Man's Land," replete with electrical light and sound effects to simulate the bombs and machine gun fire, and "All of No Man's Land is Ours."

In Chicago, where the tour was booked for a full week at Louis Sullivan's Auditorium, "the biggest and best theater west of New York," they experienced an especially warm reception. "Lieut. Jim Europe and his 369th U.S. Infantry Band is creating a great sensation," reported the *Chicago Defender*.[23] "Chicago music lovers are literally 'eating up' the offerings of 'Jim's' clever aggregation." "It is just a 'hot-stuff' musical organization, made up of 'hot-stuff' musicians, directed by a 'hot-stuff' wielder of the baton, delivering a 'hot-stuff' program." The conductor, himself, was described as making "a handsome appearance in his overseas uniform and it is apparent from the first that he 'knows his stuff,' to use the language of the times. It is almost as fascinating to see him work as it is to hear his band, and that is saying a whole lot." "Jim certainly handles the wonderful group efficiently; he is without doubt the best real director of which the Race can boast. . . ." Having attended practically all the big concerts in Chicago in the last twelve years, the writer concluded:

> [T]he work of the "Hellfighters" would not suffer by comparison with the best of them. In many ways it surpasses them all: for it is safe to say that no other organization in the world could compete with this one in the rendition of "Blues," "Jazz" and Negro folk numbers.

Such enthusiastic reviews were especially welcomed by Europe and the other members of the troupe because just prior to their Chicago engagement they had been the focus of a demonstration by the black citizens of Terre Haute against continuing racial prejudice in that city. Following the long-standing practice of the Grand Opera House where they had been booked to perform on April 21, the theater manager announced in the papers that racially segregated seating would be maintained despite the fact that Europe's band of black musicians and war heroes were the featured attraction. Community and church leaders, backed by the N.A.A.C.P., responded by organizing a boycott of the theater to protest the policy. "Never before has such unity of oneness of purpose been displayed in this city," declared the *Chicago Defender*.[24] A picket line of women "approximately a mile long" gathered outside the theater "stopping every black face" and passing out a handbill entitled "The Shame of Segregation." When the irate manager appeared swearing never to allow another "colored person to enter the house again," a woman in the crowd yelled back: "That's for the courts to decide." The result was that, although the concert was held as scheduled (the paper did not criticize Europe for appearing), it was attended by only 200 whites and two blacks ("traitors," the *Defender* labeled them). It was the only disheartening note to an otherwise triumphant tour.

Between concerts during the band's stay in Chicago, Europe and Sissle, ever on the lookout for musical talent, auditioned and hired several instrumentalists—five from Indianapolis and a quartet of singers who called themselves the Four Harmony Kings. One of the Kings, according to Sissle, was the thirty-two-year-old tenor, Roland Hayes, a veteran of the Fisk Jubilee Singers, who would later be credited as the individual most responsible for shattering racial barriers in the concert world and establishing the Negro spiritual in the repertoire of the concert stage.[25] Another musician whom Europe auditioned, but did not hire, was clarinetist Sidney Bechet. Bechet was then playing in Chicago with Lawrence Duhé's band and was unhappy with what Duhé was paying him. Europe and Sissle were told that Bechet was someone they should hear, although he did not read music. An audition was arranged with the band, and Bechet showed up with an instrument held together with tape and rubber bands. "He's not going to try to play that," Europe exclaimed, but he did indeed, performing a cadenza from "Poet and Peasant Overture" that simply blew away "the twelve clarinetists Europe already had in the band."[26]

During the entire week in Chicago, Europe was treated as a celebrity and as a musical authority; he was the guest of honor at several private and public affairs, and his opinion of local bands and musicians was constantly sought. At one such celebration at the Royal Gardens, a nightclub on East 31st Street, the *Chicago Defender* reported that he was particularly impressed by the house band, known as the Royal Gardens Jazz Band, and at the end of the evening he went up to them and said, "'Men, I have enjoyed your wonderful playing more than words can express. Beyond all others, it is the best I have ever heard; your work is unique and is played with startling precision, as well as with rare musical taste.'" "Guess that wasn't some compliment to be proud of," commented the paper.[27] Adding to Europe's sense that his musical career was about to take a major step forward was word from Pathé Record Company that the first recordings of the band were about to be released.[28]

"Lieutenant Jim Europe's 369th Infantry ("Hellfighters") Band" were recorded by Pathé in four recording sessions, three between March 3 and March 14, before the band went on tour, and a fourth session on May 7, while the band was performing in Philadelphia near the end of their trip (See Appendix B). Among the thirty sides cut on those dates are six by the band's singing groups, four by the Singing Serenaders and two by the Harmony Kings, and several others featuring the band's lead vocalists, Noble Sissle and Creighton Thompson. While each of them has something of interest, the strictly instrumental numbers are perhaps the most important for the evidence they provide of the kind of jazz interpretation Europe was then developing.

The band's recording of "Broadway Hit Medley" provides a good comparison of several different styles of performance since it includes a chorus or two of a standard march ("Madelon"), a popular ballad ("Smiles"), a waltz ("Till We Meet Again"), and a blues ("I've Got the Blue Ridge Blues"). The different pieces are taken in different tempos and meters, and all of them, with the exception of the blues, demonstrate Europe's concern with correct reading and respect for standard note values and pitch. The march segment, although short, is strong and precise. The blues theme is interjected in two places (in the introduction and between "Till We Meet" and "Smiles,"). The band's performance of this music is noticeably more relaxed and loose, and it includes a smearing clarinet obbligato and modified tonal coloration through the use of mutes. These same methods—including that "whirling tonguing" technique Europe described in the April *Literary Digest* interview—are developed further in the band's recordings of popular tunes like "Ja Da" and "Darktown Strutters' Ball" and in specialty pieces like "Indianola," with its Eastern flavor and tom-tom effects, and "That Moanin' Trombone," where the trombone section takes several slurring breaks in unison.[29]

Much of the recorded material is admittedly uneven, partly the result of recording techniques of the time (the substitution of wood blocks for drums, for instance), but, as Schuller has said, in a "real sense this was the first big band. Naturally the pieces had to be arranged. To hear a whole clarinet section take a clamorous break, as on 'That's Got 'Em' or 'Clarinet Marmalade,' is to recapture, I am sure, some of the wild abandon of the early New Orleans marching bands." Compared to the white concert bands of the time, who "could take a ragtime or early jazz piece and make it stiff and polite," Jim Europe's band "could take a polite salon piece and make it swing—in a rudimentary sort of way."[30]

Even more interesting are the band's recordings of the three pieces written by W. C. Handy: "St. Louis Blues," "Memphis Blues," and "Hesitating Blues." As Charles Hamm has noted, most of the "blues" published and recorded before the mid-1920s bear little resemblance to the formal and harmonic patterns of traditional vocal blues, and at most may contain only a twelve-bar blues phrase or two "embedded in a larger structure."[31] "Memphis Blues" is such a piece. Europe's recording begins with a short introduction followed by a twelve-measure blues phrase and then a sixteen-measure section similar to a rag or march. The final section consists of another twelve-bar blues played six times, each repetition featuring a different instrumentalist whose short solo is "surely not written into the score Europe had prepared for the band" and which may constitute the first swinging jazz breaks on record.[32] The less well-known "Hesitating Blues" was already a traditional folk-music piece before Handy copyrighted his version in 1915.[33] In the band's performance it takes the idea of the individual interpreting (embellishing/improvising) soloist a step further. In addition to the usual breaks at the end of a four-bar blues line, which invite a soloist's interpretation, the stop-time melodic theme of "Hesitating Blues" encourages such interpretation from the start. In the Europe recording the twelve-bar "hesitation" blues theme is played twice, with the expected breaks being filled by the clarinets at the end of each four-bar phrase. On the third and fourth time through, a clarinet soloist paraphrases the entire melody over the top of the band. The soloist cannot truly be said to be improvising, since he never creates a new melody, but he does (sometimes effectively, sometimes less so) rephrase the melody in his own terms. The full band takes over again, with the trumpets and trombones in the forefront, for two more blues choruses, a sixteen-measure section is played twice, and a final twelve-bar blues with the clarinet lead and a short cadenza ends the piece.

Europe referred to these "blues" pieces as fox-trots, and he had been playing them ever since his days with the Castles. The significant thing about the fox-trot is that, although the name suggests a kinship with the other prewar ragtime animal dances like the turkey trot, it actually represents a "radical slowing down of the accompanying music" and a turning away from the increasingly speeded-up 2/4 staccato of ragtime.[34] When Irene Castle, who returned to America from London in the spring of 1919, was asked to give her definition of the new term, *jazz*, her response was revealing:

Let me try to define jazz as I understand it. The colored bands jazz a tune. That is to say, they slur the notes they syncopate, and each instrument puts in a world of little fancy bits of its own. The dominating feature is brass. In the United States everyone dances to jazz music, but there are no fixed steps.

Those people who regard themselves as jazz dancers—jazzers, as they doubtless would label themselves—are making just this mistake. They are being deluded by a very old step in the fox-trot, and, believing it to be a new discovery instead of a resurrection, they call it jazz. . . .

People have come to me bubbling over with enthusiasm about the jazz dance or the jazz step. I'm just crazy about the step, these enthusiasts say. And when I've asked them to show it [to] me, they've just trotted forth the old fox-trot, pure and simple.[35]

In Jim Europe's recordings one can hear both the instrumental colorations that Irene identified with jazz and the critical rhythmic shift to the fox-trot that she (along with Vernon, Jim Europe, and Ford Dabney) had pioneered before the war. Both of these developments, it should be said, necessarily preceded the emergence of the classic blues-based jazz of the 1920s.

When the final curtain came down on the "Hellfighters" engagement in Chicago on Saturday night, May 3, and as Europe and the band prepared to return East, the *Chicago Defender* attempted to sum up what they had accomplished. They had achieved a wonderful record abroad and been given "a great ovation by the people of New York" when they returned, the editors said, and Chicago also found them "equal to advance notices," having all the "artistic finish of any band that has invaded these parts in many years. . . ." Although the audiences at the Auditorium rewarded "each number with the most spirited applause," it was not just their music as such that made Europe and his band so worthy of admiration. Of far greater importance was the message that Europe carried with his music:

The most prejudiced enemy of our Race could not sit through an evening with Europe without coming away with a changed viewpoint. For he is compelled in spite of himself to see us in a new light. It is a well-known fact that the white people view us largely from the standpoint of the cook, porter, and waiter, and his limited opportunities are responsible for much of the distorted opinion held concerning us. Europe and his band are worth more to our Race than a thousand speeches from so-called Race orators and uplifters. Mere wind-jamming has never given any race material help. It may be entertaining in a way to recite to audiences of our own people in a flamboyant style the doings of the Race, but the spellbinder's efforts, being confined almost exclusively to audiences of our own people, is of as much help in properly presenting our cause to those whom we desire most to reach as a man trying to lift himself by pulling at his own bootstraps. Experience has shown that most of our spellbinders are in it for what there is in it. The good they do us is nil.[36]

To the editors of Chicago's leading black newspaper, the warm reception that greeted Lieutenant Europe and his music as he traveled through the East and Midwest in the spring of 1919 seemed to forecast a new and better season for race relations in the United States. They did not know that it was a false spring, one that would turn bitter in the Red Summer of that same year when more than a dozen bloody race riots would erupt, and that the worst of these would occur in their own city.[37]

Heading back to Philadelphia and Boston for the return engagements that constituted the final leg of the tour, and with the happy prospect of a final concert at the Manhattan Casino in Harlem scheduled for May 10 before them, the "Hellfighters" and their leader had reason to feel pleased about the reception they had received and optimistic about the future. Between matinee and evening performances at the Academy of Music in Philadelphia on May 8, Europe took Sissle and the Harmony Kings with him to the home of Barclay Warburton where they gave a private entertainment for the members of the Wanamaker family, Europe's long-time patrons. "It was the first time that we had seen any of the Wanamaker family since the Armistice," Sissle wrote, "and to be once more in the home of those wonderful people," and to experience their "real friendship and hospitality" touched them. Due to the fact that the train taking the band to Boston the next day left promptly at 10:40 P.M., the usual post-evening concert reception on stage had to be cut short. Nevertheless, among "our host of friends, both white and colored, that were crowded on the stage to bid Jim farewell and wish him good-luck, were the members of the Wanamaker family."[38]

Thirty-nine-year-old Jim Europe must have felt himself standing at the threshold of the most brilliant chapter of his career, one that would bring him and his associates the personal rewards they sought, and one that would also see him realize his larger dreams and ambitions for African-American music. His immediate plans, following a short rest, were to take Sissle and Blake and a few others from the band to Brighton Beach to fulfill an engagement at the Chelborne. Many of the band members had not been able to get home since the war, and they needed time off. While playing at the Chelborne, Sissle, Blake, and Europe could begin planning for a worldwide concert tour for the band beginning in the fall. They could ultimately begin to think seriously about the band, and about a National Negro Symphony Orchestra and even, perhaps, about a new musical production for Broadway.[39]

16

"Flee as a Bird"

> We won France by playing music which was ours and not a pale imitation of others, and if we are to develop in America we must develop along our own lines.
>
> James Reese Europe (1919)

"Return Visit By Popular Demand: Three Jubilee Days of Sunshine in Music" by "Lieut. 'Jim' Europe and the Famous 'Hellfighters' 369th U.S. Infantry Band," announced the large ad in the Boston *Herald* on May 9, 1919.[1] Europe and the band arrived early that morning after traveling all night by train from Philadelphia, and most of the musicians spent the next several hours getting what sleep they could before it was time to collect their instruments and set out for the concert hall. Europe, who had developed a heavy cold and was feeling poorly, left to consult a local physician, Dr. Bennie Robinson, an old friend of his, and rejoined the musicians shortly before their matinee concert at 2:30 P.M.

It was a cold, rainy—altogether miserable—day for the first of "three days of sunshine in music." The atmosphere in the old and drafty Mechanics Hall on Huntington Avenue, in comparison to the Boston Opera House where they had performed previously, was also somewhat depressing. Despite the weather, a lively crowd had assembled that included singer Al Jolson and a number of his fellow cast members from the *Sinbad* company.[2] Ironically, it was due to the Jolson show's prior booking of the Boston Opera House that the Hellfighters found themselves in the barnlike auditorium. When he arrived at the hall, Europe told Sissle that Dr. Robinson had been concerned that his cold might turn into pneumonia if he were not careful, but since they were so close to the end of the tour, he wanted to keep going and finish it out. Although his illness was apparent to Sissle and the other members of the band, Europe was able to complete the matinee concert; however, immediately after it was over he asked Sissle to stand in for him at a dinner engagement and again went to see his doctor.

When Sissle returned to the concert hall for the evening performance, he was encouraged to find his leader feeling somewhat better. The Boston weather had improved not at all, but Europe had just received an invitation from Governor Coolidge for the band to play on the State House steps the next morning. As part of the ceremony, the governor also wanted to present Lieutenant Europe with a wreath that he would then place at the base of the Robert Gould Shaw

Monument in the Commons. Shaw, of course, had been the commander of the heroic 54th Massachusetts Voluntary Regiment of black soldiers in the Civil War. This was a singular honor for Jim Europe, and as the evening concert began, the news seemed to cheer both the conductor and his musicians. It was, however, never to take place. The precise details of what transpired over the next three hours are somewhat unclear, but the results—bizarre and tragic—are certain. It would be Jim Europe's last concert; at 11:45 on the evening of May 9, 1919, at City Hospital, America's first "Jazz King" was pronounced dead of a knife wound in the neck.[3] The assailant was his diminutive twenty-four-year-old drummer, Herbert Wright.

In his "Memoirs of Lieutenant 'Jim' Europe," written over a period of several years after the fact, Noble Sissle left the only extant description by an eyewitness to the events of that evening.[4] Although there are discrepancies between his account and that published in the papers the next day, including several important questions that he left unanswered, Sissle's description seems, on balance, to correspond most closely to the limited amount of evidence that remains. According to Sissle, the evening's concert was proceeding as usual, when, as he was sitting in the dressing room he shared with Europe while awaiting his turn to go on stage, one of the musicians from the band called to him saying that Europe wanted him to find Herbert Wright and send him back on stage since it was nearing the time for the "Percussion Twins" duet. Sissle immediately began searching the rooms backstage and found Wright with his uniform coat off and lying on a bench in one of the rooms. When Sissle asked him if he were sick, Wright replied that he was not, but was just upset because "Steve [the other drummer] never does anything right and he makes mistakes and then Lieutenant Europe looks back in the drummer section and commences to frowning at me." Sissle tried to console the drummer and succeeded in getting him into his uniform and back to the stage in time for him to appear on schedule.

As usual, the duet by the two drummers ended the first half of the concert, and there was a short intermission before the rest of the program began. As Europe came off stage, both Herbert and Steve Wright followed him into his dressing room:

> After about one half a minute, Jim finally spoke up and said: "Now, Herbert, you and Steve know how sick I am. The doctor says I should be in the hospital right now, but I am trying to keep going in order to finish out this engagement, that all of you may have your money and be able to go home or take your vacations and you two boys, above anybody else in the band, should cause me the least worry. I have at all times tried to be a father to both of you and there is nothing that I wouldn't do to help both of you, and I don't want either one to worry me any more."

Steve answered that he would do what Europe asked, but Herbert had something more to say. "Lieutenant Europe, you don't treat me right," he said. "I work hard for you. Look at my hands, they're all swollen where I have been drumming, trying to hold the time and yet, Steve, he makes all kinds of mistakes and you never say anything to him." Before Europe could respond, there was a knock at the door and Harold Browning, Horace Berry, Exodus Drayton, and Roland Hayes came into the room to talk to the conductor. Sissle says that he sensed that Herbert was not satisfied, but that he was able to convince him to leave until the others had finished their business.

As Europe rose to greet the Harmony Kings, Herbert burst back into the room, threw his drum into a corner, and screamed: "I'll kill anybody that takes advantage of me. Jim Europe, I'll kill you!" Everyone stood frozen with astonishment, and then they saw that Wright had a small pocket knife in his fist. Europe picked up a chair and held it in front of him as the others yelled for him to "knock the knife out of his hand, Jim!"

> Jim grasped the chair in an attitude as though he was about to carry out our warning, when all of a sudden there came over him some thought, God knows what, that caused him to completely relax his whole body and set the chair down, and was about to mutter, "Herbert, get out of here!," when . . . like a panther Herbert Wright hurled himself over the chair.

No one was aware that Wright had actually struck Europe, but they grabbed the drummer, and as Sissle recalled, Wright immediately became "as calm and as quiet as a child" and followed Sissle from the room. Sissle took Wright to the dressing room and was about to lecture him about his conduct when one of the members of the quartet called to him: "Sissle, come at once. Herbert stabbed Lieutenant Europe." Sissle rushed back to find Europe with his collar off and "a stream of blood" spurting from a small wound in his neck. Someone wrapped a towel around the wound, and an ambulance was sent for. While they waited, Europe, who appeared calm, ordered that the men go back on stage and finish the concert under the direction of Felix Weir, his assistant conductor, and that he be taken out from the back of the hall so as not to interrupt the concert. Sissle does not say how long it took for the ambulance to arrive, but he did remember Europe's last words to him. "Sissle," he said, "don't forget to have the band down before the State House at 9 in the morning. I am going to the hospital, and I will have my wound dressed and I will be at the Commons in the morning, in time to conduct the band. See that the rest of the program is gone through with." It was the last time that Sissle saw his friend alive.

The Boston daily papers, the *Globe* and the *Herald*, which had reporters most quickly on scene, gave a slightly different account of the events. The *Globe* reported that the incident occurred when Lieutenant Europe called Wright into his dressing room to criticize him for walking on and off stage while several of the other acts were performing and that Wright "became indignant and enraged," threw his drum sticks into a corner, and started toward Europe. "Go away from me," Europe said, backing away, "I am a sick man and I don't want to argue with you. Go back on stage." Before any of the others in the dressing room could respond, Wright pulled a small pen knife from his pocket and slashed Europe in the neck. He then turned on the others, slashing at Browning and Drayton when they tried to subdue him and ran from the room.[5] The Boston *Herald* also reported that the drummers (*both* Herbert and Steve Wright) had been walking back and forth in the wings "and several times stepped on the stage and showed themselves to the audience" while the Harmony Kings were singing.[6] Europe "cautioned them against this and also about making any noise which might interrupt the singing." His remarks, witnesses declared, "could have given absolutely no cause for the outburst which came from the Wrights on hearing them." Herbert then suddenly pulled a knife and leaped at Europe and "Ivan Brown [I. Harold Browning] and Charles E. Traton [C. Exodus Drayton], both members of the band, attempted to block him, but they only succeeded in throwing his arm up and the knife went deep into Europe's throat and he dropped to the floor." Both Boston papers reported that in the confusion one of the band members found Captain Thomas Goode and Patrolman William Delaney, police officers from the Back Bay Station who had been assigned to the concert, and they quickly came back stage and apprehended Wright.[7] Both papers also agreed that Europe was fully conscious and that he identified Herbert Wright to the policemen and described to them what had happened before he was taken to the hospital. All the reports also confirm Sissle's memory that although there was concern, no one suspected that Europe was critically injured and that the band members returned to the stage and completed the concert as their leader had instructed. "We all pictured that we would see him in the morning, with just probably a bandage around his neck," Sissle wrote.[8] The theater audience, of course, did notice the absence of the famous conductor, but after Al Johns announced that Lieutenant Europe had been taken ill and that Weir would lead the band for the remaining numbers, they settled back and enjoyed the rest of the concert in ignorance of what had taken place backstage.

In the meantime, Herbert Wright was taken to the police station, charged with assault, fingerprinted, booked, and locked up. According to the *Globe*, Wright "appeared to be very sorry and there were tears in his eyes."[9] Although no official statement was released, the Boston papers reported that Wright claimed that Europe had been "riding" him "a good deal of late and appeared to want to get him out of the band altogether," and that it had become "more than he could stand." Wright was also reported to have stated that he left the stage because he needed to "attend to a finger which was sore," and that he stabbed Europe in the dressing room because he was afraid that Europe "intended to strike him over the head" with a chair.

Immediately following the concert, Sissle, Browning, Drayton, and several others who had witnessed the altercation went to police headquarters and gave their statements of what had happened. Just as he had finished Sissle recalled that a call came in to the station reporting that Europe's condition was very serious, and they hurried to City Hospital. When they arrived, an orderly told them that Europe was in great danger and that they might be asked to give blood to help him pull through. A few minutes later,

> we heard steps on the stairway and stepping to the door of the office, we saw coming down the steps doctors, interns, and the chaplain. Ahead of that party was the young orderly that had asked us concerning the blood transfusion. When I asked him: "Will it not be necessary for us to give blood?," he sorrowfully whispered, "Lieutenant Europe is dead."[10]

The next day newspapers across the country carried the shocking report that the "King of Jazz" had been slain in Boston by a member of his own band.[11]

W. C. Handy, who was in New York at the time of the murder, later wrote that he remembered feeling disturbed and depressed the night Europe died. Unable to sleep, he walked out into Harlem and into the subway, which he rode back and forth until morning, nursing his "strange feeling of numbness and foreboding." When he finally emerged from the trains, it was broad daylight, and the newsboys at 135th Street were excited. "I stopped dead still," he wrote, "and heard one say, 'Extra! Extra! All about the murder of Jim Europe! Extra!'"

> The man who had just come through the baptism of war's fire and steel without a mark had been stabbed by one of his own musicians during a band performance in Boston. No wonder I couldn't sleep. No wonder the rumble of the empty subway had been a ghostly sound without music. I felt that I could at last put my finger on the strange restlessness that had troubled me. . . . The sun was in the sky. The new day promised peace. But all suns had gone down for Jim Europe, and Harlem didn't seem the same.[12]

Indeed, New York's black community was stunned by the tragedy. All the next day a steady stream of the bandleader's friends and admirers called on Willie Europe at their apartment at 67 West 133rd Street to offer their sympathy. If they hoped that Mrs. Europe could give them some explanation, some reason for what had happened, they were disappointed. "Wright, I am sure, would be the last person in the world to hurt my husband if he were in his proper senses," she said.

> Why, "Jim" was the best friend Wright had in the world. "Jim" first met Wright while the drummer was a member of Jenkins' Orphan Band, at Charleston, S.C. When my husband organized his original jazz band, which played for Mr. and Mrs. Vernon Castle, as well as many of the Broadway restaurants in the city, he brought Wright here. Wright wasn't much of a drummer at the time, but "Jim" devoted much time to him and eventually made a fine drummer out of him.[13]

"I had no intimation there were any differences between Jim and Wright until I got the telegram this morning telling what had happened," Mrs. Europe told the press.[14]

The emotional response from New Yorkers to the death of Jim Europe was so great that it was decided that his funeral should be a public one, the first ever granted to a black American in the city's history. After being released by the Boston authorities, Europe's body was brought home to Harlem where it lay in state at Paris Undertakers on 131st Street. Between 9 and 10:45 on Tuesday morning, May 13, thousands of people—some prominent, most not so—filed past the casket to take a last look at the famous bandsman and pay their respects.[15] A little before 11:00 A.M., after a brief service by the Negro Free Masons, the funeral procession led by Captain McGrath and a squad of police from the 38th Precinct began its march through the streets of Harlem. Following the police came a delegation from the Hayward Unit of the Women's League for National Defense and six automobiles carrying flowers sent by the Frogs, the Clef Club, Bert and Lottie Williams, Irene Castle Treman, and others. Next came the new 15th Infantry Regiment Band of the New York National Guard, a company of veterans from the "Old 15th" (including war heroes Henry Johnson and Needham Roberts), and then the hearse, carrying the flag-draped casket and attended by eight former members of Europe's machine gun company and a number of honorary pall-bearers. Finally, there marched a representative company of soldiers from the New York National Guard and a number of civilians, including the members of Hiram Lodge No. 4 (of which Europe had been a member) in Masonic regalia. At the very end of the procession, led by Ford Dabney, Europe's former partner during the Castle years, wearing black arm bands and carrying their instruments at their sides, silently marched "the famous 'Jimmy' Europe Jazz Band."

From the funeral parlor, the solemn parade proceeded slowly over to 7th Avenue, north to 140th Street, east to Lenox and South to 125th Street. The route along the way was lined by thousands of Harlemites who quietly saluted when Europe's casket passed by. As they turned onto 7th Avenue, the National Guard Band played the traditional funeral hymn "Flee as a Bird in the Mountains" and then "Nearer, My God, To Thee," bringing tears to the eyes of many in the crowd. "Not since the day that Jack Johnson came back to town bringing the world's heavyweight championship with him," the *Philadelphia Tribune* said, "has New York's colored population turned out in such numbers. . . ." At 125th Street, the marchers took the subway down town to Columbus Circle and there rejoined the hearse, the other automobiles, and additional thousands of sadly gazing spectators of both races for the final procession to St. Marks Episcopal Methodist Church on West 53rd Street. In paying their last respects to the bandleader, "no color line was drawn," observed the *Tribune*. As the procession approached St. Marks it was met by even larger throngs "of white and colored friends, who could get nowhere near the church" and who so jammed the sidewalks and street that "it took several police to keep order."

Inside the church every available space was occupied. Among those in the pews were Colonel Hayward, Lt. Colonel Fillmore, Majors Fish, Esperance, and

Clark, Lieutenant A. P. Gillespie (representing the French Army), Charles Canfield of the Allied Theatrical Association, and Captain John Wanamaker, Jr. The service, which was short but moving, was conducted by Reverend William H. Brooks (former Chaplain of the 369th Infantry) with assistance from Reverend Richard Bolden (Pastor of the First Emanuel Church), Reverend W. Stephenson Holder (Pastor of the Harlem Congregational Church), and Reverend A. R. Cooper of the Bethel Church. The St. Marks Choir sang "Abide with Me," and "Lead, Kindly Light," a quartet led by Creighton Thompson sang "Dear Old Pal of Mine," and Reverend Brooks talked of Europe's life and accomplishments. A second eulogy was then offered by the president of the Clef Club. "To the throngs along Broadway the passing of Jim Europe meant little more than the loss of the man to whose music many feet had kept time," said the *Tribune*, "but what it meant to the city's colored contingent was perhaps best expressed by Tanney [Deacon] Johnson. . . ."

> Before Jim Europe came to New York, the colored man knew nothing but Negro dances and porter's work. All that has been changed. Jim Europe was the living open sesame to the colored porters of this city. He took them from their porter's places and raised them to positions of importance as real musicians. I think the suffering public ought to know that in Jim Europe the race has lost a leader, a benefactor, and a true friend.[16]

Harry T. Burleigh, Europe's long-time friend and teacher, and baritone soloist at St. George's Episcopal Church, then sang "Now Take Thy Rest," and taps was played by Private Clarence Clark, bugler of the "Old 15th."[17] A resolution by the Interdenominational Ministers of New York was read endorsing "the movement started by his band for a monument in his honor." Europe's body was then taken immediately to Pennsylvania Station for transport to Washington and burial at the National Military Cemetery in Arlington.[18] A second, brief ceremony was held at his mother's and sister's beloved Lincoln Temple on the morning of May 14, 1919, and thirty-nine-year-old James Reese Europe, his remarkable career left unfinished, was buried with full military honors.[19]

In the days and weeks that followed, memorial services were held in several cities, and many tributes to Europe as a patriot, race leader, organizer, composer, and bandleader were published in the nation's newspapers and musical magazines. At the Olympia Theater in Philadelphia on May 25, Colonel William Hayward, Major Hamilton Fish, Major Charles Fillmore, Judge Robert Terrell, Irene Castle Treman, and Theodore Roosevelt, Jr., paid honor to his memory, and both at Philadelphia and at a memorial held in Washington, D.C., on June 1 music was provided by a twenty-one-year-old baritone named Paul Robeson.[20] Although considerable effort was expended by his associates and friends to establish a suitable memorial in his name, including the Jim Europe Memorial Fund to create a music school in Harlem for Negro students and the short-lived Europe Memorial Theatre Company to build a permanent home to "protect and encourage negro [sic] music," none was ever successful. Neither was the proposal for a "National Musical Memorial Day" to be set aside in his memory for patriotic speeches and music by American composers. An American Legion Post (Number 5), founded in Washington on June 27, 1919, however, was named in his honor, and despite the self-promoting nature of some of its comments, *Talking Machine World* was in part correct in writing that Europe's Pathé recordings would remain as a lasting "memorial to the skill of Lieutenant Europe" and to the "jazz music inaugurated and perfected by this wonderful leader . . ."[21]

Most of what appeared in the papers, however generous, added little to the depth of general understanding of what Europe's life had meant beyond the chronicle of his achievements. A writer or editor occasionally attempted to say more. One of these was Mrs. Addie Hunton, a YMCA worker still in France in the spring of 1919, who felt compelled to send a letter to the *New York Age* when she learned of Europe's death.[22] Writing from "'No Man's Land,' about thirty miles north of Verdun between the Meuse and Argonne Forest," she said, "I want to send this line of appreciation for the late Lieut. James Reese Europe, whose death comes to all overseas workers as a severe shock. I can think of no more fitting time or place from which to send these words of appreciation for his service to his country and his race."

> But everywhere in France the question is asked: "Did you hear the 369th Band?" or, more familiarly, "Lieutenant Europe's Band?" Down in the Savoie Leave Area, where the band spent some time, this question was asked by French and Americans alike. At Aix-les-Bains, Chambéry, and Challes Eaux we were being told how wonderful it was, months after it had gone.

In addition to Europe's role in the Great War, a number of writers attempted to evaluate his broader musical and cultural contribution. In an editorial entitled "Loss of an American Musician," the *New York Times* said that those

> who think that contemporary ragtime, however imperfect, is a stage in the evolution of a different sort of music which may eventually possess considerable merit will regret the untimely death of a man who ranked as one of the greatest ragtime conductors, perhaps the greatest, we have had. Ragtime may be negro [sic] music, but it is American negro music, more alive than much other American music; and Europe was one of the Americans who was contributing most to its development.[23]

"They buried 'Jim' Europe the other day," began an editorial in the New York *Clipper*,

> Jim, the "Jazz King" of Broadway. He was only a black man, was Jim—outside— but they laid him away as though he had belonged to the more fortunate race. Colonel Bill Hayward, white leader of the 369th Infantry, a colored regiment, of which Jim was bandmaster, was there, and so were many other white officers, and, yes, civilians who saw beneath Jim's skin, into his heart, and—loved him. . . . Hereafter, jazz music will mean more to us than it ever did before.[24]

"Some day," concurred the editors of *Outlook*, "when ragtime and kindred forms of music become recognized as distinctive and valuable material for the artist, such a man as the Negro band leader James Europe, who was murdered the other day, will be considered as more than a mere entertainer."[25]

The last word, appropriately enough, was left to the black press. "He was not ashamed of being a Negro or being called a Negro," said the *Age*, "believing instead of worrying and arguing about what he should be called, the proper thing was to dignify the term *Negro*, just as he helped dignify Negro music." "He was the Roosevelt of Negro musicians—a dynamic force that did things— big things. His death comes as a big loss to the musical world, but a still greater loss to the race of which he was proud to be a member."[26]

Coda

The surroundings did not awe him nor was his manner defer-
ential. . . . He was a professional pianist and was now more or less
permanently located in New York, having secured a job with the
Jim Europe Clef Club Orchestra. . . . "Wall Street Rag," he said.
Composed by the great Scott Joplin. He began to play. Ill-tuned
or not the Aeolian had never made such sounds.

E. L. Doctorow
Ragtime (1974)

On May 12, the day before Jim Europe's funeral in New York City, Noble
Sissle, Harold Browning, Exodus Drayton, Charles Jackson, and Steven
Wright testified before the grand jury in Boston. After hearing the evidence, the jury brought in an indictment of first degree murder against Wright,
and the drummer was arraigned two days later before Judge George A. Sanderson of the Superior Court. Wright pleaded self-defense and was ordered held
without bail until the trial, set for May 21. When it was discovered that the
Wright could not pay for his own defense, the court assigned attorney Johnson
W. Ramsey as his council. Ramsey immediately asked for additional time and
the trial was moved back to June 9.[1]

It seems clear that Defense Attorney Ramsey did the best he could to construct a line of defense for Wright in the nearly four weeks that followed.[2]
There was little doubt of the primary facts of the crime, that Wright stabbed
Europe as charged, and none of the witnesses supported Wright's claim of self-
defense, so Ramsey concentrated his efforts on building a case for extenuating
or mitigating circumstances (Was Europe's death completely attributable to the
stabbing? Was there a long pattern of abuse of Wright by Europe? Had Wright's
mental stability been affected by the war or by his childhood experiences in the
orphanage? Was Wright sane?).

On May 31, and again on June 4, two physicians on the behest of the defense attorney, examined Wright at the Charles Street Jail and found him, in
their opinion, insane. The state responded by having its own medical experts
("alienists," they were called at the time) examine the defendant. On June 9,
the day set for the trial, Judge Sanderson received the report of the state's doctors that while they did not find Wright insane, he was "of such low type of
mentality that there was a question as to his entire responsibility."[3] District At-

torney Pelletier then told Ramsey that the state would accept a charge of manslaughter if Wright would plead guilty, which he did, and Judge Sanderson immediately sentenced him to prison for a term of from ten to fifteen years. Herbert Wright spent the next eight years of his life in the Massachusetts State Penitentiary; he was paroled on April Fools Day, 1927.

With Jim Europe's death, the musicians in the Hellfighters Band found themselves without a leader and without much sense of direction. There was talk, probably by promoters, about bringing John Europe, Jim's brother, from Washington, D.C., to take over; but John was no conductor, and nothing came of it.[4] A far better prospect, although also unsuccessful in the end, was for Eugene Mikell to leave his teaching post at the Bordentown School and lead the band; Mikell at least knew most of the musicians and their music.[5] By the middle of July, Mikell had reorganized the group, held a well-attended concert and dance at the Manhattan Casino, and garnered enough support for a concert to be scheduled at Carnegie Hall on July 26 as "a tribute to the late leader of the band."[6] Times had begun to change, however, and without Europe's name and leadership popular interest faded quickly.

In September, Mikell tried to institute a semi-annual concert and dance series in Harlem as Europe had done with the Tempo Club and Clef Club before the war. A concert was held at the Manhattan Casino on September 20, 1919, and another, advertised as the "Lieut. Europe Memorial Dance and Bayonet Contest," took place the following spring.[7] By that time the band numbered only thirty-eight musicians, and the public—even in Harlem—seemed no longer especially interested in military bands or other reminders of the war. Shortly after its May 11, 1920, appearance, the musicians and singers disbanded, and Mikell returned to teaching. In the 1920s, he occasionally conducted the Clef Club Orchestra or the Jenkins Orphanage Band, and he was an influence on a younger generation of musicians, like Benny Carter, who studied with him briefly.[8] Gene Mikell died in 1932.

Noble Sissle and Eubie Blake, Europe's closest associates and friends, set off after the tragedy in a different direction. "There was only one Jim Europe," Sissle told Kimball and Bolcom. "There was years of experience behind that sweep of his arms, and anyone who tried to follow him would just be out of their mind."[9] The pair, therefore, went to Pat Casey, Europe's former agent, and asked him to find them a spot in vaudeville, where they appeared for several years as the "Dixie Duo." Jim Europe was not forgotten, however; in their act they appeared formally—dressed in tuxedos—as they had done in their society jobs with Europe before the war, and they performed the songs they had written together, like "Good Night, Angeline," and especially "On Patrol in No Man's Land," which they used as their big finale. At an N.A.A.C.P. benefit in Philadelphia in 1920, Sissle and Blake met the comedy-dancing team of Flournoy E. Miller and Aubrey Lyles, who had worked with Europe on the ill-fated musical *Darkydom* in 1915, and the four performers decided that together they would try to carry out one of Europe's dreams: to restore authentic African-American artistry to the American stage.[10] The result was *Shuffle Along*, the epoch-making musical written, performed, produced, and directed by black Americans, which opened at the Sixty-Third Street Theatre in New York on May 23, 1921. Few people at the time thought such a production possible, but as Blake later recalled, Sissle "said we'd get there, somehow, and we did. I think Sissle still felt Jim Europe's hand guiding us."[11] Without the triumph of *Shuffle Along*, as Kimball and Bolcom rightly contend, much that subsequently became distinctive and original in American musical theater might never have happened.[12]

The Clef Club also survived Europe's death and it even prospered throughout most of the 1920s. Alexander Fenner, a cello player who had worked with Ford Dabney at the New Amsterdam Theater Roof, became the club's fourth president, and under his leadership, aided once again by a strong demand for black musicians, the club was able by 1927 to pay off the mortgage on its club house.[13] During these years the Clef Club continued to attract talented members (Elliot Carpenter, Paul Robeson, and Fletcher Henderson, among others) and continued to offer concerts by its orchestra and to book its members for jobs in many parts of the world. When radio began to become commercially popular after 1920, the Clef Club was also an important source for musicians in the new medium. Even the eccentric Will Marion Cook returned to the fold after a couple of successful years abroad. Business fell dramatically during the Depression, however, and finally, after more than thirty years of pioneering service to black American musicians, the Clef Club of New York City, Inc., ceased to exist.[14]

Cook, Will Vodery, Ford Dabney, and W. C. Handy, the other comparable figures of Europe's generation, remained active and to one degree or another influential for several decades. All of them made contributions to the rejuvenation of black musical theater and except for Handy, continued to lead their own bands and orchestras. Cook was an important mentor of Duke Ellington before dying of cancer in 1945. Vodery assisted Sissle and Blake with *Shuffle Along* and several other significant productions, orchestrated Gershwin's *Blue Monday* (Gershwin's first attempt at a "Negro opera") and Kern's *Showboat*, became the first black professional on the music staff of 20th Century Fox, and helped the careers of many future stars, including Bill "Bojangles" Robinson and Jules Bledsoe. He died in 1951. Dabney wrote the music for the Broadway production of *Rang Tang* (1927), operated an entertainment bureau, and held down engagements in Palm Beach, Miami, and Newport for many years. In 1958 he died at the age of seventy-five. The subsequent career of the "Father of the Blues," W. C. Handy, who also died in 1958, is well-known.[15]

For a man who had been so successful in his professional life and who had prided himself in his ability to control nearly every situation, his unexpected death left Europe's personal affairs in a shambles. He left no will, and his estate amounted to less than $1,000.[16] Willie Europe, his wife of six years, who was aware of his relationship with Bessie Simms and knew about their son, filed the application for letters of administration in the Surrogate's Court of New York naming—perhaps understandably—only Europe's mother, brother, and sisters as "persons interested in this proceeding." Willie Europe was granted sole administrator of Jim Europe's estate on May 15.[17] In a material sense, it helped her very little. She spent the latter part of her life with her sister and her husband, Ada and Fitzherbert Howell (with whom she had lived since 1917), and was employed as a manicurist in a beauty parlor. Willie Europe died of cancer on May 20, 1930. She was fifty-three.[18]

Europe's mother, Lorraine, had been financially dependent upon her son for over fifteen years. While he was in the army, Europe named her the beneficiary of his army life insurance policy, and she began receiving payments of $57.50 per month beginning with his discharge in February 1919. In November 1925, by which time Lorraine Europe had received a total of $4,663.66, the Veterans Bureau terminated the disbursements when it was discovered that Europe had allowed the policy to lapse during the latter part of his service.[19] Mother Europe continued to live with her daughter, Mary, in the house on S Street that the two had purchased in 1910 until her health began to fail in 1934. A woman of strong will and determination, she lived to experience the great sorrow of burying all but one of her children and grandchildren (at least of those she acknowledged); she, herself, died on March 29, 1937.[20]

Mary Lorraine Europe, the last surviving member of the Europe family that had come north from Alabama at the end of Reconstruction, suffered a stroke while teaching at Dunbar High School in November 1944 and was forced to retire. In the years before her illness, she had conducted and trained dozens of student choruses for concert, radio, and army camp performances, and taught piano and organ privately and in the schools for more than forty years. Following her death on October 20, 1947, funeral rites were held at Lincoln Congregational Church where she had served as organist and choir director for thirty years; a student choir sang the Dunbar High School Alma Mater, which she composed.[21]

Bessie Simms witnessed the public funeral but did not attend the services in New York for Jim Europe, electing to remain out of the public eye for her own reasons as well as, perhaps, to protect the reputation of the murdered bandleader and his two-year-old namesake. She was just twenty-eight at the time, and although his death deprived her and James Reese Europe, Jr., of his future support, the revival of black musical theater two years later may have seemed to promise renewed opportunities for her own career. Indeed, in 1922 Bessie Simms appeared in two productions by the veterans Salem Tutt Whitney and J. Homer Tutt, *Jump Steady* and *Oh! Joy!*, and in 1923 she was in the chorus of

Barrington Carter's *7–11*. Her daughter, Madeline Belt, who lived with her and James Reese Europe, Jr., before marrying Eddie Rector (one of the premier dancers of the period), was a familiar figure in black musical theater in the 1920s and early 1930s, as were her two nieces, Margaret and Edith Simms.[22]

By the middle of the decade, and despite her many family members and friends in the business, Bessie Simms found herself no longer being called for parts in new theater productions, and her life became increasingly difficult. She was able to find a place for her son at the Cardinal Gibbons Institute, a Catholic school in St. Mary's County, Maryland, where she wrote to him almost daily and where he completed his elementary education. When he asked about his father, she never complained about him but told her son that he should be proud to carry the name of a famous and important man. She also never mentioned Willie Europe nor suggested to him that there was anything complex or unusual about his parents' relationship. The nightlife of Harlem in the 1920s is justifiably legendary for its variety and exuberance, and Bessie Simms, among many others, was able to make a living working in the clubs and restaurants. It was a fragile world, however, and when the Depression came the glittering crowds departed and a world closed down suddenly and, for many people, like Bessie Simms, shockingly. She was married again, briefly, in 1930 to Grafton Johnson, but her life had already become a hard one. She died in August 1931.

For fourteen-year-old James Reese Europe, Jr., who was too young at the time of his father's death to remember him, the loss of his mother left him completely alone. He had understood, somehow, that he had relatives in Washington, D.C., and after his mother died he tried to find them. Using the local phone book, he discovered a Europe address on S Street and he went there and rang the bell. When the door was answered he announced himself as James Reese Europe, Jr., and looking for his relatives. An old woman in a wheelchair responded from down the hall, "Where did you get that name?" "From my father," he replied. "Humph!" said the woman, and the door was closed in front of him.[23]

It is unfortunate that neither James Reese Europe nor his mother, Lorraine Europe, ever came to know James Reese Europe, Jr., for he would have pleased them both. Returning to New York City, Jim, Jr., raised himself on the streets of Harlem, mopping floors at Radio City Music Hall and sleeping in the subways. At the time of the American entry into World War II, he enlisted in the Merchant Marine and after serving for two years as a seaman, was nominated to attend the U.S. Merchant Marine Academy. Following service as an officer during the war, he returned to New York and joined the New York Police Department and, later, the Fire Department (from which he retired as a decorated lieutenant). At each stage of his career he stubbornly fought the persistent racism he encountered in employment practices, educational opportunities, and housing, and he usually prevailed—sometimes with the help of the N.A.A.C.P. In 1975 he received a graduate degree from the State University of New York, became an alcohol and drug abuse clinician, and retired as a social welfare administrator on Long Island. In 1988 James Reese Europe, Jr., was awarded the Nassau County Commission on Human Rights Leadership Award.

As for James Europe, the father, it is tempting to speculate on the contributions that he, himself, might have made had he lived. At the time of his death in 1919 he was one of the best known and respected band leaders of either race in the United States. He had already accomplished a great deal toward popularizing the music (and dance styles) that would help make the new Jazz Age possible. Still a young man, possessing great imagination and ambition for himself and the music he believed in, given his ability to engage others in his vision it is hard to believe that he would not have become in the years ahead one of the most important figures the world of American popular music ever produced. He surely would have presented a challenge to Paul Whiteman, the man who became the most commercially successful exploiter of jazz in next decade. Gilbert Seldes, a writer and editor of *Collier's* and *The Dial*, and a great admirer of the Hellfighter's Band, was certain of it. In his 1924 book, *The 7 Lively Arts*, in which he challenged the pretentiousness attached to the traditional "high arts," Seldes wrote that "Jim Europe seemed to have a constructive intelligence and, had he lived, I am sure he would have been an even greater conductor than Whiteman."[24] "Say that what he played had nothing to do with music; say that to mention the name of a conductor in the same breath with his name is an atrocity of taste," he wrote,

> I cannot help believing that Jim Europe had the essential quality of music in him, and that, in his field, however far from any other it may have been, he was as great as Karl Muck in his. The hand kept perfect time, and his right knee, with a sharp and subtle little motion, stressed the acceleration or retard of the syncope. His dynamics were beautiful because he knew the value of noise and knew how to produce it and how to make it effective; he knew how to keep perfectly a running commentary of wit over the masses of his sound; and the ease and smoothness of his own performance as conductor had all the qualities of greatness.
>
> [I]n him nearly all that is most precious [in the African-American musical consciousness] . . . came to the surface. He seemed sensitive to the ecstasy and pathos of the spirituals as he was to the ecstasy and joy of jazz.[25]

In 1926, Dave Payton, who, along with Wilbur Sweatman and Erskine Tate, was one of the pioneering black orchestra leaders in Chicago, reminded his readers in the *Chicago Defender* that James Reese Europe "was the man more than anybody else to place the Race musician before the public. It was Jim Europe, as the gang called him, who [demonstrated that] we could play music and direct it." "Everywhere Jim Europe and his band played a new field was opened for our musicians," he said.[26] Some ten years later, "New Negro" spokesman Alain Locke included Europe among his four "arrangers of genius" (Dabney, Cook, and Handy were the others), who "organized Negro music out of a broken, musically illiterate dialect and made it a national music with its own peculiar idioms of harmony, instrumentation, and technical style of playing."[27]

Seldes, Payton, and Locke are exceptions to a general pattern of neglect with which Americans, white and black, of the 1920s and after tended to treat the accomplishments of Jim Europe and, indeed, most of the members of his ragtime generation of African-American musical pioneers. Even Irene Castle, who had written in 1930 that Jim Europe's music "was the only music that completely made me forget the effort of the dance," seems to have forgotten him in her later years.[28] Europe's reputation suffered for a number of reasons, chiefly because, like the era to which he belonged, he was a transitional figure, and like all transitional figures difficult to place. While he was steadfastly committed to increasing the respect accorded to African-American music and to improving the conditions for black Americans, he was never directly involved— in a political sense—with the racial ferment of his times. His association with the Castles and with the white musical and social establishment of New York has also tended to make his position in African-American history somewhat ambiguous, as has, ironically, the very fact of his considerable success within the larger society. In addition, Europe was careful about his public image, and, unlike many of the more flamboyant entertainers of the period, he succeeded in keeping his personal and family life private, avoiding the sensational public disclosures that often make for good copy.[29]

With the revival of public and scholarly interest in ragtime music in the 1960s and with the general awakening of interest in African-American culture and history, however, there has begun a rediscovery of James Reese Europe. Beginning with Samuel B. Charters and Leonard Kunstadt's *Jazz: A History of the New York Scene* in 1962, scholars of American music, African-American music, musical theater, jazz, and ragtime have come to recognize Jim Europe as "one of the most remarkable and influential American musicians of the first decades of the twentieth century."[30] Samuel A. Floyd, Jr., following Alain Locke, for example, has identified him as one of those figures "whose accomplishments were recognized as significant and provocative by New Negro leaders" and thus helped to shape the emergence of the Harlem Renaissance in the 1920s.[31] Europe's "idea of the orchestra as a viable vehicle for the expression of musical ideas emanating from the black-American experience," Olly Wilson wrote in 1986,

> has not only continued to flourish, but also has become a reality in the work of several generations of black-American composers. At its best, that work has in the past enriched all our lives, and will in the future continue to do so, for it speaks of human experience from a unique dual perspective—a perspective that has the potential for yielding valuable insights into the human condition.[32]

Europe was active "at a moment when black American music was in transition from ragtime to jazz," Dan Morgenstern, Director of the Institute of Jazz Studies at Rutgers State University, has said, "and he did much to bring about that transition."[33] To Gunther Schuller, Europe was "the most important transitional figure in the prehistory of jazz on the East Coast," providing for orchestral jazz "the same kind of catalyst Jelly Roll Morton was for piano music."[34] An articulate musician and war hero, Jim Europe was very likely the individual most responsible for making the new music and the term jazz widely acceptable (if not completely respectable), both at home in America and on the continent as well.[35] He helped to make jazz safe for democracy.

Public appreciation of Jim Europe has grown somewhat more slowly, but the publication of a number of articles in popular magazines and journals in more recent years, reissues of his recordings by New World Records and others, and the inclusion of his compositions in the repertoire of performing groups like the New England Conservatory Ragtime Ensemble and the Black Music Repertory Ensemble (the performing unit of the Columbia College Center for Black Music Research) have helped to broaden contemporary public exposure to both his music and his remarkable career.[36] In the summer of 1989, the noted conductor Maurice Peress, a champion of American composers and "vernacular-inspired music," organized a three-part series of recreations of historic concerts at Carnegie Hall. Among these "Carnegie Hall Jazz Heritage Concerts" was the recreation of the James Reese Europe Clef Club Concert of 1912, featuring baritone William Warfield, mezzosoprano Barbara Conrad, pianist Leon Bates, the Boys Choir of Harlem and the Morgan State University Male Choir, and eighty-eight-year-old arranger, composer, actor Jester Hairston. The program followed the original concert as closely as possible and encompassed the same variety of the music of black composers—vaudeville tunes, orchestral and ensemble ragtime, formal waltzes and concert marches, liturgical choral works, and concert arias—for which the Clef Club under Europe was noted. The composers who were represented included Europe, Will Marion Cook, Harry T. Burleigh, J. Rosamond Johnson, Samuel Coleridge-Taylor, William Tyers, and Wilbur Sweatman. Peress's "New Clef Club Orchestra" did not precisely replicate the 1912 Europe instrumentation (harp-guitar and bandoris players proved difficult to find), but the large sections of banjos and mandolins, and, of course, the ten upright pianos, were there. The audience was spirited and generous (especially after James Reese Europe, Jr., and his family were introduced) and joined the orchestra by clapping along and demanding encores. The performers, this time including both blacks and whites, responded enthusiastically. It was an entirely enjoyable musical evening, but unlike the original 1912 concert, there was little of the shock of the new. Perhaps this is, itself, the best testimony to Europe's musical legacy.

As Jon Pareles concluded in his review of the concert, black musicians "have proved themselves in different ways since 1912, some (like Jessye Norman) triumphing in the classical tradition, some bypassing it completely, some (like Wynton Marsalis) conquering it as a sideline. All those ways for members of a minority to make themselves heard in the majority's musical culture were foreshadowed at the Clef Club."[37] Had the Clef Club's founder accomplished just this, his life would be one worth remembering. Jim Europe, however, did something more; he both made it possible for a minority within American culture to be heard, and he also helped to give the national culture itself a voice and an aesthetic it badly needed, one that has since been heard around the world. James Reese Europe "was just something that had to happen in America," Eubie Blake once said. "He was at a point in time at which all the roots and forces of Negro music merged and gained its widest expression. And he furnished something that was needed in time."[38] His was a life in ragtime.

Appendix 1

The Musical Compositions of James Reese Europe

In Chronological Order According to Copyright Date or Date of First Performance

1904

"Arizona" Music by James Reese Europe. Lyrics by William Estren. c. Sol Bloom 5/26/04.

"Blue Eyed Sue" Words and Music by James Reese Europe (Sung by Miss Susie Fisher in *A Little of Everything* and by Miss Neva Aymar in *Mother Goose*). c. Sol Bloom 7/14/04.

"My Heart Goes Thumping and Bumping for You" Words and Music by James Reese Europe. c. Sol Bloom 7/21/04.

"Nubiana—A Nubian Love Song without Words" Music by James Reese Europe. c. Sol Bloom 7/21/04.

"Come, Cinda, Be My Bride" Words and Music by Estren and Europe. c. Sol Bloom 9/27/04.

"Zola; Jungle Song" Words and Music by Larkins and Europe. c. G.W. Setchell (Boston) 11/23/04.

1905

"Obadiah (You Took Advantage of Me)" By James Reese Europe. c. Gotham Music 1/26/05.

"The Coon Band Parade" Music by James Reese Europe. c. Sol Bloom 10/14/05.

1906

"On the Gay Luneta" From the *Shoo-fly Regiment*. Words by Bob Cole. Music by James Reese Europe. c. Joseph W. Stern 8/23/06.

1907–1908

"A Royal Coon" Words by Jolly John Larkins. Music by James Reese Europe. c. Will Rossiter (Chicago) 6/1/07

"When I Rule the Town" From the *Black Politician*. Words by R. C. McPherson. Music by James Reese Europe. Performed 9/14/07.

"Spooney Sam" From the *Black Politician*. As cited previously.

"The Darktown Band" From the *Black Politician*. As cited previously.

"Help Yourself" From the *Black Politician*. As cited previously.

"Don't Take Him Away" From the *Black Politician*. As cited previously.

"Races, Races" From the *Black Politician*. As cited previously.

"Down Manila Bay" From the *Black Politician*. As cited previously.

"Hezekiah Doo" From the *Black Politician*. As cited previously. Title changed to "Hezekiah," 2/24/08.

"The Smart Set Carbineers" From the *Black Politician*. As cited previously.

"Society" From the *Black Politician*. As cited previously.

"Lolita" From the *Black Politician*. As cited previously.

"I Don't Like School" From the *Black Politician*. As cited previously. Title changed to "School Days," 2/24/08.

"Crow" From the *Black Politician*. As cited previously. Title changed to "Old Black Crow," 2/24/08.

"Likin' Ain't Like Lovin'" From the *Black Politician*. Words and music by James Reese Europe. c. Victoria Music Co. 11/15/07.

"Election Time" From the *Black Politician*. Words by R. C. McPherson. Music by James Reese Europe. Performed 2/24/08.

"Take Him Away, the Law Commands It" From the *Black Politician*. As cited previously.

"When the Moon Plays Peek A Boo" From the *Black Politician*. As cited previously.

"Suwanee River" From the *Black Politician*. As cited previously.

1908–1909

"I Ain't Had No Lovin' in a Long Time" From *The Red Moon*. Words by Bob Cole. Music by James Reese Europe. c. Joseph W. Stern 8/24/08.

"Ada, My Sweet Potater" From *The Red Moon*. Lyrics by Chas. A. Hunter. Music by Cole and Europe. c. Joseph W. Stern 9/22/08.

"Sambo" From *The Red Moon*. Words by Bob Cole. Music by James Reese Europe. c. Joseph W. Stern 11/18/08.

"Picanninny Days" From *The Red Moon*. Words by Bob Cole. Music by James Reese Europe. c. Jerome H. Remick 11/24/09.

"Red Moon" From *The Red Moon* of 1909. Music by James Reese Europe (according to Sylvester Russell of the *Freeman*)

1910–1911

"Pliney, Come Out in the Moonlight" From *The Red Moon*. Words by Bob Cole. Music by James Reese Europe. c. Jerome H. Remick 1/10/10.

"Sweet Suzanne" Words by Henry Troy. Music by James Reese Europe. c. F.B. Haviland 8/29/10.

"Queen of the Nile" Music by James Reese Europe. Performed by the Clef Club Orchestra at the Manhattan Casino, 10/20/10.

"The Clef Club" Grand march and two step. Music by James Reese Europe. c. F.B. Haviland 5/11/11.

"The Separate Battalion" March. Dedicated to the High School Cadets of Washington, D.C. Music by James Reese Europe. Performed by the Clef Club Orchestra at the Manhattan Casino, 5/11/11

"Lorraine Waltzes" Dedicated to his mother. Music by James Reese Europe. Performed by the Clef Club Orchestra at Manhattan Casino, 5/11/11.

"Strength of the Nation" March. Dedicated to the proposed colored regiment of New York. Music by James Reese Europe. Performed by the Clef Club Orchestra at Manhattan Casino, 11/9/11.

1912–1913

"Hula, Hawaiian Dance" Music by James Reese Europe. Performed by the Clef Club Orchestra at Manhattan Casino, 5/23/12.

"Droop Dem Eyes" Words and music by Henry Creamer and James Reese Europe. c. Waterson, Berlin, and Snyder 6/11/12.

"I've Got the Finest Man" Words and music by Creamer and Europe. c. Waterson, Berlin, and Snyder 6/12/12.

"Oh, Silvery Star" Words by Henry Creamer. Music by James Reese Europe. c. Joseph W. Stern 11/18/12.

"Someone is Waiting Down in Tennessee" Words by Cecil Mack (aka R. C. McPherson). Music by James Reese Europe. c. Waterson, Berlin and Snyder 2/21/13.

"Breezy Rag" Music by James Reese Europe. Performed by the Clef Club Orchestra at Manhattan Casino 5/8/13.

"A Hot Step" Music by James Reese Europe. Performed by the Clef Club Orchestra at the Philadelphia Academy of Music 11/4/13.

"Benefactors, a March" Music by James Reese Europe. Performed by the Clef Club Orchestra at the Philadelphia Academy of Music 11/4/13.

1914

"What It Takes to Make Me Love You—You've Got it" Words and Music by James Reese Europe. c. Joseph W. Stern 1/27/14. Words by James Weldon Johnson. c. Joseph W. Stern 2/13/14.

"Castle House Rag" Trot and one step. Music by James Reese Europe. c. Joseph W. Stern 3/9/14.

"Castles in Europe" Innovation trot. Music by James Reese Europe. c. Joseph W. Stern 3/10/14.

"Castles' Half and Half" Music by Europe and Dabney. c. Joseph W. Stern 3/18/14.

"Congratulations (Castles' Lame Duck Waltz)" Music by James Reese Europe. c. G. Ricordi 3/23/14.

"Castle Walk" Trot and one step. Music by Europe and Dabney. c. Joseph W. Stern 4/3/14.

"Castle Maxixe" Brazilian maxixe. Music by Europe and Dabney. c. Joseph W. Stern 4/8/14.

"Castle Innovation Tango" Argentine tango. Music by Europe and Dabney. c. Joseph W. Stern 4/8/14.

"Castle Perfect Trot" One step. Music by Europe and Dabney. c. Joseph W. Stern 4/28/14.

"Valse Marguerite" Dedicated to Mrs. Hawkesworth and introduced by Mrs. Hawkesworth and Mr. Basil Durant. Music by James Reese Europe. c. Joseph W. Stern 4/28/14.

"The Nell Rose Waltz" Dedicated to Miss Eleanor Wilson. Music by James Reese Europe. Performed 5/7/14.

"Castle Lame Duck Waltz" Music by Europe and Dabney. c. Joseph W. Stern 5/8/14.

"Enticement" An Argentine idyl. Music by Eporue Yenbad. c. Joseph W. Stern 5/11/14.

"Castle Combination" Waltz. Music by Europe and Dabney. c. Joseph W. Stern 6/2/14.

"Fiora" Waltz dedicated to Mrs. Hawkesworth. Music by James Reese Europe. c. G. Ricordi 9/25/14.

1915

"The Castle Doggy Fox Trot" Music by James Reese Europe. c. G. Ricordi 3/24/15.

"Queen Louise" Hesitation waltz. Music by James Reese Europe. c. G. Ricordi 4/10/15.

"At that San Francisco Fair" From *Nobody Home*. Lyrics by Schuyler Greene. Music by
    Jerome Kern, Ford Dabney, and James Reese Europe. c. T. B. Harms and Fran-
    cis, Day and Hunter 4/19/15.
"Rouge et Noir" Walk. Music by James Reese Europe. c. G. Ricordi 4/22/15.
"Father's Gone to the War" Words by Henry Creamer. Music by James Reese Europe.
    c. G. Ricordi 5/3/15.
"I'll Hit the Homeward Trail" Words by Henry Creamer. Music by James Reese Europe.
    c. G. Ricordi 5/3/15.
"Hey, There!" One step march. Music by James Reese Europe. c. G. Ricordi 5/7/15.
"Hi, There!" One step march. Music by James Reese Europe. c. G. Ricordi 5/7/15.
"Monkey Doodle" Cakewalk one step. Music by James Reese Europe. c. G. Ricordi
    5/11/15.
"I Must Have Someone Who Loves Me" Words by Henry Creamer. Music by James Reese
    Europe. c. G. Ricordi 5/13/15.
"Wait For Me" Words by Henry Creamer. Music by James Reese Europe. c. G. Ricordi
    5/13/15.
"Someday You'll Want a Home of Your Own" Words by Henry Creamer. Music by James
    Reese Europe. c. G. Ricordi 7/8/15.
"Follow On" March song. Words by Henry Creamer. Music by James Reese Europe. c. G.
    Ricordi 7/8/15.
"Boy of Mine" Words by Gene Buck. Music by Ford T. Dabney and J. R. Europe. c. T. B.
    Harms and Francis, Day, and Hunter 7/10/15.
"Myosotis" Waltz. Music by James Reese Europe. c. G. Ricordi 7/15/15.
"Syncopated Minuet" Words by Henry Creamer. Music by James Reese Europe. c. G. Ri-
    cordi 9/21/15.
"Rat-A-Tat Drummer Boy" Words by Henry Creamer. Music by James Reese Europe.
    c. g. Ricordi 9/24/15.
"Tinkle a Little Tune" Words by Henry Creamer. Music by James Reese Europe. c. G. Ri-
    cordi 10/26/15.

1916–1919

"Hilo; Hawaiian Waltz" Music by James Reese Europe. c. G. Ricordi 7/10/16.
"Good-bye My Honey, I'm Gone" Music and words by Europe, Sissle, and Blake.
    c. Joseph W. Stern 1/10/18.
"I've the Lovin'es' Love For You" Music and words by Europe, Sissle, and Blake.
    c. Joseph W. Stern 1/10/18.
"Mirandy, That Gal O'Mine" Music and words by Europe, Sissle, and Blake. c. Joseph W.
    Stern 1/10/18.
"Jazz Baby" Music by Europe, Sissle, and Blake. Recorded by Lieut. Jim Europe's 369th
    Infantry ("Hellfighters") Band 3/14/19. See Appendix 2.
"Good Night Angeline" Fox-trot. Music and words by Europe, Sissle, and Blake. c. M.
    Witmark 4/30/19
"On Patrol in No Man's Land" Music and words by Europe, Sissle, and Blake. c. M. Wit-
    mark 4/30/19.
"All of No Man's Land is Ours" Music and words by Europe, Sissle, and Blake. c. M. Wit-
    mark and Sons 5/26/19.

Appendix 2

James Reese Europe Discography

Compiled from record labels, record company recording books and announcements, newspapers, concert programs, and the following sources: Brian Rust, *Jazz Records 1897–1942* (New Rochelle, N.Y.: Arlington House, 1978); *Record Research* 1 (December 1955), pp.3–5; Michael Montgomery, "Exploratory Discography of Noble Sissle, Eubie Blake, and James Reese Europe" in Kimball and Bocom, *Reminiscing with Sissle and Blake*, pp.247–54; and Max Harrison, Charles Fox, and Eric Thacker, *The Essential Jazz Records: Ragtime to Swing*, vol.1 (Westport, Conn.: Greenwood Press, 1984), pp.19–20.

Organized under recording dates as follows:

1. Title.
2. Composer (Matrix no.) label/issue no.
   Label abbreviations:
      a. VIC—RCA Victor
      b. HMV—His Master's Voice
      c. PF—Pathé Frere
      d. PA—Pathé Actuelle
      e. PER—Perfect
3. Reissues:
      a. NW260—New World 260 *Shuffle Along.*
      b. NW269—New World 269 *Steppin' on the Gas.*
      c. SD221—Saydisc 221 (Br.) *Ragtime, Cakewalks & Stomps, vol.3: The Bands of Jim Europe and Arthur Pryor (1907–1919).*
      d. SD253—Saydisc 253 (Br.) *Ragtime, Cakewalks & Stomps, vol.4: "Rusty Rags"(1900–1917).*
      e. RCA42402—RCA PM 42402 (Fr.) *Ragtime vol.2: Cakewalks, etc. (1900–1921).*
4. U.S. Library Holdings (from the *Rigler and Deutsch Index*):
   NSY—Syracuse University
   NN—N.Y. Public Library
   DLC—Library of Congress
   CTY—Yale University
   CST—Stanford University

A. Europe's Society Orchestra

Europe, director; Cricket Smith, cornet; Edgar Campbell or John Russell, clarinet; Tracy Cooper, George Smith, Walter Scott, Allie Ross, James Van Hooten, or William Tyler, violins; Leonard Smith, Ford Dabney, piano; Buddy Gilmore or

George Jenkins, drums. Five unknown banjos/mandolins that may include Opal Cooper, Lloyd Smith, William C. Elkins, Joe Meyers, George Waters, or Joe Grey.

December 29, 1913; New York City
1. "Too Much Mustard/One Step or Turkey Trot"
   C. Macklin (14246-1) VIC 35359-A, HMV 0230588(as "Trés Moutarde")
   SD221, RCA42402
   CTY, DLC, CST, NN
2. "Down Home Rag/One Step or Turkey Trot"
   W. C. Sweatman (14247-2) VIC 35359-B
   SD221, RCA 42402
   CTT, DLC, CST, NN
3. "Irresistable/Tango Argentine"
   L. Logatti (14249-1) VIC 35360-A
   No reissues
   CTY, DLC, CST, NN
4. "Amapa/Maxixe Bresilien (Le Vrai)"
   J. Storoni (14248-1) VIC 35360-B
   No reissues
   CTY, DLC, CST, NN

February 10, 1914; New York City
Add Chandler Ford or Leonard Jeter, cello; Fred Covite, flute; George De Leon, baritone, and George Heyward, bass. Drop all banjo/mandolins

1. "Congratulations Waltz (Castles' Lame Duck)"
   J. R. Europe (14435-1) VIC 35372-A
   No reissues
   CTY
2. "Castle House Rag (Castles in Europe)"
   J. R. Europe (14433-3) VIC 35372-B
   NW269, RCA42402
   CTY, CST
3. "Castle Walk"
   J. R. Europe/F. T.Dabney (14434-2) VIC 17553-1, HMV B-258
   SD253, NW269, RCA42402
   CTY
4. "You're Here and I'm Here/One Step"
   J. D. Kern (14432-1) VIC 17553-B
   SD253, RCA42402
   CTY, NSY

October 1, 1914; New York City
Add William Parquette, violin. Drop 1 piano
1. "Fiora Waltz"
   J. R. Europe (15230-1-2) VIC-rejected
2. "Fox Trot"
   Unknown (15231-1-2) VIC-rejected

B. Lieut. Jim Europe's 369th Infantry ("Hellfighters") Band

Europe, director; Frank de Broit, Russell Smith, Pops Foster (not the bass player), Jake Porter, cornets/trumpets; Ward "Dope" Andrews, Amos Gilliard, Raphael Hernández, Herb Flemming, trombones; Elige Rijos, Antonio Gonzáles, Jesús Hernández, Arturo Ayala, Pinkhead Parker, reeds; Steve Wright, Herbert Wright, Whitney Viney, Karl Kenny, drums; Noble Sissle, violin and vocals. Other possible personnel include Piccolo Jones, Calvin Jones, Lee Perry, and Alex Jackson.

March 3–7, 1919; New York City
1. "Broadway Hit Medley"
   a. Intro: "I've Got the Blue Ridge Blues"
   b. "Madelon" (A. Bryan and C. Robert)
   c. "Till We Meet Again" (R. Whiting)
   d. "Smiles" (J. W. Callahan and L. S. Robert)
   (67470) PF 22082-A
   No Reissues
   NSY
2. "St. Louis Blues"
   W. C. Handy (67471) PF 22087
   No Reissues
   No Holdings
3. "How ya Gonna Keep 'Em Down on the Farm?" Vocal
   W. Donaldson, S. M. Lewis, J. Young (67472)
   PF 22080-A
   NW260
   DLC
4. "Arabian Hights"
   David/Hewitt (67473) PF 22080-B
   No Reissues
   CTY
5. "Darktown Strutters' Ball"
   S. Brooks (67475) PF 22081-A
   SD221
   DLC
6. "Indianola"
   D. Onivas (ne D. Savino) (67474) PF 22081-B
   SD221
   DLC

March 7, 1919; New York City
1. "That Moaning Trombone"
   T. Bethel (67485) PF 22085-A, PA 020929, PER 14111
   SD221
   CST

2. "Memphis Blues"
   W. C. Handy (67486) PF 22085-B, PA 020929, PER 14111
   NW269, SD221
   CST
3. "Hesitating Blues"
   W. C. Handy (67481) PF 22086-B
   SD221
   No Holdings
4. "Plantation Echoes" Vocal
   Coates (67484) PF 22086-A
   No Reissues
   DLC
5. "Russian Rag"
   Cobb (67487) PF 22087, PA 020928, PER 14110
   No Reissues
   No Holdings
6. "Ja-Da"
   B. Carleton (67488) PF 22082-B
   No Reissues
   NSY

March 14, 1919; New York City

1. "Jazz Baby" (Creighton Thompson, vocal)
   Sissle/Europe/Blake (67517) PF 22103-A
   No Reissues
   CTY
2. "When the Bees Make Honey"
   W. Donaldson (67520) PF 22103-B
   No Reissues
   CTY
3. "Mirandy" (Sissle, vocal)
   Sissle/Europe/Blake (67515) PF 22089-A
   NW260
   CTY, DLC
4. "On Patrol in No Man's Land" (Sissle, vocal)
   Sissle/Europe/Blake (67516) PF 22089-B
   NW260
   CTY, DLC
5. "All of No Man's Land is Ours" (Sissle, vocal)
   Sissle/Europe/Blake (67518) PF 22104-A
   No Reissues
   CTY
6. "Jazzola" (Sissle, vocal)
   Robinson/Morse (67519) PF 22104-B
   No Reissues
   CTY

May 7, 1919: New York City

1. "Dixie is Dixie Once More" (Sissle, vocal)

Turner/Kard (67670) PF 22146-A
No Reissues
CTY, NSY

2. "That's Got 'Em"
   W. C. Sweatman (67667) PF 22146-B
   No Reissues
   CTY, NSY

3. "The Dancing Deacon"
   Unknown (67666) PF 22167
   No Reissues
   No Holdings

4. "Clarinet Marmalade"
   L. Shields/H. Ragas (67668) PF 22167, PA 020928,
   PER 14110
   NW269
   No Holdings

5. "Missouri Blues"
   Brown (67669) PF 22147-A
   No Reissues
   CTY, NSY

6. "My Choc'late Soldier Sammy Boy" (Sissle, vocal)
   E. Van Alstyne (67671) PF 22147-B
   No Reissues
   CTY, DLC

C. Lieut. Jim Europe's Singing Serenaders

Acappella vocal. Personnel included Noble Sissle and Creighton Thompson and others (L. Gibbs, C. Smith, Whitney Viney, T. Lee, and Arthur Payne)

March, 1919; New York City

1. "Little David Play on Your Harp" (Sissle, lead)
   Negro Spiritual (67478) PF 22084-A
   No Reissues
   CST, NSY

2. "Exhortation/Jubilee Song" (Thompson, lead)
   W. M. Cook (67477) PF 22084-B
   No Reissues
   CST, CTY, NSY

3. "Roll, Jordan, Roll"
   Negro Spiritual (67522) PF 22105-A, PA 020851-A, PER 11056
   No Reissues
   CST, DLC

4. "Ev'rybody Dat Talks About Heave' Ain't Goin' There"
   Unknown (unk) PF 22105-B
   No Reissues
   DLC

D. Jim Europe's Four Harmony Kings

Acappella vocal. Personnel included Exodus Drayton, Harold Browning, Horace Berry, and (possibly) Roland Hayes.

March, 1919; New York City
1. "Swing Low, Sweet Chariot"
   Negro Spiritual (67672) PF 22187, PA 020851-B, PER 11056
   No Reissues
   CST
2. "One More Ribber to Cross"
   Negro Spiritual (67673) PF22187
   No Reissues
   No Holdings

Notes

Prelude

1. New York's daily newspapers, as well as the national weekly black press, gave extensive coverage to the parade. The most comprehensive account appeared in the New York *World* of February 18, 1919, a reprinting of which constitutes the chapter entitled "Homecoming Heroes" in Allison Sweeney's *History of the American Negro in the Great War* (1919; reprint, Negro University Press, 1969), 267–74.

2. *From Harlem to the Rhine: The Story of New York's Colored Volunteers* (New York: Covici and Friede, 1936) by Arthur W. Little, one of the regiment's senior officers, is the standard history. William Miles's documentary film, *Men of Bronze* (1977), is especially valuable for its interviews with four veterans of the 369th. In addition to Sweeney's *History*, which lists the officers and men awarded the Croix de Guerre (142–45), useful information is also contained in Emmett J. Scott, *Scott's Official History of the American Negro in the World War* (Washington D.C.: 1919); Robert Greene, *Black Defenders of America 1775–1973* (Chicago: Johnson, 1974); Bernard C. Nalty, *Strength for the Fight: A History of Black Americans in the Military* (New York: The Free Press, 1986); and Edward Wakin, *Black Fighting Men in U.S. History* (New York: Lothrop, Lee and Shepard, 1971).

3. "New York Gives Ovation to Its Black Fighters," *New York Herald*, February 18, 1919.

4. "Old 15th Regiment Given Rousing Reception," *New York Age*, February 22, 1919.

5. See "Fifth Av. Cheers Negro Veterans," the *New York Times*, February 18, 1919, and "New York City Acclaims Veterans of the 'Fighting 15th,'" the *Philadelphia Tribune*, February 22, 1919. Hayward is quoted in the *World*, February 18, 1919, which is reprinted in Sweeney, *History*, 268.

6. The *World*, reprinted in Sweeney, *History*, 267. The front page of the *New York Times* the morning of February 17 announced that it was the "City's Negro Fighters" who would parade that day. "WILD CHEERS GREET CITY'S OWN NEGRO REGIMENT," read the banner headlines of the *New York Herald* on February 18.

7. See the editorial page of The *New York Tribune*, February 18, 1919.

8. See "The 369th Swings Up Fifth Avenue," in William L. Katz, ed., *Eyewitness: The Negro in American History* (New York: Pitman Publishing Co., 1967), 140.

9. The *New York Times*, February 18, 1919.

10. The *New York Herald*, February 18, 1919.

11. The *New York Age*, February 22, 1919.

12. Miller was one of the four veterans who appeared in the documentary film, *Men of Bronze* (1977).

13. The article was reprinted in full in the Baltimore *Afro-American*, March 21, 1919, 4.

14. The *World*, February 18, 1919, reprinted in Sweeney, *History*, 268.

15. James Weldon Johnson, "Views and Reviews," the *New York Age*, February 22, 1919, 4.

16. The *Chicago Defender*, February 22, 1919.

17. The *World*, February 18, 1919, reprinted in Sweeney, *History*, 272, and the *New York Times*, February 18, 1919. "That's one of the biggest men in New York," commented a soldier as they marched past the Frick residence. "I used to shine his shoes. Now he's almost falling out of a window to wave to me." Quoted in the *New York Tribune*, February 18, 1919.

18. The *New York Age*, February 22, 1919.

19. See the *World*, February 18, 1919, reprinted in Sweeney, *History*, 270, the *New York Herald*, and the *New York Times*, of the same date.

20. Johnson's story, in his own words, is quoted in Sweeney, 146–47. Colonel Hayward's account can be found in a letter written to Johnson's wife and reprinted in Scott's *Official History*, 256–59. Most Americans learned about "The Battle of Henry Johnson" from Irvin S. Cobb's article, entitled "Young Black Joe," in the *Saturday Evening Post*, August 24, 1918, 7–8, 77–78.

21. See the *New York Herald*, February 18, 1919.

22. The *Chicago Defender*, February 22, 1919, described Europe and his "world famous band" as the center of attraction of the parade. For the opinion of the soldiers, see, for example, the interviews with Captain Fish and the other veterans of the 369th in *Men of Bronze*. "I concur with Irvin S. Cobb," Hayward wrote in a letter to Noble Sissle after the war (dated January 27, 1920), "who said in the *Saturday Evening Post*, that this was the best band in the American army in which he but voiced the opinion of all competent judges." See Sissle, "Memoirs of Lieutenant 'Jim' Europe," dated October, 1942, NAACP Records 1940–55, Group II, J Box 56, General Miscellany, Library of Congress, 33.

23. The *New York Times*, May 12, 1919.

24. British historian, Jeffrey P. Green, for example, is unequivocal in giving Europe the credit. See his *Edmund Thorton Jenkins: The Life and Times of an American Black Composer, 1894–1926* (Westport, Conn.: Greenwood Press, 1982), 60. Europe's place as a jazz pioneer, however, does depend upon giving the term *jazz* a somewhat more flexible definition than is usual today. For a discussion of his career and its relationship to the new music, see Reid Badger, "James Reese Europe and the Prehistory of Jazz," in *American Music* 7(Spring, 1989): 48–67.

25. The *Philadelphia Tribune*, February 22, 1919, and the *New York Times*, February 18, 1919, carried the same description.

26. The *World*, February 18, 1919, reprinted in Sweeney, *History*, 271.

27. Quoted in Katz, "The 369th Swings Up Fifth Avenue," 410. Several of the drums played by the band were gifts of the French government and one was a trophy captured from the Germans.

28. Letter from William H. Hayward to Noble Sissle, January 27, 1920, quoted in Sissle, "Memoirs," 33.

29. The lack of black officers was the only sad aspect of the day, said the *Chicago Defender* of February 22, 1919. "Had they been officers of our own Race, Harlem's cup of joy would have been filled."

30. Both Jervis Anderson in *This Was Harlem: A Cultural Portrait 1900–1950* (New York: Farrar, Straus & Giroux, 1981), and David Levering Lewis in *When Harlem Was in Vogue* (New York: Knopf, 1981) see the recruitment and service of the 15th Regiment as significant in the coming-of-age of the Harlem community.

31. The *New York Age*, February 22, 1919. Sissle ("Memoirs," 195) remembered the tune as "Whose Been There While I've Been Gone." In either case, it does not require much imagination to picture the effect upon the crowd.

Chapter One: "Down Home Rag"

1. The State of Alabama did not require birth certificates until after 1900. The extant records (military service, funeral documents, death certificate, newspaper reports) give Europe's birth date as February 22 of either 1881 or 1882; the U.S. Census for 1880, however, establishes 1880 as the correct year.

2. See Levine's *Black Culture and Black Consciousness: Afro-American Folk Thought from Slavery to Freedom* (New York: Oxford University Press, 1977), 139–40.

3. Harriet E. Amos, *Cotton City: Urban Development in Antebellum Mobile* (Tuscaloosa: University of Alabama Press, 1985) provides a general history of the city during the period. See also, Alan S. Thompson, "Mobile, Alabama, 1850–1861: Economic, Political, Physical, and Population Characteristics" (Ph.D. diss., University of Alabama, 1979), and Christopher Andrew Nordmann, "Free Negroes in Mobile County, Alabama" (Ph.D. diss., University of Alabama, 1990).

4. Amos, in *Cotton City*, 86–87, and Nordmann, "Free Negroes," 58.

5. The standard work on the subject of free blacks is Ira Berlin, *Slaves Without Masters: The Free Negro in the Antebellum South* (New York: Pantheon Books, 1974).

6. Quoted in Nordmann, "Free Negroes," 51. See, also, Amos, *Cotton City*, 89.

7. No persons with the unusual surname "Europe," white or black, have been discovered in the city directories, U.S. Census, municipal, church, or other standard sources for the pre-1865 period.

8. An obituary carried by the Washington, D.C., *Colored American* on July 8, 1899, documents his birth and involvement in the Baptist Church, but says nothing about his legal status. An entry in the *Record of Internal Revenue Employees 1863–1870, 1875–1909*, Vol. 1875–1886, entry 262, National Archives Record Group 56, confirms that he was born a slave.

9. Amos, *Cotton City*, 111.

10. Frederick D. Richardson, a current member of the Stone Street Church, has compiled the evidence in his *The Stone Street Baptist Church—Alabama's First, 1806–1982* (n.p.,n.d.), which is on file at the Mobile Public Library. In addition, Reverend T. D. Bussey's *History of Colored Baptists in Alabama* (n.p., 1949), 43, quotes from a "Brother Holcomb" who wrote in 1836 that the first white Baptist congregation (First Baptist) "met in the house belonging to the African Baptist Church. The African Church is in a prosperous condition; their number is about 90."

11. See George W. McRae, *A Concise Statement of Facts Concerning the Baptist Churches of Mobile Taken Chiefly from the Records with Occasional Remarks* (1879; reprint, as *Early Baptist History in Mobile County, Alabama*, 1951), 20.

12. See Charles O. Boothe, *The Cyclopedia of the Colored Baptists of Alabama: Their Leaders and Their Work* (Birmingham: Alabama Publishing Co., 1895), 22.

13. Henry Europe's post–Civil War employment as a reporter, editor, clerk, and Internal Revenue officer suggests that he received at least an elementary education prior to the War. Since such an opportunity was far more likely for either a free black child or one who lived as free, than for a slave, it is probable that he belonged to one of the former groups (and most probably the second, given his birth as a slave). In his *Cyclopedia of the Colored Baptists*, 24, Boothe refers to a "Judge Europe" whom he lists simply as among several "founders or antibellum [sic] members of the Colored Baptist work in Mobile." The reference can also be found in Bussey, *History of Colored Baptists*, 45. Judge Europe's relationship, if any, to Henry Europe is unknown, although he was old enough to be his father, or even grandfather. According to the 1870 Census, which mistakenly lists him as "white," Judge Europe was born in North Carolina in 1794.

14. At the time of her mother's death in 1937, Mary L. Europe described Mary Ann Saxon, her maternal grandmother (whose maiden name was Clarke), as "tall and vigorous, whose Spanish blood gave both fire and charm to her personality." Her grandfather, Armistead, was a man "of fine integrity, prominent in the business and social world of his time; loved, respected and highly honored by the eminent people of both races." Both grandparents were "staunch Episcopalians, Mr. Saxon being a lay reader in one of the finer white churches in Mobile." This typed, three-page obituary notice is among the documents in the possession of Mrs. Lorraine Johnson of Washington, D.C.

15. Support for the new church came both from Trinity Episcopal and from Christ Church, the oldest of Mobile's Episcopal congregations. A building was eventually constructed some four blocks west of Trinity, and Reverend J. J. Scott (white) was brought from Pensacola to be the first pastor. Parish Registers exist for both Trinity and Good Shepherd Churches during this period. They contain valuable information about slaves and free blacks in the city that does not exist elsewhere. See Mobile Writers Workshop, *Historic Churches of Mobile* (n.p., 1970), 79.

16. Nordmann concludes that Saxon was one of the prominent free blacks in the church. Since he acted as sponsor to "numerous slaves owned by whites," he must have "developed friendships and earned respect within the white community," as well as the African-American. See "Free Negroes," 173, which draws upon the Church of the Good Shepherd, Parish Register, Volume 2, 1855–1893. According to his granddaughter, Saxon was also a man of some property—sufficient to send his young daughters north to begin their education. He was forced to call them back to Mobile when the war broke out and his property was confiscated. This information comes from Lorraine S. Europe's obituary notice, written by her daughter, Mary, in 1937, in the possession of Mrs. Lorraine Johnson.

17. Tragedy did not avoid the Saxons. They buried their three-year-old son, William, in April 1857, and their infant daughter, Sally Ida, in March 1859. See Mobile *Daily Register*, March 20, 1859, and the Church of the Good Shepherd, Parish Register, Volume 2, 1855–1893.

18. Amos, *Cotton City*, 91 and 99–101.

19. See Church of the Good Shepherd, Parish Register, Volume 2, 1855–1893. His family seems to have survived the initial shock, however. In April 1869, both Emma and Leanna Saxon were confirmed in the Good Shepherd Church, and the U.S. Census of the following year has them still living with their mother whose occupation is listed as teacher. Leanna also became a teacher, working at the Broad Street Academy and Orange Grove School in the last decade of the century. See the Mobile City Directories for 1892–1900.

20. See Trinity Episcopal Church Marriage Records, Volume XIII, Number 2, p. 144, and the Mobile County Court Records, *Colored Marriage License Book*, 1, 157–166. The actual marriage certificate is in the possession of Mrs. Lorraine Johnson of Washington, D.C.

21. The first listing for Henry Europe in the Mobile city directory appears in the 1869 edition, where he is described as a barber in the shop of Peter Peiser, at the Battle House (Mobile's first truly first-class hotel). The *Official Register of the United States*, 384 (September 30, 1873), indicates that Europe was initially employed by the Post Office in the first quarter of 1872.

22. See "The Late H. J. Europe," Washington, D.C., *Colored American*, July 8, 1899. Noble Sissle, who received his information from Mary Europe (James's younger sister), confirms the senior Europe's post–Civil War political activity. See his "Memoirs," 7.

23. See Allen Woodrow Jones, "Alabama," in *The Black Press in the South, 1865–1979*, ed. Henry Lewis Suggs, Contributions in Afro-American and African Studies no. 74 (Greenwood Press: Westport, Conn., 1983), 23.

24. By the 1880s, 69 percent of the black population lived in Ward Seven. See Alma Ester Berkstresser, "Mobile, Alabama in the 1880s" (M.A. thesis, University of Alabama, 1951), 71. The two lots, numbers 5 and 6, of square 247, were apparently purchased by Lorraine Europe (or at least in her name), for $377.50 from Isaac and Adeline Bell and Henry Brewer of New York City. Mobile County Court records (Deed Book, 35, p. 107) of November 18, 1874, contains a record of the transaction. Taxes were paid on the property by Henry J. Europe on November 6. See the City Tax List for Mobile for 1874. The 1876 Tax list indicates that the property was transferred to Lorraine S. Europe, in whose name it remained until sold on June 19, 1889, for back taxes after the Europe's had left Mobile for Washington, D.C.

25. See Miscellaneous Book, I and J, p. 197, in the Mobile County Court House records for a record of the contract.

26. See Walter L. Fleming, *The Churches of Alabama During the Civil War and Reconstruction* (1902; reprint, in *The Gulf States Historical Magazine*, September, 1942), 19.

27. See "Minutes of the Colored Missionary Baptist Convention of the State of Alabama, Held in Zion Methodist Church, Tuscaloosa, Ala., November 25, 1873" (Mobile: Thompson & Powers, 1874) and Boothe, *Cyclopedia of Colored Baptists*, 37.

28. "Minutes of the Seventh Session of the Colored Missionary Baptist Convention of the State of Alabama, Held in St. Louis Street Baptist Church, Mobile, Ala., November 11th to 17th, 1874" (Mobile: Shields Co., 1875).

29. "Minutes of the Eighth Annual Session of the Colored Missionary Baptist Convention, of Alabama, Held in the Saint Louis Street Baptist Church of Mobile, Ala., November 17 to 24th, 1875" (Mobile: Henry Farrow & Co., n.d.), 5.

30. According to the Mobile City Directories, Henry Europe both continued his leadership of the Virginia Street Church and also served, apparently, wherever else he was needed—including a period as pastor of the Bethlehem Methodist Church and as pastor of the Marine Street Baptist Church. Europe's name is one of those that appears on the mortgage agreement with the Bank of Mobile. See Mortgage Book 19, Mobile County Courthouse, 512. The property was sold at public sale for $460 and the deed recorded on January 4, 1886. See Deed Book 52, Mobile County Courthouse, 459.

31. See letter from D. P. Bestor, a Mobile lawyer, to Secretary of the Treasury Daniel Manning, dated June 26, 1885, in *Letters Received from Collectors of Internal Revenue, 1864–1906*, 1st Alabama District, Entry 166. Documentation of Europe's service and his replacement by Butler can also be found in *Registry of Officers of the Internal Revenue*, First District of Alabama, Entry 262, Record of Internal Revenue Employees, Volume 1875–1886, and *Record of Daily Changes in Internal Revenue Personnel, 1884–1887*, Entry 265. All of the preceding are held in National Archives Record Group 56. Henry Europe's obituary (Washington *Colored American*, July 8, 1899) also suggests that politics was involved in the termination of his employment with the I.R.S.

32. The Mobile City Directories for the period after 1885 list his occupations as Pastor of both the Warren Street and the Marine Street Baptist Churches (the latter a missionary church which served an irregular congregation), and, in 1889, as editor of the *Christian Weekly*.

33. The older Europe children might have attended one of the missionary supported schools in Mobile, but it is most likely that John's and James' first school was the

Good Hope School, later called Broad Street Academy. Student records that could have confirmed this were lost when the Barton Academy where they were stored burned in 1908.

34. Sissle, "Memoirs," 7. Sissle's information concerning Lorraine Europe's role as a teacher of her children was given to him by Mary Europe (it appears, in fact, to be a direct quote from her daughter), probably in the early 1920s when "Mother Europe," as she was by then known, was still alive. A copy of Mark Twain's *A Tramp Abroad* (1880) in the possession of Mrs. Lorraine Johnson of Washington, D.C., is inscribed "To My darling, Lorraine S. Europe, from her husband," and dated April 13, 1880, just two months after James Reese was born. It suggests a great deal about the intellectual and educational climate of the Europe home.

35. See Charles Welton, "Filling France Full of Jazz," in The *World Magazine*, New York *World* Sunday supplement, March 30, 1919, 10.

36. Washington, D.C. *Colored American*, July 8, 1899.

37. See Sissle, "Memoirs," 7, and Welton, "Filling France Full of Jazz," 10. Scott's *Official History*, 303, also carries a description of his early musical activities, but it appears to be based on Welton's account.

38. See Caldwell Delaney, *The Story of Mobile* (Mobile: Gill Press, 1953), 151.

39. See the New York *News*, April 9, 1914.

Chapter Two: *"Washington Post* March"

1. See Carl Abbott, "Dimensions of Regional Change in Washington, D.C.," *The American historical Review* 95 (December 1990): 1375.

2. George Lathrop, "A Nation in a Nutshell," *Harper's New Monthly Magazine*, 62 (March 1881): 542, quoted in Abbott, "Regional Change," 1377.

3. W.E.B. Du Bois, *Black reconstruction in America: 1860–1880* (1935; reprint, New York: Atheneum, 1969), 562.

4. A local census in 1867 found that "more than two-thirds of black Washingtonians and half of all white residents had arrived since 1860." See Abbott, "Regional Change," 1375. In that same year it was "estimated that of the 32,000 Negroes in the district, one half were destitute." In March 1867, Congress appropriated $15,000 for the relief of the freemen in the city. See Du Bois, *Black Reconstruction*, 563.

5. Abbott, "Regional Change," 1383. See also, Doris Evans McGinty, "The Black Presence in the Music of Washington, D.C.," in Irene V. Jackson, ed., *More Than Dancing: Essays on Afro-American Music and Musicians* (Westport, Conn.: Greenwood Press, 1985), 102, and Letitia W. Brown and Elsie M. Lewis, *Washington in the New Era, 1870–1970* (Washington, D.C.: U.S. Govt. Printing Office, 1976), 4.

6. Mary Church Terrell, "History of the High School for Negroes in Washington," *The Journal of Negro History* II (July, 1917): 253. Author, suffragette, civil rights activist, Mary Church Terrell was one of the most notable and respected black women of the period.

7. Jervis Anderson, "Our Far-Flung Correspondents: A Very Special Monument," *The New Yorker*, 54 (March 20, 1978): 96. Anderson's piece provides an excellent discussion of the high school as a symbol of class and status divisions (and a source of continuing debate) within Washington's black community.

8. See Anderson, "Special Monument," 94.

9. Abbott, "Regional Change," 1383. The pattern had become clear enough when the 1875 Civil Rights Act was interpreted by the Supreme Court in 1883 as helpless to prevent acts of discrimination by private individuals or privately owned businesses.

10. "Man-on-the-Corner," Washington, D.C. *Colored American*, September 6, 1902, 11.

11. At the outbreak of the Civil War, the "greatest concentration was along 4th Street between the Navy Yard and East Capitol Street, with the blocks between 3rd and 5th Streets, S.E. (east of the present Folger Library and the Library of Congress Annex), having the largest number of black homeowners." See Letitia W. Brown and Elsie M. Lewis, *Washington From Danneker to Douglass, 1791–1870* (Washington, D.C.: U.S. Govt. Printing Office, 1971), 12.

12. The Washington, D.C., City Directory's first listing for Henry J. Europe is in 1890; his occupation is recorded as "clerk." Two years later, he is listed as "superintendent." His obituary (Washington, D.C., *Colored American*, July 8, 1899) says that he held the position of assistant superintendent of the Mail Bag Repair Department. The 1893 edition of the Register of Employees in the Post Office Department contains no listing for a "Mail Bag Repair Department," but does have one for a "Mail Equipment Division."

13. Howard University Scholastic Record, 1890–1891, and letter dated May 19, 1983, from William H. Sherrill, dean of admissions and records, Howard University, to Mr. James Reese Europe, Jr.

14. "Statement of the Family," dated May 13, 1919, in the James Reese Europe Funeral Documents, Moorland Collection, Manuscript Division, Moorland-Spingarn Research Center, Howard University. See also, Sissle, "Memoirs," 7.

15. See Eileen Southern, *The Music of Black Americans: A History* (New York: W. W. Norton, Co., 1983), 279.

16. Quoted in Sissle, "Memoirs," 8.

17. Ibid. See also the "Statement of the Family," in James Reese Europe Funeral Documents, May 13, 1919, Howard University Manuscript Division.

18. Mary Europe stated flatly to Noble Sissle that he "never lost a friend." See Sissle, "Memoirs," 8.

19. See, for example, Margaret Hindle Hazen and Robert M. Hazen, *The Music Men: An Illustrated History of Brass Bands in America, 1800–1920* (Washington, D.C.: The Smithsonian Institution Press, 1987), 8. The cultural significance of brass bands became a subject of some debate in the last decades of the ninteenth century, as Lawrence Levine has shown. Extreme defenders of "high culture" viewed the bands and their music as representative of "impure art, pseudo culture, and disorder." See *Highbrow/Lowbrow: The Emergence of Cultural Hierarchy in America* (Cambridge, Mass.: Harvard University Press, 1988), 165.

20. Doris Evans McGinty, "Aspects of Musical Activities in the Black Communities of Baltimore and Washington, D.C., 1840 to the Early 1920s," *Black Music Research Bulletin* 11 (Fall, 1989): 11.

21. See Paul E. Bierley, *John Philip Sousa: American Phenomenon* (Englewood Cliffs, N.J.: Prentice-Hall, 1973), 241.

22. In the opinion of Maud Cuney-Hare, his greatest compositional successes were his marches, and she quotes the *New York Tribune* in saying that "all in all they are worthy of the pen of John Philip Sousa." See her *Negro Musicians and their Music* (Washington, D.C.: The Associated Publishers, Inc., 1936), 137. See also Charles Hamm, *Music in the New World* (New York: W. W. Norton, 1983), 401.

23. See Ronald M. Johnson's "LeDroit Park: Premier Black Community," in Kathryn S. Smith, ed., *Washington at Home: An Illustrated History of Neighborhoods in the Nation's Capital* (Northridge, Cal.: Windsor Publications, 1988), 143.

24. The stretch of 7th Street that passed north from the city was known as Brightwood Avenue until 1908 when it was renamed Georgia Avenue. See Katherine Grandine, "Brightwood: From Tollgate to Suburb," in Kathryn S. Smith, ed., *Washington at Home*, 94.

25. See Alison K. Hoagland, "7th Street Downtown: An Evolving Commercial Neighborhood," in Kathryn S. Smith, ed., *Washington at Home*, 52.

26. See Marcia M. Greenlee, "Shaw: Heart of Black Washington," in Kathryn S. Smith, ed., *Washington at Home*, 123.

27. Greenlee, "Shaw," 121.

28. McGill, a follower of Andrew Jackson Downing, designed some sixty-four houses in the Eastlake, Second Empire, and Italianate styles. See Ronald M. Johnson, "LeDroit Park: Premier Black Community," in Kathryn S. Smith, ed., *Washington at Home*, 139.

29. Quoted in Johnson, "LeDroit Park," 141.

30. An announcement of the violin recital is among the documents in the possession of Mrs. Lorraine Johnson of Washington, D.C. Europe's early musical education, as well as the contest, is described in the *Crisis*, 2 (June 1912), where Europe was one of the featured "Men of the Month," 67–68. In addition, see Cuney-Hare, *Negro Musicians*, 137, and Gunther Schuller, "Europe, James Reese (1881–1919)" in Rayford W. Logan and Michael R. Winston, eds., *Dictionary of Negro Biography* (New York: W. W. Norton, Co., 1982), 214.

31. See Robert N. Mattingly, "Autobiographic Memories, 1897–1954: M Street—Dunbar High School," (privately printed in Washington, D.C., May, 1974): 10. A copy of the pamphlet can be found in the Washingtoniana Collection of the Martin Luther King, Jr., Branch of the District of Columbia Public Library.

32. See Mattingly, "Autobiographic Memories," 7, and McGinty, "Aspects of Musical Activities," 11. James C. Wright's article, "Our High School Cadets—What They Have Accomplished," in the Washington *Bee*, June 8, 1918, gives a good description of how popular the cadet competitions became, especially after the founding of the Armstrong Manual Training School in 1901 and the competitions became inter–high school. In 1917, for example, an estimated 18,000 spectators attended the annual contest. See also Mark Tucker, *Ellington: The Early Years* (Urbana, Ill.: University of Illinois Press, 1991), 7. Growing up in Washington, D.C. (where he was born in 1899), Ellington, Tucker argues, was like Jim Europe strongly influenced by the unique social and cultural character of the Nation's Capital. Although there is no evidence of direct or personal contact between the two, Ellington probably heard Europe lead the Clef Club Orchestra at the Howard Theatre before World War I and he was certainly aware of Europe's musical reputation. Ellington was apparently personally acquainted with Mary Europe because "in later years he would ask his friend Maurice Banks to 'look her up' in Washington and make sure she was getting along." Tucker, *Ellington*, 10.

33. Even the losing competitors in the drill were happy to praise him, Mary recalled, so that one would "think that 'Jim' was the whole company." Quoted in Sissle, "Memoirs," 7. See also "Statement of the Family," in Funeral Documents for James Reese Europe, Howard University; the Washington *Bee*, June 8, 1918; and the Washington *Post*, May 11, 1919.

34. Letter from James Reese Europe to Miss Mary Europe, dated May 5, 1915, in the private collection of Mrs. Lorraine Johnson of Washington, D.C.

35. In July of 1975, for instance, a letter to the *Washington Post* concluded that "the pride that Dunbar alumni rightfully have in the academic achievements of their school should be substantially tempered by sadness—the criteria for a guaranteed comfortable and successful student sojourn at Dunbar were, in order of importance (1) parents in professional jobs, (2) a minimum of melanin in the skin, and (3) a fairly high scholastic average, not necessarily deserved." Quoted in Anderson, "Special Monument," 104.

36. This was a trait of Europe's throughout his life, Mary Europe remembered. He was never self-conscious about showing affection. Whenever he met his "Ma" or little "Sis," he "cared not who saw how much he loved them." Quoted in Sissle, "Memoirs," 9.

37. See McGinty, "Aspects of Musical Activites," 10–11, and "Black Presence," 89.

38. Marva Griffin Carter's "The Life and Music of Will Marion Cook, 1869–1944" (Ph.D. diss., University of Illinois at Urbana, 1988) is the most extensive treatment of this important figure which now exists.

39. A full list of the instrumentalists was published in the *New York Age* the following day. See Carter, "Will Marion Cook," 17, and McGinty, "Black Presence," 97.

Chapter Three: "On the Gay Luneta"

1. Both John and James were devoted to their mother and sister. They both provided financial support and regarded their mother's house as their true home throughout their lives. Both sons returned to live with their mother periodically, and when they died both were buried from her house in Washington. Lorraine Europe was not a large woman, but she had a forceful personality and exerted a powerful influence over her children, especially after Henry Europe died; only the eldest, Minnie, seems to have been able to establish a successful personal life or form a long-term relationship apart from her. When she died in 1937, she had survived them all except Mary, her unmarried youngest daughter with whom she lived. It is perhaps significant that her obituary (almost certainly written by Mary, but perhaps not without prior suggestions from her mother) specifically mentions only her sons "who thought her an angel incapable of any wrong doing, and who willingly laid their gifts and their homage at her feet." Unpublished obituary written sometime after March 29, 1937, and in the possession of Mrs. Lorraine Johnson of Washington, D.C.

2. "Stage Silhouettes," Washington, D.C., *Colored American*, July 9, 1898, 6. See also, for example, "Opportunities in Entertainment in NYC for Negroes," the *Colored American*, July 29, 1899, 7.

3. Washington, D.C. *Colored American*, July 29, 1899, 7. In its September, 16, 1899 issue, the *American* reported that in New York "first class artists are commanding liberal salaries, and the supply falls short of the demand," 7.

4. "Among Negro Performers," Washington, D.C., *Colored American*, October 6, 1900, 11.

5. The Washington, D.C., City Directory indicates that Europe was employed as a porter, a clerk, and a waiter during those years. The exact nature of his musical activities is not clear, though there are reports (written later) which indicate that he continued organizing and directing amateur musical groups while expanding his knowledge of the various band and orchestral instruments. See Emmett Scott's biographical sketch of Europe in his *Official History*, 303. Mary Europe, whose abilities as a pianist were becoming quite well-known, was appointed as accompanist for the music classes in the public schools in the fall of 1903. See the announcement in the Washington,

D.C., *Colored American*, October 24, 1903, 9, and her obituary published in the Washington *Star*, October 22, 1947.

6. Sometimes referred to as the "Black Bohemia," the colorful and corrupt Tenderloin (roughly the West 20s through 40s between Fifth and Eighth Avenues) and the surrounding area had become a major locus for black New Yorkers since the 1890s. See Edward Berlin, *Reflections on Ragtime*, Institute for Studies in American Music Monograph No. 24 (New York, 1987), 44–58, and also in Anderson, *This Was Harlem*, 13–20.

7. Noble Sissle, "Show Business," *New York Age*, October 23, 1948, and quoted in Berlin, *Reflections*, 52.

8. Willie "The Lion" Smith (with George Hoefer), *Music on My Mind: The Memoirs of an American Pianist* (New York: Doubleday & Co., 1964), 55.

9. Sissle, "Memoirs," 12.

10. Tom Fletcher, *100 Years of the Negro in Show Business: The Tom Fletcher Story* (1954; reprint, New York: DaCapo Press, 1984), 252.

11. The New York *News*, April 9, 1914.

12. James Weldon Johnson, "Negro Songmakers," in *The Negro in Music and Art*, ed. Lindsay Patterson, *International Library of Negro Life and History* (New York: Publishers Co., Inc., 1967), 44.

13. Lorraine Saxon Europe obituary manuscript. Among the Europe memorabilia that Mrs. Johnson holds is a photographic portrait of John Wanamaker. Tom Fletcher also understood that "Jim Europe's father had long worked" for the Wanamakers. See *100 Years of the Negro in Show Business*, 263.

14. Letter from John W. Love to Noble Sissle, dated January 28, 1920, and quoted in full in Sissle's "Memoirs," 14–15. Among the occasions at which Europe performed, Love mentions "two of the largest celebrations inaugurated by Mr. Wanamaker and given at Sherry's [New York restaurant]," "at the Ritz-Carlton Hotel, Philadelphia, with a seventy-five-piece orchestra when Miss Marie Louise Wanamaker had her debut," "when Marie Louise was married at 'Lindenhurst,' Pennsylvania," "at the Ritz-Carlton Hotel, New York City, when Captain John Wanamaker, Jr., gave his farewell bachelor dinner, in 1917, and then again for his wedding at Newport in the same year." The composition and name (if there was one) for Europe's first ensemble is not known for certain, but it may have been the same "Metropolitan Quartet," managed by James Hunt, which was reported in February of 1905 to be going to Philadelphia to entertain "ex-General Postmaster Wanamaker and guests." The Indianapolis *Freeman*, February 18, 1905, 2.

15. "Of His Trip To Africa," "The Stage," Indianapolis *Freeman*, October 29, 1904, 2. *A Trip to Africa* of 1904 was not a major theatrical achievement by any stretch of the imagination, and, in fact, very little information about it remains. One complicating factor is that it had the same title as a more famous German comic opera which starred Lillian Russell in 1884. Neither of two recent studies of black musical theater, Allen Woll's *Black Musical Theatre: From Coontown to Dreamgirls* (Baton Rouge: Louisiana State University Press, 1989) or Thomas Riis's *Just Before Jazz: Black Musical Theater in New York, 1890–1915* (Washington, D.C.: Smithsonian Institution Press, 1989), mentions it. Riis, however, does provide a brief description of a 1910 "musical farce comedy" of the same name that starred Sissieretta Jones ("Black Patti") and John Larkins (p. 146).

16. "A Trip to Africa," in "The Stage by Woodbine," Indianapolis *Freeman*, October 29, 1904, 5. In the midst of the confusion of opening night, Europe still found a moment to dash off a birthday greeting to Mary back home in Washington (signed "Jas"). Postcard dated October 16, 1904, in the collection of Mrs. Lorraine Johnson.

17. Bloom, an amazing American character, started in publishing as the head of the Chicago branch of M. Witmark and Sons after the World's Columbian Exposition closed (where he had run the famous Midway). He then moved to New York and after a few successful years as a publisher himself, entered politics and was elected to Congress representing New York State numerous times. For Bloom's role in the 1893 Chicago Fair, see Reid Badger, *The Great American Fair: The World's Columbia Exposition and American Culture* (Chicago: Nelson Hall, 1979). See also David A. Jasen, *Tin Pan Alley: The Composers, the Songs, the Performers and Their Times* (New York: Donald I. Fine, Inc., 1988), 8, and Sol Bloom, *The Autobiography of Sol Bloom* (New York: Putnam, 1948).

18. Five years younger than Europe, Vodery (1885–1951) was just beginning his long and important career as songwriter, arranger, musical director, and bandleader. Born in Philadelphia and educated at the University of Pennsylvania, Vodery's first big successes came as composer of the scores for *The Time, the Place, and the Girl* (1907) and Ernest Hogan's *The Oyster Man* (1909). Later, he led the dance band at the Coconut Grove and supervised the music for the Ziegfeld Follies. For additional information see Southern, *The Music of Black Americans*, 346, and Fletcher, *100 Years of the Negro in Show Business*, 154–56.

19. See the Indianapolis *Freeman*, March 11, 1905, 5.

20. Additional information about Ernest Hogan can be found in Riis, *Just Before Jazz*, 37–40.

21. An ad in the *Freeman* of July 15, 1905, 5, announced: "W.L. Lykens presents The Unbleached American Ernest Hogan, King of his Race, and his Big Funny Folk Company in the three act musical melange 'The Birth of the Minstrel.' Book by William D. Hall. Music by Will Marion Cook. Staged by J. Ed Green." The ad also calls for musicians to "complete the Memphis Students."

22. Mose McQuitty, who had a long career on the road, lists a number of "Nashville Student" minstrel companies with whom he worked around the turn of the century, including P. T. Wright's Nashville Students, (P. G.) Lowery and Green's Nashville Student Company, and M. L. Swain's Nashville Students. See Alex D. Albright, "Mose McQuitty's Unknown Career: A Personal History of Black Music in America," *Black Music Research Bulletin* 11 (Fall, 1989): 2.

23. James Weldon Johnson, *Black Manhattan* (New York: Alfred A. Knopf, 1930), 120. In January 1905, Europe (in collaboration with Ernest Hogan) published "Obadiah (You Took Advantage of Me)," a "coon" song in the manner of "All Coons Look Alike to Me," with the Gotham Music Company. See Sylvester Russell, "Stage Notes and Logic," in the Indianapolis *Freeman*, April 15, 1905, 2. See Appendix 1 for the other songs which Europe wrote in that style. Gotham Music, which was owned by Will Marion Cook and R. C. McPherson, merged with the first black owned and operated Tin Pan Alley firm, the Attucks Music Publishing company, to form Gotham-Attucks Music Company in mid-1905. See Jasen, *Tin Pan Alley*, 32–33.

24. The review was reprinted in the Indianapolis *Freeman* on July 8, 1905, 5.

25. "Interview with Ernest Hogan," *The New York Age*, August 24, 1905, 7.

26. Johnson, *Black Manhattan*, 120. See, also, Marva Carter, "Will Marion Cook," 102–7.

27. Johnson, *Black Manhattan*, 120.

28. Sylvester Russell listed the Memphis Students musicians in his "Gotham Gossip" column in the *Freeman* of September 30, 1905 (p. 5). They included Will H. Dixon—conductor; Joseph Gray, Peter J. Staples, Theo Watts, Will Brown, Will Blacklock, Ike Smith, Cleaner Jackson, E. J. Harper, William Thomas, John Hoffman, and

Adolphus Hastor—mandolin; Charles A. Wilson, Lewis Wise, and Victor Joyner—cello; Walter Gray, Thomas Harris, F. D. Beaumont—harp guitar; Frank Price, and George Chase—banjo. This translates to an orchestra of nineteen instruments (eleven mandolins, three celli, three harp guitars, and two banjos). In addition, in his advertisement for musicians to "complete the Memphis Students," which ran for several weeks in the *Freeman* in July, Hogan called for singers who could play mandolin, guitar, cello, and banjo only. There was a further stipulation: "Each must be able to read music at sight." See the Indianapolis *Freeman*, July 8 and 15, 1905.

29. See Russell, "Gotham Gossip," Indianapolis *Freeman*, September 30, 1905, 5. Hogan's musical, *Rufus Rastus*, which began touring in late 1905 and opened at the American Theatre in New York on January 29, 1906, is described in some detail by Riis in *Just Before Jazz*, 125–27.

30. "Memphis Students Sail," *New York Age*, 1, and Southern, *The Music of Black Americans*, 344. Sylvester Russell reported in the *Freeman* that Cook had "stolen" the troop and that Abbie Mitchell had been particularly deceptive (or clever, or both): "It was a very slick trick if that is what we might otherwise term it," he wrote. "Miss Abbie Mitchell had to steal away all alone by another ship in order to escape Hogan's injunction. The writs served on the Students at sea were valueless." See "Sylvester Russell Notes," the Indianapolis *Freeman*, November 4, 1905, 5.

31. See Carle Browne Cooke, "New York Society and Stage Comment," the Indianapolis *Freeman*, December 16, 1905, 6. In October, Europe published his "The Coon Band Parade" with his old publisher, Sol Bloom, and not, perhaps significantly, with Cook's Gotham Music.

32. Whatever differences might have existed between Hogan, Europe, and Cook seemed to have been patched-up fairly quickly, at least according to a report in the March 17 Indianapolis *Freeman* (p. 6) that "Mr Cook honored *Rufus Rastus* with a visit at the Saturday matinee and seemed highly pleased with the great production. He was accompanied by Mr. James Reese Europe, the composer and song writer." Abbie Mitchell was also a member of the 1908 group, for which Jordan, who took Dixon's part as the dancing conductor, wrote virtually all of the songs and music. Fletcher's memoir is less reliable for information about the original Memphis Students of 1905, but there is an interesting photograph (p. 130) in his book (Europe and Hogan are clearly visible) of what may be the first edition. See Fletcher, *100 Years of the Negro in Show Business*, 129–31.

33. For excellent discussions of the careers of Bob Cole and the Johnson brothers and the background of the *Shoo-Fly Regiment*, see Riis, *Just Before Jazz*, 33–37, and 129–35, and Woll, *Black Musical Theatre*, 14–24.

34. "Cole and Johnson to Star in 'The Shoo-Fly Regiment,'" *New York Age*, July 26, 1906, 5, and Indianapolis *Freeman*, August 4, 1906, 5. The supporting cast listed by the *Age* (A. A. Talbort, Andrew Tribble, Matt Harshall, Nettie Glenn and Fanny Wise) differs from that of the *Freeman* (Tom Brown, Sam Lucas, Bob A. Kelly, Theodore Pankey, Inez Clough, Siren Navarro, and Anna Cook) suggesting, perhaps, that the company's personnel was still unsettled with less than three weeks until opening.

35. Johnson, *Along This Way*, 239. See also, the Indianapolis *Freeman* for September 29 and October 27, 1906.

36. Woll, *Black Musical Theatre*, 24.

37. Riis, *Just Before Jazz*, 133.

38. Program dated December 9, 1906, theater unknown, and the program (February 16, 1907) from the Nesbitt Theater in Wilkes Barre, Pennsylvania. Billy Rose Theater Collection, New York Public Library.

39. Riis, *Just Before Jazz*, 131–32. A facsimile of "On the Gay Luneta," arranged for voice and piano, as published by Joseph W. Stern in October of 1906, is included (pp. 286–88).

40. Johnson, *Along This Way*, 240.

41. Riis, *Just Before Jazz*, 130.

42. Franklin, *From Slavery to Freedom*, 442.

43. See Sylvester Russell, "The Sixth Annual Review," in The Indianapolis *Freeman*, January 5, 1907, 5.

44. Woll, *Black Musical Theatre*, 23.

45. An unidentified clipping dated May 27, 1907, and quoted in Riis, *Just Before Jazz*, 187.

46. Johnson, *Along This Way*, 240.

47. See Riis, *Just Before Jazz*, 141.

48. Walter Crumbly to Marshall and Jean Stearns in *Jazz Dance: The Story of American Vernacular Dance* (New York: Macmillan, 1968), 76–77, and quoted in Riis, *Just Before Jazz*, 142.

49. *The Black Politician* program for October 21, 1906 (Toledo, Ohio—theater unknown), Billy Rose Theatre Collection, New York Public Library. Dudley's most lasting contribution was not as a performer, but as the founder of the Dudley Circuit, a precursor of the Theatre Owners' Booking Association (TOBA). See Riis, *Just Before Jazz*, 145.

50. Among the cities in the East that *The Black Politician* played were Pittsburgh, Philadelphia, Atlantic City, Boston, Baltimore, and New York (but not a theater on Broadway).

51. Quoted in Riis, *Just Before Jazz*, 142.

52. Russell, "The Stage," in the Indianapolis *Freeman*, October 12, 1907, 5. Also see Russell's column of September 21, 1907 ("Europe and McPherson fairly outdid themselves in their contribution of new lyrics and music."), 5.

53. Sylvester Russell, "The Stage," in the Indianapolis *Freeman*, October 12, 1907, 2. Henry T. Sampson in his *Blacks in Blackface: A Sourcebook on Early Black Musical Shows* (Metuchen, N.J.: Scarecrow Press, 1980), 148, carries the same list of songs for the show. A comparison to the listing in the program for February 24, 1908 (the Bijou Theater in Pittsburgh) indicates that a few changes were made over the previous five months. "Election Time" was substituted for "Darktown Band," "When the Moon Plays Peek A Boo" for "Likin' Ain't Like Lovin'," and "Suwanee River" for "Lolita." "I Don't Like School" was simply dropped, "Crow" was changed to "Old Black Crow," and by February "Don't Take Him Away" was called "Take Him Away, The Law Commands It." The program still lists Europe as composer of the music and McPherson as lyricist. The Billy Rose Theater Collection, New York Public Library.

54. One of the reasons Europe had to feel genial was that he had just acquired the services of G. W. "Cricket" Smith of Pittsburgh as his lead cornetist. See the Indianapolis *Freeman*, November 2, 1907, 5.

55. Nagol Mot [Tom Logan], "Smart Set Notes," in the Indianapolis *Freeman*, November 30, 1907, 5.

56. "Smart Set," in the Indianapolis *Freeman*, February 29, 1908, 5.

57. See "Smart Set Pickups," in the Indianapolis *Freeman*, February 29, 1908, 5.

58. After 1912, Dudley began concentrating more of his time in an attempt to build a circuit of theaters independent of white control. He died on February 29, 1940. See Riis, *Just Before Jazz*, 141–45.

59. In addition to Dudley, Cole, Johnson, and Europe the planning committee for

the benefit included: George Walker, Bert Williams, Tom Brown, Will Marion Cook, Sam Corker, Jr., Alex Rogers, D. E. Tobias, J. A. Shipp, R. C. McPherson, Walter Craig, Joe Jordan, W. H. Tyers, James Vaughan, Charles H. Moore, and Lester Walton (the latter two of the *New York Age*). The Memphis Students (with Tom Fletcher, Abbie Mitchell and Joe Jordan) appropriately closed what Fletcher remembered as "one of the greatest shows ever put together." Fletcher, *100 Years of the Negro in Show Business*, 143.

60. See Ann Charters, *Nobody: The Story of Bert Williams* (New York: Macmillan Co., 1970), 93.

61. "Frogs Organized," the Indianapolis *Freeman*, July 18, 1908, 5, and Lester Walton, "Frogs Elect Officers," the *New York Age*, May 26, 1910.

62. The ad in the *New York Age*, July 9, 1908, 6, promised the "Season's Greatest Novelty," "Dancing from twilight till dawn," and prizes for "the ladies wearing the most unique and picturesque costumes emblematic of the Frogs."

63. Lester Walton's column, "The Frogs," The *New York Age*, August 6, 1908, 6.

64. The other officers were: J. Rosamond Johnson, vice president; R. C. McPherson, secretary; and Jesse Shipp, treasurer. Walton, "The Frogs," The *New York Age*, August 6, 1908, 6.

65. See Woll, *Black Musical Theatre*, 24–27. Jean Toomer employed the image with chilling effectiveness ("The full moon in the great door was an omen. Negro women improvised songs against its spell.") in his "Blood-Burning Moon," a tale of racial bigotry and violence from *Cane* (1923; reprint, New York: Liveright, 1975), 28.

66. See Woll, *Black Musical Theatre*, 27 and Riis, *Just Before Jazz*, 135.

67. Riis, *Just Before Jazz*, 138.

68. Ibid. As Riis suggests, the music and the lyrics seem to anticipate the future. In their subject matter and female point of view, Cole's words are comparable to the blues (or blues influenced popular songs) of the 1920s. He is probably correct that Eubie Blake, consciously or otherwise, found Europe's melody appropriate for reworking into his 1921 *Shuffle Along* hit "If You've Never Been Vamped by a Brownskin."

69. The Indianapolis *Freeman*, October 24, 1908, 5. The *Freeman*, which was pleased by the positive reception *The Red Moon* was given by the Chicago press and by Chicago theater-goers, believed that the outstanding features of the production were the music ("The music is the best that was ever offered by Negroes.") and the female chorus ("There never was such a collection of colored girls"). The music publisher E. B. Marks, who was familiar with the great black shows of the twenties, still maintained in 1934 that *The Red Moon* was "the most tuneful colored show of the century." Quoted in Riis, *Just Before Jazz*, 141.

70. The *Freeman*, October 24, 1908, 5.

71. As both Riis and Woll document, *The Red Moon* was reviewed favorably by a number of periodicals (*The Dramatic Mirror*, *The Dramatic News*, *Theatre Magazine*, and The *New York Times*, among them) that rarely took notice of black musical shows. The black press, which had struggled for years with the dilemma of reporting positively the increasing commercial and popular successes of a black show business which also denigrated and belittled the race, began referring to *The Red Moon* in what was then understood to be the highest possible terms of musical theater artistry (i.e., opera). "Under the personal direction of Mr. James Reese Europe, the chorus is full, strong, sweet and brilliant. Such support can hardly be seen outside of grand opera," said the *Freeman* of November 28 (p. 5). Abbie Mitchell was not just the singing star, she was now "the prima donna."

72. See the Indianapolis *Freeman*, December 5, 1908, 5.

73. Lester Walton, "Music and the Stage," the *New York Age*, January 28, 1909, 6. *The Red Moon* opened at the Folly Theater in Brooklyn on February 1, and from there moved on to Boston.

74. See Lester Walton, "Music and the Stage," the *New York Age*, March 25, 1909, 6, and "Rays from The Red Moon," the *New York Age*, April 15, 1909, 6. The popularity of baseball among the black touring companies goes back to the nineteenth-century minstrel troops like the Georgia Minstrels and the Rabbit's Foot Comedy Company. Williams and Walker had their "nine," and Ernest Hogan his "Black Rats." A company would typically come into a new town, do their shows, and challenge the local amateur ball team to a game.

75. Riis, *Just Before Jazz*, 135. The review of *Red Moon* in *Theatre Magazine* (June 1909, xii) observed that it was an "unusual kind of theatrical entertainment in which all the ingredients—book, music, players are furnished by colored talent."

76. *Theatre Magazine* (June 1909), xii.

77. New York *Mirror*, May 15, 1909, quoted in Woll, *Black Musical Theater*, 27.

78. Lester Walton, "Music and the Stage," the *New York Age*, June 3, 1909, 6.

79. For additional discussions of *Bandanna Land*, see Riis, *Just Before Jazz*, 117–22, and Woll, *Black Musical Theatre*, 46–48.

80. George Walker died on January 6, 1911, at a sanitarium in Islip, Long Island. He was thirty-nine. It would be hard to overestimate the pioneering role of Williams and Walker in opening Broadway musical comedy to black actors, directors, and writers. For an excellent summary of their achievement, see Woll, *Black Musical Theatre*, 32–49.

81. Riis, *Just Before Jazz*, 123. An unidentified review in the Billy Rose Theater Collection of the New York Public Library described the music as "really tuneful and pleasing, and the whole makes as good a score as Mr. Johnson has ever contributed to such an entertainment," and *Theatre Magazine* (December, 1909, p. xviii) said that the music of *Mr. Lode of Koal* was further proof that Johnson was "an Afro-American musical composer of marked talent and scholastic cultivation."

82. The Indianapolis *Freeman*, December 4, 1909, 5.

83. See the *New York Age*, December 16, 1909, 7. "Did anyone ever see so many changes in the big wheel shows as this season?," asked The Indianapolis *Freeman* of February 5, 1910 (p. 5). "There will be a real battle in New York next summer; just you wait. Here are some of the changes and drops from *Red Moon*: James Europe, Abbie Mitchell, Bennie Jones, Charles Hunter, Tootsie Hunter—all on account of trouble. From 'Mr. Lode of Koal:' Jim Vaughan, Will Elkins, Babe Foster, and Hattie Hopkins— all to cut down on expenses." Bob Cole's health had also begun to deteriorate and he began to exhibit symptoms of general paresis similar to those that afflicted George Walker. Like Walker, Cole would never fully recover.

84. "Music and the Stage," the *New York Age*, July 14, 1910, 6.

85. See Salem Tutt Whitney's column, "Seen and Heard While Passing," in the Indianapolis *Freeman*, January 15, 1916, 6.

86. Woll, *Black Musical Theatre*, 48.

Chapter Four: "Lorraine Waltzes"

1. Mary Europe's musical activities are often remarked upon in the pages of the Washington, D.C., *Colored American*. See, for example, the following issues: April 6,

1901 (p. 13), May 17, 1902 (p. 10), April 4 (p. 16), June 13 (p. 5), October 3 (p. 15), and December 5 (p. 6) of 1903, and February 13, 1904 (p. 5). See, also, McGinty, "The Black Presence," 101.

2. Mary was a graduate of the M Street School in 1900 and Minor Normal School in 1902. She attended the Teachers College of Columbia University during several summer sessions and received her A.B. degree from Howard University in 1922. She was a much loved and admired teacher, who founded the Cantoren (a group of Dunbar graduates who regularly performed in the Washington area and appeared on the Major Bowes radio program). During World War II she trained students for concert, radio, and army camp performances. Among her students were Lawrence Whisonant (Larry Winters), an internationally noted baritone; Turner Layton, an accomplished concert pianist and composer; and Frank Wess, an outstanding jazz instrumentalist and arranger. According to her students, Mary Europe possessed an absolute sense of pitch and could read and transpose accurately the most difficult music at sight. For additional information about Mary Europe, see Doris E. McGinty, "Gifted Minds and Pure Hearts: Mary L. Europe and Estelle Pinkney Webster," in *The Journal of Negro Education*, 51 (Summer 1982): 266–72, and Mary Gibson Hundley, *The Dunbar Story: 1870–1955* (New York: Vintage Press, 1965), 138. Obituaries from the Washington *Evening Star* (October 22, 1947) and the Washington-Pittsburgh *Courier* (November 1, 1947) are also useful and can be found in the vertical file of the Washingtoniana Collection, Martin Luther King Branch, Washington, D.C., Public Library.

3. As McGinty says, at that time he was "a musical hero to Afro-Americans." See "Gifted Minds and Pure Hearts," 269. Even into the the 1920s, most of the leading black composers were followers "of Dvořák's brand of romantic nationalism or had been inspired and influenced by the Anglo-African composer Samuel Coleridge-Taylor." See Samuel Floyd, Jr., "Music in the Harlem Renaissance: An Overview," in *Black Music in the Harlem Renaissance*, ed. Samuel A.Floyd, Jr., Contributions in Afro-American and African Studies no. 128(Westport, Conn.: Greenwood Press, 1990), 16.

4. W. C. Berwick Sayers, *Samuel Coleridge-Taylor, Musician: His Life and Letters*, (London: Cassell and Company, LTD, 1915; rpt. Chicago: Afro-American Press, 1969), 28. "Dvořák was my first musical love," Coleridge-Taylor wrote to Andrew Hilyer in May of 1901, "and I have received more from his works than from anyone's, perhaps." Quoted in Sayers, 117. See, also, William Tortolano, *Samuel Coleridge-Taylor: Anglo-Black Composer, 1875–1912* (Metuchen, NJ: The Scarecrow Press, 1977), 15–38.

5. The *New York Herald*, May 21, 1893, and quoted in John Clapham, *Dvořák* (New York: W. W. Norton, 1979), 198.

6. Dvořák's American-inspired compositions include a quartet (Op. 96), a quintet (Op. 97) and the celebrated Symphony No. 9 in E Minor *From the New World*, which was given its premiere performance on December 15. Ellington studied informally with Will Marion Cook, and both Gershwin and Copeland studied with Rubin Goldmark at Juilliard.

7. Perhaps the most widely reprinted quotation from Dvořák's letters to the *New York Herald* appeared on May 25, 1893, when he stated simply,

[I]n the Negro melodies of America I discover all that is needed for a great and noble school of music. They are pathetic, tender, passionate, melancholy, solemn, religious, bold, merry, gay or what you will. It is music that suits itself to any mood or any purpose. There is nothing in the whole range of composition that cannot be supplied with themes from this source. The American musician understands these tunes and they move sentiment in him. They appeal to his imagination because of their associations.

Quoted in Clapham, *Dvořák*, 197; and Southern, *The Music of Black Americans*, 265. The precise use that Dvořák made of Negro spirituals or folk melodies in the *New World* has been the subject of some debate. For a useful discussion of the question, see Paul Burgett, "Vindication as a Thematic Principle in the Writings of Alain Locke on the Music of Black Americans," in *Black Music in the Harlem Renaissance*, ed. Samuel A. Floyd, Jr., Contributions in Afro-American and African Studies no. 128 (Westport, Conn.: Greenwood Press, 1990), 30–33. There is no question at all, however, that Dvořák was strongly influenced by hearing Burleigh's singing of Negro spirituals. For a more detailed description of the Madison Square Garden concert see the *New York Herald*, January 23, 1894, which is quoted in Maurice Peress, "Dvořák and African-American Musicians, 1892–1895," in *Black Music Research Bulletin* 12 (fall 1990), 26–9.

8. Sayers, *Samuel Coleridge-Taylor*, 48. His *African Romances* was composed as a setting for six of Dunbar's poems. For a brief and appreciative sketch of his life, see Cuny-Hare, *Negro Musicians and Their Music*, 308–14.

9. Willard B. Gatewood, *Aristocrats of Color* (Bloomington, Indiana: Indiana University Press, 1990), 28.

10. Ibid., 217.

11. McGinty, "Gifted Minds and Pure Hearts," 269.

12. Sayers devotes an entire chapter, "The Apostle of Colour," to the composer's evolving race consciousness, his desire to do for black music "what Brahms has done for Hungarian folk-music, Dvořák for the Bohemian, and Grieg for the Norwegian" (p. 258). "Other and greater musicians have lived," writes Sayers, "but he was the first of his race to reach recognition as a world musician." See *Samuel Coleridge-Taylor*, 280. *Hiawatha* was a very popular work in the first two decades of the century; indeed, it was "the most popular English oratorio from 1898 to 1912" according to Tortolano. See his *Anglo-Black Composer*, 31.

13. See the letter from Coleridge to Hilyer dated May 12, 1901, and quoted in Sayers, 117.

14. See "'Hiawatha,' Musical Triumph," in the Boston *Guardian*, May 2, 1903, 2. The *Guardian* reported that the "white orchestra that had been engaged for the occasion proved itself incompetent to play the music" and so two pianos and a vocalion (a small organlike instrument) were substituted. The *Guardian* was also pleased that both the Washington *Evening Star* and the *Washington Post* (a paper not known for showing great sympathy toward blacks) printed glowing reviews. "The Coleridge-Taylor Choral Society has scored a splendid triumph for the race," the article concluded, "and we are proud of them."

15. See Gatewood, *Aristocrats of Color*, 217.

16. Quoted in the Washington *Colored American*, May 2, 1903, 2.

17. During this time, Coleridge-Taylor's estimation of the significance of this unique choral society to African-Americans and to people of African descent grew considerably, aided in part by his reading of Du Bois's *Souls of Black Folk*. "In some ways," writes his biographer, "this unique chorus was the most interesting thing in Coleridge-Taylor's world." See Sayers, 141–44.

18. The Washington *Colored American*, for example, reported that the choral society's performance of *Hiawatha* before a packed house at the Music Hall the previous week was a "triumph," and, once again, Mary Europe's accompaniment was singled out as "particularly commendable." See the *Colored American*, December 5, 1903, 6.

19. Sayers, *Samuel Coleridge-Taylor*, 158. The London *Musical Times* of September 1, 1903, described the chorus as

excellent and deserving of all praise. Even several eminent white musicians have borne testimony to its high achievement, and even the white press acknowledge that the performance was a splendid success. Considering the deep-rooted racial feeling among the white and coloured people this is all the more gratifying and encouraging. Moreover we understand that it is the first time that white singers have applied in hundreds for admission to an entirely coloured Society (in the U.S.A.) and have been refused because there was not room for them!

The article is reproduced in Tortolano, *Anglo-Black Composer*, 31–33.

20. See Gatewood, *Aristocrats of Color*, 217.

21. Quoted in Sayers, 116.

22. Ibid., 171.

23. "I must say that the band last year was not a tenth good enough for the chorus, especially in its string department," he wrote. Ibid., 185.

24. Quoted in Cuney-Hare, *Negro Musicians and Their Music*, 246. For documentation as to the importance of the event to Mary Europe, see McGinty, "Gifted Minds and Pure Hearts," 269.

25. Quoted in Sayers, 250.

26. The concert was "pronounced by white critics to have been the finest choral singing heard here this season." See The *New York Age*, April 26, 1906, 1.

27. Mary Europe performed with Melville Charlton on a number of public occasions, the last of which was in 1932 when she and Charlton accompanied a performance of Coleridge-Taylor's *Atonement*. See McGinty, "Gifted Minds and Pure Hearts," 269.

28. See "The Negro's Genius for Music," in The Indianapolis *Freeman*, June 8, 1907, 5.

29. "I shall always love the S. Coleridge-Taylor Choral Society," tenor J. Arthur Freeman wrote Andrew Hilyer, "because it is doing more than any similar society in the world for the culture and refinement of our race." Letter dated December 4, 1904, and quoted in Gatewood, *Aristocrats of Color*, 218.

30. Letter from Andrew Hilyer to Samuel Coleridge-Taylor, dated April 26, 1908, and quoted in Sayers, *Samuel Coleridge-Taylor*, 218.

31. Interview at Washington, D.C., quoted by Sylvester Russell in "S. Coleridge Taylor [sic] Answered," the Indianapolis *Freeman*, December 31, 1904, 2.

32. Quoted in Sayers, *Samuel Coleridge-Taylor*, 206.

33. Sousa's comments and the responses that Walton solicited were published in the latter's column, "Is Ragtime Dead?," in the *New York Age*, April 8, 1909, 6. All quotes are from this source.

34. Quoted from an editorial written by the publisher of the *New York Age* in response to a remark of President Roosevelt's (following Dvořák) that the Negro Spirituals and Indian folk song would constitute the source of a new American music. See The *New York Age*, February 22, 1906, 4. The leading theater and stage critics of the national black newspapers, Lester Walton of the *New York Age* and Sylvester Russell of the Indianapolis *Freeman* in particular, were more ambivalent toward the music than their publishers. Russell, while admitting that "coon songs" and ragtime were "the lighter class of true genuine American Negro music," nevertheless rejected Coleridge-Taylor's dismissal of it as worthless: "I deny Mr. Taylor's assertion that there is no melody in 'coon' songs," he wrote in 1904. "They are light and airy and very often full of variety, for ragtime is something that Mr. Taylor has not understood and will not understand until he visits some low Negro concert hall and sees how naturally it is executed in music, song and dance." Dvořák, he regretted to say, recognized this and, therefore, his

name "lives nearer to us in musical relationship than Taylor's, although Mr. Taylor is a Negro." See "S. Coleridege Taylor [sic] Answered," the Indianapolis *Freeman*, December 31, 1904, 2.

Chapter Five: "The Clef Club March"

1. Johnson, *Black Manhattan*, 170. Also see Woll's discussion in *Black Musical Theatre*, 50–57.

2. Lewis A. Erenberg, *Steppin' Out: New York Nightlife and the Transformation of American Culture, 1890–1930* (Chicago: The University of Chicago Press, 1981), xi.

3. See Erenberg's Chapter 5, "Everybody's Doin' It: Irene and Vernon Castle and the Pre-World War I Dance Craze," in *Steppin' Out*, 146–71.

4. Ibid., 151.

5. *A History of Popular Music in America* (New York: Random House, 1948), 369, and quoted in Marshall and Jean Stearns, *Jazz Dance*, 95.

6. The New Amsterdam Musical Association established its headquarters in a room on West 59th Street and sponsored concerts at the New Amsterdam Opera House and the Palm Gardens, but in the end was unable to make much headway in opening up the hotels to black orchestras largely due to its "high" musical standards. See Samuel Charters and Leonard Kunstadt, *Jazz: A History of the New York Scene* (New York: Doubleday and Co., 1962), 25–26. The New Amsterdam Musical Association enjoyed a long, if bumpy, career that eventuated in 1922 in the purchase of a permanent building at 107 West 130th Street in Harlem that was still operating in the 1970s. In 1974, Sammy Heyward, president of the Association, composed a short history entitled "Resume of the New Amsterdam Musical Association, Inc.," which is available from that organization.

7. Fletcher's account of the genesis of the Clef Club can be found in his *100 Years of the Negro in Show Business*, 252–64. According to Fletcher, an original member, one of the Marshall regulars had been sent a couple of opossums from home, the hotel agreed to cook them, and he "invited the gang to help eat them." Over a down-home opossum dinner, then, the Clef Club was born.

8. The other original officers included Daniel Kildare, vice-president; Arthur Payne, secretary; William C. "Kid" Thomas, treasurer; and John Barnes, sergeant-at-arms. See Lester Walton's "Music and the Stage" column in the *New York Age* for April 28, 1910, 6. The organization date of April 11 appears on the same page in an advertisement for the first Clef Club entertainment scheduled for the following month. The ad, which also ran in the previous week's edition (see the *New York Age*, April 21, 1910, 6), confirms Walton's list of the officers. Tom Fletcher remembered correctly that Europe was the first president and that William Thomas was the first treasurer, but he was mistaken in the original vice-president and first secretary. See *100 Years of the Negro in Show Business*, 252.

9. Quoted by Lester Walton in his "Music and the Stage" column in the *New York Age* of February 20, 1912, 6. Walton, along with Jimmy Marshall, Baron Wilkins, and a few other nonmusician supporters, were named honorary members of the Clef Club when it was formed in 1910.

10. The objectives of the Amsterdam Musical Association were:

[T]o voluntarily promote and encourage the study and production of instrumental music in all the various branches; to draw together trained musicians in the State of New York, in a musical association for mutual intercourse and encouragement and to establish in the City of New York, a central meeting place for the instruction and for social intercourse between its members.

Quoted in Heyward, "Resume of the New Amsterdam Musical Association, Inc.," 2.

11. Walton, "Music and the Stage," The *New York Age*, April 28, 1910, 6.

12. "It was at the Clef," recalled the great stride pianist Willie "The Lion" Smith in his autobiography, "that I met Irving (Kid Sneeze) Williams—a legit pianist who loved to sneak off and rag it by ear—bandleader Happy Rhone, and other celebrated personalities of the period." See *Music on My Mind*, 62.

13. The C.V.B.A. held annual fund-raising picnics until it disbanded around the beginning of World War I. See Fletcher, *100 Years of the Negro in Show Business*, 176. The Frogs had also been sponsoring an annual summer social event, a formal ball that they called "The Frolic of the Frogs," since 1908. Europe participated in all of these high-spirited affairs until they were discontinued during the war. The last Frolic of the Frogs in New York was held on June 30, 1913.

14. Ibid., 255.

15. The *New York Age*, April 21, 1910, 6. Admission was fifty cents and those wanting boxes were directed to apply to Henry Creamer at the Gotham-Attucks Music Company office.

16. The announced program was as follows:

> "Cackles" . . . . Alford
> "Indian Summer" (Intermezzo) . . . . More
> "Beautiful Spring" (Concert Waltz) . . . . Lincke
> "That Teasing Rag" . . . . Jordan
> Orch. conducted by the Composer
> "The Clef Club" (A Novelty) . . . .
> "The Clef Club March" . . . . Europe
> Specially written and dedicated to the Clef Club by James Reese Europe.
> Words to the trio by Henry S. Creamer

A variety, or vaudeville, show, featuring some twenty individual song, dance, and comedy acts, was to follow the concert; a reprise of the "Clef Club March" by the combined orchestras of Walter Craig, Hallie Anderson, and the Clef Club would signal the end of the entertainment portion and the beginning of the dance (accompanied by Craig's and Anderson's orchestras). See The *New York Age*, May 26, 1910, 6.

17. See Lester A. Walton, "Music and the Stage," The *New York Age*, June 2, 1910, 6. Among the variety acts that appeared were a boxing skit by Creamer and Billy Farrell, several songs each by George Walker, Jr., and Tom Bethel, the "Marshall Trio" (composed of John Europe-piano, Anthony Tuck-mandolin, and William Patrick-vocals), and a piano/banjo trio featuring Clarence Williams, piano, and Will Humphreys and Isaac Johns playing banjos.

18. The *New York Age*, September 15, 1910, 6.

19. The *New York Age*, October 20, 1910, 6.

20. The complete program, as reported by Lester Walton in the *New York Age* of October 27, 1910, 6 and as published in the official program (a copy of which can be found in the Schomburg Center for Research in Black Culture, New York Public Library), is as follows:

> Part One
> "Crackles" (Overture) . . . . Orchestra
> "Lovie Joe" (solo) . . . . William Patrick

"Suffragette" (solo) . . . . Al Brown
"When the Bell on the Lighthouse Rings" (solo)
 . . . . James Rivers w/quartet
"Come Along, My Mandy" (solo) . . . . Tom Bethel
"Grizzly Bear" (solo) . . . . Joe Weatherly
"Bon Bon Buddy" (solo) . . . . George Walker, Jr.
 Part Two (Composers)
"Maori," "Smyrna," "Panama" . . . . William Tyers
"Dear Old Moonlight," "Sweetness," . . . . Henry
 Creamer and Tom Lemonier w/Will Dixon
"For the Last Time Call Me Sweetheart,"
 "Araby" . . . . Al Johns
"Oh, You Devil," "Minor Strain". . . . Ford Dabney
 Part Three (Orchestra)
"Clef Club March" . . . . Europe
"To A Wild Rose" . . . . McDowell
"Every Little Movement" . . . . Hoschna
"Queen of the Nile" . . . . Europe
"Unrequited Love" . . . . Lincke
"Little Mikado" . . . . Lange
"Beautiful Spring" (by request) . . . . Linke
"The Clef Club Chant" . . . . Creamer

21. "Both demonstrated that they were conductors of no little ability," Walton remarked. See the *New York Age*, October 27, 1910, 6.

22. Ibid.

23. Ibid.

24. The article suggests that the address may not be permanent, but will be "the home of the 'Clefties' for several months at least. The Club has taken possession of two floors and the six rooms are being tastefully furnished. James Reese Europe will be in charge." See the *New York Age*, December 15, 1910, 3.

25. See *100 Years of the Negro in Show Business*, 264.

26. Ibid., 261.

27. The *New York Age*, March 2, 1911, 6.

28. The *New York Age*, April 27, 1911, 6.

29. Lester Walton's two column review of the third Clef Club concert appears in "Music and the Stage," the *New York Age*, May 18, 1911, 6.

30. The *New York Age*, May 18, 1911, 6. The complete program is as follows:

Grand Opening Medley . . . . Entire Company
"That Long Lost Chord" . . . . Clarence Bush & Chorus
"Way Down in Georgia" . . . . William Parquette & Chorus
"Bamboola" (A Samoan Idle) (c. Frederick Bryan)
 . . . . Clef Club Symphony Orchestra
"Toddlin' the Todelo" . . . . Paul Simmons & Chorus
"The Suffragette" . . . . Al Brown
"Love's Menu" and "Smyrna" (c. William Tyers)
 . . . . C.C.S.O. conducted by the composer
"Danse La Ballet Grotesque" . . . . Henry Creamer and Joe Grey
"Porto Rico" (c. Ford Dabney) . . . . C.C.S.O.
"The Barbershop Chord" . . . . George Henry & Chorus

"Don't Wake Me Up I Am Dreaming" .... Henry Troy & Octette
"A Jubilee" and "On Bended Knee" (c. Harry T. Burleigh) .... C.C.S.O.
Song and Wooden Shoe Dance .... Irving Williams·
"Trans-mag-ni-fi-can-ban-dan-u-al-i-ty" .... Percy Robinson & Chorus
"Lorraine Waltzes" (c. J. R. Europe and "Dedicated to My Mother")
      .....C.C.S.O.
"Grizzly Bear" .... Tom Bethel & Chorus
"She's Everything and Then Some More" .... William Patrick &
      Henry Creamer
"Lovie Joe" .... John Christian and Chorus
"The Separate Battalion" (c. J.R. Europe & Especially written and dedicated
      to the High School Cadets of Washington, D.C.) .... C.C.S.O.
"Darktown is Out To-night" (c. Will Marion Cook)
      .... Entire Company
"Clef Club March" (c. J.R. Europe) .... Entire Company

31. The *New York Age*, May 18, 1911, 6.

32. One of the pieces he led the band in was his "Clef Club March." See the *New York Age*, March 30, 1911, 6. Advertisements for the Walker Memorial appear in the May 18 and 25 issues of the *New York Age* on page 6.

33. The *New York Age*, May 18, 1911, carries a full listing of the notables who had volunteered to appear. The Indianapolis *Freeman* of June 10, 1911, gives a short review of the memorial.

34. See "Frogs Elect New Officers," in the *New York Age*, June 15, 1911, 6. The fourth annual "Frog Frolic" was held on June 26.

35. A summary of the remarkable career of John Thomas Douglass, master violinist and the first black composer to write an opera (1868), can be found in Southern, *The Music of Black Americans*, 249. The Douglass/Mannes' story was first printed in an article, "Negro Put Mannes on Road to Fame," in the *New York Times*, March 20, 1912, 9, reprinted in "Black-Music Concerts at Carnegie Hall, 1912–1915," *The Black Perspective in Music* 6 (Spring 1978): 72–74. See also, Elbridge L. Adams, "The Negro Music School Settlement," in *The Southern Workman* 44 (1915): 161–62.

36. For additional discussions of the formation of the Music School Settlement, see George Martin, *The Damrosch Dynasty: America's First Family of Music* (Boston: Houghton Mifflin, 1983), 211–15, and David Mannes's autobiographical *Music is My Faith* (New York: Norton, 1938), 219.

37. See "Negro Put Mannes on Road to Fame," The *New York Times*, March 20, 1912, 9, and reprinted in "Black-Music Concerts in Carnegie Hall, 1912–1915," 74, and Mannes, *Music is My Faith*, 219. The officers of the Board of Directors, as of February, 1912, were Elbridge Adams, chairman; Natalie Curtis and Mrs. Percival Knauth, treasurers; David Mannes, supervisor; and David Martin, director. See the *New York Age*, February 20, 1912, 6.

38. See Martin, *The Damrosch Dynasty*, 214.

39. David Martin directed the school from 1911 until 1914, when J. Rosamond Johnson replaced him. In 1912, he joined with Helen E. Smith (later Mrs. Nathaniel Dett) in forming the Martin-Smith School of Music, which for many years was one of the most important black musical education institutions in the country. See Southern, *The Music of Black Americans*, 284.

40. As of 1915, Adams maintained, "no deserving child was turned away for want of means to pay for lessons." Adams, "The Negro Music School Settlement," 162.

41. The *New York Age*, October 5, 1911, 6.

42. Walton, "The Clef Club Concert," The *New York Age*, November 16, 1911, 6.

43. Walton, "The Clef Club Concert," The *New York Age*, November 16, 1911, 6. Among the popular numbers performed in the vaudeville/cabaret program was Irving Berlin's hit of 1911, "Alexander's Ragtime Band," which is not, in terms of form, a rag at all, but a mild version of the then-popular coon song. In addition to Europe's "Strength of the Nation," the orchestra concert included Will Dixon's "Thoughts," Burleigh's "On Bended Knee," Europe's "Hula," "The Lorraine Waltzes," and "Clef Club March," James Shaw's "Queentano," Woolford's "Dance of the Marionettes," "Tout a Vous" and " Panama" by Tyers, and Creamer's "Clef Club Chant."

44. "The Clef Club Concert," The *New York Age*, November 16, 1911.

45. See The Indianapolis *Freeman*, November 11, 1911, 5, and December 2, 1911, 2. Europe's continuing love of black musical theater and his admiration for its early pioneers is manifested in his being named to the board of directors (along with Bert Williams and Barron Wilkins) of a group organized to raise funds for a theater at 138th Street between Fifth and Lenox Avenues to be named the Walker–Cole–Hogan Theatre. An announcement of the offering of shares of stock in the new theater, along with the names of the officers and directors, was carried in the *New York Age*, March 21, 1912, 6. The first ad for the Frogs' January "Frolic" appears in the *New York Age*, November 16, 1911, 6.

46. See the *New York Age*, December 14, 1911, 6.

47. Mannes, *Music is My Faith*, 217.

48. See "Clef Club Plans to Expand," The *New York Age*, February 29, 1912, 6. A picture of Europe and a list of the current Clef Club officers accompanied the article.

49. Mannes, *Music is My Faith*, 217.

50. Adams, "The Negro Music School Settlement," 162, and Martin, *The Damrosch Dynasty*, 211.

51. As part of the legacy of the European art music tradition, Scott DeVeaux has written,

[T]he concert is a solemn ritual, with music the object of reverent contemplation. Certain formalities are imposed upon the concert audience: people attend in formal dress, sit quietly and attentively with little outward bodily movement, and restrict their response to applause at appropriate moments only.

They do not dance or engage in other forms of active public behavior that may be perfectly acceptable in other places where music is performed, and these differences reflect "the distance between 'high' and 'low' musical culture in the United States." See DeVeaux's interesting discussion in "The Emergence of the Jazz Concert, 1935–1945," *American Music* 7 (Spring, 1989): 6–29.

52. Martin, *The Damrosch Dynasty*, 211.

53. A copy of the program for the May 2, 1912, "Concert of Negro Music, under the auspices of The Music School Settlement for Colored People, Inc." can be found in the Carnegie Hall library. Clef Clubber Tom Fletcher, who thought Carnegie Hall was "run by what might be termed the 'long hair' musicians and singers," was certain that the church choir was added primarily to make it appear that it was not just a popular concert. See *100 Years of the Negro in Show Business*, 258.

54. Few of the players in the "great band" had received any formal musical training, she recalled. "They were—by profession—elevator men, bell-boys, porters, janitors, or followers of still humbler tasks, for few trades-unions then admitted colored men, so that the vocations open to the Negro were about as restricted and over-crowded

as the Negro streets themselves." See Natalie Curtis-Burlin, "Black Singers and Players," in *The Musical Quarterly* V(1919): 502–3.

55. Curtis-Burlin was especially impressed with how quickly the band picked up the music, even though most of what she heard them play was relatively simple dance and march music, and with Europe's confidence in them. See "Black Singers and Players," 504.

56. Mannes, *Music is My Faith*, 217. He was also concerned that some of Europe's musicians were being asked to learn instruments that were new to them in a very short period of time. The bassoon player, for instance, Mannes claimed, had learned his difficult instrument in a week (p. 218). "David had moments when he feared the result would be chaos," wrote George Martin, "but watching Europe work, he was impressed by him as a conductor and impresario. Europe could make happen what he said would happen." See *The Damrosch Dynasty*, 211.

57. Sissle, "Memoirs," 22–23. Sissle was not a first-hand witness to this, acquiring much of his information from discussions he had with Europe a few years later. His story, however, is consistent both with Cook's well-known behavior and was also one "often told around the circles of the boys who took part in that concert."

58. See Fletcher, *100 Years of the Negro in Show Business*, 258.

59. Ibid.

60. The New York *Evening Journal*, May 1, 1912, 24, and quoted in Adams, "The Negro Music School Settlement," 163, and Martin, *The Damrosch Dynasty*, 212. The author of the editorial, as Martin says, "reads very much like the kind of statement the school's board constantly published about its aims."

61. Mannes described the hall as "packed from the floor to the roof, thousands being turned away for lack of even standing room." See *Music is My Faith*, 218.

62. Adams, "The Negro Music School Settlement," 163, and Fletcher, *100 Years of the Negro in Show Business*, 259. The "Clef Club March," Adams recalled in 1915, is the one "so well known to every Hampton student, and the refrain of which has been adopted by the boys of Andover Academy in Massachusetts as one of their marching songs."

63. Johnson, *Black Manhattan*, 123–24.

64. The program for the first "Concert of Negro Music," May 2, 1912, at Carnegie Hall is:

PART ONE

1. "The Clef Club March" . . . . Europe
   The Clef Club Orchestra
2. "Lit'l Gal" . . . . J. Rosamond Johnson, words by Paul Laurence Dunbar
   Sung and played by the composer
3. a) "Dance of the Marionettes" . . . . Woolford
   b) "You're Sweet to Your Mammy Just the Same" . . . . Johnson
   The Versatile Entertainers Quintette
4. a) "Tout a Vous" . . . . Tyers
   b) "Panama—Characteristic dance" . . . . Tyers
   Orchestra conducted by the composer
5. a) "Jean" . . . . Burleigh
   b) "Mon Coeur s'Ouvre ta Voix" from *Samson and Delilah* . . . . Saint-Saens
   (a last minute substitution for Stephen Foster's "Old Folks at Home")
   Miss Elizabeth Payne, Contralto
6. "Benedictus" . . . . Bohlen

Choir of St. Phillip's Church
Paul C. Bohlen, Organist
PART TWO
7. "Swing Along" .... Cook
   Clef Club Chorus
8. "Danse Heroique" .... Johnson
   Piano solo by the composer
9. a) "Hula—Hawaiian Dance" .... Europe
   b) "On Bended Knee" .... Burleigh
      Clef Club Orchestra
10. "By the Waters of Babylon" .... Coleridge-Taylor
    Choir of St Phillip's Church
11. a) "Dearest Memories"
    b) "The Belle of the Lighthouse"
    c) "Take Me Back to Dear Old Dixie"
    d) "Old Black Joe"
       The Royal Poinciana Quartette
12. "The Rain Song" .... Cook, words by Alex Rogers
    Clef Club Chorus and Deacon Johnson's
    Martinique Quartette
13. a) "Lorraine Waltzes" .... Europe
    b) "Strength of the Nation," dedicated to the proposed Colored
       Regiment .... Europe
       Clef Club Orchestra

65. Walton, "Music and the Stage," The *New York Age*, May 9, 1912, 6, and reprinted in "Black-Music Concerts in Carnegie Hall, 1912–1915," 74–76.

66. Curtis-Burlin, "Black Singers and Players," 502–4.

67. Mannes, *Music is My Faith*, 218.

68. Ibid., and Curtis-Burlin, "Black Singers and Players," 503.

69. Curtis-Burlin, "Black Singers and Players," 503.

70. "Negro Talent Revealed: New York Concertgoers Treated to Novel Entertainment," *Musical America*, May 11, 1912, 19, and reprinted in "Black-Music Concerts in Carnegie Hall, 1912–1915," 77. As long as the selections were "in their native vein," the reviewer stated, "much success was attained, but when one of singers essayed to sing an aria from Saint-Saens's 'Samson et Dalila,' of which she had not the slightest conception, and of which her accompanist knew even less, an emphatic mistake of judgment was shown." It should be noted, however, that Lester Walton also thought Ms. Payne's treatment of "Mon Coeur s'Ouvre ta Voix" was not particularly well done.

71. See Sissle, "Memoirs," 22. Sissle wrote that Europe introduced Cook, and also turned the baton over to him to conduct his compositions. Europe, a generous man, had made a practice of having black composers conduct their own works, so the story is consistent.

72. Fletcher, *100 Years of the Negro in Show Business*, 260. Neither Fletcher, who was present, nor Eubie Blake, who was not (but who, like Sissle, became a close associate of Jim Europe's in later years) could corroborate Sissle's contention that Cook actually conducted the orchestra that night. For Blake's version, see Al Rose, *Eubie Blake* (New York: Schirmer Books, 1979), 43.

73. *The Crisis* 2(June, 1912): 66–67. William Tyers, the Clef Club Orchestra's As-

sistant Conductor, was also named as one of the "Men of the Month." "Fully to appreciate the worth of James Reese Europe to the Negro musicians of New York City," the article said, "one would have to know how the Negro entertainers in cafes, hotels, at banquets, etc. were regarded before the organization of the Clef Club, and how they have been regarded since. Before, they were prey to scheming head waiters and booking agents, now they are performers whose salaries and hours are fixed by contract."

74. See Sissle, "Memoirs," 24, and Fletcher, *100 Years of the Negro in Show Business*, 260.

75. Lester Walton, "Clef Club Plans to Build," The *New York Age*, February 20, 1912, 6.

76. Fletcher, *100 Years of the Negro in Show Business*, p. 260, and Mannes, *Music is My Faith*, 219.

77. Johnson, *Black Manhattan*, 123.

78. Fletcher, *100 Years of the Negro in Show Business*, 261.

Chapter Six: "What It Takes to Make Me Love You—You've Got It"

1. McGinty, "Gifted Minds and Pure Hearts," 268. Mary Europe had hoped to attend Oberlin University after graduating from Minor Normal School in 1902 (a copy of the application, signed by Mrs. Anna Cooper of M Street High School, is in the possession of Mrs. Lorraine Johnson of Washington, D.C.). She did enroll in Howard University but—probably for financial reasons—left after a year. Later, she did continue her education at Columbia University, attending summer programs from 1913 to 1919. She received the A.B. from Howard in 1922.

2. The *Philadelphia Tribune* of January 18, 1913, reported that the couple was married by Reverend Hutchins C. Bishop, Rector of St. Phillips P. E. Church, the bride being given in marriage by her brother, Thomas Angrom, and that a reception followed the ceremony "which was attended by a few relatives and friends."

3. Ibid. The *Tribune*, which carried the only known announcement, described her as "one of New York's most charming widows." Her death certificate indicates that she was born on February 25, 1877, to George and Georgia Coffey Angrom, and that she died on May 20, 1930. She is buried in Woodlawn Cemetery in New York.

4. The *Freeman* regularly carried short, anecdotal "notes" from the various touring companies. Between February and May 1908, Bessie Simms is mentioned six or eight different times, not a great deal, perhaps, but enough to convey a sense of her charm and liveliness. After reporting on an enjoyable party given for the company in St. Louis, and listing Ms. Simms as one of those in attendance, for example, the writer quipped that "Miss Bessie Simms, the girl with wavy hair, expects a great big time in Cleveland, Ohio." See "Notes from Cole and Johnson's Shoo-Fly Regiment," in the Indianapolis *Freeman*, February 29, 1908, 5. In reporting on Cleveland's Smart Society Ball, held while *The Shoo-Fly Regiment* was in town, the *Freeman* (March 28, 1908, 5) reporter wrote: "Well, Daisy Brown, Oriena Howard, [and] Bessie Simms certainly did look sweet at that ball." "For the last couple of months Miss Bessie Simms of the Shoo-Fly Regiment has been carrying a cold with her every place she went," began a longer piece in the February 15 edition (Charles D. Marshall, "Before the Stage Mirror," 5).

A day or so ago while at St. Louis, Miss Simms got up early, as she does not always do, and went to a nearby drug store. She admitted she felt a little cross that morning, being burdened with such a heavy cold. "Give me a dime's worth of two-grain quinine capsules, quick," she said hoarsely to a very polite drug clerk. "Will you have them wrapped up?," he asked. "No," she said, as she snatched them from his hands. "I want them rolled over to my rooms."

The following March 14 *Freeman* reported that "Bessie Simms is well and doing well, thank you. With best wishes to New York town," and on May 23, 1908, 5, the *Freeman* reported on the closing of *The Shoo-Fly Regiment* that "Bessie Sims [*sic*] will spend a few weeks in Baltimore this summer. I guess it will be a few at that. Baltimore doesn't look like New York to Bessie."

5. See "Sylvester Russell's Tenth Annual Review," in the Indianapolis *Freeman*, December 25, 1909, 14.

6. No marriage certificate has as yet been located.

7. The Simms–Europe relationship had some serious ups and downs, if the Indianapolis *Freeman* is to be believed. Sylvester Russell's "Musical and Dramatic" column of February 3, 1912, 5, a year before Europe's marriage to Willie Angrom, carried the sensational news that "James Reese Europe, the well-known composer and leader, is reported to have been shot by Bessie Sims [*sic*], an actress, in New York, and is said to be in a serious condition." No corroboration for this incident has been discovered, and it may simply be a rumor without factual basis. Such things occasionally happened. The *Age* of February 20, 1912 (p. 6), which carried a story about the Clef Club and included a picture of Europe, makes no mention of a shooting or any injury suffered by the club's president. Europe's friend, dramatic and music editor, Lester Walton, of course, may have simply not wished to print the story.

8. There were numerous concerts, in addition to that of the Clef Club, of various sizes, held all across the nation in honor of the anniversary. See Joshua Berrett, "The Golden Anniversary of the Emancipation Proclamation," *The Black Perspective in Music* 16 (Spring 1988): 67–69.

9. See the reviews of the concert by Lucien H. White, "Concert at Carnegie Hall," in the *New York Age*, February 20, 1913, 6, and reprinted in "Black-Music Concerts in Carnegie Hall, 1912–1915," 77–79, and "The Negro in New York: Concert of Negro Music Given at Carnegie Hall," in the Indianapolis *Freeman*, March 1, 1913, 2.

10. Moton's address is printed in full in "Concert at Carnegie Hall," the *New York Age*, February 20, 1913, 6.

11. See the Indianapolis *Freeman*, March 1, 1913, 2.

12. "Concert at Carnegie Hall," the *New York Age*, February 20, 1913, 6.

13. See "Emancipation Concert," in *Musical America*, 22 February 1913, 10.

14. See "Legitimizing the Music of the Negro," *Current Opinion* 13 (May 1913): 384–85. Under the picture of the full orchestra, the New York *Press* is paraphrased as saying that they play with "extraordinary rhythmical precision and contagious swing" and that they sing in "robust harmony." "The Clef Club," it concludes, "has been called the American Balalaika."

15. Krehbiel, who heard the first northern concert of the Fisk Jubilee Singers nearly a half-century earlier, was concerned that more recent performances of their songs, even by such technically excellent groups as the Hampton Quartet, had also "overlooked the same intervallic element in so familiar a song as 'Roll, Jordan, Roll,' and that they [such groups] robbed other songs of their charm by harmonic sophistication." Quoted in "Legitimizing the Music of the Negro," 384. Krehbiel's observation of the dropping of the flatted seventh in modern performances by highly trained black choral groups is particularly interesting because the interval is (along with the flatted third) a

defining feature of the blues scale, and these notes are generally called "blue notes." Europe read Krehbiel's book and was influenced by his emphasis upon authenticity. Europe was also the first band leader to perform W. C. Handy's "Memphis Blues," published just a few months earlier.

16. Natalie Curtis, "The Negro's Contribution to the Music of America," in *The Craftsman* (February 1913), and quoted in "Legitimizing the Music of the Negro," 385.

17. A program/schedule of events and activities for the Exposition is reprinted in Berrett, "The Golden Anniversary of the Emancipation Proclamation," 76–77.

18. Ibid., 78.

19. "The Clef Club Galaxy of Stars," in the *Afro-American Ledger*, November 1, 1913, and quoted in Berrett, "The Golden Anniversary of the Emancipation Proclamation," 69. See "The Clef Club," in the Washington *Bee*, October 25, 1913, 5, for a listing of the names and instruments of the musicians, among whom are John Europe, Tim Brymn, Will Dixon, Al Johns, Clarence Williams, David Irwin Martin, E. E. Thompson, and C. Arthur Rhone.

20. "The Clef Club," in the Washington *Bee*, October 25, 1913, 5.

21. See Berrett, "The Golden Anniversary of the Emancipation Proclamation," 69.

22. The complete program was published in the *Philadelphia Tribune*'s review of the concert at the Academy of Music on November 4. See "Clef Club Orchestra Renders an Inspiring Program," the *Philadelphia Tribune*, November 8, 1913.

23. Europe, apparently against the advice of some friends in Philadelphia, scheduled the concert for the same week at the Academy of Music as a popular black musical production was being promoted. Publicity for the New Yorkers' concert suffered, and so did the size of their audience. The relevant correspondence between Europe and G. Grant Williams of the *Philadelphia Tribune* concerning the difficulty was later published, with apologies to the Clef Club. See "The Clef Club vs. The Ambassador," in the *Philadelphia Tribune*, November 22, 1913.

24. Quoted in "Clef Club Tonight," in the *New York Age*, November 13, 1913, 6.

25. See the Indianapolis *Freeman*, November 1, 1913, 2.

26. "Famous Clef Club Gives Concert," in the Indianapolis *Freeman*, November 22, 1913, 1. Europe made one slight concession to Washington's musical taste in the orchestra's program; he added a violin/cello duet by the conservatory-trained Felix Weir and Leonard Jeter.

27. See "Clef Club Tonight," in the *New York Age*, November 13, 1913, 6.

28. See "The Clef Club Concert," in the *New York Age*, November 20, 1913, 6. White's review is also quoted by Charters and Kunstadt in *Jazz: A History of the New York Scene*, 32.

29. Dissention was apparent at least as early as the spring of 1912, when Lester Walton, in the pages of the *Age*, reminded the club members that their current success was due to "the willingness of each and every member to work in harmony and to hold in high esteem the heads of the organization." Furthermore, he warned them, the only way to continue to develop was by hard work, cooperation, and "by showing marked respect for superior officers." See the *New York Age*, May 30, 1912, 6. Gene Fernett, in *Swing Out: Great Negro Dance Bands* (Midland, Mich.: Pendell Publishing Company, 1970), 19, claims that some of the Clef Club members were so envious of Europe's personal success "that they more than hinted that he was using the Clef Club telephone as a booking office exclusively for Jim Europe—not for colored musicians in general." Fernett, however, offers no documentation.

30. The *New York Age* reported on January 1, 1914, 6, without explanation, that

Europe had tendered his resignation "several days ago" and that Daniel Kildare had been elected the new president of the organization. The *Age* did remark, however, that "much of the Clef Club's success has been in a large measure due to the activities of Mr. Europe." The Tempo Club was officially formed on January 4, 1914. "According to the leaders of this new movement," reported the New York *News* of April 9, 1914, "Europe aims to keep the colored musical world up to a certain standard morally, socially, and artistically."

31. Lucien White was particularly admiring of Europe's skills as a conductor, and he often noted them. See, for instance, his review of the May 8 Manhattan Casino concert of the Clef Club in the *New York Age*, May 15, 1913, 6.

Chapter Seven: "Castle House Rag"

1. The story of the Castles is recounted in Mrs. Irene Castle, *My Husband* (1919; reprint, New York: DaCapo Press, 1979), and Irene Castle (as told to Bob and Wanda Duncan), *Castles in the Air* (1958; reprint, New York: DaCapo Press, 1980), with a foreword by Ginger Rogers. See, also, the extensive collection of newspaper and magazine clippings in the Vernon and Irene Castle scrapbooks, Robinson Locke Collection, in the Billy Rose Theater Collection at the New York Public Library. In addition, there are two semi-biographical feature-length films. *The Whirl of Life* (1915) is a melodrama written by Vernon in which Vernon and Irene Castle play themselves. The only known original copy of the silent film is in the Museum of Modern Art in New York. The second is the RKO movie *The Story of Vernon and Irene Castle* (1939), a romantic musical starring Fred Astaire and Ginger Rogers as Vernon and Irene Castle. The principal value of both films is the documentation of the Castle's dances and their wardrobes. In the earlier film, Jim Europe appears on screen on several occasions conducting the Castle's orchestra, but in order "to satisfy southern exhibitors" of the 1939 musical neither he nor any other African-American is represented; even the role of Walter Ash, the Foote's black valet, is played by a white actor—Walter Brennan. See *Castle's in the Air*, 247.

2. Among those traveling from England to the United States with the Blyths and Grossmiths was the young American composer, Jerome Kern.

3. Irene Foote came to her unconventional nature honestly enough; her mother was the first woman to make a balloon ascension in the United States (and once shot a gardener for cursing her when she dismissed him), and her father had been expelled from Cornell for blasting the chemistry building with an old Civil War cannon. See Irene Castle, *Castles in the Air*, 9–11.

4. Douglas Gilbert, *Lost Chords: The Diverting Story of American Popular Songs* (New York: Doubleday, 1942), 345.

5. Castle, *My Husband*, 21.

6. Ibid., 38.

7. *Castles in the Air*, 56–57.

8. Vernon Castle, "How the Castles Began to Dance," in the Philadelphia *Ledger*, undated clipping, Castle Scrapbooks, Billy Rose Theater Collection, New York Public Library.

9. See Charles Hamm, *Yesterdays: Popular Song in America* (New York: W. W. Norton, 1979), 379.

10. Clipping from an unknown Toronto, Canada, newspaper dated May 30, 1914, 93, in the Castle scrapbooks.

11. "Perhaps it was the informality of our first cabaret performance, perhaps it was because the audience thought that we were guests, perhaps because we were new at the game; in any event, our little dance was much applauded," was how Irene explained the response to their first night at the Café de Paris. See *My Husband*, 38. As their reputation grew and their financial situation improved, Irene might have been expected to wear more elaborate costumes and expensive jewelry. Instead, and wisely, she decided to keep herself "demure and simple, unadorned with jewelry." *Castles in the Air*, 58.

12. De Wolfe first created a stir at the turn-of-the-century by the very un-Victorian manner in which she decorated the small house she shared with Elisabeth Marbury on Irving Place. "Her 'white decor,' so named because of her penchant for enamelling dark Victorian furniture white, her use of simple, striped wallpapers, her banishment of bric-a-brac, all led," according to David Lowe, "to bright, well-composed interiors that were a breath of fresh air in gloomy brownstone Gotham." See his *Chicago Interiors: Views of a Splendid World* (Chicago: Contemporary Books, Inc., 1979), xxi.

13. Elisabeth Marbury died in January 1933 at the age of seventy-six. Her obituary, carried in the New York *Herald Tribune* of January 25, 1933 (a copy of which is in the Billy Rose Theater Collection, New York Public Library), describes her villa at Versailles, which she shared with Elsie de Wolfe and Anne Morgan (J. P. Morgan, Sr.'s, daughter), as a "headquarters for literary and diplomatic celebrities in the era preceding the war."

14. See the article by Vance Thompson in the *New York Sun*, April 26, 1914, 3, a copy of which can be found in the Castle Scrapbooks, the Billy Rose Theater Collection, New York Public Library.

15. "After that," she later wrote, "we always felt like Pavlova, who, when she was asked to dance at a fashionable party, gave her price as fifteen hundred dollars. 'Of course, my dear,' the hostess hinted subtly, 'you won't be required to meet the guests.' 'In that case,' Pavolva said, 'my price will only be a thousand.'" See *Castles in the Air*, 72.

16. *Castles in the Air*, 79. In 1919, Irene Castle described the origin of the Castle Walk as nearly accidental. "More as a rest than anything else, we fell into a reverse of the usual proceeding," she wrote. "In all dances the weight is thrown down on the foot. For a change we threw the weight up. It is difficult to describe, but easy to do." "It wasn't very graceful to be sure, but it did provide a variation and a great deal of amusement." See *My Husband*, 54.

17. *Castles in the Air*, 78. One of those who remembered the Castle's "stiff-legged walk" in the *Sunshine Girl* was F. Scott Fitzgerald. It was a walk, he wrote, "that gave the modern dance a social position and brought the nice girl into the cafe, thus beginning a profound revolution in American life." "The Perfect Life," in *The Basil and Josephine Stories* (1928), 158–59, and quoted in Erenberg, *Steppin' Out*, 146.

18. Irene made her own conquests, including Anastasia's nephew, Grand Duke Dmitri. See *Castles in the Air*, 81–83. Palmer was owner of the famous Palmer House hotel in Chicago. His wife, Bertha Honoré Palmer, had been a figure of national importance since the World's Columbian Exposition of 1893, where she played a highly visible and influential role as president of the board of lady managers.

19. See Erenberg, *Steppin' Out*, 147. By February 1912, *Life* magazine estimated that the "dancing set" in New York was "at least half a million strong." Quoted in Mark Sullivan, *The War Begins*, vol. 4 of *Our Times, 1900–1925* (New York: Charles Scribner's Sons, 1932), 255–56.

20. Quoted in Roland Gelatt, *The Fabulous Phonograph: From Edison to Stereo* (New York: Appleton-Century, 1954), vol. 2, 188.

21. Quoted in Sullivan, *The War Begins*, 223.

22. The anti–dance hall and antiragtime sentiment of the time was interrelated with the larger progressive social reform movement. This broader, national movement included the antisaloon and prohibitionist campaigns that succeeded in first segregating and then closing down the red-light districts of New Orleans (Storyville in 1916) and San Francisco (the Barbary Coast in 1913), and led also to the licensing of dance halls and cabaret performers in New York and elsewhere.

23. Quoted in Sullivan, *The War Begins*, 250–51.

24. Ibid., 254. Additional useful accounts of the ragtime controversy can be found in Erenberg, *Steppin' Out*, Irene Castle, *Castles in the Air*, and Ian Whitcomb, *After the Ball: Pop Music from Rag to Rock* (New York: Simon and Schuster, 1972).

25. Vernon had established a reputation as a dancing instructor before the couple left for Europe in 1913. The *Atlanta Journal* of March 16 called him not only the most popular of the cabaret dancers, but also "the most sought after dancing teacher in America." Quoted in Erenberg, *Steppin' Out*, 173.

26. *Castles in the Air*, 86.

27. See Gilbert, *Lost Chords*, 347.

28. Ibid., 349.

29. The program included familiar numbers by the Clef Club Orchestra ("Swing Along," "Exhortation," and "Deep River," among them), as well as several popular songs by Clef Club singers, but new pieces like Gus Edward's "English Rag," and Tim Brymn's "La Rumba" (conducted by the composer) were also introduced. See Lucien H. White, "The Clef Club Concert," in the *New York Age*, May 15, 1913, 6. As far as the orchestra's performance was concerned, White was especially taken by Europe's addition of a brass section, which he used for the first time for the final selection, the "Clef Club Chant."

30. See Marshall and Jean Stearns, *Jazz Dance*, 128–29, and Erenberg, *Steppin' Out*, 151. For a discussion of "Darktown Follies," see Riis, *Just Before Jazz*, 173–82.

31. Quoted in Stearns, *Jazz Dance*, 129.

32. Stearns, *Jazz Dance*, 129. This would seem both to establish the Texas tommy as the predecessor of the Lindy hop and the jitterbug, and also create an unmistakable, and perhaps significant, parallel to the instrumental solo "break" that became such a common feature of later jazz performances.

33. Arlene Croce, *The Fred Astaire and Ginger Rogers Book* (New York: Vintage, 1972), 159. In making the film, although he and Rogers had a copy of the Castle's *Whirl of Life* (1915), Astaire could draw upon his own memory in recreating the Castle dances. When he was fourteen he saw the Castles in *The Sunshine Girl* nine times.

34. See Lester Walton, "Monster Show Planned," in the *New York Age*, July 24, 1913, 6.

35. "Historic Pilgrimage," in the *New York Age*, August 7, 1913, 6.

36. See Lester Walton, "An Unusual Bill," in the *New York Age*, August 14, 1913, 6.

37. See "Theatrical Jottings," in the *New York Age*, August 28, 6, which reported that

James Reese Europe and his band finished a successful engagement at Newport, R.I. last week. With the band were James Reese Europe, George Watters, William Parquette [banjoline], Lawrence Morris [cello], Tracy Cooper, George Smith, George DeLeon, Cricket Smith, Chandler Ford, and Dennis Johnson.

"Mrs. Europe spent the week with her husband," the article added.

38. Charters, *Nobody*, 125. Despite the Jim Crow, the Richmond audience, according to Charters, numbered some 3,000 people.

39. See "Musicians Play for 400, " in the *New York Age*, September 4, 1913, 6.

40. Castle, *Castles in the Air*, 88, and also quoted by Erenburg, *Steppin' Out*, 160.

41. See "Women of Society to Open Dancing Academy," in the *New York Herald*, December 6, 1913, and "Castle House Backed by Group of Smart NY Women," un-identified clipping in Castle Scrapbooks, Billy Rose Theatre Collection, New York Public Library. The *Herald* article also reported that while the women are financing Castle House, they have no desire to profit from it, and indeed are "willing to operate it at a small loss." No alcohol would be served, either.

42. "Castle House Memories," unidentified New York newspaper, date unknown (probably April 1939) in the Castle Clipping File, Museum of the City of New York.

43. "Castle House Memories," says simply that "Jim Europe, the Paul Whiteman of his day, provided music with his Negro orchestra." Twenty years later when she wrote *Castles in the Air*, her memory of Europe, his music, and their importance to her and Vernon had faded considerably. In 1958 she wrote merely that the two rooms of Castle House "would hold a colored band for jazz enthusiasts and a string orchestra for the tango and maxixe." See *Castles in the Air*, 88.

44. Ibid.

45. Unidentified Worcester *Telegram* clipping (from the early spring of 1914) in the Castle Scrapbooks, Billy Rose Theater Collection, New York Public Library.

46. *Castles in the Air*, 92.

47. Ibid.

48. Europe and the Castles had been working together barely a month before Vernon was taking drum lessons from Buddy Gilmore, the Society Orchestra's principal drummer. Vernon took up the drums about the time Sans Souci opened and "Buddie [Gilmore], the drummer in our orchestra, trained him so well," Irene later claimed, "that by the following winter his drumming was as good as that of most professionals, but with a personality and character that most of them lacked." See *My Husband*, 58. There is no question about Vernon's attraction to the drums once he had heard Gilmore. He insisted on playing them in the 1914 musical *Watch Your Step*, and he kept a set with him in England and in France after he joined the Royal Air Force. "I simply love to play the drums," he wrote his wife from camp. See *My Husband*, 60.

49. Gilbert, *Lost Chords*, 349.

50. Castle, *Castles in the Air*, 92.

51. This interpretation is in substantial agreement with Charters and Kunstadt, *Jazz: A History of the New York Scene*, 32–33.

52. See the *New York Age*, January 1, 1914, 6. Europe did not completely sever his relationship with the organization, however, or with his many long-term friends among its membership, and he remained a "financial member" of the Clef Club throughout his life. See, for example, the *New York Age*, March 2, 1918, 6.

53. The announcement of the ball was carried on the front page of the *Age* on January 1, 8, and 15, and the review of the affair ("Brilliant Gathering at Fourth Charity Ball," the *New York Age*, January 29, 1914, 1) reported that over 1,000 people attended and that Mrs. Vanderbilt was among those purchasing tickets.

54. See the New York *News*, April 9, 1914.

55. The Victor Talking Machine Company had produced a fairly substantial catalog of dance records, made by its studio band primarily, that included recordings of compositions by Europe's associates William Tyers ("Maori—Tango") and Luckey Roberts ("Junk Man Rag") among others. In late 1913 they contracted the Castles for their endorsement (as "supervisors of their dance records") and at the same time received "the exclusive services of the Castle House orchestra." See the ad for Victor Dance Records from early 1914

that is reproduced in Irene Castle, *My Husband*, supplemental illustrations.

56. See Lester Walton's column in the *New York Age*, January 15, 1914, 6.

57. The *New York Age*, January 15, 1914, 6, and the Indianapolis *Freeman*, January 24, 1914, 6. Also see the January 16 and 23 issues of *Variety* magazine, which covered the story. Copies of these articles can be found in the Robinson Locke Scrapbooks, Billy Rose Theater Collection, New York Public Library. The orchestra that Europe used at the Palace and at the Victoria was composed of four violins (William Tyler, Alfred [Allie] Ross, Tracy Cooper, and James Van Hooten), a single cello (Leonard Jeter), bass (George Heyward), baritone (George De Leon), clarinet (John G. Russell), flute (Fred Covite), trombone (William Fairfax), and drums (George Jenkins).

58. See the informative liner notes by Thornton Hagert for *Come and Trip It: Instrumental Dance Music 1780s–1920s*, New World 293, in *The Recorded Anthology of American Music* (New York: New World Records, 1978), 1–4.

59. Gunther Schuller, *Early Jazz: Its Roots and Musical Development* (New York: Oxford University Press, 1968), 248.

60. A reissue of the Brown Brothers' recording of "Down Home Rag" can be heard on *Steppin' on the Gas*, New World 269, in *The Recorded Anthology of American Music* (New York: New World Records, 1976).

61. Alec Wilder, in *American Popular Song: The Great Innovators, 1900–1950* (New York: Oxford University Press, 1972), says that if the piece were printed today, it would carry 4/4, rather than 2/4, time signature (p. 36). Peter Clayton, writing in the London *Sunday Telegraph* of August 7, 1983, claims that Kern "wrote the melody at ten one morning, and by the same afternoon, Feb. 2, 1914, the complete duet was being performed on stage. On the tenth, Jim Europe's Orchestra was in the studio setting down its version for a quick sale." See "The Riches of Ragtime," reprinted in *Ragtimer* (September–October 1983), 13. "You're Here and I'm Here" also caught the attention of another young songwriter, sixteen-year-old George Gershwin, who found the "tune so exciting in its melodic and harmonic construction," when he heard it in *The Girl from Utah*, according to David Ewen, "that he rushed to the bandstand to inquire after its title and composer." See *A Journey to Greatness: The Life and Music of George Gershwin* (New York: Henry Holt and Co., 1956), 57.

62. See Gushee's excellent liner notes to *Steppin' on the Gas: Rags to Jazz*, New World 269, 3.

63. Charles Hamm calls the last measures of the piece the "first time that music so dominated by percussion had been captured on a phonograph record." See his *Music in the New World*, 402.

64. Gushee, *Steppin' on the Gas*, 3.

65. *Castles in the Air*, 114–15.

66. See Irene Castle McLaughlin, "Jim Europe—A Reminiscence," *Opportunity*, March 1930, 91.

Chapter Eight: "The National Negro March"

1. Lester Walton, in the *New York Age* of January 1, 1914, announced the intention of Cook (and Burleigh) to put together a Negro Choral Society of Greater New York, much like the one that had been in existence in Washington, D.C., for a number of years. Walton quotes Cook in appealing for greater support from the general black population for the development of an African-American music other than "ragtime or primitive spirituals." See "Negro Music," in the *New York Age*, January 1, 1914, 6.

2. See "Negroes Give a Concert," in the *New York Times*, March 12, 1914, 3, and reprinted in "In Retrospect: Black-Music Concerts in Carnegie Hall, 1912–1915," 80–81.

3. W.E.B. Du Bois referred to the "sorrow songs" extensively in *The Souls of Black Folk* (1903; reprint New York: New American Library, Inc., 1969). Krehbiel's *Afro-American Folksongs* (New York: G. Schirmer, Inc., 1913) was one of the earliest attempts to analyze the strictly musical characteristics of African-American folk music. It had reached its fourth edition by 1914. Krehbiel, music editor of the *New York Tribune*, was the author of numerous books on classical music and opera and an occasional lecturer at the Music School Settlement for Negroes.

4. "Negroes Perform their own Music," in *Musical America*, March 21, 1914, 37, and reprinted in "In Retrospect: Black-Music Concerts in Carnegie Hall, 1912–1915," 81–82. If *Musical America* was critical of what the National Negro Orchestra played, because it was not African-American enough, others, including Elbridge Adams of the Music School thought that the use of conventional European orchestral instruments made the sound less African-American. He wrote:

> The experiment, while interesting and furnishing evidence of the Negro's ability to play instruments of the violin family, particularly the 'cello, was not, on the whole, a success. It was the opinion of pretty nearly everyone who had heard the orchestra play in former years, that Negro music is best interpreted by instruments played with a plectrum, supplemented by instruments of percussion, including always the "ten pianos."

See "The Negro Music School Settlement," 163–64.

5. See "Tango Breaks in the Field of Classic Music," in the *New York Herald*, March 15, 1914, in the Robinson Locke Scrapbooks, Billy Rose Theater Collection, New York Public Library.

6. Cook had appealed for a greater race consciousness among black people and a greater appreciation for the "great beauty of its own legends, stories and melodies" from which could come a "school of Negro writers and composers who will build from these simple stories and themes imperishable works of art." He also argued, however, that black choral societies should study "the works of the masters, for we can only learn to understand and render what is good of our own by studying and rendering the best of the masters." See Cook's interview with Lester Walton, "Negro Music," in the *New York Age*, January 1, 1914, 6, and reprinted in "Black-Music Concerts in Carnegie Hall, 1912–1915," 79–80.

7. See "The Negro's Place in Music, " the New York *Evening Post*, March 13, 1914, 7, and reprinted in Robert Kimball and William Bolcom, *Reminiscing with Sissle and Blake* (New York: Viking, 1973), 60–61.

8. See his "James Reese Europe and the Infancy of Jazz Criticism," in *Black Music Research Journal*, 7 (1987), 35–44.

9. See "The Black-American Composer and the Orchestra in the Twentieth Century", in *The Black Perspective in Music*, 14 (Winter 1986): 26–34.

10. "The Black-American Composer," 29.

11. *The Souls of Black Folk*, 45.

12. Ibid., 265.

13. *Afro-American Folksongs*, 27.

14. Wilson, "The Black-American Composer," 28. This was well understood at the time, and it is why the symphonic orchestra (and the compositions written for it) were regarded, and are still regarded, as the supreme musical expressions of any civilization.

15. According to the article, plans were already in place to secure four horn players from Honduras and two from West Africa. See "Philanthropists to Back Assembly of Big Orchestra," in the New York *News*, March 26, 1914.

16. See the New York *News*, April 9, 1914.

17. The *New York Age*, March 26, 1914, 6. Miss Wilson was apparently pleased with Europe's music; at her wedding on May 7, she had the Marine Corps Band play "The Nell Rose Waltz," a piece he had composed for her. The story was carried in the New York *Evening Sun*. See "The Woman Who Saw" gossip column, date (late spring of 1914) and page unknown, in the Castle Scrapbooks, Billy Rose Theater Collection, New York Public Library. "Later," the columnist wrote, "she [the president's daughter] sent him a handwritten note of thanks which Mr. Europe shows only to the fortunate few, one of whom is the Woman Who Saw."

18. The Boston concert was sponsored by the Harmony Club, a leading black musical organization in the city. Lester Walton's brief review of the concert appears in "An Evening in Boston," *New York Age*, April 9, 1914, 6.

19. In the three months following the defection of its former leader, the Clef Club had chosen new officers, held an organizational dinner meeting at Reisenweber's Cafe, and published an announcement disassociating themselves with Europe's March 11 Carnegie Hall Concert. Otherwise, the papers had little to report about the club's current or future activities. See the *New York Age*, February 19, 1914, 1, and March 5, 1914, 1.

20. It may be significant that the *Age*'s report of the Tempo Club entertainment appeared on the front page, a place reserved for general news, rather than on the music and entertainment page. Perhaps it was thought to be of more than entertainment interest that a celebrated white couple should appear at an entertainment primarily for blacks. Perhaps it reflects the ambivalence of the *Age*'s music editor, Lester Walton, a long-time friend of Europe's, but a loyal supporter of the Clef Club, toward the Tempo Club–Clef Club split. Or, perhaps it reflects a combination of the two. In any case, see "Mr. and Mrs. Castle to Dance at Benefit" and the Tempo Club ad, in the *New York Age*, March 19, 1914, 1.

21. See "Race is Dancing Itself to Death," in the *New York Age*, January 8, 1914, 1.

22. A copy of the "Castle House Program" can be found in the Castle Scrapbooks, Billy Rose Theater Collection, New York Public Library. It is quoted from in Erenberg, *Steppin' Out*, 160–61. The description of public dance halls is drawn from "TANGO is Condemned in City Club Report," an unidentified news article that contains excerpts from a report of the City Club Committee on Public Amusements and Morals, in the Castle Scrapbooks, Billy Rose Theater Collection, New York Public Library.

23. For the Yale story, see an unidentified *New York Tribune* article, dateline January 31, 1914, in the Castle Scrapbooks, Billy Rose Theater Collection, New York Public Library. The description of the Castle Walk appears in "TANGO is Condemned in City Club Report."

24. Unidentified article from the Worchester *Telegram*, in the Castle Scrapbooks, Billy Rose Collection, New York Public Library. Social dancing was not the only area that Marbury saw in need of improvement. The following year she convinced F. Ray Comstock, the owner of the small Princess Theater, that the time was right "to do something about elevating musical comedy" by putting on a series of low-budget shows that emphasized coherent texts, good music, and good performances and dispensed with much of the usual extravagant Broadway nonsense. Possessing a sharp eye for talent as well as business, she was responsible for bringing Jerome Kern and Guy Bolton together (and later P. G. Woodhouse) to create a series of successful Princess Theater productions that in-

cluded *Nobody Home* (1915), *Very Good Eddie* (1915), and *Oh Boy!* (1917). The influence of the "Princess Theater Show," according to David Ewen, was "decisive and permanent . . . a pronounced step forward from the musical comedies of George M. Cohan." See Ewen, *The Story of America's Musical Theater* (Philadelphia: Chilton, 1961), 82–83. Elisabeth Marbury's role in American musical theater did not end here; in 1916 she also produced *America First*, the first musical comedy written by Cole Porter.

25. The Castle's reliance on Bessie Marbury was well known in New York. "The Castles have never made a move" without consulting her, reported the New York *Star* of May 23, 1914, for example (clipping in the Robinson Locke Collection, Billy Rose Theater Collection, New York Public Library). In the "Foreword" to their book *Modern Dancing* (1914; reprint, New York: DaCapo, 1980), 17, the Castles, in a very Marbury-like manner, explained their objectives:

> Our aim is to uplift dancing, purify it, and place it before the public in its proper light. When this has been done, we feel convinced that no objection can possibly be urged against it on the grounds of impropriety, but rather that social reformers will join with the medical profession in the view that dancing is not only a rejuvenator of good health and spirits, but a means of preserving youth, prolonging life, and acquiring grace, elegance, and beauty.

When it finally opened the following year, *Whirl of Life*—the Castle's motion picture—did very well, at least according to *Variety* (November 26, 1915, p. 26), which reported that the police had to be called out to control the crowds in Philadelphia.

26. Unidentified article in the Worcester *Telegram* in the Castle Scrapbooks, Billy Rose Theater Collection, New York Public Library. Another less idealistic incentive was that Arthur Hopkins guaranteed the Castles a small fortune for doing the tour.

27. See the *New York Age*, March 26 and April 2, 1914, 1.

28. The New York *News*, who sent its society editor to cover the event, listed many of the notables of both races who occupied the boxes, including W.E.B. Du Bois, Joseph Stern, Natalie Curtis, Aida Overton Walker, and Will Marion Cook. See "Tempo Club Gives Classic Dansant Before Big Throng," the New York *News*, April 13, 1914.

29. The full program for the concert is as follows:

1. "The Tempo Club March"/"La Mariposa"—Tyers
2. Original songs by Smith and Burris
3. "Sari—Waltz"—Kalman
4. "In Der Nacht"—Gilbert
5. Songs by Abbie Mitchell
6. "La Creole—Porto Rican Waltz"—Thompson
7. "Exhortation"—Cook
8. "Peer Gynt Suite"—Greig
9. "Delicioso—Characteristic Tango"—Dixon
10. Songs by Abbie Mitchell
11. "A Fabian Romance"—Tyers
12. "Una Sensuale Diablo"—Dabney and "Castle Lame Duck"—Europe
13. Songs and humor by C. Happy Rhone
14. "Tango Dreams"—Johnson and a violin/cello duet by Jeter and Wier
15. Songs and humor by Jolly John Larkins
16. "The Tango—Characteristic Dance"—Jordan
17. Songs and humor by Criswell and Bailey

18. "Valse Marguerite"/"Castle House Rag"—Europe
19. S. H. Dudley and Co.
20. "At the Ball"—Hill

Mr. and Mrs. Vernon Castle interpreting the following modern dances (music especially written for them by Europe and Dabney): The Castle Half and Half, The Castle Tango, The Castle Maxixe, and The Castle Walk.

21. "The Tempo Club March"—Tyers

The *New York Age*, April 16, 1914, and the New York *News*, April 13, 1914, both published the entire program.

30. The other two were "Nighttime is the Right Time" and "Rock Me in the Cradle of Love," all of which were written by Hill. See Rennold Wolf, "Ziegfeld Buys Material From 'The Darktown Follies,'" in the New York *Telegraph*, December 5, 1913, in the Robinson Locke Scrapbooks, Billy Rose Theater Collection, New York Public Library, and Sampson, *Blacks in Blackface*, 28, 270. The Darktown Follies Company did well at Hammerstein's, and the white press reviewed them favorably. See, for example, *Variety*, June 5, 1914, 14.

31. See *Jazz Dance*, 128–29. Thomas Riis, who gives considerable attention to the music and dancing in *My Friend From Kentucky*, argues that the importance of the show was that Hill realized "that the novel impact of black performers lay in the special ways they could use their bodies and their voices, making the trappings of the nineteenth-century extravaganza or European operettas seem irrelevant." See *Just Before Jazz*, 173–82.

32. See the New York *News*, April 13, 1914.

33. See "Vernon Castles Dance Before Big Negro Club," in the New York *Sun*, April 9, 1914, and reprinted in Kimball and Bolcom, *Reminiscing with Sissle and Blake*, 63.

34. "The Castles in Unique Enterprise," the *Musical Leader*, April 16, 1914, a clipping in the Robinson Locke Collection, Billy Rose Theater Collection, New York Public Library. The article credits David Mannes with stimulating interest in musical development among black people and H. E. Krehbiel's *Afro-American Folksongs* as an inspiration on "Mr. Europe, Will Marion Cook, J. Rosamond Johnson, Harry Burleigh and others to study their racial literature and to produced works which find speedy popularity." Mannes and Krehbiel did provide useful encouragement, but Europe, Cook, Johnson, and Burleigh were "stimulated" and "inspired" long before.

35. "The Castles in Unique Enterprise," the *Musical Leader*, April 16, 1914.

36. "The Tempo Club Concert," in the *New York Age*, April 16, 1914, 6.

37. Irene Castle, *Castle's in the Air*, 118, *My Husband*, 60–61, and "Jim Europe: A Reminiscence," 90–91. Elisabeth Marbury may also have joined the company for at least part of the trip. Reports in the papers vary slightly on the actual size of the Europe Orchestra, but eighteen seems to be the consensus. In addition to Europe and Ford Dabney, the other musicians who are named include violinists William Tyler and Tracy Cooper, trombonist William Fairfax, cellist Leonard Jeter, banjo player William Elkins, and drummer Buddy Gilmore. Irene Castle, who wrote that every member of the orchestra was "a star at his own particular instrument," recalled an African french horn player who "had won medals of honor at the Conservatory of Music in London" (see "Jim Europe: A Reminiscence," 90), and Tom Fletcher, in his memoir, *100 Years of the Negro in Show Business*, 261, says that Europe was the first to add a saxophone to the dance orchestra during the Castle tour.

38. The benefit concert in Brooklyn was reported by the *New York Age*, April 23, 1914, 1, and the Indianapolis *Freeman*, May 2, 1914, 6. The Castle "Whirlwind Tour" included performances in Boston, Springfield, Washington, D.C., Baltimore, Philadelphia, Pittsburgh, Rochester, Buffalo, Chicago, St. Louis, Kansas City, St. Joseph, Omaha, St. Paul, Minneapolis, Milwaukee, Detroit, Cincinnati, Cleveland, Youngstown, Akron, Columbus, Albany, Toronto, Syracuse, Utica, Hartford, New Haven, Worcester, Providence, and New York.

39. See the review published in the Boston *Record*, April 29, 1914, which was reprinted (along with several others) under the headline "Colored Orchestra Plays at Boston Opera House," in the Boston *Guardian*, May 2, 1914. The *Guardian*, one of the leading black newspapers in the country, and its readers were naturally very interested in the Castle's unique orchestra and how the mixed-racial entertainment was received by the Opera House audience.

40. See "James Reese Europe and His Orchestra—With the Castles," which is included in the reviews reprinted in "Colored Orchestra Plays at Boston Opera House," in the Boston *Guardian*, May 2, 1914. Clark may actually have been a *Guardian* writer since no other newspaper citation is attached to his review. If so, this would explain why he, unlike the other reporters, never reveals the race of the orchestra; he would not need to because Jim Europe's name would have been sufficient. Coverage of the tour by the black press in other cities reflected a similar sense of pride. Tony Langston, for example, writing in the *Chicago Defender* after the Castles' performance at Chicago's Orchestra Hall, wrote of the orchestra that

> the very fact that the Castles use it exclusively on this, their initial tour, testifies to the extreme quality of the orchestra. It must have been a revelation to the uninitiated when they heard the wonderful music produced by the colored orchestra, which was actually the first of its kind to handle the entire program of a white organization of class in this house; but the Castles are entirely justified in their choice, as we doubt that it would be possible to assemble a better qualified and more thoroughly competent orchestra than this one."

See "Review of the Theaters," *Chicago Defender*, May 9, 1914, 6.

41. See the Boston *Transcript*, April 26, 1914, in the Robinson Locke Scrapbooks, Billy Rose Theater Collection, New York Public Library. The date marked on the clipping is clearly in error, since the Castles did not perform in Boston until April 27.

42. See "Whole Audience in Rhythm," the Boston *Post Report*, no date, reprinted in "Colored Orchestra Plays at Boston Opera House," in the Boston *Guardian*, May 2, 1914.

43. The Boston *Record*, April 29, 1914, and reprinted in "Colored Orchestra Plays at Boston Opera House, in the Boston *Guardian*, May 2, 1914.

44. Irene Castle, *Castles in the Air*, 119.

45. Croce, *The Fred Astaire and Ginger Rogers Book*, 154–55. *Variety* also noted that the audiences (and the size of the revenue) were smaller as the company moved farther west. "The management," said *Variety*, "could not decide whether the cold shoulder was induced by a lack of interest in dancing or the prices of admission." See "Castles Finish Weak," in *Variety*, May 22, 1914, 6.

46. See Erenberg's excellent analysis "New Woman and the Fun Home," in *Steppin' Out*, 165–71.

47. See "The Castles," in the Syracuse *Post Standard*, May 21, 1914, clipping in the Robinson Locke Scrapbooks, Billy Rose Theater Collection, New York Public Library.

Among the other aspects of Irene Castle's "New Woman" behavior that became the subject of popular comment were rumors of her smoking, posing nude for artists, advocating professional careers for women, riding astride, wearing men's pants and hats, and designing her own more individualistic and freer clothing. Her most celebrated innovation, the Castle Clip—cutting her hair in a short bob, came after the Castle Tour, as did her encouraging women to attend boxing matches.

48. Irene Castle, *Castles in the Air*, 44.

49. Unidentified Toronto magazine (dated about May 30, 1914), 93, clipping in the Robinson Locke Scrapbooks, Billy Rose Theater Collection, New York Public Library. A headline in the Detroit *News* the day following the Castles' appearance at the Armory read "Honest, the Castles Are Really Awful Thin—and Vernon Looks Like a Bar of Music and He's Very Perpendicular." See the Detroit *News*, May 13, 1914, a clipping of which is also in the Robinson Locke Scrapbooks. See also "Vernon Castle Dictator of the Dancing World of New York: Vance Thompson Tells How the Modern Napoleon Blazed a Road to Fame and Fortune With His Legs—And Refinement—Giving Refinement at $25 a Refining," in the New York *Sun*, April 26, 1914, 3.

50. See Noble Sissle's "Show Business" column in the *New York Age*, September 28, 1948, 8, which carries an interview with Elkins about the Castle Tour.

51. Erenberg, *Steppin' Out*, 170.

52. See "Europe's Society Orchestra," in the *Philadelphia Tribune*, May 9, 1914

53. Irene Castle, "Jim Europe—A Reminiscence," 90.

54. "The Castles," the Syracuse *Post Standard*, May 21, 1914.

55. See "'Butch' Dempsey Fails to Enthuse Over the Castles," in the Minneapolis *Journal*, unknown day, May, 1914, clipping in the Robinson Locke Scrapbooks, Billy Rose Theater Collection, New York Public Library.

56. "The Vernon Castles," in the Cincinnati *Tribune*, May 13, 1914, clipping in the Robinson Locke Scrapbooks, Billy Rose Theater Collection, New York Public Library.

57. Headline in the St. Louis *Post*, date unknown (May, 1914), clipping in the Robinson Locke Scrapbooks, Billy Rose Theater Collection, New York Public Library. The announcement further states that Europe will be "performing the Argentine tango as it is really danced in Argentine [sic]."

58. During his talk Vernon thanked the clergy for being kind to them on the tour; perhaps, commented the paper, he appreciated "the fact that no St. Joseph clergy were present." See the St. Joseph *Gazette*, May 7, 1914, clipping in the Robinson Locke Scrapbooks, Billy Rose Theater Collection, New York Public Library. Other newspaper clippings from Chicago, Detroit, and Syracuse in the Robinson Locke Scrapbooks reflect the same kind of ambivalence. "The orchestra of 'gen'lmen of color' was reported by one well informed in such matters to be a very choice and very costly specimen," wrote a reviewer in Chicago, to give one last example. "It certainly filled the welkin [sic] with racket and rhythm." See Eric Delamarter, "When the Castles Walk Abroad," in the Chicago *Inter Ocean*, May 5, 1914.

59. Irene Castle, *Castles in the Air*, 119.

60. See the interview in Sissle, "Show Business," the *New York Age*, September 28, 1948, 8.

61. Irene Castle, *Castles in the Air*, 119. Irene described the Kangaroo court routine on several occasions. See *My Husband*, 61, and "Jim Europe—A Reminiscence," 90–91, as well.

62. Quoted by Sissle from his interview published in "Show Business," the *New York Age*, September 28, 1948, 8.

63. See *Variety*, May 29, 1914, clipping in the Robinson Locke Scrapbooks, Billy Rose Theater Collection, New York Public Library, and Irene Castle, *Castles in the Air*, 120. The New York *American* agreed with Irene's estimation of a large crowd, and the *New York Herald* estimated the audience at "1,000 or more." See the New York *American*, May 24, 1914, and "Dancing Championship Won by NY's Team," an unidentified *New York Herald* clipping, both of which are in the Robinson Locke Scrapbooks, Billy Rose Theater Collection, New York Public Library. As a final benediction for the evening, and for the tour, Europe presented the Castles with a loving cup from the orchestra.

64. The second prize went to a Mr. Chamberlain and his sister of Boston.

65. Both the *Variety* and *New York Herald* articles reported the same $85,000 total for the tour, *Variety* quoting $30,000 as the Castles' share. The Indianapolis *Freeman*, which congratulated Europe and the orchestra for making "quite an impression on the road with the Castles," said the Castles made $31,000. See Billy E. Jones, "Eastern Theatrical News," in the Indianapolis *Freeman*, May 30, 1914, 5.

66. The operation took place the following day. See the Pittsburgh *Post*, May 28, 1914, clipping in the Robinson Locke Scrapbooks, Billy Rose Theater Collection, New York Public Library, and Irene Castle, *Castles in the Air*, 85.

67. Irene's description of the origin of the "Castle Clip" is as charmingly innocent as any of her other innovations, and perhaps she is right to play down her role as a true reformer. "Evidently women were just waiting for someone to do it first and give them enough nerve to face their outraged husbands," she wrote. Her first public appearance with the bob was at a dinner at the Knickerbocker Hotel, at which songwriter Irving Berlin was among the guests. See *Castles in the Air*, 116–17.

68. Unidentified photograph (and caption), Castle Scrapbooks, Billy Rose Theater Collection, New York Public Library.

Chapter Nine: *Watch Your Step*

1. The New York *Evening Sun* even announced that an agreement had been struck and that "James Reese Europe of Alabama, U.S.A., sails this month to show Europe of Europe how to put time into ragtime." Undated clipping in the Castle Scrapbooks, Billy Rose Theater Collection, New York Public Library.

2. See "The Clef Club at Manhattan Casino," in the *New York Age*, June 11, 1914, 6. White concentrated his review on the orchestral and choral performances, which were apparently well-done; he says little about the Clef Club's attempt to catch-up on the Tempo Club's lead in the area of popular dance.

3. Tyers, as well as Europe's brother, John, were listed as members of the piano section.

4. The psychological climate of Paris on the eve of the war, as well as the Castles' difficult experience getting out of France and back to the United States, is described by Irene in *Castles in the Air*, 123–31

5. See Billy E. Jones' "Eastern Theatrical News" column in the Indianapolis *Freeman*, July 18, 1914, 5, which announced that "James Reese's European Society Orchestra [sic] now featured in the last act of Ziegfeld's Follies." By August, Dabney's name was being routinely used as the orchestra's leader. See the Indianapolis *Freeman*, August 22, 1914, 4.

6. The undated clipping from the Brooklyn *Citizen* is in the Castle Scrapbooks, Billy Rose Theater Collection, New York Public Library.

7. Tutt and Whitney had replaced S. H. Dudley when he temporarily retired from the Smart Set. Their 1913–14 production, *The Wrong Mr. President*, was reported to be doing well in Washington. See "News of the Nation's Capital," in the Indianapolis *Freeman*, March 28, 1914, 1.

8. The article suggests that Europe and the others were willing to invest both their time and talent, and their capital as well. See the *New York Age*, August 27, 1914, 6.

9. The Indianapolis *Freeman*, September 26, 1914, 2.

10. See Margaret Knapp, "*Watch Your Step*: Irving Berlin's 1914 Musical," in *Musical Theatre in America: Papers and Proceeding of the Conference on the Musical Theatre in America*, ed. Glenn Loney, Contributions in Drama and Theatre Studies no. 8 (Westport, Conn.: Greenwood Press, 1981), 246.

11. Letter from W. C. Handy to James Reese Europe, Jr., dated February 5, 1947.

12. Quoted in ""Negro Composer on Race's Music: Jesse Rees Europe [sic] Credits Men of His Blood with Introducing Modern Dances," in the *New York Tribune*, November 22, 1914, and reprinted in the *New York Age*, November 26, 1914, 6. Europe's account of the evolution of the fox-trot is essentially the same as that given by Irene Castle in a letter to Noble Sissle dated January 12, 1920, which can be found in Sissle, "Memoirs," 25, and by W. C. Handy in his autobiography, *Father of the Blues*, ed. by Arna Bontemps, (1941; reprint, New York: Collier Books, 1970), 233. Tom Fletcher in his memoirs gave a different version of the origin of the fox-trot. He says that pianist Hughie Woolford developed the tempo while playing at a restaurant on Long Island. Fletcher does not give any dates for his version, so it is difficult to evaluate. See Fletcher, *100 Years of the Negro in Show Business*, 163. It is possible that roughly the same dance was evolving in New York from several sources at the same time; indeed, the slower dance (actually there was a wide variety in the steps done to the tempo) caught on very rapidly during the summer of 1914. Still, the Castles were the leaders, and it was their public dancing of it in vaudeville that provided the catalyst.

13. According to Irene, the Castles first referred to the new dance as the fish walk, but that while they were abroad during the summer they learned that "fox-trot" was being attached to the slower step and they—believing "in letting the public name our dances"—therefore cabled *The Ladies Home Journal* to make the change. The *Journal* article, which appeared in three installments beginning with the October issue, can be seen as yet another indication of the Castle's victory in the battle to gain respectability for social dancing, although the only modern dance they described was the fox-trot (the other two were the Castle Polka, and the Castle Gavotte). See "Mr. and Mrs. Vernon Castle's New Dances for this Winter," *The Ladies Home Journal*, October 31, 1914, 24–25; November 1914, 22–23; and December 1914, 24–25. Bok, the reserved editor of *Ladies Home Journal*, had formerly been among the opponents of the dances and had, if the story widely circulated about him is accurate, at one point fired fifteen young women employees discovered turkey-trotting on their lunch break. See Sullivan, *The War Begins*, 256.

14. Liner notes for *Come and Trip It: Instrumental Dance Music 1780s–1920s*, 4.

15. "Mr. and Mrs. Vernon Castle's New Dances for this Winter; III: The Castle Fox Trot," *Ladies Home Journal*, 31 December 1914, 24.

16. See "Castles Dance Foxtrot; Call It Negro Step," in the *New York Herald*, no date (Fall, 1914), clipping in the Castle Scrapbooks, Billy Rose Theater Collection, New York Public Library.

17. "Negro Composer on Race's Music," in the *New York Tribune*, November 22, 1914. Europe is not entirely correct in giving Tyers credit for the first tango composed by an American. The honor probably belongs to Louis Moreau Gottschalk (1829–1869), the New Orleans–born concert artist and composer who included a tango section in his

"Ojos Criollos" of 1859. He is quite right, however, in claiming an original African or African-American (in this case Argentinean, later Cuban) source for the characteristic rhythm. See also, "Says Colored People First to do Modern Dances," in the Indianapolis *Freeman*, March 6, 1915, 1.

18. See "Cabarets," in *Variety*, 35 (August 28, 1914), 8.

19. Knapp, "*Watch Your Step*: Irving Berlin's 1914 Musical," 246–50. One of the Castles popular dance routines, the hesitation waltz, with its suspension on the second beat, seems to have made an impression on Berlin. Nine years after *Watch Your Step*, he incorporated the hesitation into one of his most enduring popular songs, "What'll I Do." "What'll I Do," a waltz was "substantially influenced by the Castles' hesitation style, and the hesitation on the third beat is one of the song's great charms, creating a feeling of uncertainty and tentativeness that beautifully supports the lyric." See James R. Morris, J. R. Taylor, and Dwight B. Bowers, *Six Decades of Songwriters and Singers of American Popular Song* (Washington, D.C.: Smithsonian Institution Press, 1984), 97.

20. Gilbert, *Lost Chords: The Diverting Story of American Popular Songs*, 349. "The show went into rehearsal and was booked to open in Bridgeport, Connecticut," he wrote. "A few nights before opening, Europe, listening to the siren call of a girl in Chicago, walked out on the show." No corroboration for this intriguing account, written in 1942 and undocumented, has yet been found in any contemporary sources (an undated and unspecified newspaper column titled "Carnival," by Dick Turner exists in the vertical files at the Schomburg Center for Research in Black Culture, New York Public Library. It gives the same account, verbatim, but it is impossible to tell whether Gilbert got his story from this article or whether Turner got it from Gilbert). Laurence Bergreen, in his biography of Berlin, pays considerable attention to Berlin's first musical but says nothing about Europe or a black orchestra ever being involved. See *As Thousands Cheer: The Life of Irving Berlin* (New York: Viking, 1990), 97–111. On the face of it, the Gilbert account contains errors and inconsistencies that make it difficult to accept, at least in full. It is, of course, not unlikely that the Castles wanted Europe, and it is conceivable that he agreed but later pulled out. To be consistent with Europe's character, and knowing as he would have the importance of breaking the color barrier in a major (white) musical production, the reason would have had to have been very compelling indeed. The Indianapolis *Freeman* did report (See Sylvester Russell's "Chicago Weekly Review," for the November 21, 1914 issue, p. 5) that Europe "who has been on a visit in Columbus, Ohio, was also a few day's visitor in Chicago." His purpose was understood to be to "import good musicians to New York," which Russell did not think in Chicago's interests and therefore "not deemed advisable." It seems, therefore, that Europe was in Chicago during this period. As far as the mystery woman is concerned, it is possible that there is also something to this aspect of the Gilbert account. Bessie Simms was touring the Midwest with *Darktown Follies* at the time, and she might have cabled Europe to join her. Until additional information surfaces, however, it is all at best conjecture.

21. Knapp, "*Watch Your Step*: Irving Berlin's 1914 Musical," 247.

22. The New York *American*, undated (October 1914) clipping in the Castle Scrapbooks, Billy Rose Theater Collection, New York Public Library, estimated the crowd at above 2,600.

23. "Negroes Dance to Aid Native Music," the New York *Sun*, undated (October 1914) clipping in the Castle Scrapbooks, Billy Rose Theater Collection, New York Public Library.

24. A description of the "Autumn Exposition," planned for September 28 to October 2, and which included a variety of musical and vaudeville acts and a children's concert, can be found in the *New York Age*, September 24, 1914, 2–3. Accounts of the Clef Club tour to Richmond, Norfolk, Washington, D.C., Baltimore, and Philadelphia appear in the

Philadelphia Tribune, October 31 and November 7, 1914, and the Indianapolis *Freeman*, November 7, 1914, 1. The fact that not everyone was thrilled with the new Clef Club Orchestra (anymore than they were with the old one), is documented in an article by Nannie Burroughs of the National Training School for Women and Girls in Washington, D.C., reprinted in the *New York Age*, December 10, 1914, 6. To her, the Clef Club performance was not dignified enough, contained too much vaudeville, and the conductor and musicians "wore anything." The acting was "coon straight," and "our good old jubilee songs are being ruined by these late interpreters" and their "American balalaika."

25. The purpose of the Castles appearance with the Tempo Club, the New York *World* reported, was "to help raise a fund for the establishment of a permanent National Negro Orchestra, under the direction of James Reese Europe." "The idea of the promoters is to found a negro [sic] orchestra that shall give a racial expression to negro music, exploit the existing wealth of negro folk songs and encourage the development of musical art by negroes." See the undated clipping (October, 1914) in the Castle Scrapbooks, Billy Rose Theater Collection, New York Public Library.

26. White's review of the Tempo Club entertainment was carried on the front page of the *New York Age* along with a picture of Europe, "Founder and President of the Tempo Club." See "Europe and the Castles and the Tempo Club Affair," the *New York Age*, October 15, 1914, 1.

27. A copy of the official program (with a large photograph of the Castles on the cover) for the October 13, 1914, Tempo Club entertainment at the Manhattan Casino can be found in the Castle Scrapbooks, Billy Rose Theater Collection, New York Public Library. The Versatile Entertainers had accompanied the Castles in Paris two years earlier, and they would do so again in London over Christmas of 1916 while Vernon was on leave from the R.A.F. See Irene Castle, *Castles in the Air*, 153.

28. Lucien White, "Europe and the Castles and the Tempo Club Affair." Among the things that Castle said was that the music for some of his dances "could only be played by Europe's orchestra, and consequently those dances had to be omitted from his program when that orchestra was not available."

29. New York *Sun*, "Negroes Dance to Aid Native Music," undated (October 1914) clipping, and Lucien White, "Europe and the Castles and the Tempo Club Affair."

30. New York *Sun*, "Negroes Dance to Aid Native Music," undated (October 1914) clipping.

31. For a description of the funeral, see Sylvester Russell's columns in the Indianapolis *Freeman* of October 24, and December 26, 1914.

32. See "Negro Composer on Race's Music: Jesse Rees [sic] Europe Credits Men of His Blood with Introducing Modern Dances," in the *New York Tribune*, November 22, 1914.

33. The Castles had been dancing there in the evenings since Halloween when it was known as the Follies Marigny. Opening night under Castles' management brought out such society and entertainment personalities as their friends the Dillinghams, Baruchs, Elisabeth Marbury, Al Jolson, Irving Berlin, Lew Fields, and Elizabeth Brice, who danced to the music of "Europe's well-known band, which has played for the Castles ever since this clever couple first danced into the limelight of popularity," until sunrise. See "Castles Open Castles in Air Above Theatre," in the *New York Herald*, undated (December 1914), among several clippings in the Castle Scrapbooks, Billy Rose Theater Collection, New York Public Library.

34. See "Tempo Club Notes," in the *New York Age*, December 24, 1914, 6.

35. The instrumentation for "Europe's Lady Orchestra" appears similar to the male versions: Marie Wayne and Mildred Franklin, violins; Maude Sheldon, viola; Alice Callo-

way, cello and traps; Nellie Sheldon, bass; Ruth Reed, cornet; Lottie Brown, drums; Mattie Gilmore (wife of Buddy Gilmore), piano; and Marie Lucas, trombone and leader. The existence of a female Europe orchestra does not mean that the Tempo Club (or Clef Club) had changed its attitude and now admitted women, however. See the *New York Age*, December 3, 1914, 6.

36. The modification of the examination was necessary because many of the black musicians played by ear only. Black musicians were also permitted to pay the usual $100 initiation fee in installments rather than up front. See Lester Walton, "Colored Musicians Invided to Join Musical Union," in the *New York Age*, March 26, 1914, 6. Tom Fletcher says that the union offered to waive the examination entirely. Fletcher, *100 Years of the Negro in Show Business*, 262.

37. See the article by "Scrip," "What's the matter With New York Vaudeville," the Indianapolis *Freeman*, November 28, 1914, 4.

38. Sammy Heyward, "Resume of the New Amsterdam Musical Association, Inc.," 3. Another important professional organization, a new one, that admitted blacks in 1914 was ASCAP (American Society of Composers, Authors, and Publishers). Among the 170 charter members were Harry Burleigh, Will Marion Cook, James Weldon and J. Rosamond Johnson, and Cecil Mack (R. C. McPherson). George Maxwell, managing director of Ricordi's American branch, was the first president. It was likely due to Burleigh's influence (Burleigh worked for Ricordi and was friends with Maxwell) that Europe shifted publishers from Stern to Ricordi, and it is therefore curious that Europe's name does not appear with the others.

39. "Negro Composer on Race's Music: Jesse Rees [sic] Europe Credits Men of His Blood with Introducing Modern Dances," in the *New York Tribune*, November 22, 1914.

40. See "Seen and Heard While Passing," in the Indianapolis *Freeman*, May 29, 1915, 6.

41. See Fletcher, *100 Years of the Negro in Show Business*, 264, and also Walton's column in the *New York Age*, May 6, 1915, 6. Before the war, Walton wrote, German musicians were in charge of the cabaret circuit, but now because of the war it should be "possible for colored entertainers to ultimately corner the cabaret work in London." Kildare, who remained in London throughout the war period, was replaced by Fred "Deacon" Johnson as the third president of the Clef Club in March of 1915.

42. Eugene de Bueris's letter to the *Globe*, dated September 8, 1915, was reprinted in James Weldon Johnson's "Views and Reviews" column in the *New York Age*, September 23, 1915, 4.

43. Johnson, "Views and Reviews," the *New York Age*, September 23, 1915, 4. In addition to his comments on black and white musicians, Johnson also reiterated a theme that he had written about previously, that the war in Europe presented proof positive that Western Civilization was not the superior culture its champions had for so long claimed.

44. Europe's comments, dated September 20, were printed in Walton's column, "The Negro Musician," in the *New York Age*, September 30, 1915, 6. To illustrate his position, Europe related an earlier experience from his days in musical theater:

> Some years ago in Cole and Johnson's show, of which the writer was musical director, there was a number containing a peculiarly syncopated passage which not a single white orchestra ever succeeded in playing correctly, while colored orchestras played it without effort, unconscious of its intricacies.

45. "Theatrical Jottings," in the *New York Age*, February 25, 1915, 6. By the end of May, Europe's Orchestra at the New York Roof Garden was being hailed as the "best orchestra engaged in this class of work in the city." The orchestra's personnel by that time

included a number of Europe's better musicians: Felix Weir, conductor and violin; William Tyler, William Carrol and George Smith, violins; F. Herrera, flute; A. Mazwell, clarinet; Wilson "Peaches" Kyer, piano; Leonard Jeter, cello; William Tallifari, baritone; George Hayward, bass; William Fairfax, trombone; William Hicks and Thomas Henson, cornets; and Carl Kenny and Billy Butler, drums. See Whitney, "Seen and Heard While Passing," in the Indianapolis *Freeman*, May 29, 1915, 6.

46. See the clipping from *Variety*, February 26, 1915, in the Castle Scrapbooks, Robinson Locke Collection, Billy Rose Theater Collection, New York Public Library.

47. See the review of the event in the *New York Age*, April 29, 1915, 6. Also see the Indianapolis *Freeman*, April 3, 1915, 5.

48. As late as March 25, the advertisements for the concert in the *New York Age* indicated that Europe and the Tempo Club Orchestra were on the program. By the next week, April 1, the *Age* announced, without comment, that the New Amsterdam Orchestra had been substituted.

49. Europe and the Tempo Club were the headliners for the event, which the *Age* described as a "splendid" musical program and the Indianapolis *Freeman* as "noble because it was clean and inspiring." Johnson and Europe comprised the program committee, and the concert raised $1,000 for the orphanage. See the *New York Age*, March 25, 6, and April 1, 1915, 1; and the Indianapolis *Freeman*, April 3, 1915, 1.

50. See Mannes, *Music is My Faith*, 219, and Martin, *The Damrosch Dynasty*, 214.

51. Martin, *The Damrosch Dynasty*, 215.

52. Ibid., 214.

53. Europe had expressed his feelings about Coleridge-Taylor's music in the New York *Evening Post* interview of March 13, 1914 and again in the *New York Tribune* on November 22, 1914.

54. "Concert Aids Music Settlement Work," in *Musical America*, April 17, 1915, 41, and "Negro Musicians Heard," in the New York *Times*, April 13, 1915, 11. Both of the articles are reprinted in "In Retrospect: Black-Music Concerts in Carnegie Hall, 1912–1915," 88, 84.

55. Roland Hayes, destined to become one of the leading black artists of the period, made his New York debut in January at Walter Craig's annual recital, singing "Celeste Aida." Box holders for the "high-class" affair included Mr. and Mrs. James Weldon Johnson, W.E.B. Du Bois, and Mr. and Mrs. James R. Europe. See the *New York Age*, January 28, 1915, 6. Lucien White, whose preference for classical music over popular music is clear, wrote the most comprehensive review of the April 12 Carnegie Hall Concert. Even he had to admit, however, that there were difficulties in the program. See "Music School's Annual Concert," in the *New York Age*, April 15, 1915, 1, reprinted in "In Retrospect: Black-Music Concerts in Carnegie Hall, 1912–1915," 85–88.

56. Martin, The *Damrosch Dynasty*, 215.

57. Quoted in "Vernon Castle Dies by Airplane Smash to Avoid Collision," in the New York *Telegraph*, February 16, 1918, a clipping in the Castle Scrapbooks, Billy Rose Theater Collection, New York Public Library.

58. Irene later wrote:

> He had never been a man's man in the public eye, and I can remember the snide remarks made by other men when Vernon was one of the first to wear a wrist watch in this country; an ornament considered effeminate in the early 1900s. That may have been part of his motive for wanting to go to war in the first place, to silence the very few critics who might blame him for not going.

See Irene Castle, *Castles in the Air*, 150.

Chapter Ten: "Rat-A-Tat Drummer Boy"

1. See the advertisement in the *New York Age*, October 7, 1915, p. 6. The affair was so unspectacular that the *Age* did not even bother to review it.

2. See "Way Down South," in the *New York Age*, September 16, 1915, 6.

3. R. W. Thompson, "Darkydom," in the Indianapolis *Freeman*, October 23, 1915, 4.

4. Lester Walton, "The Negro Renaissance," in the *New York Age*, September 30, 1915, 6.

5. Ibid.

6. Thompson, "Darkydom," in the Indianapolis *Freeman*, October 23, 1915, 4.

7. Four of the numbers were subsequently published by Cook ("Live and Die in Dixie Land," lyrics by Cecil Mack; "Mammy," lyrics by Lester Walton; "My Lady's Lips," lyrics by James Weldon Johnson; and "Ghost Ship;") and a fifth ("Dreaming Town") was probably a piece Cook had written ten years before in collaboration with Paul Laurence Dunbar. "Mammy," a sentimental "plantation" song with similarities to Stephen Foster's "Old Black Joe," was the most popular piece from the show and was later sung as a solo piece by Roland Hayes and Ethel Waters. As a black version of the perennially popular Victorian "mother songs," it was the likely inspiration for Young, Lewis, and Donaldson's more famous "Mammy" that Al Jolson introduced five years later as well as for George Gershwin's "Swanee." Cook's biographer, Marva Griffin Carter, has described the chorus of "Mammy," as "one of Cook's most beautiful melodies." See "Will Marion Cook," 298. Europe's contribution to the music of *Darkydom* appears to have been advisory, at most; none of the published pieces from the show is attributed to him.

8. Thompson, "Darkydom," in the Indianapolis *Freeman*, October 23, 1915, 4. The *Freeman*, which also carried the news of the opening on the front page, made particular mention of the role of Cook and Europe ("these two gifted artists") in creating music that will "further perpetuate" their names. "The appearance of the new production," it said, "will be hailed with delight throughout the country by the entire race who is interested in the renaissance of the Negro stage." See "News of the Nation's Capital," the Indianapolis *Freeman*, October 23, 1915, 1.

9. See the Indianapolis *Freeman*, October 30, 1915, 4.

10. Thompson made the recommendation again the following week, saying that not only does the name offend "the sensibilities of self-respecting colored people," but also that it does not "make any 'hit' with white people of real class" either. See the Indianapolis *Freeman*, October 30, 1915, 4.

11. See "400 to be at Opening," in the *New York Age*, October 21, 1915, 6. Among the capacity crowd reported to have attended the opening were F. Ray Comstock (underwriter of *Bandanna Land* and *Mr. Lode of Koal*), Charles Dillingham, Irving Berlin, and Joseph F. Stern. The review in *Variety* praised the comedy of Miller and Lyles, but found "nothing startling about the music." The ballads were thought to be the strongest part of the score, and the drummer in the Lafayette Theatre's female orchestra that provided the accompaniment, made a notable contribution to the "Rat a Tat" drill number. See "Darkydom," in *Variety*, 5 November 1915, 18.

12. One problem was that there were too many stars. As Thompson had predicted after the Washington debut, the "use of stars where fireflies do as acceptably, may lead to dangers before the season is old." Abbie Mitchell quit the show after the first week at the Lafayette. Another specific difficulty was that Lester Walton found himself the defendant in a breach of contract suit brought by an act that he had precipitously fired to

make room for *Darkydom* at the Lafayette Theatre. Although the production never made it to Broadway (or to London), the show played a couple of weeks in Philadelphia and was booked by an independent white theater owner for a tour of his circuit in the West. See "Court Backing 'Darkydom'," in *Variety*, 3 December 3 1915, 10; 24 December 1915, 3; and Riis, *Just Before Jazz*, 183.

13. Riis, *Just Before Jazz*, 182.

14. "Washington Stage Notes," in the Indianapolis *Freeman*, October 9, 1915, 5. The "two very talented young men . . . gave a knockout piano and singing act."

15. Kimball and Bolcom's *Reminiscing with Sissle and Blake*, an engaging documentary account drawn from interviews and the personal memorabilia of the two veterans, is the best single source for information about the early lives and careers of both Noble Sissle and Eubie Blake.

16. The Indianapolis *Freeman*, which began reporting Sissle's activities as early as 1912, was, by the end of April, printing his picture and calling him "Cleveland's Famous Tenor Boy," See the Indianapolis *Freeman*, April 13, 1912, 5, and April 27, 8. A review of his New Years' Eve recital of 1914 gives a good description of the kind of religious and sentimental songs he was then noted for singing. On that occasion, Sissle interpreted "Ave Maria," De Koven's "I Promise Thee," "Rose in the Bud," "I Know Two Bright Eyes," " and the Spanish love song, "Nita Gitana." See "Sissle-Cable Recital a Grand Affair," in the Indianapolis *Freeman*, January 10, 1914, 6.

17. *Reminiscing with Sissle and Blake*, 34.

18. Ibid.

19. "He had heard several colored bands in the big spots of the big cities," Sissle told *Down Beat*'s Buddy Howard in 1942. "These bands were playing a new kind of music that had four beats to the bar. And, most amazing of all was the fact that people were crazy about it. He had to have such a band." See "Noble Sissle, International Star," in *Down Beat*, October 1, 1942, 21.

20. In keeping with the pattern established at least as far back as the Memphis Students of 1905, vocalists in black dance orchestras were not specialists (as they would become in the swing bands of the late 1930s); rather, they were expected to be instrumentalists who sometimes sang. Sissle, who did not play an instrument, was therefore given a bandolin "to hold and make motions until I could learn to play it." See *Reminiscing with Sissle and Blake*, 35. In the Indianapolis *Freeman*'s description of the "Hoosier Society Orchestra" at the Severn Hotel, which offered "regular New York style entertainment," the six-member band included a violin, mandolin, piano, and saxophone. Sissle was listed as the trap drummer; the leader was Russell Smith. See the Indianapolis *Freeman*, March 6, 1915.

21. Both of his parents could write, however, his father having been taught as a slave by the plantation owner's daughter "at great peril of discovery." *Reminiscing with Sissle and Blake*, 38.

22. Ibid., 42.

23. Ibid., 49. Blake also liked the melodies of MacDowell, his "Memories of You" was in fact based upon MacDowell's "To a Wild Rose," which he first heard in the 1890s, and Victor Herbert, whose "Gypsy Love Call" was the inspiration for Blake's own "Gypsy Blues." He was also exposed to the music of Tin Pan Alley, including that of Irving Berlin, whose "Alexander's Ragtime Band" (a pop song, despite the title) he frequently played when he worked in Atlantic City.

Now I already knew Izzy because he used to hang around the Boathouse asking me to play his songs, and I always did because they were very good. You know he could only play in one key. Well, he always used to like the way I play. He used to come by the place wearing his little derby hat and his yellow—I don't mean tan, I mean yellow—pointed shoes, and he'd say in his raggedy voice, "Hey, Eubie, play my tune, play my tune!"

See Rose, *Eubie Blake*, (New York: Shirmer Books, 1979), 18, 51.

24. Quoted in Rose, *Eubie Blake*, 56.

25. On September 11, the Indianapolis *Freeman*, always interested in the achievements of an "Indianapolis boy," reported that he was doing nicely at the Kernan and writing songs with J. Edward Dowell and Eubie Blake, "young men of Baltimore." See the Indianapolis *Freeman*, September 11, 1915, 6.

26. Among the songs they performed were "It's All Your Fault," and "Have a Good Time, Everybody," and Blake played "his famous fox-trot, 'Chevy Chase.'" See the Indianapolis *Freeman*, October 9, 1915, 5.

27. Young's group, who dressed in formal attire, was the first black act to play the Palace without using burnt cork. See *Reminiscing with Sissle and Blake*, 52, and Rose, *Eubie Blake*, 57.

28. See the Indianapolis *Freeman*, March 25, 1916, 6.

29. Prior to joining Europe, Sissle had made it a practice to cultivate the good will of the rich and the powerful; "he was full of the practical conviction that this couldn't do his career any harm," Blake recalled. See Rose, *Eubie Blake*, 57.

30. Quoted from a conversation in 1972 and published in *Reminiscing with Sissle and Blake*, 239.

31. It may be that Sissle did not recall Europe's words exactly when he wrote them down in his "Memoirs" (pp. 27–30), but the substance is consistent with Europe's own published statements.

32. The Black Patti Troubadours and the Darktown Follies companies both gave their final performances in 1916, and later in the year, two more of the veteran leading figures in black musical comedy—J. Leubrie Hill and Sam Lucas—died.

33. *Reminiscing with Sissle and Blake*, 329.

34. Quoted in Rose, *Eubie Blake*, 60.

35. Sissle, "Memoirs," 34.

36. Interviews with Eubie Blake by Vivian Perlis, January and May 1972, at his home in Brooklyn, New York, Series 9D, transcript, Yale University School of Music Oral History Collection, 8. "We were only twelve men sounding like sixty," Blake told Rudy Blesh in 1970. "Jim would come in, bow, raise his baton, count, 'One, Two,' (Lawrence Welk didn't invent that), hand me the stick, and walk out." See *Combo: USA, Eight Lives in Jazz* (Philadelphia, Chilton Book Company, 1971), 205.

37. "I want that to come out in the record," Blake told Vivian Perlis. "He was the first one invented that word—gig. Now you hear everybody say that." See the interviews with Eubie Blake, Yale University School of Music Oral History Collection, Series 9D, 8.

38. Rose, *Eubie Blake*, 59.

39. Blesh, *Combo: USA*, 205.

40. Rose, *Eubie Blake*, 59. At more informal jobs, like college parties, Europe sometimes allowed members of the audience to play with his band. One such amateur who often sat in when they played fraternity house parties at Yale was a young piano-playing student named Cole Porter. See Buddy Howard, "Noble Sissle, International Star," in *Downbeat*, 1 October 1942, 21.

41. Blesh, *Combo: USA*, 205. When Europe's musicians played in the homes of New York's millionaires, it was essential that they maintain an almost military discipline. Sometimes that was difficult to do, given the fairyland opulence in which these people

lived. In 1979, Blake related a couple of instances when he was in charge and one of the orchestra members crossed the line of acceptable behavior. His orchestra was once nearly fired because, despite Blake's efforts to stop him, one of the musicians could not resist playing the hostess's gilded harp, which stood grandly at the top of the stairs. On another occasion, they were playing a birthday party and the presents (wrapped in 5-cent red handkerchiefs) had been stacked on a large table. While they waited to perform, one of the orchestra's members began peeking into them. He was immediately grabbed by a Pinkerton detective who would have arrested him had he not heard Eubie trying to keep him away. By the time all the guests had arrived, the detective said, there would be as much as $30,000 worth of jewelry on that table and they'd "'better pray to God that nothing comes up missing.'" See Laurence T. Carter, *Eubie Blake: Keys of Memory* (Detroit: Balamp Publishing Company, 1979), 93–94.

42. Rose, *Eubie Blake*, 58–59.

43. Europe, however, eventually forgave Cook. See Rose, *Eubie Blake*, 94.

44. Blake remembered John Europe as "a great musician," who possessed a "phenomenal memory," and who was very well-liked. Getting someone to replace him, however, was difficult, since John never kept any music scores, having committed them all to memory. In order to be prepared when he was needed, therefore, Blake had to learn all of John's piano music by heart himself. See Carter, *Eubie Blake: Keys of Memory*, 89.

45. Jack Trotter's "New York Notes of Stage and Sport," the Indianapolis *Freeman*, November 11, 1916, 4.

46. See "Mr. and Mrs. Vernon Castle Visit Lafayette Theatre," in the *New York Age*, December 9, 1915, 6. In 1979 Blake told Carter of an interesting incident, the facts of which may be accurate except that Eubie was probably not present, involving Europe and the Castles in Harlem at about this time.

> One night Eubie and Jim Europe were out with Vernon and Irene Castle taking them on a tour of all of the nice black clubs in Harlem. The Castles wanted to see the dancing. It was an enjoyable evening until they got to Leroy's place [Leroy Wilkins was the brother of the famous Baron Wilkins and both ran clubs in Harlem] and discovered that he wouldn't let them in. Eubie was stunned, because as well as he knew Leroy, he had never before realized that he refused to allow whites into his club. Angry and embarrassed, Jim and Eubie stood outside the door and begged Leroy to let them in. "You know me, Leroy," said Jim. "You know I wouldn't bring anybody in your place that wasn't all right. Why, this is the famous, the great Mr. and Mrs. Vernon Castle." Jim was probably the best-known man in Harlem and his feelings were hurt. "Jim," said Leroy, "I know you all right, and I respect you. But I don't care who they are. They're white, and they can't come in here. That's my policy, and I'm sticking to it." And he wouldn't let them in.

Unlike Europe and Blake, the Castles were not used to being discriminated against, and "they felt very hurt." See Carter, *Eubie Blake: Keys of Memory*, 75.

47. *Castles in the Air*, 141. For reviews of the performances, see "Farewell Performance at the Hippodrome, NY," in the New York *Clipper*, January 29, 1916, 5, and "Notable Evening at Hippodrome," in the New York *Telegraph*, January 31, 1916, both of which can be found in the Castle Scrapbooks, New York Public Library.

48. See the letter dated February 26, 1916, reprinted in Irene Castle, *My Husband*, 113. Although he had not gone himself, Europe had been sending Tempo Club musicians to London and Paris for several months to take advantage of the shortage of musicians caused by the war. See Sissle, "Memoirs," 46.

49. *My Husband*, 74–75.

50. In May, for example, "James Reese Europe's Castles in the Air Band played for Holbrook Blynn, who is posing for a picture which is being made at Fort Lee, N.J.," the *New York Age* reported. William Tyers was the conductor of the group whose instrumentation included Joe Lynas and Hall Johnson, violins; Elias Bowman, bandolin; Clarence Jones, flute; Sylvester Williams, saxophone; Russell Smith, cornet; Frank Withers, trombone; Nelson Kincade, clarinet; Lawrence Costner, bass; Isadore Meyers, piano; and Buddy Gilmore, drums. It would be interesting to know how this ensemble sounded since the instrumentation (violins, flute, and bandolin, excepted) is basically that of the standard jazz band of the 1920s. See the *New York Age*, May 11, 1916, 6.

51. See "Tempo Club Moves," in the *New York Age*, July 6, 1916, 6.

52. See the advertisements for the Tempo Club entertainment carried on the front page of the *New York Age* of September 28 and October 5, 1916.

53. See Jack Trotter's column "New York Notes of Stage and Sport," in the Indianapolis *Freeman*, October 14, 1916, 4.

54. Castle's letter, written from France, is dated November 4, 1916, and is partially reprinted in Irene Castle, *My Husband*, 231.

55. Europe appeared, personally, only at the debut of the group. He was not one of the regular performing members. They included Sissle, bandolin and tenor; Opal Cooper, bandolin and tenor; William Elkins, banjophone and baritone; John Ricks, bass violin and basso; Ralph Jones, violin; Joe Myers, bandolin; Harry Williams, piano and cello; and Buddy Gilmore, drums. The two remaining musicians are unknown. See "Europe at the Lafayette," in the *New York Age*, October 19, 1916, 6. Jack Trotter's "New York Notes of Stage and Sport," in the Indianapolis *Freeman* for October 21, 1916, and December 2, also mentions the group.

56. Black leaders were distressed by the Wilson administration's acceptance of segregation and discrimination against black employees in the federal government, and by its unwillingness to do anything to counter the increasing disfranchisement of black citizens or even to curb the growing instances of physical violence against blacks. "A Negro's place is in the cornfield," announced one of Wilson's officials in Georgia (quoted in Samuel Eliot Morison, *The Oxford History of the American People* [New York: Oxford University Press, 1965], 847.) The release of the extremely negative motion picture *Birth of the Nation*, coupled with the death of Booker T. Washington, the nation's most respected black leader, in late 1915 only added to the depressing domestic picture.

57. See Sampson, *Blacks in Blackface*, 231–33.

58. Salem Tutt Whitney in his column "Seen and Heard While Passing," in the Indianapolis *Freeman*, October 7. 1916, 6, lists, along with Europe, Jesse Shipp, Will Marion Cook, Tim Brymn, Luckey Roberts and his wife, Dora Dean, and a half-dozen others.

Chapter Eleven: "The Separate Battalion"

1. See Little, *From Harlem to the Rhine*, 111. A brief history of the regiment can also be obtained from The 369th Historical Society, One 369th Plaza, New York, N.Y. 10037. While its main purpose is to document the prejudicial treatment afforded the black soldier by the army, Arthur E. Barbeau and Florette Henri's *The Unknown Soldiers: Black American Troops in World War I* (Philadelphia: Temple University Press, 1974) also provides an excellent general summary of African-American service during the war.

2. The front page of the *New York Age* of April 13, 1916, expressed the early hope that since "preparedness" meant an expanded military then, perhaps, blacks would be given an opportunity to earn commissions, "especially if colored regiments are authorized." See "More Army Officers: A Chance for Commissions Seen in the Formation of New Regiments." The hostility toward black officers in the regular army in the years prior to the war was so well known that when the one black officer who held the rank of colonel, Charles Young, a West Point graduate, was forced into retirement for what was announced as high blood pressure, few people (white or black) believed the army's explanation. Even after the United States entered the war, and it was decided to use black soldiers, it proved extremely difficult to get the president or his army officials to establish facilities for the training of black officers.

3. Quoted in Little, *From Harlem to the Rhine*, 112.

4. See Charles T. Magill, "All New York Honors Brave 15th," in the Chicago *Defender* of February 22, 1919, 11.

5. "Whenever I got up against a blank wall with the Quartermaster's Department and their prejudices against us, I would have to go either to Stotesbury [Louis Stotesbury, Whitman's Adjutant General] or to Gov. Whitman himself, and get such stuff as I could get in the way of supplies, by specific orders," Hayward later told Arthur Little. See *From Harlem to the Rhine*, 115.

6. See "Negro Troops of N.Y.C.N.G.," in the *New York Age*, June 29, 1916, 1; "15th Regiment is Fast Filling," July 20, 1916, 1; and "15th Regiment, N.G. Nearly Completed," 1. Several of the church leaders in Harlem also endorsed the plan for the black regiment. A good example of the kind of problems Hayward faced (and also his resourcefulness in overcoming them) is contained in his description of how the regiment got its rifles:

> We paraded around with broom sticks and what-nots for so long that the people of Harlem commenced to believe that the whole thing was a fake, and that we were not going to be soldiers at all. I figured that if we could get some rifles that would be of great help to us, so I went over to the state quartermaster, took my hat in my hand, and asked for rifles. Of course I didn't get any. But I didn't get right out, either, and some of the laborers over there at the Arsenal commenced to develop human instincts, and commenced to whisper to me a little bit about where I could find things that I needed, if I only knew how to look for them. I found that there were between 500 and 1,000 rifles available—all nice new ones too—which had been earmarked to be reserved for civilian shooting clubs. This civilian shooting club idea, I believe, was an off-shoot of some of General Leonard Wood's military preparedness program. He couldn't get any action from the government in the line of military preparedness, but he applied his resourcefulness to seeing what he could do about getting preparedness under a camouflage. So he got either a law or a regulation put on the books, encouraging the formation of civilian shooting clubs, or rifle clubs, with the right to draw rifles from the Ordinance Department of the United States Army.
>
> Well, I started the darndest set of rifle or civilian shooting clubs that you ever heard of. There was a regular boom. Practically everybody in the regiment in the early days became the president or the secretary of a civilian shooting club, and we put in our requisitions and got the rifles delivered to us . . . nobody did discover it until we had all the rifles that were available for shooting clubs.

See *From Harlem to the Rhine*, 115–16.

7. Europe's complete military file was lost in a fire that destroyed many of the personnel records held in the National Archives repository at St. Louis. His officer's card and military pay records do provide the basic dates of his service, however.

8. Quoted in Sissle, "Memoirs," 36. Europe had been generally interested in the idea of a black unit for New York for at least five years. In 1911 he dedicated his "Strength of the Nation" march to the proposed regiment. See Appendix 1.

9. Fish was a member of a well-known and distinguished New York political family. Prior to joining the New York 15th Regiment, he had himself been an all-American and captain of the Harvard football team, a state assemblyman, and a lieutenant in the 71st Infantry of the New York National Guard. See *Hamilton Fish: Memoir of an American Patriot* (Washington, D.C.: Regnery Gateway Inc., 1991), his autobiography, and the informative interviews in Jon Guttman, "Regiment's Pride," in *Military History* 8, no. 3 (October, 1991), 35–41, and in the film *Men of Bronze*.

10. Sissle, "Memoirs," 36.

11. Europe's quick promotion was due to his former high school cadet training in Washington, D.C. Sissle, "Memoirs," 37.

12. See the editorial in *New York Age*, October 5, 1916, 4, which made special mention of "Chief Musician Thompson and his band." Thompson, nicknamed the "Black Sousa," was a respected musician, and Europe and the Tempo Club supported him in his attempt to provide the regimental band for the 15th by featuring his band at the Tempo Club entertainment on October 12, 1916. See the front page advertisements in *New York Age*, September 28 and October 5, 1916.

13. See "NY Notes of State and Sport," in the Indianapolis *Freeman*, November 4, 1916, 4.

14. "I do not think," Hayward later told the *New York Age*, "the failure to secure enlisted men for the band was through lack of diligent and earnest efforts on Mr. Thompson's part. He had a difficult task. I felt, however, that progress would be made by making a new start from the beginning." See "15th Regiment is Now Under U.S. Government Supervision; Hayward Makes a Statement," in the *New York Age*, April 19, 1917, 1.   ·

15. Sissle, "Memoirs," 42. Hayward's account of the formation of the band, which is contained in Little's *From Harlem to the Rhine*, 119–22, follows Sissle's in terms of factual detail fairly closely, but does not mention Europe's initial resistance to the idea.

16. Quoted in Little, *From Harlem to the Rhine*, 119.

17. Ibid., 120.

18. Quoted in Sissle, "Memoirs," 44. Sissle also said that once Europe was sure that he understood Hayward correctly and that the money had been found, he made no additional protests.

19. Quoted in Little, *From Harlem to the Rhine*, 120. There were other philanthropists who helped the 15th with donations. One of these, who gave over $1,000, was John D. Rockefeller, Jr. See *From Harlem to the Rhine*, 122.

20. Sissle, "Memoirs," 45.

21. Quoted in Little, *From Harlem to the Rhine*, 120.

22. See Ruth Glasser, "'Que Vivío Tiene la Gente Aquí en Nueva York': Music and Community in Puerto Rican New York, 1915–1940," (Ph.D. diss., Yale University, 1991), 217–18. Glasser's study is to be published by the University of California Press as *My Music Is My Flag: Puerto Rican Musicians and Their New York Communities, 1917–1940*.

23. In his desire to convince Hayward to grant his rather unusual request, to give him the proper orders and permit him to "pay some bonuses where needed," Europe argued that the scarcity of black reed players in the United States was do to "the lips of the colored man." "I don't know whether it was thick lips or thin lips," Hayward told Arthur Little, "but Jim Europe knew," and he also knew that the Puerto Ricans' "lips

were all right, and that they were well educated; that he had corresponded and found out about it. . . ." See Little, *From Harlem to the Rhine*, 120. If the story is true, it may illustrate the length to which Europe was willing to go (it is hard to believe that he actually accepted the notion that such physical characteristics explained the scarcity of black woodwind players in the U.S.) to get approval for his plan.

24. Sissle, "Memoirs," 47. Sissle's tendency to exaggerate and overdramatize his story is hardly subtle, and it does limit the value of the "Memoirs" somewhat. Nevertheless, if account is made for this problem, the "Memoirs" does contain factual information that can be found nowhere else.

25. Ibid., 52.

26. Sweeney, *History of the American Negro in the Great War*, 135. See also "15th Regiment Is Now Under U.S. Government Supervision," in the *New York Age*, April 19, 1917, 1. In response to criticism for the appointment of white officers, Hayward explained that he had tried, without much luck, to get "leading colored professional men" to enlist and accept nomination for commission. He had himself nominated fifteen members of the 15th, he said, everyone who asked to be, and ten had passed the test. Two of these had since dropped out, leaving the regiment with eight black officers and ten whites (whites were serving under blacks in three companies). Had he not added the whites, the unit would not have been mustered into service. The article also announced that "plans are on foot to organize a regimental band of sixty-five pieces. E. E. Thompson has resigned as band master. An effort will be made to get together one of the finest military bands in the country, to be comprised of Negro musicians residing in greater New York and other cities." An advertisement at the bottom of the same page read:

An Opportunity for Musicians
Crack Colored Musicians wanted for the famous 15th Infantry Band of N. Y. Write or wire Lieut. Jas. Reese Europe, 15th Infantry Armory, 2217 7th Av. N. Y.

27. Lester Walton noted in his newspaper column of April 5 that Europe was back in the city after several months in Palm Beach and that he is "spending most of his time at the Fifteenth Regiment Armory, being a first lieutenant of the regiment." See the *New York Age*, April 5, 1917, 6. The *Age* also carried the announcement that the "King" of the ragtime composers, Scott Joplin, had died in New York on April 1. Joplin's death, the release of the first jazz recording of the Original Dixieland Jass Band a month before, and America's entry into World War I the next day mark the end of an era.

28. Quoted from an interview in Rose, *Eubie Blake*, 60. Blake was in charge of Europe's business for the next nearly two years while Europe was in the army. "I had a swell office," he told Laurence Carter, "I had a secretary and everything. It was on the sixteenth floor of this building, and I used to look down on Broadway." See Carter, *Eubie Blake: Keys of Memory*, 90.

29. Glasser, "'Que Vivío Tiene la Gente Aquí en Nueva York': Music and Community in Puerto Rican New York, 1915–1940," p. 224. The *New York Age* also reported that Europe was in Puerto Rico "securing musicians for the regimental band." See "News of Greater New York: 15th Regiment Notes," May 3, 1917, 8. I am indebted to Donald Thompson of Rio Piedras, Puerto Rico, for generously sharing his findings in the San Juan newspapers and for providing copies of the service cards of the Puerto Rican members of the 15th Regiment that he obtained from the New York State Archives. Reports in the *Boletín mercantil de Puerto Rico* and *La correspondencia de Puerto Rico* establish Europe's arrival and departure as well as providing (along with the service records which reflect some name changes) the following musicians as the ones Europe recruited:

Rafael J. Duchesne	clarinet
Antonio González	clarinet
Gregorio Felix Delgado	clarinet
Genaro (Jenaro?) Torres	clarinet
Arturo B. Ayala	clarinet
Pablo Fuentes	bassoon
Ceferino (Severino?) Hernández	saxophone
Francisco Meléndez	horn
Eleuterio Meléndez	horn
Nicolas Vázquez	baritone
Froilan Jiménez (Jimenez Froilan?)	baritone
José Rivera Rosas (Rosa?)	tuba
Sixto Benitez	unknown

30. Little, *From Harlem to the Rhine*, 7.

31. A capable performer on a number of instruments, especially violin and cornet, Mikell's talents had been noted in the black press as early as 1900, when the *Colored American* reported that the well-known violinist of the South Carolina State College had written a new march "pronounced by critics as one requiring extraordinary ability." See the Washington *Colored American*, December 29, 1900, 14. See, also, the Indianapolis *Freeman*, October 15, 1910, 10, for a summary of his career to that point.

32. The *New York Age*, May 10, 1917, 6, and also reprinted in Charters and Kunstadt, *Jazz: A History of the New York Scene*, 65–66. As the advertisement indicates, the regimental headquarters had recently been moved from the Lafayette Theatre building to the Harlem Casino.

33. Little, *From Harlem to the Rhine*, 10.

34. Sissle's lengthy memoir is both humorous and distorted. See "Memoirs," 51–62. His description of the Puerto Ricans, whose musicianship he admired, as Ruth Glasser has noted, is also ironic. Sissle depicts them as childlike, pathetic, demanding, and—in the end—loyal, not unlike the familiar white conceit about black Americans. See Glasser, "'Que Vivío Tiene la Gente Aquí en Nueva York': Music and Community in Puerto Rican New York, 1915–1940," 225.

35. Little, *From Harlem to the Rhine*, 13, 22.

36. See "Raw Recruits of the Fifteenth Learn Quickly at Peekskill; Complemented on Deportment," in the *New York Age*, May 24, 1917, 1.

37. "'The players say I'm toast,'" Europe told Blake. "In the band 'toast' meant 'nuts.' We picked up the term playing a benefit at an asylum. We heard a couple of the inmates talking. One says, 'Got any butter?' 'No, why?' 'I'm a piece of toast and I need to be buttered.'" See Blesh, *Combo: USA*, 205–6.

38. Sissle, "Memoirs," 48–50.

39. State of New York Certificate and Record of Birth, number 7678, Bureau of Vital Records, City of New York, Department of Health, dated February 19, 1917.

40. R. W. Thompson reported in April that she had "a fine offer to join a big act in New York, numbering ten girls, eight of whom are to be white." See his "Passing Show" in Washington" column in the Indianapolis *Freeman*, April 8, 1916, 3.

41. The evidence for this, while not absolute, is compelling. James Reese Europe, Jr., who lived with his mother until her death in 1931, was called "Little Jim" (as opposed to "Big Jim," his father's nickname) by his mother and by the throngs of theatrical people who frequented their apartment. He also has recalled playing as a child with his father's military helmet and gas mask. Moreover, Sissle and Blake, with

whom James Reese Europe, Jr., was acquainted for many years thereafter, always treated him unquestionably as their former partner's child. It was, in fact, only after James Reese Europe, Jr., began to conduct his own genealogical research following his retirement in the 1980s that he discovered his father's marriage to someone other than his mother.

42. In a telephone conversation held on October 1, 1992, James Reese Europe, Jr., told the author that he could not recall in the fourteen years he lived with his mother her ever speaking negatively of his father. He did remember her telling him that Europe had intended to send both him and his half-sister, Madeline (Bessie Simms's daughter from her former marriage), to be educated in Europe after the war.

43. The first announcement of the concert appeared in the *New York Age* on June 7, 1917, 6.

44. See Lester Walton, "15th Regiment Band," in the *New York Age*, June 28, 1917, 6. Sissle estimated the throng at over 4,000 people. "Memoirs," 64.

45. Walton, "15th Regiment Band," *New York Age*, June 28, 1917, 6.

46. Sissle, "Memoirs," 65.

47. Sissle, "Memoirs," 68.

48. Franklin, *From Slavery to Freedom*, 455, and Scott, *Official History*, 33–34.

49. Sissle, "Memoirs," 72.

50. Sissle, "Memoirs," 72–73.

51. Sissle, "Memoirs," 73. Sissle's memory is confirmed by the *New York Times*, May 10, 1919, 1. In the 1920s and 1930s, Jenkins' alumni (notably "Jabbo" Smith, Tommy Benford, and "Cat" Anderson) played in bands led by such leading jazz figures as Jelly Roll Morton, Duke Ellington, Fletcher Henderson, Jimmie Luncefored, Count Basie, and Lionel Hampton. See John Chilton's *A Jazz Nursery: The Story of the Jenkins' Orphanage Bands of Charleston, South Carolina* (London: the Bloomsbury Bookshop, 1980). Additional useful information is provided in Jeffrey P. Green's "A South Carolina Band in London, 1914," in *Black Music Research Bulletin* II(Fall 1989): 5–9, and his *Edmund Thorton Jenkins*, a life of Daniel Jenkins's son who studied in England at the Royal Academy and became a prize winning composer following the war.

52. Chilton, *A Jazz Nursery*, 23. Green also says that there were three recruits from the orphanage but does not identify the third musician (*Edmund Thorton Jenkins*, 60). Sissle, however, only recalled the two drummers.

53. See Chilton, *A Jazz Nursery*, 14. Historically, perhaps the most important theatrical appearance of the Jenkins' band came in October 1927, when it appeared in the stage version of Du Bose Heyward's *Porgy* at the Guild Theatre in New York. Chilton, *A Jazz Nursery*, 38.

54. Ibid., 15. Tommy Benford, who later recorded with Jelly Roll Morton and Coleman Hawkins and who replaced Steven Wright as the Jenkins' band's "ace percussionist," credited Steven and Herbert Wright with giving him his "real education in percussion." "They both gave me lessons, taught me everything about drumming from the bottom up," Benford told *Melody Maker* (see Max Jones, "Benford: Drum Pioneer," in the May 28, 1977 issue of the British weekly, p. 40). Asked if the Jenkins' bands played any "jazz" at the time, he answered:

That's what started everything. And we played against all the bands in America, every band that you know; Arthur Pryor, Sousa, everybody. And we were only twenty-five pieces but we played everything. Play them with swing? Yes we did. Look, we used to swing when we played overtures. Talk about swinging; we used to swing on "Poet and Peasant."

Jenkins' bands may even have played a major role in the development of "The Charleston," the dance (not the familiar tune composed by James P. Johnson) which became a symbol of America's postwar "Roaring Twenties." See Chilton, *A Jazz Nursery*, 25.

55. Sissle, "Memoirs," 74.

56. "Fifteenth Goes to Camp Whitman Monday," the *New York Age*, July 12, 1917, 1.

57. Quoted in a letter from Love, John Wanamaker, Sr.'s secretary, to Noble Sissle, dated January 28, 1920, and printed in Sissle, "Memoirs," 15.

58. Sissle, "Memoirs," 76–77. One of the pieces that Sissle recalled them performing was "Little Bit of Honey," by Carrie Jacob-Bond.

59. On September 10, for example, Sergeant Mikell conducted the band in a concert at the Bordentown (New Jersey) Industrial School, where he had been musical director. Over 1,000 people attended. See "15th Regiment Band at Bordentown School," in the *New York Age*, September 13, 1917, 1.

60. Hayward felt insulted and bitter by this treatment, and he did not forget it. Later, after the regiment finally arrived in France, he called his officers together and made them promise that "whichever of us may be in survival as commanding officer of this regiment when we get back to New York, that we see to it that the glory and honor of the Negro race of America may be served by having our welcome home parade celebrated all alone—in the same manner as we have been born and trained. . . ." Quoted in Little, *From Harlem to the Rhine*, 124.

61. The problem of training black soldiers within the United States plagued the War Department from the outset of the war. The army was committed to a policy of segregation, and yet no arrangements or facilities had been established for training the proposed "all-Negro Division," the 92nd (a second division, the 93rd, was established later though never brought up to strength).

62. To many black Americans, the army's precipitous action simply confirmed their sense of the racial prejudice and injustice of the military. "Nothing since the Brownsville incident," wrote John Hope Franklin, "had done so much to wound the pride of American Negroes or to shake their faith in their government." See *From Slavery to Freedom*, 460. See, also, "Houston Race Riot," in the *New York Age*, August 30, 1917, 1.

63. The mayor's metaphor was more appropriate than he knew; since the animals are color-blind, waving a red flag is to the bull the same as waving a black flag. "Fear Negro Troops in Spartanburg," in the *New York Times*, August 31, 1917, 4, and reprinted in Little, *From Harlem to the Rhine*, 49–50.

64. See "Men of 15th Resent Insult," in the *Philadelphia Tribune*, October 6, 1917

65. Little, *From Harlem to the Rhine*, 54–55. See, also, "Fifteenth Regiment May Soon See Active Service in France," in the *New York Age*, October 18, 1917, 1, and Sissle, "Memoirs," 78. The *Age* reported that the greatest hostility toward the regiment came from the poorer white citizens, but that Hayward told the men that he was depending on them to "break the ice in this country for the entire race." "We are about to win the regiment's greatest victory," he said, if they would promise to stay away from areas and places where they were not wanted, keep their tempers even if called "niggers," and report to him any incidents of abuse or insult.

66. Little, *From Harlem to the Rhine*, 55.

67. Ibid., 56. Drum-Major Sissle, who provided the vocal solos that evening, estimated the size of the crowd, which "applauded and cheered very vigorously," at several thousand. See "Memoirs," 77.

68. Sissle, "Memoirs," 78. See also, "Fifteenth Regiment May Soon See Active Service in France," in the *New York Age*, October 18, 1917, 1.

69. Quoted in Little, *From Harlem to the Rhine*, 57.

70. Sissle, "Memoirs," 78. The complex roots of the antagonisms that underlay the situation at Spartanburg in 1917 involve more than the legacy of Negro slavery in the American South. They extend to vestiges of a primal honor system that remained not only in Southern society, but in the military tradition itself. Thus, white soldiers tended to view the insults directed at black soldiers as attacks upon the collective self-esteem and honor of the U.S. Army, and indeed their country (whose uniform they both wore). Such attacks required an immediate, preferably violent, response. For a discussion of honor as an ethical system see Bertram Wyatt-Brown's *Southern Honor: Ethics and Behavior in the Old South* (New York: Oxford University Press, 1982).

71. Little reported the incident in detail as it was told to him by Colonel Hayward immediately afterward. See *From Harlem to the Rhine*, 59–62. According to his account, a local white truck driver was responsible for starting the rumor.

72. Ibid., 65–66.

73. Emmett Scott had been appointed on October 5, 1917, to serve Secretary Baker as his "confidential advisor in matters affecting the interest of the 10 million Negroes of the United States and the part they are to play in connection with the present war." Quoted in Franklin, *From Slavery to Freedom*, 457. Following the first serious incident in Spartanburg, Scott was sent immediately from Washington to investigate. In his *Official History*, 79–81, he confuses, somewhat, the two near riots that occurred during the week of October 17.

74. Sissle, "Memoirs," 79. There is general agreement on the series of events that occurred that Sunday evening (see, for example, the accounts given in Scott, *Official History*, 79–80, and Franklin, *From Slavery to Freedom*, 460–61). Sissle, who was a participant, and Little, who was immediately on the scene and wrote out the official report, differ on only one possibly important point. Sissle remembered that the man, a waiter at the hotel, who told them it was all right to buy papers there, was black; Little reported that it was the white head waiter who assured them that it was permissible.

75. Sissle, "Memoirs," 80.

76. Sissle and Little agree that the hotel owner, and his hotel, were in serious jeopardy, although Sissle suggests that he had most to fear from the angry black soldiers, and Little tends to emphasize the hostility of the white soldiers.

77. Sissle, "Memoirs," 82.

78. Little, *From Harlem to the Rhine*, 69. "The officer who had quelled that riot by the power and majesty of command was a black man," Little wrote, "a full-blooded negro [sic], 1st Lieutenant James Reese Europe." There are two interesting aspects of the incident that reflect upon the continuing influence of the ancient principles of honor. First, the hotel proprietor became incensed beyond self-control (and beyond considerations of the consequences to himself and his property) by what might appear a minor infraction of the local racist customs—a black man wearing his cap in a "white" hotel. Sissle was certainly puzzled by the intensity of the violence it provoked. As Wyatt-Brown has written, however, "honor was a state of grace linking mind, body, blood, hand, voice, head, eyes, and even genitalia," but of greatest importance was "the head, the seat of the social self." See Wyatt-Brown, *Southern Honor*, 49. Moreover, covering the head by headdresses, wigs, crowns, or caps was historically a clear sign of social status. A black man could buy papers in a "white" hotel without drawing comment, but if he wore a hat he was threatening the entire Southern social system. As the accounts indicate, Lieutenant Europe was able to calm down the hotel owner to find out what had happened only after he removed his own cap. In doing so, however, from the standpoint of military honor, Europe was in danger of demeaning both the army and his status as an officer. He avoided this problem, as Major Little emphasized in his report,

by "staring down" the hotel owner, his steady gaze looking down (Europe was over six feet tall) into the face of the man and rejecting any implication of deference.

79. Little, *From Harlem to the Rhine*, 71–72.

Chapter Twelve: "Over There"

1. Sissle, "Memoirs," 85.

2. For the officers, at least, the two-week layover was anything but relaxing. Overseas equipment had to be drawn and issued (the original regimental equipment having been shipped with the convoy), inoculations had to be given, all sorts of paperwork had to be completed, and 2,000 homesick and nervous soldiers had to be kept in tow. One evening, in an incident widely reported in the papers, troops of the 15th Regiment at Camp Mills nearly became engaged in a battle with a national guard unit from Alabama that was also stationed there. "I learned that the Alabamians intended to attack us during the night," Hamilton Fish recalled. "For our defense, I had to borrow ammunition from another New York regiment, as we had none. After arming our soldiers, I and my fellow officers told them that if they were attacked, they were to fight back; if they were fired on, they were to fire back." See Fish, *Memoir of an American Patriot*, 26–27. When the Alabama troops discovered that the black troops were prepared to fight back, they changed their plans. The story that Captain Fish had "offered to fight singlehanded any five white officers from the Alabama regiment" (which he, to no avail, denied) became a part of the folklore of the regiment. See, for example, Charles T. Magill's recounting of the incident in his "New York Honors Brave 15th," in the Chicago *Defender*, February 22, 1919, 11.

3. Little, *From Harlem to the Rhine*, 78.

4. Ibid., 92, and Sissle, "Memoirs," 87–91.

5. Sissle, "Memoirs," 94–95. It may also constitute the only time in American history that a state militia was sent to foreign soil to serve against a nation at war with the United States without first having been made, officially, a part of a unit of the national armed forces. In effect, the 15th Regiment was going to war with Germany under the colors of the state of New York.

6. Sissle, "Memoirs," 96–99. Little recalled that Europe liked to joke about being scared. On one occasion when the ship slowed to conduct target practice and the first gun went off,

> Jim made a jump, and was on deck almost in time to see the shell splash the water near the target. Later, he was laughing at himself, and telling the colonel how he felt sure we were in a battle, and probably sinking. The Colonel said: "Jim, did you stop to put on your life preserver?" "No Siree!" answered Europe. "I didn't do no stopping. But, when I calmed down, I found I had my life preserver on—and Cheeseman's too."

Little, *From Harlem to the Rhine*, 95. The favorite songs of the officers, which they requested Sissle and Europe to play in the evenings, tended to be popular sentimental ballads like "I Never Knew What Love Could Do," and "You Said Something When You said You Loved Me." Sissle, "Memoirs," 98–99.

7. Sissle, "Memoirs," 99.

8. Ibid., 106–7.

9. Quoted in Guttman, "Regiment's Pride," 37. See also, Barbeau and Henri, *The Unknown Soldiers*, 111–13.

10. The band, led by Mikell, awakened the regiment each morning with "a good ragtime tune to try to cheer the boys up before they departed for their day's drudgery," and met them coming back to camp in the evening. There were also regular concerts on the drill field after supper. See Sissle, "Memoirs," 113. In a letter to Fred Moore, publisher of the *New York Age*, dated January 18, 1918, Hayward reported that the band was "making a favorable impression 'over there.'" See "15th Regiment Give Concert in France," in the *New York Age*, March 9, 1918, 6. Despite the band, the "pick and shovel work was most destructive of the morale of men who had enlisted to fight." "We put up with it," Little wrote, "and the incidental indignities, for a long time, however, but the condition was not one to be endured indefinitely." *From Harlem to the Rhine*, 99.

11. Quoted by Guttman in "Regiment's Pride," 37. Sissle and Little also support Fish's recollection that the men, themselves, were keen to get into action and found the labor work demoralizing.

12. See Allan M. Brandt, *No Magic Bullet: A Social History of Venereal Diease in the United States Since 1880* (New York: Oxford University Press, 1985), 99, and Little, *From Harlem to the Rhine*, 100–101. An early advocate of sex hygiene education, Little instituted an educational and prophylactic treatment program for the 15th Regiment before it left for France. American and French attitudes toward venereal disease differed considerably, and in fact, went beyond questions of military efficiency and civil health.

13. "You run a good show out [t]here in the hall. It keeps the boys in and the chippies don't get them," J. H. McCurdy, director of Recreational Activities for the YMCA in France, was told. Quoted in Brandt, *No Magic Bullet*, 109.

14. Letter from Winthrop Ames to Noble Sissle, dated February 10, 1920, and reprinted in Sissle, "Memoirs," 125.

15. Sissle, "Memoirs," 115. The success of the band was almost immediately broadcast by the black press back home. The front page of the Baltimore-Washington *Afro-American* of March 22, for example, printed a letter to Colonel Hayward from Johnson De Forest of the American Red Cross thanking him for allowing the band to play for the patients in the base hospital at St. Nazaire. "Every window in the hospital was open," the letter read, adding:

> I may say every man [was] straining his hearing not to lose a note. I have talked with a number of patients—there are about 750 of them, unfortunately—the nurses, doctors and corps men, about 1,000 in all, and I have yet to find a single one who does not seem to have been stimulated in spirit by just hearing those colored boys of yours play.

"I don't want to seem to lay it on too thick," De Forest concluded. "I'm not when I say that I think every one who heard, who hears those boys play, is a better soldier and better able to help win the war." See "Soldiers at the Front Cheered by New York's Famous Band," in the Baltimore-Washington *Afro-American*, March 22, 1918, 1. The paper also quoted from a letter from Hayward to New York City official Alfred J. Johnson, to whom he wrote:

> Our band is the most wonderful thing over here. I don't believe any money ever bought as much pleasure and happiness for human beings as did Daniel G. Reid's in this instance. If Mr. Reid could see tired, exhausted men straighten up, shift packs a little higher and step like school kids when they play, or see the thin, wan faces lean out of hospital windows to catch every note of melodious cheer of Southern melody or the sextette from "Lucia," he would be pleased with his investment.

16. See Little, *From Harlem to the Rhine*, 108. "As a matter of fact," Major Little continued, "nobody was in the same class with Jim Europe, who was a most extraordinary man without qualification of limitation as to race, color, or any other element."

17. Ibid., 109.

18. According to Little, when the general rose to say goodnight at the end of the evening, he remarked that:

Something must have happened to your bandsmen tonight, Colonel, I have never heard them play so before, in fact, I have never heard such music from a military band in all my life. You must have been putting them through some wonderful practice since you got the preparing orders about that trip to Aix. I have listened to every concert down in the Park, and of course, I have dined with you a number of times and heard them, and I have even sneaked in on the outskirts of the crowd and listened to your general afternoon concerts here, but nothing ever happened such as happened tonight. I'm all stirred up.

Quoted in Little, *From Harlem to the Rhine*, 110.

19. Ibid., 128.

20. "Ragtime by U.S. Army Band Gets Everyone 'Over There,'" St. Louis *Post-Dispatch*, June 10, 1918, reprinted in Kimball and Bolcom, *Reminiscing with Sissle and Blake*, 67–68, and in Sissle, "Memoirs," 118–20. Sissle, who almost missed the trip because of illness, remembered (incorrectly) that the concert was in Tours rather than Nantes.

21. Little, *From Harlem to the Rhine*, 129.

22. Little thought the speech effective in reminding his detachment that they had duties beyond entertaining American soldiers, and perhaps it was so. Europe, Sissle, and the other more experienced members of the band, however, surely needed no such reminders of the responsibility that they carried. In any case, the "American army in general had no cause for complaint in its representation by the men of my command," Little wrote, and neither did the "cause of the colored race" suffer in any way. Little, *From Harlem to the Rhine*, 130.

23. Letter from Winthrop Ames to Noble Sissle dated February 10, 1920, and reprinted in Sissle, "Memoirs," 126–8. Sissle later told Buddy Howard that the band's playing of the "Marseillaise" caught the soldiers' attention, but that they really went wild when Europe followed it up with "Memphis Blues." "They threw their hats in the air and started a procession through town that Aix Lesbains [sic] probably remembers to this day . . . hundreds of American soldiers marching happily to a strange tune . . . Memphis Blues." See "Noble Sissle, International Star," *Downbeat*, October 1, 1942, 21. See also, "French Royalty Welcome Americans: Colored Band of New Army Led the Troops for Uncle Sam," in the *Philadelphia Tribune*, February 23, 1918, 1.

24. Letter from Ames to Sissle dated February 10, 1920, and reprinted in Sissle, "Memoirs," 128. Franklin S. Edmonds, secretary of the YMCA workers at Aix-les-Bains was of the same opinion. "The music of the Band [sic] has been easily the most important single element in the programme provided for the amusement and refreshment of the men sent here from the camps and trenches," he wrote in an official letter to the band written in March 1918, and reprinted in Little, *From Harlem to the Rhine*, 136. Sothern's appraisal of the band appeared in a letter to the *New York Times* and reprinted in the *New York Age*. See "Tells of Colored Regiment in France," in the *New York Age*, April 27, 1918, 1.

25. See Sissle, "Memoirs," 133.

26. Little, *From Harlem to the Rhine*, 133.

27. Ibid., 137.

28. Letter from Winthrop Ames to Noble Sissle dated February 10, 1920, reprinted in Sissle, "Memoirs," 128–29.

29. Sissle, "Memoirs," 129.

30. Shortly after the regiment joined the French, Hayward described the assignment as the "most wonderful thing in the world." Letter to Colonel Reginald L. Foster, dated March 18, 1918, reprinted in Little, *From Harlem to the Rhine*, 145–47.

31. Hayward to Foster, in Little, *From Harlem to the Rhine*, 146.

32. Ibid., 141. In his official report, Major W. F. Alcorn, assistant provost marshal of the leave center praised the band for their playing as well as their conduct as "of the very highest order." It is most telling, however, that Alcorn requested that a band "be kept here at all times." The report is printed in Little, *From Harlem to the Rhine*, 141.

33. Sissle, "Memoirs," 129–30, and Little, *From Harlem to the Rhine*, 142.

34. Sissle, "Memoirs," 131.

Chapter Thirteen: "On Patrol in No Man's Land"

1. See Guttman, "Regiment's Pride," 37.

2. Wakin, *Black Fighting Men in U.S. History*, 112–13. The black troops' boxing skills served them well in the trenches. One soldier from the 371st, who joined the 369th with the French Army in June, recalled a particularly bloody battle in which the Germans "tried to fight with their bayonets, but we could all box pretty well, and boxing works with the bayonet. A few feints and then the death stroke was the rule. Most of the Huns quit as soon as we got at them." Quoted in Wakin, 113.

3. Sissle, "Memoirs," 135.

4. Guttman, "Regiment's Pride," 37.

5. Hayward to Colonel Reginald L. Foster, dated March 18, 1918, and reprinted in Little, *From Harlem to the Rhine*, 146.

6. Letter dated June 13, 1918, from Europe to Fred R. Moore and printed in "Europe Writes From Europe," in the *New York Age*, July 28, 1918. The "some people" to whom Europe referred were the American officials, especially in the A.E.F., who were fearful that if black troops were treated fairly by the French Army and French civilians, that serious repercussions would result when the troops came home to the United States. The A.E.F. had already begun trying to tell the French how to treat American blacks; this was the subject of the A.E.F.'s report "Secret Information Concerning Black American Troops," whose intention was to instruct French officers in the practice of racial prejudice. For a discussion of this infamous document, see Johnson, *Black Manhattan*, 245, and Barbeau and Henri, *The Unknown Soldiers*, 114–15.

7. Letter from Europe to Eubie Blake, dated April 9, 1918, in the Eubie Blake Papers, Maryland Historical Society, and reprinted (in part) in Kimball and Bolcolm, *Reminiscing with Sissle and Blake*, 66.

8. Letter from Europe to Blake, dated April 9, 1918, in the Eubie Blake Papers, Maryland Historical Society.

9. See Irene Castle, *Castles in the Air*, 169–72, and *My Husband*, 3–4. Six weeks after his funeral, Irene received the letter Vernon had left for her with his sister in case he should be killed. It was addressed to "My poor little widow." *Castles in the Air*, 174.

10. Nahum Daniel Brascher wrote that Europe told him this after he returned from France. See "'Jim' Europe Lives," the Chicago *Defender*, May 17, 1919, 15.

11. Letter from Europe to Blake, April 9, 1918.

12. See, for example, "Vernon Castle Dies by Airplane Smash to Avoid Collision," in the New York *City Telegraph*, February 16, 1918, in the Castle Scrapbooks, Billy Rose

Theatre Collection, New York Public Library, and "Military Rites Held for Captain Castle," in the *New York Times*, February 17, 1918, 14, which reported that in Fort Worth "the streets were lined with thousands of soldiers and civilians." The *Times* also carried a eulogistic poem by O.C.A. Child, entitled, simply, "Castle." In New York, hundreds of military, entertainment, and society people met the train carrying his body. "Society matrons cried by the side of bit players from the shows Vernon had played in," Irene Castle remembered (*Castles in the Air*, p. 173), and many notable society and entertainment figures (including Ethel Barrymore) attended the funeral. See, for example, "Notables at Bier of Vernon Castle," in the Brooklyn *Eagle*, February 19, 1918, in the Castle Scrapbooks, Billy Rose Theatre Collection, New York Public Library.

13. "Last Honors Paid Vernon Castle As Aviator and a Trap Drummer," in the *New York Tribune*, February 20, 1918, in the Castle Scrapbooks, Billy Rose Theatre Collection, New York Public Library.

14. Sissle, "Memoirs," 135–36. See, also, the excerpts from a letter to his father by Hamilton Fish reprinted in "Fighting 15th in Front Line Trenches," in the *New York Age*, May 11, 1918, 1.

15. Sissle, "Memoirs," 139.

16. Ibid., 143.

17. Captain Little was made 1st Battalion Commander, and promoted to Major, just before the 369th moved forward into the battle zone.

18. "My platoons in the first lines were stationed in Groupes de Combat (combat groups)" Fish told Guttman ("Regiment's Pride," 38–39), "very strongly protected on all sides by numerous rows of wire entanglements and Annamite (barbed wire) doors, closing off both ends of the trench. Practically all fighting was done at night or in the early morning."

19. See Guttman, "Regiment's Pride," 39.

20. Letter to Emmett Scott from William Hayward, reprinted in full in Scott, *Official History*, 204–7.

21. The "Heavy Foot" Regiment was an early nickname the 369th had earned by virtue of having been ordered from one place to another so often by the army command. It was not the last they would earn.

22. This section of Sissle's narrative (titled "Memoirs of Lt. 'Jim' Europe by Noble Lee Sissle, Ex. Lieut. U.S.A., IN NO MAN'S LAND") constitutes most of Chapter 19, 155–64, of the "Memoirs," and is written quite differently from the rest. It appears to have been the earliest part that Sissle completed, perhaps based on notes he made at the time or shortly after the end of the war. Because it contains such extensive dialog, it comes the closest of any of the chapters to actually being a "Memoir of Jim Europe, as told to Noble Sissle."

23. Ibid., 166. The words may seem outrageously sentimental to modern taste, but they would not have been thought so at the time. The entry of America into the war gave new life to a kind of Victorian sentimentality in American popular music that one might have thought had been put to rest by ragtime and the blues.

24. Ibid., 167.

25. Little, *From Harlem to the Rhine*, 199, and Sissle, "Memoirs," 146–47.

26. Sissle, "Memoirs," 147.

27. Ibid., 148. "Flee as a Bird in the Mountains" was widely known and performed by black and white musicians in various regions of the United States. Louis Armstrong, for example, cited the hymn as one of those familiar tunes the brass bands of his youth would play in funeral processions. A recording of Armstrong's description and a performance of

"Flee as a Bird" (arrangement by Dick Hyman) by the New York Jazz Repertory Company, can be heard on *Satchmo Remembered: The Music of Louis Armstrong at Carnegie Hall*, Atlantic SD 1671 (New York: Atlantic Recording Corporation, 1975).

28. Sissle, "Memoirs," 147.

29. Sissle calls the song "Swanee River," a relatively common mistake do to the confusion with George Gershwin's "Swanee" made popular by Al Jolson. Gershwin's song, however, was not written until the following year. Sissle, "Memoirs," 150.

30. As Charles Hamm has written, "Old Folks at Home" was a major advance over Foster's early minstrel show songs. The most popular of his songs during his lifetime, "Old Folks" "still retains traces of dialect, but the text is a lament for lost home, friends, and youth, cutting across racial and ethnic lines and almost identical in substance (if not in style) to many of Moore's "Irish Melodies." See Hamm, *Yesterdays*, 214.

31. See Irvin S. Cobb, "Young Black Joe," 7–8, 77–78.

32. Anita Lawson, *Irvin S. Cobb* (Bowling Green, Ohio: Bowling Green State University Popular Press, 1984), 164. The black press reprinted Cobb's article and, much to his surprise, he found himself a hero to blacks all over the country. During a lecture tour in the fall of 1918, he found himself approached by black porters, railway workers, and others who thanked him for what he had written. When invited to join Theodore Roosevelt at the Circle for a Negro War Relief Benefit at Carnegie Hall on November 2, 1918, he told the audience that "the color of a man's skin hasn't anything to do with the color of his soul. The value of your race has been proven over there and [your] value here at home is unquestioned." In his autobiography, *Exit Laughing* (New York: Bobbs-Merrill Company, 1941), 435, he wrote:

> I had seen black men actually under fire and despite that it was their debut at that scary sort of thing, had seen them acquitting themselves as men, too. It struck me that the color of a man's skin might not altogether determine the color of his soul and, purely as a biological proposition, that a black man might die just as painfully— and just as gamely—as the white comrade dying alongside him. So, in fairness to a race, I shaped my scripts into that current.

This is not to say that Cobb refrained from treating blacks humorously, even in the *Post* article; he continued to do so. His humorous treatments, however, were no longer solely of the demeaning nature of his earlier writing.

33. Johnson and Roberts were members of Captain Little's 1st Battalion, and because he was on the scene quickly his reconstruction of the battle is probably the most accurate of the many accounts that were later written. Little was also responsible for writing the official report and the recommendation that resulted in the two men being awarded the Croix de Guerre. See Little, *From Harlem to the Rhine*, 193–200.

34. Ibid., 201.

35. See "Europe Writes From Europe," which reprints his letter of June 13, 1918 to Fred Moore, in the *New York Age*, July 28, 1918, 1–2. In fact, the *Age* had run the story on the front page when it first broke, but Europe added additional details. See "French Decorate 2 Men of 15th," in the *New York Age*, May 25, 1918, 1.

36. Sweeney, *History*, 149.

37. As a matter of policy, the French discouraged senior officers from leading their troops into the line; Hayward's action was thus intended to hide his rank. Jaminson's account appeared in the Baltimore-Washington *Afro-American*, February 7, 1919, 1, under the title "'We Go Forward or Die,' Say Troops Who Know No Fear." See also, Barbeau and Henri, *The Unknown Soldiers*, 117, and Scott, *Official History*, 208.

38. Sissle, "Memoirs," 168–69.

39. "On Patrol in No Man's Land" became one of Europe's and his band's most popular pieces when they began performing it in 1919, after the war. It is even possible that he taught it to the band and that they played it in France in the fall of 1918. In any case, if Sissle's memory is correct, Europe had virtually completed the composition while convalescing in June 1918. The words to the chorus are:

> There's a minnenwerfer coming, Look out! Bang!
> Hear that roar! It's one more.
> Stand fast! There's a Very light.
> Don't gasp, or they will find you all right.
> Don't start to bombing with those hand grenades,
> There's a machine gun! Holy spades!
> Alert! Gas! Put on your mask.
> Adjust it correctly and hurry up fast.
> Drop! There's a rocket for the Boche Barrage,
> Down! Hug the ground close as you can,
> Don't stand! Creep and crawl.
> Follow me, that's all.
> What do you hear, nothing near.
> Don't fear, all's clear.
> That's the life of a stroll when you take a patrol
> Out in no man's land. Ain't life grand,
> Out in no man's land.

40. Sissle, "Memoirs," 170.

41. The detailed records of Lieutenant James Reese Europe's service in the war were unfortunately lost by a fire in July 1973 that destroyed many of the army records kept by the General Services Administration. It is not, therefore, possible to be sure of the manner of his service during the major German offensive of July 15. Europe, himself, later wrote that he served in the trenches until August 1918 and that he was a participant in the defense against the German attack in July. See "A Negro Explains 'Jazz,'" in the *Literary Digest*, April 26, 1919, 28–29, since reprinted in Eileen Southern, *Readings in Black American Music* (New York: W. W. Norton, 1983), 238–41.

42. "Order to the French and American Soldiers of the 4th Army," dated July 7, 1918, and reprinted in Little, *From Harlem to the Rhine*, 219–20.

43. Letter dated July 15, 1918, and excerpted in "What One of the Boys of the 15th New York Saw," in the *Philadelphia Tribune*, August 17, 1918, 1. Marshall had just returned to the regiment from a week's leave in Paris and St. Etienne. "Being the first American officer to visit St. Etienne," he remarked, "I was the object of much observation on the streets."

44. Little, *From Harlem to the Rhine*, 225.

45. Quoted in Barbeau and Henri, *The Unknown Soldiers*, 118.

46. Gouraud's famous message of July 16, 1918, to his soldiers of the 4th Army is reprinted in full in Little, *From Harlem to the Rhine*, 228. The Battle of Champagne-Marne has been seen—correctly—as a major turning point of the war. After four years of aggression, German ambitions were dealt a major blow from which they did not recover.

47. Butler single-handedly intercepted a German patrol that had entered the American trenches and captured five privates and a lieutenant. Butler, amazingly, killed ten of

the Germans, freed all of his American comrades, and took a German officer prisoner himself. See Scott, *Official History*, 211–12. In his statement, the German officer "said he had been forced to let the Americans escape because he was attacked by an 'overwhelming number of blutlustige schwartzemaenner!'" That overwhelming number "being one elevator operator." See Sweeney's *History*, 229.

48. Barbeau and Henri, *The Unknown Soldiers*, 119–20.

49. Quoted in Guttman, "Regiment's Pride," 40. See, also, the American Battle Monuments Commission report, *The 93rd Division, Summary of Operations in the World War* (Washington, D.C.: U.S. Government Printing Office, 1944).

50. Little, *From Harlem to the Rhine*, 311.

Chapter Fourteen: Filling France Full of Jazz

1. This is not to say that the regiment avoided all problems. Major Little, by July the commander of the 1st Battalion, felt certain that Captain Fillmore "was of the opinion that every correction ever offered him by me was offered on account of his being a colored man, and not on the merits of the good of the service." "Of course," Little recognized, "no amount of explanation can remedy a situation like that." See *From Harlem to the Rhine*, 239. Whatever the misunderstanding, it did not seem to interfere with their working relationship. It was Little who recommended Fillmore for the Croix de Guerre.

2. See "Losses of 369th Are Reported to be Moderate; Well Known Line Officers Go to Other Regiments," in the *New York Age*, August 24, 1918, 1, which quotes from a letter to Fred Moore from Hayward, dated July 26. After praising his troops' performance in the recent fighting, Hayward reported that Lacy, Fillmore, and Marshall had been transferred and that Reid and Europe, who was "away sick," were "also ordered, *without application*, to [other units of] the 93rd Division."

3. See Scott, *Official History*, 213. Hayward further told Scott that he "felt then and feel now, that if colored officers are available and capable, they, and not white officers, should command colored troops. I hope, if the 15th is reconstructed, as it should be, colored men will have the active work of officering it, from top to bottom."

4. Ibid.

5. Letter from Europe to Lorraine and Mary Europe, no date [1918], courtesy of Mrs. Lorraine Johnson. The letter is written on stationery from the Hotel Moderne in Paris, where, apparently, Europe resided during his leave.

6. Europe's band may have been the first, but several other regimental bands—in particular those led by former Clef Club musicians Tim Brymn, E. E. Thompson, and Will Vodery (now all officers)—had also been making names for themselves. There was also the non–Clef Clubber, Lieutenant Jack Thomas, whose 368th Regimental Band was noted for superb precision.

7. Quoted in "369th on Banks of Rhine," in the *New York Age*, December 28, 1.

8. The source of the information that Europe asked Major Warburton to use his influence on General Pershing is Gilbert, *Lost Chords*, p. 350. See also, Fletcher, *100 Years of the Negro in Show Business*, 263. While this part of Gilbert's undocumented story is plausible enough, his suggestion that Europe did so to avoid Colonel Hayward's threat to "put you in charge of a machine-gun nest," makes no sense at all.

9. Letter from Hayward to Sissle, dated January 27, 1920, and reprinted in Sissle, "Memoirs," 31–33. Hayward repeated what he said many times before, that without the

band "the regiment never could have performed the long and difficult service it did both in America and in the A.E.F., and that without Lieutenant Europe, there would have been no band." Barbeau and Henri state flatly that Europe was "returned to the 369th so that the famous regimental band he led could maintain its excellence." See *The Unknown Soldiers*, 122.

10. Europe, "A Negro Explains 'Jazz,'" 28–29. The historical significance of this interview, as Ron Welburn has pointed out, stems not only from the perceptiveness of Europe's description, but also because it is, in fact, "the first published discussion of a music called 'jazz' by a practicing black musician." See Welburn, "James Reese Europe and the Infancy of Jazz Criticism," in *Black Music Research Journal* 7(1987): 40.

11. See Addie W. Hunton and Kathryn M. Johnson, *Two Colored Women with the American Expeditionary Forces* (1920; reprint, New York: AMS Press, 1971), 219–20. "Time and time again the playing of these colored Americans thrilled the house into rapturous applause," they wrote.

12. See "Mrs. Hunton Writes about Old 15th Band," in the *New York Age*, date unknown, 1919, in the vertical file, Schomburg Center for Research in Black Culture, New York Public Library. "That night's work alone would put the name of Lieutenant Europe among the foremost of American bandmasters, but it was just one of the many laurels he won on French soil," she said.

13. Sissle, "Memoirs," 170.

14. A pair of photographs, marked U.S. Signal Corps #21879 and #21880, showing Europe leading the band outside of Hospital Number 9 (across from the Hotel Tunis) in Paris on September 4, are reprinted in Little, *From Harlem to the Rhine*, between 214–15. Another, published in the New York *Musical America* of November 16, 1918, shows Europe and the band performing for Red Cross Hospital Number 5 at Auteuil on the east side of Paris. Tim Brymn, leader of the 350th Field Artillery Band wrote to Lester Walton of the *New York Age* that he had run across Europe in Paris during September and that he was "well and doing fine." See Walton's column of October 26, 1918, 6. Finally, in his column of November 2, 1918, 5. (under the caption "369th Band Under Fire"), Walton quoted from a recent letter from Charles L. Saunders, a private in the 369th, describing a visit by the band to the regiment at the front in September or early October.

15. Letter from James Reese Europe to Mrs. Lorraine Europe dated September 10, 1918, courtesy of Mrs. Lorraine Johnson.

16. Letter from James Reese Europe to Mrs. Lorraine Europe dated September 16, 1918, courtesy of Mrs. Lorraine Johnson.

17. Quoted in "369th on Banks of Rhine," the *New York Age*, December 28, 1918, 1.

18. Quoted in "A Negro Explains 'Jazz'," 29; reprinted in Southern, *Readings in Black American Music*, 240. In a letter dated October 14, 1918, Sissle wrote to Blake that all the black officers had been transferred from the 15th, except Europe, who was back in charge of the band. "He thought he would get the bounce—that's one reason I went to school. Well it will all come out in the wash—you know," he wrote. Reprinted in Kimball and Bolcom, *Reminiscing With Sissle and Blake*, 69.

19. The *New York Age*, October 5, 1918, 6.

20. See Welton, "Filling France Full of Jazz," 7, portions of which are quoted in Scott, *Official History*, 303.

21. Quoted in "A Negro Explains 'Jazz'," 28; reprinted in Southern, *Readings in Black American Music*, 239.

22. Welton, "Filling France Full of Jazz," 7. The French music critic, Gerard Conté, has confirmed the importance of Europe's band "qui est sans doute la toute première

dans l'histoire du jazz en France." See "Jim Europe et les Hellfighters," *Jazz Hot* 243 (October 1968), 8.

23. Little, *From Harlem to the Rhine*, 323.

24. Ibid., 329.

25. The interview with seventy-five-year-old Melville Miller, one of the 369th's individual metal winners, can be seen and heard in the documentary film *Men of Bronze*.

26. The letter is reprinted in full in Little, *From Harlem to the Rhine*, 336.

27. Letter to Miss Mary L. Europe dated November 28, 1918, courtesy of Mrs. Lorraine Johnson.

28. Barbeau and Henri, *The Unknown Soldiers*, 167.

29. Little, *From Harlem to the Rhine*, 347. Little mistakenly recalled that Noble Sissle was also there, and sang his speciality, "Joan of Arc." After leaving the 369th in August for two months of officer training, Sissle had been reassigned to the 370th Regiment, which was stationed with the 10th French Army on the Belgium border when the war ended.

30. Sissle, "Memoirs," 186.

31. Little, *From Harlem to the Rhine*, 349.

32. Ibid., 351.

33. Ibid., 352.

34. Ibid., 354.

35. Ibid., 354. In fairness, Little notes that it should also be said that the social workers of the Red Cross and other agencies at Brest did "everything that they could do, for the physical and spiritual and mental welfare of men and officers."

36. Ibid., 355.

37. Ibid., 355–56.

38. Little, *From Harlem to the Rhine*, 356.

39. Sissle, "Memoirs," 191.

40. Little, *From Harlem to the Rhine*, 360–61.

41. See "Europe's Crack Band to Tour Country," dateline Camp Upton, February 28, in the *Chicago Defender*, March 1, 1919, 8. See also "Jim Europe Killed in Boston Quarrel," in the *New York Times*, May 10, 1919, 1.

Chapter Fifteen: "All of No Man's Land is Ours"

1. James Reese Europe to Eubie Blake, dated April 9, 1918. Henry "Broadway" Jones was active in vaudeville and musical theater into the 1930s. In fact, Jerome Kern and Oscar Hammerstein wrote "Ol' Man River" with Jones in mind.

2. Fletcher, *100 Years of the Negro in Show Business*, 265.

3. See "Clef Club Concert Packs Academy," in the *Philadelphia Tribune*, April 27, 1918, 1.

4. See "The Clef Club," in the Washington *Bee*, September 21, 1918, 8.

5. Schuller, *Early Jazz*, 251.

6. For a detailed account of the 1918–1919 tour of the New York Syncopated Orchestra, see Carter, " Will Marion Cook," 123–36.

7. For example, see Southern, *The Music of Black Americans*, 354–55, Schuller, *Early Jazz*, 195, and Neil Leonard, *Jazz and the White American* (Chicago: University of Chicago Press, 1962), 142.

8. Fletcher, *100 Years of the Negro in Show Business*, 265.

9. The *New York Age* reported that Lieutenant Europe called the 368th Infantry Band the best in the A.E.F. and that, while it "specializes in singing jazz numbers . . . the men say they prefer to play classical pieces." See "Colored Military Bands to Delight American Audiences," in the *New York Age*, February 22, 1919, 6.

10. The nickname given the 350th Field Artillery of the 92nd Division, according to Willie "The Lion" Smith, the regiment's drum major (and also one of the great pianists in jazz history), came as an off-shoot of the "Blue Devils," a name the French had given to their Senegalese colonial troops. Smith had intended to enlist in the 15th Regiment but was assigned instead to the 350th. See Smith, *Music on My Mind*, 74, 70. The *New York Age* of December 21, 1918 (p. 6), quoted from a letter Vodery wrote to Alex Rogers reporting the French President's great pleasure in hearing his band play at Verdun on November 20th.

11. "Welcome Concert for 15th Saturday Night," in the *New York Age*, February 15, 1919, 6.

12. Ad for the "Big Welcome Concert," in the *New York Age*, February 15, 1919, 6.

13. See the review of the concert in the *Chicago Defender*, February 22, 1919, 9.

14. Handy, *Father of the Blues*, 195. Handy's memory was probably better about having been invited by Deacon Johnson in 1918 to conduct "Beale Street Blues" with the Clef Club Orchestra at the Selwyn Theater (West 42nd near Broadway).

15. See "Europe's Crack Band to Tour Country," in the *Chicago Defender*, March 1, 1919, 8.

16. Mikell decided to return to his former teaching position at the Bordentown School. See the *New York Age*, April 12, 1919, 2.

17. Sissle, "Memoirs," 197–200. The attempt to describe the evening, though it consumes four pages, clearly taxed his capacities. But it needs to be remembered that it was Sissle's first appearance on a major concert stage.

18. See "Jim Europe's Band Scores Great Hit," in the New York *Sun*, March 17, 1919, portions of which are also quoted in Southern, *The Music of Black Americans*, 354. "Many people who went to the Manhattan Opera House last night—most of them, perhaps," said the *Sun*'s reporter, "never had heard a real band in their lives. They just thought they had. But as they wended their way homeward with the jazzing echoes of Jim Europe's 'Hellfighters' still titillating their eardrums they understood the difference between musical pink lemonades and gin fizzes." This group is more than just a band, "they are a complete circus."

19. Handy, *Father of the Blues*, 234.

20. Sissle, "Memoirs," 220.

21. Lester Walton was especially encouraged. See "Colored Attractions Winning OK of Broadway," in the *New York Age*, March 22, 1919, 6. James Weldon Johnson devoted his "News and Reviews" editorial column to the same theme. For Johnson, the important thing was that the general public seemed to be acknowledging that the credit for originating ragtime—"the most universally known and most popular artistic thing that America has ever produced"—belonged to the Negro, despite the fact that for the "past decade nearly all syncopated music that has been written has been written by white men, most of it by Jews, who seem to have a special genius for Ragtime." See Johnson's "Comeback of Negro Music and Musicians," in the *New York Age*, March 22, 1919, 4.

22. "Europe's Negro Jazz Band Makes Big Hit," in the Buffalo *News*, April 11, 1919.

23. See "Europe's Band: Famous Organization Making Great Record at Auditorium Theater," in the *Chicago Defender*, May 3, 1919, 9.

24. "Theater Boycotted: Band Embarrassed," in the *Chicago Defender*, May 3, 1919, 13.
25. Sissle, "Memoirs," 221. The other three members of the Harmony Kings were Harold Browning, Horace Berry, and Exodus Drayton. It is possible that Hayes did not actually meet Europe until the band returned to Boston; at least that is what Blake told Vivian Purlis in 1972. See her interview with Blake in the Yale University School of Music Oral History Collection.
26. See John Chilton, *Sidney Bechet: The Wizard of Jazz* (London: Macmillan Press, 1987), 32–33. Chilton's sources include the article by Buddy Howard, "Noble Sissle International Star," in *Down Beat*, October 1, 1942, 21, and a 1957 interview with Willman Braud, who played with Bechet and Lil Hardin in Duhé's band, which can be found in the oral history collection of the Hogan Jazz Archives, Tulane University.
27. See "Jim's Opinion," in the *Chicago Defender*, May 10, 1919, 9.
28. See "Lieut. Jim Europe and Famous Band Record Jazz Exclusively for Pathé," in New York *Music Trades*, April 26, 1919.
29. "A Negro Explains Jazz," 28.
30. Schuller, *Early Jazz*, 247, 249.
31. Hamm, *Music in the New World*, 404.
32. Ibid. Also see Schuller, *Early Jazz*, 249.
33. An interesting Anglo-American folk version of the same song, recorded as "Yodeling Blues" by the Buck Mountain Band in 1929, can be heard on *Let's Get Loose: Folk and Popular Blues Styles from the Beginnings to the Early 1940s*, New World 290, in *The Recorded Anthology of American Music* (New York: New World Records, 1978).
34. See Gushee, *Steppin' on the Gas*, 1.
35. "Jazz Music is Now All the Rage Throughout United States," in the *New York Age*, May 3, 1919, 6. Following the death of her husband, Irene Castle completed the film she had been working on and went to Europe to entertain the American troops. She returned to the United States about the time that the 369th did, and she and Jim Europe had dinner together and "both sat and cried at Mr. Castle's tragic death." Europe wanted to establish a memorial to Castle and while he was in Chicago was "arranging with musicians and singers of national renown to give a memorial in the Madison Square Garden" in Vernon's honor. See "Lieut. 'Jim' Europe Killed," in the *Chicago Defender*, May 17, 1919, 2, and Brascher, "'Jim' Europe Lives," in the same issue of the paper, 15.
36. See "Jazzing Away Prejudice," in the *Chicago Defender*, May 10, 1919, 20.
37. The riot in Chicago began on July 27 at a beach on the lake front. Thirteen days later, when it was finally over, thousands had their homes destroyed, hundreds had been injured, and thirty-eight (twenty-three blacks) were dead. See, for example, David M. Kennedy, *Over Here: The First World War and American Society* (New York: Oxford University Press, 1980), 279–84.
38. Sissle, "Memoirs," 222. Jim Europe's earliest patrons continued to support African-American music and musicians after his death. In the mid-1920s, Rodman Wanamaker, in cooperation with National Association of Negro Musicians, established the Wanamaker Music Contest, which awarded cash prizes for a number of years to black composers. While in Philadelphia, in addition to seeing the Wanamakers, Europe apparently also got the opportunity to hear the young singer who had been causing such a stir since appearing with the Clef Club the previous year. Before leaving the city for Boston, the bandleader told G. Grant Williams of Phillips Academy of Music that "Marian Anderson has the greatest contralto voice I have ever heard." See the Philadelphia *Tribune*, May 31, 1919, 5.

39. Sissle, "Memoirs," 224–25, and Kimball and Bolcom, *Reminiscing With Sissle and Blake*, 239.

Chapter Sixteen: "Flee as a Bird"

1. The Boston *Herald*, May 9, 1919, 10.

2. Sissle later remembered the audiences for both the matinee and evening performances as uncharacteristically small, with many empty seats. His memory of everything that happened that day, however, was colored by the tragedy that took place later. The papers described the audiences as "unusually large," even jamming "the house to the rafters." See, for example, the Boston *Herald*, May 10, 1919, 1, and the Washington *Herald*, May 11, 1919, 6.

3. Commonwealth of Massachusetts Medical Examiner's Certificate of Death, dated May 13, 1919, Registry of Vital Records and Statistics, State Department of Public Health.

4. Sissle's detailed account of the tragedy was recorded in his "Memoirs," 227–35.

5. See "J. R. Europe, Band Leader, Murdered," in the Boston *Globe*, May 10, 1919, front page. There also appears to be some confusion about exactly when the confrontation between Wright and Europe occurred. Some of the reports agree with Sissle that it happened during intermission; others (the *Chicago Defender*, for example) say that the second half of the concert had begun and that Europe had finished conducting a Brazilian overture by Gomez and was in his dressing room during Al Johns's pianologue.

6. "Jazz Band Leader Stabbed to Death During Concert," in the Boston *Herald*, May 10, 1919, front page.

7. The *Globe* reported that the policemen found Wright in his dressing room and "placed him under arrest without any difficulty." The *Herald*'s version was that they found Wright "struggling in the arms of several other band members. . . ."

8. Sissle, "Memoirs," 234.

9. See "Call Back Grand Jury About Europe Murder," in the Boston *Globe*, May 10, 1919.

10. Exactly what took place during the roughly two hours that Europe was being attended to at Boston City Hospital cannot be known for certain since the hospital does not retain patient records for more than thirty years. None of the papers, black or white, however, suggested that there were any irregularities or that Europe received anything less than proper treatment. The *Chicago Defender*, for example, whose banner headlines of May 17 carried the news of the tragedy and whose account essentially followed that reported in the Boston papers, reported that "several physicians were at the bedside when the end came." Wright's defense attorney, who interviewed the doctors and reviewed the hospital records within a week of Europe's death in preparing for trial, also found nothing useful to the defense to argue that anything other than the actions of his client were responsible. As with the death of any celebrity, however, rumors persisted. In the late 1970s, Eubie Blake (who was in New York, not in Boston, at the time of the stabbing) told Lawrence Carter that it was his understanding that the doctors had been successful in stopping the bleeding, but that an unnamed black doctor from Washington, D.C., "one of these self-important take-over fellows," who had been at the concert rushed to the hospital and bullied his way into the emergency room. Before anyone could stop him, he "tore off the bandage and resevered the vein. Jim gave a gasp

and he was dead." See Carter, *Eubie Blake*, 92. Neither Al Rose, nor Vivian Perlis, who also interviewed Blake in the 1970s, recorded this version of events.

11. The Boston *Herald*, Washington *Herald*, *Washington Post*, and *New York Herald* used the title of "Jazz King" or "King of Jazz" in the headlines or text of their stories. Others, like the *New York Times* described him having "Won Fame by 'Jazz' Music." Most of the nation's black newspapers were weeklies that appeared on Friday or Saturday at the end of each week. The news of Europe's death was consequently carried initially by the major white papers; the *Age*, the *Defender*, and other black papers could not report it until the following week.

12. *Father of the Blues*, 235–36.

13. Quoted in "All 'Little Africa' Mourns Killing of 'Jazz King' Europe," in the *New York Herald*, May 11, 1919, 1st Section, Part 2, 5:

> "Little Africa" went into mourning yesterday when the thousands of admirers of Lieutenant James Reese Europe, bandmaster of the famous Fifteenth (colored) Infantry, of this city, learned the man who had made "jazz" music popular on the fighting front in France had been murdered by one of his musicians during a concert Friday night in Mechanics Hall, Boston.

The news of the killing was "mystifying to his relatives and friends. . . ."

14. Quoted in "Jim Europe will have a Public Funeral Here," in the New York *World*, May 11, 1919, a copy of which can be found in the clipping file, Schomburg Center for Research in Black Culture of the New York Public Library.

15. See, in particular, "Throngs Pay Last Tribute to Lieutenant Europe," in the *New York Herald*, May 14, 1919, Part 2, 8; "Thousands, White and Colored, Attend the Funeral of Lieut. James Reese Europe," in the *Philadelphia Tribune*, May 17, 1919, 1; "Lieut. 'Jim' Europe Killed: The Funeral," in the *Chicago Defender*, May 17, 1919, 1; and "Lieut. Europe's Funeral," unknown paper dated May 14, 1919, in the clipping file of the Music Division, New York Public Library. Useful details are also contained in other reports including "Country Mourns Death of Great Colored Bandmaster," in the Baltimore-Washington *Afro-American*, May 16, 1919, and "Lieutenant James Reese Europe Buried with Honors," in the *New York Age*, May 17, 1919, 1, 6.

16. Quoted in "Thousands, White and Colored, Attend the Funeral of Lieut. James Reese Europe," in the *Philadelphia Tribune*, May 17, 1919, 4.

17. Several of the papers reported that Burleigh sang "The Victor" and that it had been composed by Europe. It is likely that this song was actually "Now Take Thy Rest," a copy of which can be seen in the Music Division of the New York Public Library with words by George F. O'Connell and music attributed to Burleigh.

18. "Ministers Approve Plan for Europe Monument," in the *New York Age*, May 17, 1919, 8.

19. "There was a dense crowd at the church, who reviewed the remains," and many floral tributes were sent from Washington's theatrical performers. A contingent of military pall bearers and a large number of high school cadets were also present at the service. See "Lieut. James Reese Europe," in the Washington *Bee*, May 17, 1919, 8. The *Bee* had not always looked favorably on Europe's popular musical activities while he was alive, but in death the paper called him "the Greatest Musician of the Age. . . ." See, also, "'Jim' Europe Rests in Arlington Cemetery," in the *Chicago Defender*, May 24, 1919, 1. The James Reese Europe Funeral Documents that exist in the Moorland Collection, Manuscript Division of the Moorland-Spingarn Research Center, Howard University, contain a list of the pall bearers, Reverend Moorland's handwritten notes for his sermon,

the Order of Service, and a statement by the Europe family. The service, according to this information, consisted of prayers, the singing of hymns, a scripture reading, and Reverend Moorland's sermon. Reverends Brown, Grimke, and Wallace assisted, and a poem by John Bostic and dedicated to Europe was read.

20. See "Memorial to Lieut. Europe," in the Washington *Bee*, June 14, 1919, 2, and "'Jim' Europe Rests in Arlington Cemetery," in the *Chicago Defender*, May 24, 1919, 1. A program for the memorial at Lincoln Temple in Washington is held by Mrs. Lorraine Johnson. The family also received many letters from individuals and organizations praising Europe and offering condolences. In one such letter, Henry Lee Grant, president of the National Organization of Negro Musicians and Artists, described the bandleader as "a genius and pioneer in the realm of musical organization." The letter, dated May 12, 1919, can be found among the James Reese Europe Funeral Documents, Moorland Collection, Manuscript Division of the Moorland-Spingarn Research Center, Howard University.

21. A copy of the "Lieut. Europe Memorial Theatre Company, Fitz Herbert Haynes, President" brochure advertising stock to black Americans at $10.00 a share is held by Mr. James Reese Europe, Jr., of New York, as is a letter from John C. Lormans, chairman, Trustee Board of the James Reese Europe Post No. 5, Inc., including a short history of the post, dated October 25, 1983. See also, "James Reese Europe," in the Baltimore-Washington *Afro-American*, May 23, 1919, 4, for a description of the proposed memorial day, and "Death of Lieut. James R. Europe," in *Talking Machine World*, 15 May 1919, 154. The latter article described Europe as "not only a conductor of individuality, but a composer of no mean skill, an accomplished pianist and a musician who could play any instrument in the band."

22. "Mrs. Hunton Writes About Old 15th Band," in the *New York Age*, June or July 1919, in the clipping file, Schomburg Center for Research in Black Culture, New York Public Library.

23. "Topics of the Times: Loss of an American Musician," in the New York *Times*, May 12, 1919, 12.

24. "To 'Jim' Europe," in the New York *Clipper*, May 21, 1919, in the clipping file of the Schomburg Center for Research in Black Culture, New York Public Library.

25. "An American Minstrel," in *Outlook* 122 (May, 1919).

26. "Lieutenant James Reese Europe Buried with Honors," the *New York Age*, May 17, 1919, 6. See, also, "'Jim' Europe Lives," in the Chicago *Defender*, May 17, 1919, 15.

Coda

1. The existing court records of the case (number 3,410) are not complete (the transcripts are missing), but the grand jury indictment is among them, as are detailed statements of expenses incurred by the defense attorney in the preparation of Wright's case. See also, "Lieut. Europe's Slayer Arraigned," in the *New York Times*, May 15, 1919, 32, "Drummer Denies Murder of Lieutenant Europe," in the *New York Herald*, May 15, 1919, p. 3, and "Murderer of Jim Europe Pleads Self-Defense," in the *Chicago Defender*, May 17, 1919, 2.

2. "Bill of Johnson W. Ramsey for Services, Counsel Fees, etc.," dated June 10, 1919, and "Bill of Joseph P. Cutter, In Re COMMONWEALTH OF MASSACHUSETTS VS. HERBERT WRIGHT," dated June 13, 1919, in the court records. Cutter was the investigator who assisted Ramsey and whose services were also paid for by the state.

3. "Herbert Wright Sentenced from 10 to 15 Years," in the *New York Age*, June 14, 1919, 1.

4. See "Brother Leads Lieut. Europe's Band," in the *New York Times*, June 12, 1919, 18.

5. "Mikell Now Leader of 'Hell Fighters Band,'" in the *New York Age*, June 21, 1919, 6.

6. See "Hellfighters Band at Carnegie Hall July 26–27," in the *New York Age*, 6. A percentage of the proceeds was intended for the "Jim Europe Memorial Fund" to create a music school in Harlem.

7. See the advertisements in the *New York Age*, on September 20, 1919, 6, and May 8, 1920, 6.

8. See Morroe Berger, Edward Berger, and James Patrick, *Benny Carter: A Life in American Music*, Studies in Jazz no. 1, vol. 1 (Metuchen, N.J.: Scarecrow Press, 1982), 19.

9. Quoted in *Reminiscing with Sissle and Blake*, 78.

10. Ibid., 86. "One thing he [Europe] wanted to do, when he got back to the U.S.A. and into civilian life," Blake told Al Rose, "was for the three of us to do a Broadway show." See Rose, *Eubie Blake*, 60.

11. Quoted in *Reminiscing with Sissle and Blake*, 89. Aside from the four principals in *Shuffle Along*, the orchestra of the musical included Felix Weir, Leonard Jeter, Hall Johnson, Edgar Campbell, William Grant Still, and Russell Smith, all of whom had worked with Europe. In tribute to Europe, Sissle and Blake even incorporated "On Patrol in No Mans Land" into the score.

12. Ibid., 2.

13. Fletcher, *100 Years of the Negro in Show Business*, 266–68.

14. The club's last president was Irving Williams, who succeeded Fenner when he resigned in 1927.

15. Composer/arranger William Tyers, who led his own band for several summers at the Mount Washington Hotel in Breton Woods, New Hampshire, and who served as Cook's assistant conductor of the New York Syncopated Orchestra, took a group of Clef Club musicians on the vaudeville circuit for several years before his death in 1924. James Tim Brymn, leader of the 350th Infantry "Black Devils," toured with the band briefly after the war and in 1921 cut a series of recordings. In 1923, he wrote the music for the musical *Dinah*, which is notable for featuring the "blackbottom," a dance that rivaled the "Charleston" for popularity in the 1920s. Brymn died in 1946.

16. See the *New York Herald*, May 16, 1919, part 2, 6.

17. The "Letters of Administration" were filed on May 13, and the decision to name Willie Europe as sole administrator was recorded on May 15. Records of the Surrogate Court of New York County, City of New York, State of New York, May 15, 1919. In a handwritten note, no date, from John Europe to Mary after their brother's death, John advised Mary that either she or Willie Europe would have to hire an attorney to make a disposition of James Reese Europe's music rights. As virtually all of the copyrights were held initially by the music publishing houses, John implied (correctly, it appears) that it might not be worth the costs involved. Courtesy of Mrs. Lorraine Johnson of Washington, D.C.

18. Death Certificate, State of New York, Department of Health of the City of New York, Bureau of Records. The funeral service, held at St. Phillips Protestant Episcopal Church, was attended by many friends and baritone Harry T. Burleigh sang "One Sweetly Solemn Thought" and "On Easter Morning." She was buried at Woodlawn Cemetery on May 32. See the obituary in the New York *Amsterdam News*, May 28, 1930, in the clipping file of the Schomburg Center for Research in Black Culture, New York Public Library.

19. Letter from the Veterans Bureau to Mrs. Lorraine Europe dated July 14, 1926. The Bureau asked for a full repayment, but Mrs. Europe replied (in a letter dated February 22, 1927) that she was unable to repay the money and that "in his lifetime [her son] was her principal support." The documents are in the possession of Mrs. Lorraine Johnson of Washington, D.C.

20. Minnie (Mayfield) and Ida, the oldest of the Europe children, died in the 1920s, and John, who was never able to keep his career on track, died on September 15, 1932.

21. See McGinty, "Gifted Minds and Pure Hearts," 271–72, and the obituaries in the Washington *Star*, October 22, 1947, and the Washington-Pittsburgh *Courier*, November 1, 1947, both of which can be found in the clipping file of the Washingtoniana Collection, Martin Luther King Branch, Washington, D.C. Public Library.

22. Madeline Belt appeared in such productions as *Plantation Days* (1925) with Florence Mills, *Pepper Pot Revue* with Bill Robinson, and the *Hot Chocolates of 1932* with Louis Armstrong, Baby Cox, and the Chick Webb Band. Margaret Simms and Edith Simms, daughters of Bessie Simms's sister, Kathrine, appeared in a number of Irvin C. Miller's productions and in Sissle and Blake's *In Bamville* (1924) that featured Josephine Baker and Valaida Snow, the *Hot Chocolates of 1929* (with Louis Armstrong and Cab Calloway, and music by Fats Waller), and the 1930 version of *Shuffle Along* (music by Fats Waller and James P. Johnson). The full listing of their shows can be found in Sampson, *Blacks in Blackface*.

23. James Reese Europe, Jr., has given this description of the incident to the author on several occasions since 1986.

24. Gilbert Seldes, *The 7 Lively Arts* (1924; reprint, New York: Sagamore Press, 1957), 103.

25. Ibid., 150–51.

26. See Peyton, "The Musical Bunch," in the Chicago *Defender*, August 21, 1926, clipping file, Music Division, New York Public Library.

27. Alain Locke, *The Negro and His Music* (1936; reprint, New York: Arno Press and the *New York Times*, 1969), 66.

28. Irene Castle McLaughlin, "Jim Europe—A Reminiscence," in *Opportunity*, March 1930, 91. A poem, "Ballad of Esau's Son," was dedicated to "Lieut. James Reese Europe" by Martha Keller and published in the *Saturday Review*, March 31, 1945, 15. The refrain is:

> The boys of black America,
> They march to the harmonica,
> The homesick concertina,
> And band's bravissimo . . .
> But near the Aisne they played a blues,
> A music the machine-guns use—
> And all God's Chillun got their shoes,
> And chariots swung low.

The Pittsburgh *Courier* also remembered Europe by naming its "Male Blues Singer" award for 1953 in his honor. "New faces, many of whom were not born when some great stars passed away can be reminded that these men and women made the path easier for them," the paper said. See the *Courier*, September 5, 1953, 23.

29. Trumpeter Howard McGhee, who worked with bebop innovator Charlie Parker in the late 1940s, told Scott DeVeaux that Parker would "play something from 1918, man.

And I said, 'Man, I've heard that before; where's that from?' And he'd tell you, 'Well, this is from such-and-such a march out of Jim Europe's band, and Europe used to play that thing.' And he could play it note for note and put it in anywhere." See "Conversations with Howard McGhee," in *The Black Perspective in Music* 15 (Spring 1987), 76.

30. Hamm, *Music in the New World*, 401.

31. Floyd, "Music in the Harlem Renaissance: An Overview," 6–7. Burgett's article, "Vindication as a Thematic Principle," in the same volume, pp. 29–40, contains additional material on the subject.

32. "The Black-American Composer and the Orchestra in the Twentieth Century," 33–34.

33. "The Night Ragtime Came to Carnegie Hall," in the *New York Times*, July 9, 1989, 32.

34. *Early Jazz*, 249–50. See also Badger, "James Reese Europe and the Prehistory of Jazz," 48–67.

35. "His role and place in the development of genuine jazz criticism is important given that he himself was not a writer-journalist. When the newspapers quoted him on Negro dance and symphonic music, his articulate descriptions and reasoning served the new music well by elevating it in the minds of his readers and by establishing a paradigm for jazz criticism." See Welburn, "James Reese Europe and the Infancy of Jazz Criticism," 36.

36. See Badger, "The Conquests of Europe: The Remarkable Career of James Reese Europe," in *Alabama Heritage* 1 (Summer 1986), 34–49; Rochelle Larkins, "James Reese Europe: A Forgotten Life," in *The World and I* (September 1986), 302–8; Tony Scherman, "When Europe Took Europe by Storm," in *American Visions* 2 (April 1987), 28–31; and Leonard Goines and Mikki Shepard, "James Reese Europe and His Impact on the New York Scene," in *Black Music Research Bulletin* 10 (Fall 1988), 5–8.

37. "Re-creating a Night When History Was Made," in the *New York Times*, July 17, 1989, C13.

38. Quoted in Carter, *Eubie Blake*, 88.

Index